One Man's America

Other Books by George F. Will

WITH A HAPPY EYE BUT . . .
America and the World, 1997–2002

BUNTS
*Curt Flood, Camden Yards, Pete Rose, and
Other Reflections on Baseball*

THE WOVEN FIGURE
Conservatism and America's Fabric, 1994–1997

THE LEVELING WIND
Politics, Culture, and Other News, 1990–1994

RESTORATION
*Congress, Terms Limits, and the Recovery of
Deliberative Democracy*

SUDDENLY
The American Idea Abroad and at Home, 1986–1990

MEN AT WORK
The Craft of Baseball

THE NEW SEASON
A Spectator's Guide to the 1988 Election

THE MORNING AFTER
American Successes and Excesses, 1981–1986

STATECRAFT AS SOULCRAFT
What Government Does

THE PURSUIT OF VIRTUE AND OTHER TORY NOTIONS

THE PURSUIT OF HAPPINESS, AND OTHER
SOBERING THOUGHTS

GEORGE F. WILL

One Man's America

The Pleasures and Provocations of
Our Singular Nation

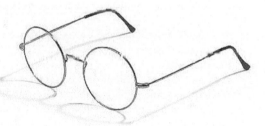

Three Rivers Press

NEW YORK

All essays with the exception of the seven credited below were originally published in
Newsweek and the *Washington Post,* and are reprinted courtesy of their publishers.

"The Game's Gifted Eccentrics" (August 15, 2004), "An Intellectual Hijacking"
(October 22, 2006), "Raising Michael Oher" (November 11, 2006), "Remember 1908!"
(April 1, 2007), and "Roberto Clemente: 'We Think He Can Hit' " (May 7, 2006) were
originally published in *The New York Times Book Review,* and are reprinted here
courtesy of the *New York Times.*

"James Madison" originally appeared in the *Princeton Alumni Weekly* (January 23, 2008).

"Barry Goldwater: Cheerful Malcontent" originally appeared as the foreword to *The
Conscience of a Conservative* by Barry Goldwater, edited by C. C. Goldwater (Princeton
University Press, 2007). Reprinted by permission of Princeton University Press.

Library of Congress Cataloging-in-Publication Data
Will, George F.
    One man's America : the pleasures and provocations
of our singular nation / George F. Will.—1st ed.
    Includes index.
    1. United States—Civilization. 2. National
characteristics, American. 3. Popular culture—United
States. 4. Political culture—United States. 5. United
States—Social conditions. 6. United States—Biography.
7. Will, George F. 8. Journalists—United States—
Biography. I. Title.
    E169.1.W4895   2008
    973—dc22   2007051281

ISBN 978-0-307-45436-2

Printed in the United States of America

DESIGN BY BARBARA STURMAN

10 9 8 7

First Paperback Edition

To the memory of

William F. Buckley Jr.

1925–2008

CONTENTS

CHAPTER TWO

PATHS TO THE PRESENT

CHAPTER THREE

GOVERNING

CHAPTER FOUR

SENSIBILITIES AND SENSITIVITIES

CHAPTER FIVE
LEARNING

CHAPTER SIX
GAMES

CHAPTER SEVEN
THE GAME

CHAPTER EIGHT
WONDERING

CHAPTER NINE

MATTERS OF LIFE AND DEATH

One Man's America

INTRODUCTION

Among the shortcomings of the current administration of the universe is the fact that Alistair Cooke is gone. The British-born journalist, who died in 2004 at age ninety-five, was one of the scarce bits of evidence that there really is an Intelligent Designer of the universe. Cooke lived in this country for sixty-seven years, producing a body of work of unrivaled perceptiveness, affectionateness, and elegance. One of his books, published in 1952, was titled *One Man's America*. The title of the book you are holding is one man's homage to Cooke.

Living in Manhattan and traveling around the forty-eight, and then the fifty, states, Cooke developed a thoroughly American sensibility—cheerful, inquisitive, egalitarian, droll, and enthralled without being uncritical. His delicate sensibility was apparent in his description of Harold Ross, founder of *The New Yorker* in 1925 and editor of it until his death in 1951, as a man "who winced for a living." Cooke was so well-disposed toward America, and so utterly at home and so exquisitely well-mannered, that he did not wince promiscuously or ostentatiously. Still, wincing is, inevitably, what conscientious social commentators often do, not only in America, but especially in America.

Matthew Arnold, for example, was a fastidious social critic and hence an accomplished complainer. When he died, an acquaintance (Robert Louis Stevenson, no less) said: "Poor Matt, he's gone to Heaven, no doubt—but he won't like God." American social critics wince when this country, in its rambunctious freedom, falls short, as inevitably it does, of the uniquely high standards it has set for itself. But different things make different people wince, because sensibilities differ. And nearly four decades of observing American politics and culture have convinced me that, in both, sensibility is fundamental.

That is, people embrace a conservative (or liberal) agenda or ideology, or develop a liberal (or conservative) political and social philosophy, largely because of something basic to their nature—their temperament, as shaped by education and other experiences. Broadly—*very* broadly—speaking, there are, I believe, conservative and liberal stances toward life, conservative and liberal assumptions about how history unfolds, and conservative and liberal expectations about how the world works. This is one reason why we have political categories like "liberal" and "conservative": People tend to cluster. That is one reason why we have political parties.

This collection of my writings is not designed to recapitulate the large events of recent years. Consider this volume an almost entirely Iraq-free zone. Rather, it is intended to illustrate, regarding smaller (but not necessarily minor) matters, how one conservative's sensibility responds to myriad provocations and pleasures. At a moment when there is considerable doubt and rancor about what it means to be a conservative, perhaps this collection will provide a useful example.

Time flies when you're having fun, and also when you're not. Time is, of course, magnificently indifferent to whether or not people enjoy what occurs as it passes. The first years of the twenty-first century have not been, on balance, enjoyable for Americans. These have been years characterized by a miasma of anxiety about a new and shadowy terrorist threat to security, and a torrent of acrimony about the dubious inception and incompetent conduct of a war that became perhaps the worst foreign policy debacle in the nation's history. (Well, I said this book would be an *almost* entirely Iraq-free zone.)

Lucretius (as translated by Dryden) wrote about the enjoyment people sometimes derive from watching other people in peril:

> 'Tis pleasant, safely to behold from shore,
> The rolling ship, and hear the tempest roar.

But Americans have not felt safe ashore—not safe from foreigners who wish them ill, not safe from unusually virulent domestic squabbles.

And Americans have not suffered from any insufficiency of journalism and other hectoring. The simultaneous arrival of saturation media (broadcast, podcast, Internet, etc.) and uncivil discourse might be a matter of mere correlation, not causation. It would, however, not be rash to think otherwise.

Anyway, it would be almost impertinent to ask readers to revisit commentary focused on the largest, and painfully familiar, events of these bleak years. I do not do so in this, the eighth collection of my columns, book reviews, and other writings. If, in any given year, more than a dozen of my columns were not about books, I would think that I had not done my job properly. This is because, for all the fascination with new media, I believe that books remain the most important carriers of ideas, and ideas are always the most important news. Hence books themselves are often news.

With this volume, I am taking a different approach. The essays in the first seven were selected and arranged in order to give readers a retrospective *tour d'horizon,* a look back at the political and cultural controversies of the four or five years from which the writings were drawn. In this volume, I hope to illustrate how one conservative's sensibility responded to disparate people, stories, and events.

In the past forty or so years, conservatism has grown from a small, homogenous fighting faction in an unconverted country to a persuasion at least at parity with liberalism in terms of political muscle and intellectual firepower. In the process, conservatism has become large enough to have schisms, and hence an identity crisis. This volume makes no attempt to distill a coherent political philosophy from episodic writings in response to disparate events. Perhaps, however, the skeleton and ligaments of one conservative's philosophy can be discerned in the response of his sensibility, or temperament, to the people, events, and controversies featured herein. This is, I think, even so (perhaps especially so) when considering the ethics of competition and craftsmanship on what General Douglas MacArthur called "the fields of friendly strife"—that is, sports.

The basic approach to writing columns and other periodic journalism resembles what used to be the unwritten but understood rules regarding Catholic confession: Be brief, be blunt, and be gone. In commentary, this approach is not optional, because print journalism is governed by two scarcities. One is a scarcity of space: Columnists who cannot get said what they want to say in 750 words should consider another vocation. The other scarcity is of time: Americans are harried, and their attention spans are not lengthening. Increasingly clamorous media, covering an always turbulent world, are constantly tugging at Americans' sleeves, urgently saying, "Pay attention to *this!*"

Saturation journalism, ravenous for the attention of a jaded and distracted public, ratchets up the hyperbole, like the character in a Tom Stoppard play who exclaims, "Clufton Bay Bridge is the fourth biggest single-span double-track shore-to-shore railway bridge in the world bar none." Gosh. One character in the American drama, Richard Nixon, said of the first landing by men on the moon, "This is the greatest week in the history of the world since Creation." A friend and supporter, the evangelist Billy Graham, thought that was a bit over the top and notified the president that there had been three bigger events: "1. The first Christmas. 2. The day on which Christ died. 3. The first Easter." Nixon, not exactly chastened but certainly prudent, scrawled a note to his chief of staff, Bob Haldeman: "H—Tell Billy RN referred to a week not a day."

The first human step on the moon, although not quite competitive with Creation as a headline, was a grand event. But with the passage of time—usually not very much time; a day often suffices—the subjects of most media cacophonies turn out to seem small indeed. But from many unheralded events and obscure people, large and durable lessons can flow, as I hope the essays in this volume demonstrate. Be that as it may, the essays that follow will perhaps remind readers how endlessly entertaining and instructive the unfolding American story invariably is.

The passing American scene certainly is that, always. Still, any sensible journalist should develop the habit of periodically lifting his or her gaze from the crisis du jour in order to remind himself or herself of this: Journalism is evanescent. But, then, this, too, is true: Under the eye of Eternity—or, less grandly, just given time—almost everything is evanescent. Everything, that is, other than the value of the simple virtues and decencies that can make communities flourish and that have made America great and exemplary. That is what Alistair Cooke believed, and what this conservative's sensibility tells him.

Chapter One

PEOPLE

The Fun of William F. Buckley

In his fortieth anniversary toast to his Yale class of 1950, William F. Buckley said, "Some of us who wondered if we would ever be this old now wonder whether we were ever young." Those who were not young forty years ago, in 1965, can have no inkling of what fun it was to be among Buckley's disciples as he ran for mayor of New York vowing that, were he to win, his first act would be to demand a recount.

Murray Kempton, the wonderful liberal columnist who later joined Buckley's eclectic legion of friends, wrote after Buckley's first news conference that the candidate "had the kidney to decline the customary humiliation of soliciting the love of the voters, and read his statement of principles in a tone for all the world that of an Edwardian resident commissioner reading aloud the 39 articles of the Anglican establishment to a conscript assemblage of Zulus." For conservatives, happy days were here again.

Back then, espousing conservatism was regarded by polite society, then soggy with that era's barely challenged liberalism, as a species of naughtiness, not nice but also not serious. Buckley, representing New York's Conservative Party, which was just three years old, won 13 percent of the vote. When the winner, John Lindsay, limped discredited from office eight years later, Bill's brother Jim had been elected, on the Conservative line, U.S. senator from New York.

Buckley, for whom the nation should give thanks, turns eighty on Thanksgiving Day, and *National Review,* the conservative journal he founded in the belly of the beast—liberal Manhattan—turned fifty this month. It is difficult to remember, and hence especially important to remember, the slough of despond conservatism was in 1955.

Ohio senator Robert Taft, for more than a decade the leading conservative in elective office, had died in 1953. Joseph McCarthy had tainted conservatism in the process of disgracing himself with bile and bourbon. President Eisenhower had so placidly come to terms with the flaccid consensus of the 1950s that the editor of *U.S. News & World*

Report, the most conservative newsweekly, suggested that both parties nominate Eisenhower in 1956.

National Review demurred. When it nailed its colors—pastels were not encouraged—to its mast and set sail upon the choppy seas of American controversy, one novel on the bestseller list was Sloan Wilson's *The Man in the Gray Flannel Suit,* voicing the 1950s' worry about "conformity." *National Review*'s premise was that conformity was especially egregious among the intellectuals, that herd of independent minds. The magazine is one reason why the phrase "conservative intelligentsia" is no longer an oxymoron.

In 1964, *National Review* (circulation then: 100,000) did what the mighty Hearst press had never done—determined a major party's presidential nomination. Barry Goldwater's candidacy was essentially an emanation of *National Review*'s cluttered office on East 35th Street. Which is why an audience of young Goldwaterites took it so hard when, two months before the election, Buckley warned them that bliss would be a bit delayed:

"The point of the present occasion is to win recruits whose attention we might never have attracted but for Barry Goldwater; to win them not only for November the third, but for future Novembers; to infuse the conservative spirit in enough people to entitle us to look about us, on November fourth, not at the ashes of defeat, but at the well-planted seeds of hope, which will flower on a great November day in the future, if there is a future."

There was. It arrived sixteen years later.

Author of more than four thousand columns, and still adding two a week; author of forty-seven books, eighteen of them novels; host of the *Firing Line* television program for thirty-four years; a public speaker, often making as many as seventy lectures and debates a year, for almost fifty years; ocean mariner; concert harpsichordist—his energy reproaches the rest of us. Married to a woman who matches his mettle, his proposal to her, made when he called her away from a card game, went like this:

He: "Patricia, would you consider marriage with me?"

She: "Bill, I've been asked this question many times. To others I've said no. To you I say yes. Now may I please get back and finish my hand?"

Buckley, so young at eighty, was severely precocious at seven when he wrote a starchy letter to the king of England demanding payment of Britain's war debts. Seventy-three years on, Buckley's country is significantly different, and better, because of him. Of how many journalists, ever, can that be said? One.   [NOVEMBER 24, 2005]

Buckley: A Life Athwart History

Those who think Jack Nicholson's neon smile is the last word in smiles never saw William F. Buckley's. It could light up an auditorium; it did light up half a century of elegant advocacy that made him an engaging public intellectual and the twentieth century's most consequential journalist.

Before there could be Ronald Reagan's presidency, there had to be Barry Goldwater's candidacy. It made conservatism confident and placed the Republican Party in the hands of its adherents.

Before there could be Goldwater's insurgency, there had to be *National Review* magazine. From the creative clutter of its Manhattan offices flowed the ideological electricity that powered the transformation of American conservatism from a mere sensibility into a fighting faith and a blueprint for governance.

Before there was *National Review,* there was Buckley, spoiling for a philosophic fight, to be followed, of course, by a flute of champagne with his adversaries. He was twenty-nine when, in 1955, he launched *National Review* with the vow that it "stands athwart history, yelling Stop." Actually, it helped Bill take history by the lapels, shake it to get its attention, and then propel it in a new direction. Bill died Wednesday in his home, in his study, at his desk, diligent at his lifelong task of putting words together well and to good use.

Before his intervention—often laconic in manner, always passionate in purpose—in the plodding political arguments within the flaccid liberal consensus of the post–World War II intelligentsia, conservatism's face was that of another Yale man, Robert Taft, somewhat dour, often sour, wearing three-piece suits and wire-rim glasses. The word *fun* did not spring to mind.

The fun began when Bill picked up his clipboard, and conservatives' spirits, by bringing his distinctive brio and élan to political skirmishing. When young Goldwater decided to give politics a fling, he wrote to his brother: "It ain't for life and it might be fun." He was half right: Politics became his life, and it was fun, all the way. Politics was not Bill's life—he had many competing and compensating enthusiasms—but it mattered to him, and he mattered to the course of political events.

One clue to Bill's talent for friendship surely was his fondness for this thought of Harold Nicolson's: "Only one person in a thousand is a bore, and *he* is interesting because he is one person in a thousand." Consider this from Bill's introduction to a collection of his writings titled *The Jeweler's Eye: A Book of Irresistible Political Reflections*:

"The title is, of course, a calculated effrontery, the relic of an impromptu answer I gave once to a tenacious young interviewer who, toward the end of a very long session, asked me what opinion did I have of myself. I replied that I thought of myself as a perfectly average middle-aged American, with, however, a jeweler's eye for political truths. I suppressed a smile—and watched him carefully record my words in his notebook. Having done so, he looked up and asked, 'Who gave you your jeweler's eye?' 'God,' I said, tilting my head skyward just a little. He wrote that down—the journalism schools warn you not to risk committing anything to memory. 'Well,'—he rose to go, smiling at last—'that settles that!' We have become friends."

Pat, Bill's beloved wife of fifty-six years, died last April. During the memorial service for her at New York's Metropolitan Museum of Art, a friend read lines from "Vitae Summa Brevis" by a poet she admired, Ernest Dowson:

> They are not long, the days of wine and roses:
> Out of a misty dream
> Our path emerges for a while, then closes
> Within a dream.

Bill's final dream was to see her again, a consummation of which his faith assured him. He had an aptitude for love—of his son, his church, his harpsichord, language, wine, skiing, sailing.

He began his sixty-year voyage on the turbulent waters of American controversy by tacking into the wind with a polemical book, *God and Man at Yale* (1951), that was a lovers' quarrel with his alma mater. And so at Pat's service the achingly beautiful voices of Yale's Whiffenpoofs were raised in their signature song about the tables down at Mory's, "the place where Louis dwells":

> *We will serenade our Louis*
> *While life and voice shall last*
> *Then we'll pass and be forgotten with the rest*

Bill's distinctive voice permeated, and improved, his era. It will be forgotten by no one who had the delight of hearing it.

[FEBRUARY 29, 2008]

David Brinkley: Proud Anachronism

To have worked alongside David Brinkley on television is to have experienced what might be called the Tommy Henrich Temptation. Henrich, who played right field for the Yankees when Joe DiMaggio was playing center field, must have been constantly tempted to ignore the game and just stand there watching DiMaggio, who defined for his generation the elegance of understatement and the gracefulness that is undervalued because it makes the difficult seem effortless.

Brinkley, who died Wednesday, a month shy of his eighty-third birthday, was a Washington monument as stately, and as spare in expression, as is the original. Long before high-decibel, low-brow cable shout-a-thons made the phrase "gentleman broadcaster" seem oxymoronic, Brinkley made it his business to demonstrate the compatibility of toughness and civility in journalism.

He was the most famous son of Wilmington, North Carolina, until

Michael Jordan dribbled into the national consciousness. Brinkley arrived in Washington in 1943, an era when a gas mask occasionally hung from the president's wheelchair and the city—then hardly more than a town, really—fit John Kennedy's droll description of it as a community of Southern efficiency and Northern charm.

It was a town in which the second-most-powerful person was the Speaker of the House, Sam Rayburn, a Texan whose office wall was adorned with five portraits of Robert E. Lee, all facing south, and who said he did not socialize because "these Washington society women never serve chili." Washington had fifteen thousand outdoor privies and a cleaning establishment that handled white flannel suits by taking them apart at the seams, hand-washing each piece, drying the pieces in the sun, then reassembling each suit. The process took a week—longer during cloudy weather—and cost $10.

By the time Brinkley retired from ABC in 1996, he had covered (in the subtitle of his 1995 autobiography) "11 Presidents, 4 Wars, 22 Political Conventions, 1 Moon Landing, 3 Assassinations, 2,000 Weeks of News and Other Stuff on Television." Like Walter Cronkite, the only other journalist of comparable stature from television's founding generation, Brinkley began his career in print journalism. Indeed, Brinkley began at a time when the phrase "print journalist" still seemed almost a redundancy.

During the Second World War, Edward R. Murrow and his CBS radio colleagues, such as Eric Sevareid, Charles Collingwood, Robert Trout, and William Shirer, elevated broadcast journalism. But television took awhile to get the hang of it.

In 1949, John Cameron Swayze's *Camel News Caravan*, for which young Brinkley, who had joined NBC in 1943, was a reporter, was carried for fifteen minutes five nights a week. NBC's network consisted of four stations, in Boston, New York, Philadelphia, and Washington. The sponsor required Swayze, who always wore a carnation in his lapel, to have a lit cigarette constantly in view. Not until 1963 did Cronkite's *CBS Evening News* become the first thirty-minute newscast.

In 1981, after thirty-eight years with NBC, Brinkley became host of ABC's *This Week*. He understood a fundamental truth about television talk shows: what one does on them one does in strangers' living rooms. So mind your manners; do not make a scene. Those thoughts guided Brinkley as he provided adult supervision to others on *This Week,* the first hour-long Sunday morning interview program.

How anachronistic the maxim "mind your manners" seems in the harsh light cast by much of today's television. How serene, even proud, Brinkley was about becoming somewhat of an anachronism.

Evelyn Waugh's novel *Scott-King's Modern Europe* (1947) concludes on what can be called a Brinkleyesque note. The protagonist, Mr. Scott-King, a teacher at an English boys' school, is warned by the school's headmaster that the boys' parents are only interested in preparing their boys for the modern world.

"You can hardly blame them, can you?" said the headmaster. "Oh, yes," Scott-King replied, "I can and do," adding, "I think it would be very wicked indeed to do anything to fit a boy for the modern world."

Brinkley's backward-looking gentility made him regret, among much else, the passing of the days when it was unthinkable for a gentleman to wear other than a coat and tie when traveling by air. It is, then, an irony of the sort Brinkley savored that he was not merely present at the creation of television as a shaper of the modern world, he was among the creators of that phenomenon. Like the Founders of this fortunate Republic, Brinkley set standards of performance in his profession that still are both aspirations and reproaches to subsequent practitioners. [JUNE 13, 2003]

Barry Goldwater: "Cheerful Malcontent"

In 2007, I was asked to write the foreword for a new edition of Goldwater's book *The Conscience of a Conservative,* the first in a series of important political books republished by Princeton University Press.

When Barry Goldwater ran for president in 1964, he was Arizona's *junior* senator. But, then, measured by length of Senate service, ninety-eight other senators also were junior to Arizona's senior senator, Carl Hayden, who was a former sheriff in Arizona territory. Hayden had entered the House of Representatives at age thirty-five when Arizona acquired statehood in 1912, and entered the Senate at age forty-nine, where he served until 1969. The Western frontier, so vivid in the national imagination and so associated with American libertarianism, *lived* in Goldwater's Senate colleague.

When I visited Goldwater at his home in Phoenix a few years before his death in 1998, he said he had built his house on a bluff to which, when he was young, he would ride his horse and sleep under the stars. When he was a boy, about one hundred thousand people lived in the Valley of the Sun. When Goldwater died, the population of a *suburb* of Phoenix—Mesa—was larger than St. Louis, and the population of the Phoenix metropolitan area, the nation's fourteenth largest, was approaching three million.

You must remember this: Goldwater was a conservative from, and formed by, a place with precious little past to conserve. Westerners have no inclination to go through life with cricks in their necks from looking backward. When Goldwater became the embodiment of American conservatism—partly by his own efforts, and partly because he was conscripted by others for the role—that guaranteed that the mainstream of American conservatism would be utterly *American*. The growing conservative intelligentsia would savor many flavors of conservatism, from Edmund Burke's to T. S. Eliot's, conservatisms grounded on religious reverence, nostalgia, and resistance to the permanent revolution of conditions in a capitalist, market society. Such conservatisms would have been unintelligible, even repellent, to Goldwater, if he had taken time to notice them.

In the beginning, which is to say in the early 1950s, America's modern conservative movement was remarkably bookish. It began to find its voice with Whittaker Chambers' memoir *Witness* (1952), Russell Kirk's *The Conservative Mind* (1953), and the twenty-five-year-old William F. Buckley Jr.'s *God and Man at Yale* (1951). The books most congruent with what came to be Goldwaterism included one published in London in 1944 by an Austrian and future Nobel laureate in economics—Friedrich Hayek's *The Road to Serfdom*. Another book by another winner of the Nobel prize for economics was Milton Friedman's *Capitalism and Freedom* (1962). Like Hayek and Friedman, Goldwater's central preoccupation was freedom, and the natural tendency of freedom's sphere to contract as government's sphere expands.

Goldwater was a man of many parts—politician and jet pilot, ham radio operator and accomplished photographer—but no one ever called him bookish. And if anyone ever had, Goldwater, a man of action and of the West, might have said—echoing the protagonist of the novel that invented the Western, Owen Wister's *The Virginian* (1902)—"When you call me that, *smile!*"

Then Goldwater would have smiled, because although he could be gruff, he could not stay out of sorts. He was, as journalist Richard Rovere said, "the cheerful malcontent." In that role, he also was an early symptom—a leading indicator—of the 1960s ferment.

The 1960s are rightly remembered as years of cultural dissent and political upheaval, but they are wrongly remembered as years stirred only from the left. Actually, they were not even stirred first, or primarily, or most consequentially from the left. By the time the decade ended, with Richard Nixon in the White House, conservatism was in the saddle, embarked on winning seven of the ten presidential elections from 1968 through 2004.

But because of the political complexion of the journalists who wrote the "first rough draft of history," and because of the similar complexion of the academic historians who have written subsequent drafts, and because much of the decade's most lurid political turbulence, such as the turmoil on campuses and at the riotous 1968 Democratic Convention in Chicago, were episodes of dissent by the left—because of all this, the decade is remembered as one dominated by dissent from the left. Nevertheless, it can reasonably be said that dissent in the 1960s began on the right, and it is certain that the most nation-shaping dissent was from the right.

Some say we should think of the sixties as beginning on November 22, 1963, and ending in October 1973—that is, as beginning with a presidential assassination that supposedly shattered the nation's sunny postwar disposition, and ending with the Yom Kippur War and the oil embargo that produced a sense of scarcity and national vulnerability. Arguably. But although it may seem eccentric—or banal—to say so, the sixties, understood as a decade of intellectual dissent and political insurgency, began in 1960.

On July 27, to be precise, when an Arizona senator strode to the podium of the Republican Convention in Chicago and barked: "Let's grow up, conservatives. If we want to take the party back—and I think we can—let's get to work."

Back from whom? In two words, "moderate" Republicans. In one word, Northeasterners. What that word denoted, to those who used it as an epithet, was the old Republican establishment that had nominated Wendell Willkie (the "barefoot boy from Wall Street" was from Indiana, but not really), New York's Governor Tom Dewey twice, and Dwight Eisenhower twice. (Eisenhower was from Texas and Kansas, long ago, but had sojourned in Paris and in Manhattan's Morningside Heights—as Supreme Allied Commander and president of Columbia University—before winning the 1952 Republican nomination by defeating "Mr. Republican" and the conservatives' favorite, Senator Robert Taft of Ohio.)

The Republican establishment, speaking through the *New York Herald-Tribune,* represented what Goldwater and kindred spirits considered a flaccid postwar Republican consensus. Goldwater's complaint was that timid Republicans challenged neither the New Deal notion of the federal government's competence and responsibilities nor the policy of mere containment regarding the Soviet Union.

The GOP establishment against which Goldwater rose in rebellion is, like the *Herald-Tribune,* which ceased publication in 1966, a mere memory. As is the subject of Goldwater's last chapter, "the Soviet menace." But what makes this book of lasting interest, and what makes it pertinent to the Republicans' deepening intramural conflicts in the first decade of the twenty-first century, is this: Goldwater's primary purpose was to refute the perception that conservatism was an intellectually sterile and morally crass persuasion.

In the first sentence of his first chapter, Goldwater wrote: "I have been much concerned that so many people today with Conservative instincts feel compelled to apologize for them." Nearly half a century later, people calling themselves "progressives" are in flight from the label "liberal." It is difficult to remember, but well to remember, how rapidly and thoroughly political fashions can change: There was a time in living memory when . . . well, in 1950, a man was arrested for creating a public disturbance and a witness said: "He was using abusive language, calling people conservative and all that."

In 1960, the common caricature was that liberals had ideas and ideals, whereas conservatives had only material interests. Goldwater set out to refute the idea that conservatism is merely "a narrow, mechanistic *economic* theory that may work very well as a bookkeeper's guide, but cannot be relied upon as a comprehensive political philosophy." Goldwater insisted that it was liberalism that had become thin intellectual gruel. He said it produced government that saw the nation as a mere aggregation of clamorous constituencies with material itches that it was Washington's duty to scratch with federal programs. The audacity of *The Conscience of a Conservative* was its charge that the post–New Deal political tradition, far from being idealistic, was unworthy of a free society because it treated citizens as mere aggregations of appetites.

In recent years, the intellectual energy in American politics has been concentrated on the right side of the spectrum, and today two kinds of conservatives are at daggers drawn with each other. The last twenty-five years or so produced the rise of "social conservatives," a group generally congruent with the "religious right." These conservatives, alarmed by what they consider the coarsening of the culture, believe in "strong government conservatism." They argue that government can, and urgently must, have an active agenda to defend morals and promote virtue, lest freedom be lost. Other conservatives, the political descendants of Goldwater, agree that good government is, by definition, good for the public's virtue. They also believe, however, that limited government *by its limitations* nurtures in men and women the responsibilities that make them competent for, and worthy of, freedom.

Had Goldwater lived to see the republication of his book in this supposedly conservative era, he might have made some characteristically blunt remarks about the impotence of books. This edition of *The Conscience of a Conservative* comes after a Republican president and a Republican-controlled Congress enacted in 2001 the largest federal intervention in primary and secondary education (the No Child Left Behind law) in American history. And, in 2002, enacted the largest farm subsidies. And, in 2003, enacted the largest expansion of the welfare state (the prescription drug entitlement added to Medicare) since Lyndon Johnson, the president who defeated Goldwater in 1964, created Medicare in 1965. In *The Conscience of a Conservative,* Goldwater insisted that most Americans embraced conservative principles, and he blamed conservatives for failing to persuade the country of the "practical relevance" of conservatism.

Was he mistaken about what most Americans believe? Are they now ideologically, meaning rhetorically, conservative, but operationally liberal?

If so, Goldwater might say this vindicates his argument: One consequence of unlimited government is unlimited dependency—*learned* dependency, a degrading addiction of citizens to public provisions.

But that gloomy conclusion could not long withstand Goldwater's Western cheerfulness. Besides, it does not begin to do justice to the changes conservatism has wrought, or helped to bring about, since Goldwater summoned conservatives to take back the Republican Party. In 1960, the top income tax rate was 90 percent, there was a lifetime entitlement to welfare, the economy was much more regulated than it is now, and the Iron Curtain looked like confirmation of George Orwell's image of totalitarianism: "Imagine a boot stamping on a human face—forever." That "forever" expired twenty-five years after Goldwater's presidential campaign.

Most historians probably think that Goldwater's 1964 run for the White House was the apogee of his public life, which began with his election to the Phoenix city council in 1949 and lasted until his retirement from the Senate in 1987. Goldwater, I suspect, thought otherwise.

Before and after 1964, he was a man of the Senate; he probably thought of his presidential run as a brief detour in a career otherwise as level as the surface of a Western mesa. The Senate suited him as a venue for taking stands and enunciating views. He was a "conviction politician"—a term later minted to describe a soul mate, Margaret Thatcher—who thought the point of public life was to advance a creed. Therefore, this book, more than his presidential candidacy, was, in a sense, the essence of the public man.

When he delivered his acceptance speech to the 1964 Republican Convention in San Francisco's Cow Palace, and thundered that "extremism in defense of liberty is no vice" and "moderation in pursuit of justice is no virtue," a journalist rocked back in his chair and exclaimed: "My God, he's going to run as Goldwater!" Indeed. Goldwater ran as the author of *The Conscience of a Conservative,* with the book as his platform.

He had been an eager author of that book, although an author with the assistance of a professional polemicist—L. Brent ("Hell Bent") Bozell, William Buckley's brother-in-law. Bozell helped Goldwater weave various speeches and other pronouncements into a coherent argument.

Goldwater was, however, a reluctant presidential candidate, especially after the Kennedy assassination. Even before that, he did not have the monomania requisite for a successful candidate. It has been well said that anyone who is willing to do the arduous things necessary to become president probably is too unbalanced to be trusted with the office. Goldwater preferred flying himself around Arizona to photograph Native Americans to being flown around the country in pursuit of convention delegates.

Before the Kennedy assassination, however, Goldwater rather fancied the idea of challenging Kennedy's reelection effort. Goldwater liked Kennedy—they had been freshmen senators in 1953—and he suggested to Kennedy that they might share a plane and hopscotch around the country debating each other. After the assassination, Goldwater knew that the outcome of the 1964 election was not in doubt because, as he put it with the pungency that sometimes got him in trouble, the country was not going to assassinate two presidents in less than twelve months. But a merry band of Republican insurgents, many of them associated in one way or another with Buckley's *National Review*—

which was not yet nine years old when Goldwater was nominated—disregarded his reluctance and launched him on a campaign that would lose forty-four states.

But it was a spectacularly creative loss. In the process, conservatives captured the Republican Party's apparatus. And in October 1964, when Goldwater was shown a speech he was supposed to deliver to a national television audience, he said: "This is good, but it doesn't quite sound like me. Get Ronald Reagan to give it." After Reagan won the presidency, conservatives liked to say that Goldwater won in 1964, but it took sixteen years to count all the votes.

Another way of understanding Goldwater's constructive defeat involves a dialect that a Marxist might relish. In 1938, there was backlash in congressional elections against President Franklin Roosevelt's plan to "pack" the Supreme Court. From 1938 through 1964, there never was a reliably liberal legislating majority in Congress. A coalition of Republicans and conservative, mostly Southern, Democrats held the balance of power. But Goldwater's landslide defeat swept liberal majorities into the House of Representatives and Senate. For two years, liberalism was rampant, until the 1966 elections began to correct the partisan imbalance. During those two years, when the prestige of government was perhaps higher than ever before or since in American history, the Great Society initiatives became an exercise in political overreaching, made possible by Goldwater's defeat. Disappointment with the results laid the predicate for Reagan's victory.

Which was followed by President George Herbert Walker Bush's "kinder and gentler" conservatism, then William Clinton's centrism, then George W. Bush's "compassionate conservatism." And so continues an American political argument about how much government we want, and how much we are willing to pay for it in the coin of constricted freedom. That argument gathered steam when Goldwater threw down a gauntlet—this book.

Forty-seven years after the publication of *The Conscience of a Conservative,* Goldwater, a seasoned politician and a child of the West, probably would look equably upon America as, like Phoenix—today approaching four million people—a work forever furiously in progress. He knew that popular government rests on public opinion, which is shiftable sand. With this book, and with his public career that vivified the principles expressed herein, he shifted a lot of sand.

[FOREWORD TO *THE CONSCIENCE OF A CONSERVATIVE*, APRIL 2007]

John F. Kennedy's Thoughts on Death

L anding in New York on a speaking trip, the president impulsively decided not to have a motorcade into Manhattan, so his limousine stopped at ten traffic lights. At one, a woman ran to the car and snapped a photograph inches from his face. A policeman exclaimed, "Oh, my God. She could have been an assassin." It was November 15, 1963.

On the Sunday night of October 28, 1962, at the conclusion of the Cuban Missile Crisis, John Kennedy quipped to his brother Robert, "This is the night I should go to the theater," a reference to Lincoln's visit to Ford's Theatre after the Civil War was won. Thoughts of death were not new to the man whose father had medicines stored for him in banks around the world. They were to treat chronic illnesses so serious that he had been given the last rites of the Catholic Church at least three times before he became president at age forty-three.

Even if he had not gone to Dallas, he probably would have died long before now. He would have been killed partly by the horrifying cocktails of pills and injections—sometimes six Novocain shots in his back in a day; one drug drove his cholesterol count above 400—mixed by doctors sometimes unaware of what the others were administering just to keep him ambulatory and alert.

The soaring arc of Kennedy's truncated life combined success achieved by discipline, and sexual recklessness—seventy calls through the White House switchboard to a mistress he shared with a Mafia don; said another woman, Marilyn Monroe, "I think I made his back feel better"—that risked everything.

In *President Kennedy: Profile of Power,* much the best book on Kennedy, Richard Reeves says that Kennedy—"very impatient, addicted

to excitement, living his life as if it were a race against boredom"—
was well matched to his moment. He was a man in a hurry at a time
when the pulse of communication was accelerating.

In seeking the presidency, Reeves wrote, "he did not wait his turn."
One of the elders he elbowed aside, Adlai Stevenson, said, "That young
man! He never says 'please' . . ." When a friend urged Kennedy to wait
beyond 1960, he said, "No, they will forget me. Others will come
along."

Always there was his fatalistic sense of how perishable everything
was, and his ironic awareness of how nothing is what it seems—least
of all himself. Campaigning in 1960 as a vessel of "vigor," his health
often forced him to spend about half of the day in bed.

The Kennedy years had, as Reeves writes, "an astonishing density
of events," from the building of the Berlin Wall to the Birmingham
church bombing, and the integration of the University of Mississippi a
month before the Cuban Missile Crisis. Kennedy was a quick study,
with much to learn.

Astonishingly callow when inaugurated, he was unable to stem or
even discern the intragovernmental delusions and deceits that propelled
the Bay of Pigs invasion just eighty-seven days into his presidency.
Much flowed from that debacle. Kennedy said that in order to reverse
Nikita Khrushchev's assessment of him as weak, he had to find somewhere to show U.S. resolve: "The only place we can do that is in Vietnam. We have to send more people there." Soon he was at the Vienna
summit, where Khrushchev, impervious to his charm, concluded that
he was "a pygmy."

Only foreign affairs held Kennedy's attention. His response to the
"freedom riders" who lit a fuse of the civil rights revolution was to
ask his civil rights adviser, who was white, "Can't you get your god-
damned friends off those buses?" But foreign affairs were plentiful
enough.

Plentiful, and a sure cure for boredom. When on May 30, 1961,
Rafael Trujillo, dictator of the Dominican Republic, was assassinated,
Kennedy asked Secretary of State Dean Rusk: "Were we involved?"
Rusk replied: "I don't think so. There's some confusion."

In 1963, too, the days were eventful. Twenty-two days after a Saigon coup encouraged by the United States—it produced regime change through the assassination of South Vietnam's two principal leaders— and on the day a ballpoint pen containing poison intended to kill Fidel Castro was scheduled to be delivered by CIA agent Desmond Fitzgerald to a potential assassin, Kennedy awoke in Fort Worth. He was to speak there, then fly to Dallas.

Looking down from his hotel room at the platform from which he would speak, he said to an aide, "With all these buildings around it, the Secret Service couldn't stop someone who really wanted to get you." It was Friday, November 22, 1963.   [NOVEMBER 20, 2003]

Eugene McCarthy: The Tamarack Tree of American Politics

I love you so. . . . Gone? Who will swear you wouldn't have
done good to the country, that fulfillment wouldn't have
done good to you.
    —ROBERT LOWELL, "For Eugene McCarthy" (July 1968)

By August 1968, Senator Eugene McCarthy was gone and his supporters were left to wonder how—whether—his fulfillment was connected to doing good to the country. When the Democratic convention nominated another Minnesotan, Hubert Humphrey—who in 1964 won the vice presidential nomination McCarthy had craved— McCarthy went to the south of France, then covered the World Series for *Life* magazine. Had he campaigned for Humphrey, who narrowly lost, there probably would have been no Nixon presidency.

McCarthy died last Saturday in his ninetieth year, in this city which he sometimes seemed to include in his capacious disdain but which, for a while, he leavened with a distinctive sensibility. In 1980, he endorsed Ronald Reagan, reasoning that Reagan could not be worse than Jimmy Carter. But even in 1968 he had a sometimes ill-disguised disdain for many who flocked to his diffidently unfurled banner.

Disgusted by Vietnam policy, he laconically announced himself "willing" to be an "adequate" president, and went to New Hampshire to unseat his party's president. McCarthy got 41.9 percent of the vote. Johnson got 49.6 percent—all write-ins; his name was not on the ballot—and three weeks later withdrew from the race.

McCarthy's 1968 achievement elevated New Hampshire's primary to the status it has subsequently enjoyed. His death occurred the day the Democratic Party gingerly suggested modifying its primary schedule in a way that might diminish New Hampshire's potency.

The sacramental status of Iowa's caucuses and New Hampshire's primary as the first two nominating events testifies to the power of the mere passage of time to sanctify the accidental, even the unreasonable. Now the Democratic Party suggests allowing one or two states to hold caucuses—not primaries—between Iowa and New Hampshire.

The case against caucuses is that they take hours, often at night, and thus disproportionately attract the ideologically fervid—not what the Democratic Party needs. The case against New Hampshire's primary is that its power is disproportionate for a state so unrepresentative of America's demographic complexities. The case for New Hampshire can be put in a name: Gene McCarthy. The small state gives an unknown underdog challenger, practicing retail politics, a fighting chance.

McCarthy's insurgency, the most luminous memory of many aging liberals, would today be impossible—criminal, actually—thanks to the recent "reform" most cherished by liberals, the McCain-Feingold campaign regulations. McCarthy's audacious challenge to an incumbent president was utterly dependent on large early contributions from five rich liberals. Stewart Mott's $210,000 would be more than $1.2 million in today's dollars. McCain-Feingold codifies two absurdities: Large contributions are inherently evil, and political money can be limited without limiting political speech. McCain-Feingold criminalizes the sort of seed money that enabled McCarthy to be heard. Under McCain-Feingold's current limit of $2,100 per contributor, McCarthy's top five contributors combined could have given just $10,500, which in 1968 dollars would have been just $1,834.30. But, then, McCain-Feingold was written by incumbents to protect what they cherish: themselves.

McCarthy first seized national attention with a theatrical act, a gesture of elegant futility. At the 1960 convention, when John Kennedy's nomination was already certain, McCarthy delivered an eloquent philippic urging a third nomination for the man who had been trounced in 1952 and 1956, Adlai Stevenson.

Witty, elegant, and problematic, Stevenson was the intelligentsia's darling and a harbinger of liberalism curdled by condescension toward ordinary Americans. When an aide assured Stevenson he had the votes of thinking people, Stevenson quipped: But I need a majority. A majority of the disdained?

McCarthy's acerbic wit sometimes slid into unpleasantness, as when, after Governor George Romney, the Michigan Republican, said that briefers in Vietnam had "brainwashed" him, McCarthy said that surely a light rinse would have sufficed. McCarthy's wit revealed an aptitude for condescension, an aptitude that charmed intellectuals but not Americans condescended to.

A talented poet, McCarthy, in his mordant "The Tamarack," surely summarized his experience of being beaten by Robert Kennedy after New Hampshire:

> *The tamarack tree is the saddest tree of all;*
> *it is the first tree to invade the swamp,*
> *and when it makes the soil dry enough,*
> *the other trees come and kill it.*

Never mind his subsequent lackadaisical presidential campaigns. After 1968, he adhered to the fourth of the commandments in his "10 Commandments":

> *Do not relight a candle*
> *whose flame has drowned*
> *in its own excess of wax.*

[DECEMBER 13, 2005]

What George McGovern Made

The former bomber pilot's spry walk belies his eighty-five years; he dresses like a *boulevardier*—gray slacks, blue blazer, shirt with bright-red stripes and a white collar—and tucks into a robust breakfast. Long ago, he began shaping the Democrats' presidential nomination process into the one that has his party's two contenders locked in a long march to Pennsylvania's April primary. He has seen important aspects of American politics move in his direction in the thirty-six years since he lost forty-nine states to Richard Nixon.

The belittling of George McGovern, especially by Democrats, only waned as memory of him faded after he lost his bid for a fourth Senate term in the 1980 Reagan landslide. But his story is fascinating, and pertinent to current events.

This minister's son was raised on South Dakota's parched prairies during the Depression. He remembers hiking home to the town of Mitchell by following the railroad tracks in a blinding dust storm. He was only the second major-party nominee with a Ph.D. (Woodrow Wilson was the first), which he earned at Northwestern University under Arthur Link, Wilson's foremost biographer.

Like Wilson, also a minister's son, McGovern was a political moralist. And he was a tenacious politician, who, inspired by the untenacious Adlai Stevenson's presidential campaign the year before, went to work for the South Dakota Democratic Party in 1953, when it held only 2 of 110 seats in the state legislature. Just four years later, McGovern was in Congress, where his first roll-call vote was in opposition to granting President Eisenhower broad authority for military intervention in the Middle East.

In tumultuous 1968, with the Tet Offensive and two assassinations (of Martin Luther King and Robert Kennedy) in five months, two insurgent candidates, Eugene McCarthy and Robert Kennedy, sought the Democratic nomination. It was won by Vice President Hubert Humphrey, *who competed in no primaries*. More than one-third of the delegates to the riotous convention in Chicago had been selected *in 1967,* months before President Lyndon Johnson decided to retire.

McGovern was named chairman of a commission to reform the nomination process, which put the party on a path to the proliferation of caucuses and primaries allocating delegates proportionally rather than winner-take-all—the long, winding path Obama and Clinton are on. In 1972, McGovern became the first winner under the democratized process. Then he was buried by the demos, Nixon vs. McGovern.

Nixon was, McGovern notes, running nationally for the fifth time (only FDR had done that) and was at his pre-Watergate apogee, fresh from the opening to China and a strategic-arms agreement with Moscow. McGovern was bitterly opposed all the way to the Miami convention by the Democratic constituencies he was displacing. He says Barry Goldwater had warned him, "Don't get fatigued," but he reached Miami exhausted, lost control of the convention (he delivered his acceptance speech at 2:30 a.m.), and disastrously selected a running mate, Missouri senator Tom Eagleton, who did not disclose previous psychiatric problems and was forced off the ticket.

Still, McGovern thinks he could have won with a running mate then called "the most trusted man in America"—Walter Cronkite. Before choosing Eagleton, McGovern considered asking Cronkite, who recently indicated he would have accepted.

Bruce Miroff, a political scientist and an admirer of McGovern, argues in his new book, *The Liberals' Moment: The McGovern Insurgency and the Identity Crisis of the Democratic Party,* that although McGovern's domestic proposals featured redistributions of wealth, this was Ivy League, not prairie, populism. Branded the candidate of "acid, amnesty, and abortion" (the Democrats' platform, adopted six months before the Supreme Court in *Roe v. Wade* legislated a liberal abortion policy, did not mention abortion), McGovern became the first candidate since the New Deal to lose the Catholic and labor union vote. So 1972, more than 1968, was the hinge of the party's history. In 1972, Miroff writes, "college-educated issue activists" supplanted the "labor/urban machine coalition."

George Meany, head of the AFL-CIO, had dropped out of high school at age fourteen. Speaking about McGovern's 1972 convention, where 39 percent of the delegates had advanced degrees, he said: "We heard from people who look like Jacks, acted like Jills, and had the odor of Johns about them." The Reagan Democrats of 1980 were incubated eight years earlier.

McGovern won only 14 percent of Southern white Protestants. This, Miroff notes, made Democrats susceptible four years later to the appeal of a pious Southerner. Thus did a disaster compound itself.

In September 1963, McGovern became the only senator who opposed U.S. involvement in Vietnam during the *Kennedy* administration. He came by his horror of war honorably in thirty-five B-24 missions over Germany, where half the B-24 crews did not survive—they suffered a higher rate of fatalities than did Marines storming Pacific islands. McGovern was awarded a Distinguished Flying Cross with three oak-leaf clusters. In his seventies, he lost a forty-five-year-old daughter to alcoholism. Losing a presidential election, he says softly, "was not the saddest thing in my life." Time confers a comforting perspective, giving consolations to old age, which needs them.   [FEBRUARY 25, 2008]

Daniel Patrick Moynihan:
The Senate's Sisyphus

Many of America's largest public careers have been those of presidents. Many, but by no means all. Chief Justice John Marshall was more consequential than all but two presidents—Washington and Lincoln. Among twentieth-century public servants, General George Marshall—whose many achievements included discerning the talents of a Colonel Eisenhower—may have been second in importance only to Franklin Roosevelt. And no twentieth-century public career was as many-faceted, and involved so much prescience about as many matters, as that of Daniel Patrick Moynihan, who died Wednesday at seventy-six.

He was born in Tulsa but spent his formative years on Manhattan's Lower East Side, from which he rose to Harvard's faculty and the administrations of Presidents Kennedy, Johnson, Nixon, and Ford, serving as, among other things, ambassador to India and the U.S. representative at the United Nations. Then four Senate terms. Along the way he wrote more books than some of his colleagues read, and became something that, like Atlantis, is rumored to have once existed but has not recently been seen—the Democratic Party's mind.

His was the most penetrating political intellect to come from New York since Alexander Hamilton, who, like Moynihan, saw over the horizon of his time, anticipating the evolving possibilities and problems of a consolidated, urbanized, industrial nation. A liberal who did not flinch from the label, he reminded conservatives that the Constitution's framers "had more thoughts about power than merely its limitation."

But he was a liberal dismayed by what he called "the leakage of reality from American life." When in 1994 the Senate debated an education bill, Moynihan compared the legislation's two quantifiable goals— a high school graduation rate of "at least 90 percent" by 2000, and American students "first in the world in mathematics and science"— to Soviet grain production quotas.

The Senate's Sisyphus, Moynihan was forever pushing uphill a boulder of inconvenient data. A social scientist trained to distinguish correlation from causation, and a wit, Moynihan puckishly said that a crucial determinant of the quality of American schools is proximity to the Canadian border. The barb in his jest was this: High cognitive outputs correlate not with high per-pupil expenditures but with a high percentage of two-parent families. For that, there was the rough geographical correlation that caused Moynihan to suggest that states trying to improve their students' test scores should move closer to Canada.

For calling attention, four decades ago, to the crisis of the African-American family—26 percent of children were being born out of wedlock—he was denounced as a racist by lesser liberals. Today the percentage among all Americans is 33, among African-Americans 69, and family disintegration, meaning absent fathers, is recognized as the most powerful predictor of most social pathologies.

At the U.N., he witnessed that institution's inanity (as in its debate about the threat to peace posed by U.S. forces in the Virgin Islands, at that time fourteen Coast Guardsmen, one shotgun, one pistol) and its viciousness (the resolution condemning Zionism as racism). Striving to move America "from apology to opposition," he faulted U.S. foreign policy elites as "decent people, utterly unprepared for their work."

Their "common denominator, apart from an incapacity to deal with ideas, was a fear of making a scene, a form of good manners that is a kind of substitute for ideas." Except they did have one idea, that "the behavior of other nations, especially the developing nations, was fundamentally a reaction to the far worse behavior of the United States."

Moynihan carried Woodrow Wilson's faith in international law, but he had what Wilson lacked—an understanding that ethnicity makes the world go 'round. And bleed. The persistence of this premodern sensibility defeats what Moynihan called "the liberal expectancy." He meant the expectation that the world would become tranquil as ethnicity and religion became fading residues of mankind's infancy.

Moynihan's Senate campaigns were managed by as tough-minded and savvy a pol as New York's rough-and-tumble democracy has ever produced, a person who also is a distinguished archaeologist—his wife, Elizabeth. In his first campaign, in 1976, Moynihan's opponent was the incumbent, James Buckley, who playfully referred to *"Professor Moynihan"* from Harvard. Moynihan exclaimed with mock indignation, "The mudslinging has begun!"

His last home was an apartment on Washington's Pennsylvania Avenue. That "Avenue of Presidents" was transformed from tattiness to majesty and vibrancy by three decades of his deep reflection about, and persistent insistence on, proper architectural expressions of the Republic's spiritedness and reasonableness, virtues made wonderfully vivid in the life of Daniel Patrick Moynihan.   [MARCH 27, 2003]

John Kenneth Galbraith's Liberalism as Condescension

John Kenneth Galbraith, the Harvard economist who died last week in his ninety-eighth year, has been justly celebrated for his wit, fluency, public-spiritedness, and public service, which extended from New Deal Washington to India, where he served as U.S. ambassador. Like two Harvard colleagues—historian Arthur Schlesinger Jr. and Senator Pat Moynihan, another ambassador to India—Galbraith was among liberalism's leading public intellectuals, yet he was a friend and skiing partner of William F. Buckley. After one slalom down a Swiss mountain, inelegantly executed by the six-foot-eight Galbraith, Buckley asked how long Galbraith had been skiing. Thirty years, he said. Buckley mischievously replied: About as long as you have been an economist.

Galbraith was an adviser to presidents (John Kennedy, a former student, and Lyndon Johnson) and presidential aspirants (Adlai Stevenson and Eugene McCarthy). His book *The Affluent Society*, published in 1958, was a milestone on liberalism's transformation into a doctrine of condescension. And into a minority persuasion.

In the 1950s, liberals were disconsolate. Voters twice rejected the intelligentsia's pinup, Stevenson, in favor of Dwight Eisenhower, who elicited a new strain in liberalism—disdain for average Americans. Liberals dismissed the Eisenhower administration as "the bland leading the bland." They said New Dealers had been supplanted by car dealers. How to explain the electorate's dereliction of taste? Easy. The masses, in their bovine simplicity, had been manipulated, mostly by advertising, particularly on television, which by 1958 had become the masses' entertainment.

Intellectuals, that herd of independent minds, were, as usual, in lockstep as they deplored "conformity." Fear of that had begun when the decade did, with David Riesman's *The Lonely Crowd* (1950), which was followed by C. Wright Mills's *White Collar* (1951), Sloan Wilson's novel *The Man in the Gray Flannel Suit* (1955), William Whyte's *The Organization Man* (1956), and Vance Packard's *The Hidden Persuaders* (1957).

Galbraith brought to the anticonformity chorus a special verve in depicting Americans as pathetic, passive lumps, as manipulable as clay. Americans were what modern liberalism relishes—victims, to be treated as wards of a government run by liberals. It never seemed to occur to Galbraith and like-minded liberals that ordinary Americans might resent that depiction and might express their resentment with their votes.

Advertising, Galbraith argued, was a leading cause of America's "private affluence and public squalor." By that he meant Americans' consumerism, which produced their deplorable reluctance to surrender more of their income to taxation, trusting government to spend it wisely.

If advertising were as potent as Galbraith thought, the advent of television—a large dose of advertising, delivered to every living room— should have caused a sharp increase in consumption relative to savings. No such increase coincided with the arrival of television, but Galbraith, reluctant to allow empiricism to slow the flow of theory, was never a martyr to Moynihan's axiom that everyone is entitled to his own opinion but not to his own facts.

Although Galbraith coined the phrase "conventional wisdom," and thought of himself as the scourge of groupthink, *The Affluent Society* was the distilled essence of the conventional wisdom on campuses. In the 1960s, that liberalism became a stance of disdain, describing Americans not only as Galbraith had, as vulgar, but also as sick, racist, sexist, imperialist, etc. Again, and not amazingly, voters were not amused when told that their desires—for big cars, neighborhood schools, and other things—did not deserve respect.

But for liberals that was precisely the beauty of Galbraith's theory. If advertising could manufacture demands for whatever corporations wanted to supply, there was no need to respect markets, which bring supply and demand into equilibrium.

The Affluent Society was the canonical text of modern liberalism's disparagement of the competence of the average American. This liberalism—the belief that people are manipulable dolts who need to be protected by their liberal betters from exposure to "too much" advertising—is one rationale for McCain-Feingold. That law regulating campaigns embodies the political class's belief that it knows just the right amount of permissible political speech.

Of course if advertising really could manufacture consumer wants willy-nilly, few new products would fail. But many do. *The Affluent Society,* postulating the awesome power of manufacturers to manufacture whatever demand they find it convenient to satisfy, was published nine months after Ford Motor Company put all of its marketing muscle behind a new product, the Edsel.

Small wonder that a conservative wit has surmised that the wisdom of economists varies inversely with their heights. Milton Friedman, ninety-three, is five feet tall.   [MAY 4, 2006]

Milton Friedman: Ebullient Master of the Dismal Science

At Oxford University in 1962, a small coterie of students, mostly Americans, merrily rowed against the leftist political currents predominant among intellectuals everywhere. Some of these rowers had been at the University of Chicago, others had come within the ambit of people from there, and all of us were infused with the doctrines of laissez-faire political economy prevalent in that university's economics department.

A conservative member of Parliament, meeting with these free-market firebrands, began by saying, "Well, presumably we agree that at least the roads should be owned by the government." The group greeted with stony silence this heresy against limited—*very* limited—government.

In one of the group's favorite periodicals—the *New Individualist Review,* published at the University of Chicago—a theorist argued that the government must own lighthouses because no market mechanism could price a lighthouse's service. That provoked this spirited rebuttal: When the light sweeps the ocean's surface, it improves the surface, which becomes the property of the lighthouse owner, who can charge whatever the market will bear for ships to cross the illuminated surface.

Ah, but does the property right lapse when fog obscures the beam of light? Hairs were split as ideological purity hung in the balance.

These contumacious students were, as students frequently are, inebriated by ideas to the point of silliness. But they were early acolytes of the extraordinary man who, as he celebrates his ninetieth birthday this month, merits celebration as America's most consequential public intellectual of the twentieth century.

By 1962, when he published his great manifesto *Capitalism and Freedom,* Milton Friedman, then a University of Chicago economist, had done much of the scholarly work for which he would receive the 1976 Nobel Prize in economics. He has been the foremost champion of "monetarism," the theory that money supply and interest rates can do more than government fiscal policy ("demand management" and other Keynesian fine-tuning measures) to control business cycles. The theory that stable growth of the money supply can control inflation and moderate recessions is an important ingredient in the recipe for modest government.

Capitalism and Freedom inserted into political discourse such (then) novel ideas as flexible exchange rates, a private dimension of Social Security, tuition vouchers to empower parents with school choice, and a flat income tax. Gary Becker (Nobel Prize, 1992), Friedman's colleague at the University of Chicago and the Hoover Institution, notes that when Friedman began arguing the case, most nations had top tax rates of at least 90 percent (91 percent in America). Today most top rates are 50 percent or less, so the world has moved far toward Friedman's position.

Friedman was a charter member of the most influential society you have never heard of—the Mont Pelerin Society, named after the Swiss community where this association of laissez-faire thinkers first gathered in 1947. Its animating spirit was Friedrich Hayek, soon to be at the University of Chicago. In 1955, Hayek prompted the founding of the like-minded Institute of Economic Affairs in London, which around 1962 caught the attention of a junior member of Parliament who seventeen years later brought Friedman's monetarism and respect for markets into No. 10 Downing Street—Margaret Thatcher.

Many intellectuals disdain the marketplace because markets function nicely without the supervision of intellectuals. Their disdain is ingratitude: The vulgar (as intellectuals see them) people who make markets productive make the intellectual class sustainable. As another of Friedman's Chicago colleagues, George Stigler (Nobel Prize, 1982), says, "Since intellectuals are not inexpensive, until the rise of the modern enterprise system, no society could afford many intellectuals." So "we professors are much more beholden to Henry Ford than to the foundation which bears his name and spreads his assets."

Economics is not the "dismal science" when infused with Friedman's ebullient spirit and expressed in his sprightly prose. So as President George W. Bush said in May when honoring Friedman, it was fortunate for the nation and the world that Friedman "flunked some of his qualifying exams to become an actuary and became an economist instead."

John Maynard Keynes, whose preeminence among economists Friedman eclipsed, said the world is mostly ruled by the ideas of economists and political philosophers: "Practical men, who believe themselves to be quite exempt from any intellectual influences, are usually the slaves of some defunct economist." But Friedman is far from defunct as he strides jauntily into his tenth decade, still an intellectual dynamo.

Adam Smith, whose banner Milton Friedman has borne high, said, "There is much ruin in a nation." There is much less of it in ours than there would have been were it not for Milton Friedman.

[JULY 14, 2002]

Alan Greenspan: High-Achieving Minimalist

F requently the fate—gratifying, yet melancholy—of consequential public persons is this: They so transform an ominous social landscape that, by the time they leave the public stage, the public no longer remembers the banished dangers, and hence cannot properly value the banisher. So as Alan Greenspan heads to the end, in January, of more than eighteen years as head of the Federal Reserve, recall that thirty years ago the intelligentsia worried that democracies, including this one, had become "ungovernable."

The worrying was caused by inflation, then thought to be the systemic disease of democracies. The theory was that democratic electorates would reward governments that delivered the pleasure of public

spending and would punish those that inflicted the pain of taxation sufficient to pay for that spending. Hence democracies would run chronic
deficits. These, it was assumed, both caused inflation and gave government a powerful incentive to tolerate inflation as a means of steadily reducing the real value of its debts—inflation as slow-motion repudiation.

Furthermore, deficit spending—giving the public a dollar's worth
of government goods and services and charging the public only, say,
eighty cents for them—produced big government and, by making big
government inexpensive, reduced public resistance to making it even
bigger. And because of affluent voters' low and steadily lowering pain
thresholds, democracies would not tolerate the discomforts associated
with wringing inflation out of the economy.

That supposition was slain by a fact: President Reagan and Paul
Volcker, Greenspan's predecessor, put the country through the rigors
of wringing inflation out of the economy, and in 1984 Reagan carried
forty-nine states. Between 1945 and 1982 the economy was in recession 22.4 percent of the time. In the 276 months since the recession
ended in 1982, it has been in recession fourteen months—just 5.1 percent of the time.

Because of Americans' low pain threshold, the Reagan-Volcker recession was considered hideous. It was the worst since the Depression,
but the economy contracted less than 3 percent. In the years between
1890 and 1945, America's period of hard learning about managing an
industrial economy, three times there were contractions of 5 percent,
twice contractions of 10 percent, and twice contractions of 15 percent.

Since 1945, and especially since 1982, we have learned the real secret of managing the economy: Do not try to manage it. If you refrain
from trying to "fine-tune" business cycles, the cycles will be less frequent and less severe.

Greenspan's tenure has illustrated an axiom to which his successor, Ben Bernanke, should subscribe: Minimalist missions by government produce maximum results. He has not defined the Fed's primary
purpose as achieving this or that level of employment or economic
growth. Rather, its mission is to preserve the currency as a stable store
of value—to control inflation. However, Greenspan's impeccable cre-

dentials as an inflation fighter have enabled him to keep inflation rates low even during very low unemployment without kindling inflationary expectations, which can be self-fulfilling.

America's economy is so dynamic that in any five-year period, approximately 45 percent of Americans move from one income quintile to another. Twenty percent move up from the bottom quintile in any twelve-month period, and 40 percent to 50 percent move up over ten to twenty years. Because of the constant transformation of dynamic economies, the study of economics has become a science of single instances. Its practitioners are constantly in uncharted waters, reasoning inferentially. Just as astronomers inferred the existence of Pluto from the behavior of known planets, Greenspan inferred a rate of productivity growth higher than most estimates because inflation and unemployment were falling simultaneously.

The Federal Reserve system—to give the devil his due, it is one of Woodrow Wilson's unregrettable undertakings—annoys some populists who think every U.S. senator and representative should write on his or her bathroom mirror, and read every morning, this thought: "The Fed is a creature of Congress." Indeed, Congress made it and could dictate to it—could dictate interest rates and the money supply. A terrifying thought.

Greenspan's famously, at times hilariously, circumspect rhetoric has been prudent because some word, or inflection, or even arched eyebrow could have caused vast sums to slosh in this or that direction in capital markets. His rhetorical style—or perhaps antistyle—is a high-stakes illustration of Voltaire's idea that men use speech to conceal their thoughts.

Greenspan's wife has said he had to propose marriage three times before she understood what he was saying. And he was being droll when he said—if he said it; apocrypha collect around legends—that "if I have made myself clear I have misspoken." His achievements speak clearly for him. [OCTOBER 25, 2005]

The Not-at-All Dull George Washington

Tonight, after you have given up trying to get the mustard stains off the dog, and after you have treated the fingers singed by sparklers, pour a beer—a Sam Adams would be apposite—and settle down to watch on PBS the documentary biography of the man most responsible for there being an Independence Day. Ninety minutes later, Richard Brookhiser's *Rediscovering George Washington* will have convinced you that its subject, whom many historians have managed to mummify into dullness, may have been the most interesting and indispensable American.

"Indispensable"? Advanced thinkers instruct us that we are not supposed to believe anyone is more important than anyone else. Not democratic. We are supposed to prefer "history from below," meaning "history with the politics left out," explaining the past not with reference of event-making individuals, but in terms of the holy trinity of today's obsessions—race, gender, class.

But Brookhiser begins his film standing at Yale in front of a portrait of Washington and says: "An empire might break on that forehead." Then he explains why an empire did: Washington's character.

Character, particularly that of someone dead two centuries, is difficult for a camera to capture. Besides, Washington's army, unlike Caesar's or Napoleon's, lost more battles than it won. It is said that America won the war because of its superior retreats, such as the one after the British landed an army on Long Island—an army larger than the population of New York City. Still, Brookhiser's script summons Washington to life.

Brookhiser's camera takes us to the Brooklyn scene—now an auto body shop—where brave Marylanders enabled Washington to escape to fight another day. Washington's next defeat occurred at what is now Thirty-fourth and Lexington Avenue. Brookhiser refutes the myth that Washington's troops usually fought "Indian style," in forest skirmishes and ambushes. As in most eighteenth-century battles, close combat—the bayonet—caused most casualties.

Washington understood that the creation of a nation depended on creating a regular army that could slug it out with Britain's. The tide began to turn in New Jersey, at Monmouth.

The most powerful person in American history, Washington had less formal education than any subsequent president, other than Lincoln. This six-foot-three leader of soldiers who averaged five-foot-eight was charismatic before the term was coined. Abigail Adams, no swooning teenager, described Washington with lines from Dryden: "Mark his majestic fabric. He's a temple sacred from his birth and built by hands divine."

He was not the only one of that era who learned showmanship from studying theater and popular entertainments such as Punch and Judy puppet shows. Joseph Addison's play *Cato* was the source of Nathan Hale's dying words ("I only regret that I have but one life to lose for my country") and Patrick Henry's "Give me liberty, or give me death!" In the play, Cato held mutinous officers in line by force of personality, as Washington was to do at Newburgh, New York.

Brookhiser, a senior editor of *National Review* magazine and frequent contributor to other magazines and to C-SPAN, is also known for his slender, sprightly biographies of Washington, Alexander Hamilton, the Adams dynasty. The longest, on Hamilton, is just 240 pages long. His next subject will be Gouverneur Morris. Brookhiser's capsule summary of Morris is characteristically pithy: "Peg-legged ladies' man who polished the Constitution's language."

Brookhiser does not write "pathographies"—biographies that present historic figures as the sum of their pathologies. His Washington adopted a noble character, then grew into it. Intensely interested in manners, Washington pioneered a civic etiquette suitable for a democracy in which preeminence was to be based on behavior, not birth.

And of the nine presidents who owned slaves, only Washington freed his at his death. Brookhiser visits a family reunion of descendants of those slaves—one of whom is a guide at Mount Vernon. Congress wanted Washington's body to rest in a room beneath the Capitol rotunda, like Napoleon's in the Invalides. But Washington's remains are at Mount Vernon. So, Brookhiser says:

"The Capitol is not his tomb but the people's house. This reflects his wishes and the goal of his life. Washington wanted to establish a government that would prove that mankind was not made for a master—not even the mastership of a hero's memory."

"They wanted me to be another Washington," whined Napoleon in his exile, as stunned as the rest of the world by Washington's voluntary yielding of power. The final component of Washington's indispensability was the imperishable example he gave by proclaiming himself dispensable.   [JULY 4, 2002]

George Washington's Long Journey Home

H is goal, 220 years ago, was to sleep Christmas Eve in his six-foot six-inch bed at his Virginia home on the bank of the Potomac. It would be nicer than some other recent Christmas Eves.

Such as in 1776, when he led soldiers across Delaware River ice floes to one of his greatest—and, truth be told, relatively few—victories, at Trent Town, as Trenton was then known. Only four Americans died that night, two—probably shoeless—from frostbite.

George Washington spent Christmas Eve 1777 with an army leaving bloody footprints in the Valley Forge snow. Six years later, he was heading to a home he had left in 1775 to lead farmers and shopkeepers against the British Empire.

Since Yorktown, Washington, like his embryonic nation, had lived in a peculiar limbo as negotiators, two months' travel away in Paris, codified peace with Britain. In late November, from headquarters along the Hudson River north of Manhattan island, he began his trek from strenuous public service into a placid future of private enjoyments, or so he thought.

His journey was through a nation deep in the throes—it would be in them for many years—of regime change. To the extent that there was a national regime, he was it, and he was retiring.

In January 1783, Congress had fled Philadelphia, going to ground in Princeton, New Jersey, to escape a mutiny of unpaid soldiers. Congress was a place of empty palaver by representatives of states that retained virtually untrammeled sovereignty. By July 1783, with Congress sitting in Annapolis, only South Carolina—seven decades later, it would be the least cooperative state—had paid its full assessment to the national treasury. Of the other twelve, only Washington's Virginia had contributed half its quota. The two weightiest states, Pennsylvania and New York, had contributed one-fifth and one-twentieth, respectively.

What united the barely united states was six feet three inches of American in a blue coat and buff trousers, carrying a sword and buckle engraved "1757" that testified to his frontier service for the British against the French, whose fleet, twenty-four years later, sealed the victory at Yorktown. If on his trip home this fifty-one-year-old man had caught a chill and died, as he would do sixteen Decembers later, national unity might have been unattainable.

The story of his triumphal trip home, itself an act of nation building, is well told by historian Stanley Weintraub in his new book *General Washington's Christmas Farewell: A Mount Vernon Homecoming, 1783*. It evokes the frail seedling from which the mighty American nation grew. In a seven-year (1775–1781) war in which fewer than forty five hundred American soldiers died in combat, Washington lost more battles than he won. But he won the battle that mattered most—the last one—and adulation unlike any ever bestowed on an American.

His homeward journey paused at Harlem, a Manhattan village nine miles north of New York City, a community of twenty-one thousand on the island's southern tip that Washington had never captured. As Washington's party entered the city, Loyalist emigrants were being ferried to departing British ships in the harbor. A British officer marveled:

"Here, in this city, we have had an army for more than seven years, and yet could not keep the peace of it. Scarcely a day or night passed without tumults. Now we are gone, everything is in quietness and safety. These Americans are a curious, original people; they know how to govern themselves, but nobody else can govern them."

Then it was four days to Philadelphia, passing along what is now U.S. Route 1 through difficult New Jersey. In 1776, Washington had urged Jerseymen in the village of Newark to join his cause. Thirty did—but three hundred joined the British. In Annapolis, he surrendered his commission after a ball at which, Weintraub reports, fashionable ladies wore their hair in the *dress à l'independence*—thirteen curls at the neck.

Washington's journey to Mount Vernon, which he reached after dark, December 24, was a movable feast of florid rhetoric and baked oysters. It also was a foretaste of what was to be, for more than a century, his central place in America's civic liturgy. Abraham Lincoln wore a ring containing a sliver from the casket Washington was buried in until his body was moved to its current tomb in 1831. At his inauguration in 1897, William McKinley wore a ring containing strands of Washington's hair. Presidents no longer inspire such reverence, perhaps because America is different, perhaps because presidents are.   [DECEMBER 25, 2003]

John Marshall: The Most Important American Never to Have Been President

A nation's identity consists of braided memories, which are nourished by diligence at civic commemorations. It is, therefore, disappointing that at this moment of keen interest in the Supreme Court and the office of chief justice, scant attention has been paid to the 250th anniversary of the birth of the nation's greatest jurist, Chief Justice John Marshall.

The oldest of the family's fifteen children, he was born September 24, 1755, into Virginia rusticity where women pinned their blouses with thorns. Yet he developed the most urbane and subtle mind of that era of remarkable statecraft. He was a member of Virginia's ratifying convention, and in nearly thirty-five years as chief justice he founded American constitutional law. That kind of legal reasoning by Supreme Court justices is a continuous exegesis of the Constitution and is sometimes not easily distinguished from a continuing writing of the document.

Marshall is the most important American never to have been president. Because of his shaping effect on the soft wax of the young republic, his historic importance is greater than that of all but two presidents—Washington and Lincoln. Without Marshall's landmark opinions defining the national government's powers, the government Washington founded might not have acquired competencies—and society might not have developed the economic sinews—sufficient to enable Lincoln to preserve the Union.

Article I, Section 8, enumerates Congress's powers, and then empowers Congress "to make all laws which shall be necessary and proper for carrying into execution the foregoing powers." Marshall's capacious construction of the "necessary and proper" clause shaped the law, and the nation's consciousness of itself.

Did Congress have the power—unenumerated but implied—to charter a national bank? In 1819, forty-two years before Lincoln grappled with unprecedented exigencies, Marshall ruled:

"Throughout this vast republic, from the St. Croix to the Gulph of Mexico, from the Atlantic to the Pacific, revenue is to be collected and expended, armies are to be marched and supported. The exigencies of the nation may require that the treasure raised in the north should be transported to the south. . . . Is that construction of the constitution to be preferred which would render these operations difficult, hazardous, and expensive?"

Two years later he held that "we are one people" in war, in making peace, and—third, but not of tertiary importance—in "all commercial regulations." The Framers' fundamental task was to create a federal government with powers impervious to encroachments by the states. The Framers had been frightened by the states' excesses in using political power on behalf of debtors against creditors and to limit competition by mercantilistic practices such as granting monopolies. Marshall made constitutional law a bulwark of the sanctity of contracts, the bedrock of America's enterprise culture. And by protecting the private rights essential to aspirational individualism, Marshall's court legitimized an inequality—not of opportunity but of outcomes—compatible with a republic's values.

When in 1801 Marshall was nominated to be chief justice—one of the last things, and much the best thing, President John Adams did—

the nation still largely had an Articles of Confederation mentality. For-mally, it was a nation; emotionally—hence, actually—it was still in many ways many countries, most states being older than and more warmly embraced than the nation. Marshall's jurisprudence built the bridge to 1862, the year it became clear that many men would have to die in a protracted conflict to preserve the Union, and that many would be willing to do so.

Marshall had been willing to die to help midwife the nation's birth, seeing much hard action during the Revolutionary War. Ami-ably sociable and broadly tolerant, he had friends of vastly different political persuasions, and the only adversary he seems to have steadily disliked was a second cousin named Thomas Jefferson, in part because of Jefferson's partisan criticisms of Washington, who Marshall cele-brated, in an immense biography, as the symbol of a national identity transcending state loyalties.

Among the many recent fine biographies of America's Founders, none is finer than Jean Edward Smith's *John Marshall: Definer of a Nation* (1996). Smith locates Marshall's greatness in this fact: Unlike Britain's constitutional documents, which are political documents that it is Parliament's prerogative to construe, the U.S. Constitution is a legal document construed by courts, not Congress. When judicial su-pervision of our democracy seems tiresome, consider the alternative.

Marshall's life of strong, consequential prose had, Smith writes, a poetic coda. Marshall died in Philadelphia, birthplace of the Constitu-tion into which he breathed so much strength and meaning. The Lib-erty Bell, while tolling his death, cracked. It never rang again.

[SEPTEMBER 25, 2005]

James Madison: Well, Yes, of Course

In 2007, a *Princeton Alumni Weekly* panel voted—unanimously—that James Madison was the university's most influential graduate. I was asked to write something about that for the magazine.

I am writing this wee tribute to the greatest Princetonian on a morning which began, as most of my mornings do, with a predawn walk accompanied by my dog. His name is Madison. I am wearing my favorite necktie. It is blue, with silver profiles of James Madison. Later this morning, I shall work on a book I am writing. It is to be titled "The Madisonian Persuasion." I am not one who needs to be persuaded that Madison merits being ranked as Princeton's greatest gift to the nation.

Before I turned to journalism—or before I *sank* to journalism, as my father, a professor of philosophy, put it—I was, briefly, a professor of political philosophy. I cheerfully accepted that I would never be nearly as original and consequential as the philosophic Madison had been. Then I became a newspaper columnist, in which role I have always known that I could never be nearly as original and consequential as was Madison, America's foremost columnist.

The Federalist Papers, of which Madison wrote the two most important, were, of course, columns written to advance the ratification of the Constitution, in the drafting of which Madison was the most subtle participant. If a student of American thought fully unpacks the premises and implications of Federalist 10 and 51, that student comprehends not only this nation's political regime but also the Madisonian revolution in democratic theory.

Before Madison, almost all political philosophers who thought about democracy thought that if—a huge if, for most of them—democracy were to be feasible, it would be so only in a small, face-to-face society, such as Pericles' Athens or Rousseau's Geneva. This was supposedly true because the bane of democracies was thought to be self-interested factions, and only a small society could be sufficiently homogenous to avoid ruinous factions.

But America in the second half of the eighteenth century, although small compared with what it would become, was in size already a far cry from a Greek polis. Besides, Americans had spacious aspirations. A small nation? They were having none of that. At a time when 80 percent of them lived on a thin sliver of the eastern fringe of the continent, within twenty miles of Atlantic tidewater, what did they call their political assembly? The Continental Congress. They knew, more or less, where they were going: California.

Madison understood the need for philosophic underpinnings for an "extensive republic," a phrase that seemed oxymoronic to others. He can be said to have had a political catechism, which went approximately like this:

What is the worst outcome of politics? Tyranny.

To what form of tyranny are democracies susceptible? The tyranny of a single, durable majority.

How can this threat be minimized? By a saving multiplicity of factions, so that majorities will be unstable and transitory.

Hence, in Federalist 10, he wrote that "the first object of government" is "the protection of different and unequal faculties of acquiring property." From these differences arise different factions in their freedom-preserving multiplicity.

Having said in Federalist 10 that "neither moral nor religious motives can be relied on as an adequate control" of factions, Madison turned, in Federalist 51, to the institutional controls established in the Constitution—"this policy of supplying, by opposite and rival interests, the defect of better motives":

"Ambition must be made to counteract ambition. . . . It may be a reflection on human nature, that such devices should be necessary to control the abuses of government. But what is government itself but the greatest of all reflections on human nature? If men were angels, no government would be necessary. If angels were to govern men, neither external nor internal controls on government would be necessary. . . . You must first enable the government to control the governed; and in the next place, oblige it to control itself." In a masterpiece of understatement, Madison said, "Enlightened statesmen will not always be at the helm." No kidding. And Madison did not mince words regarding those about whom no one nowadays dares to say a discouraging word—"the people."

"There is," he said, "a degree of depravity in mankind which requires a certain degree of circumspection and distrust." Let the record show that once we had a president who had spoken of the voters' de-

pravity. Those were the days. Madison did qualify his astringent judgment about the people by acknowledging that there "are other qualities in human nature which justify a certain portion of esteem and
confidence." But notice the carefully measured concession to the public's sensibilities: "a certain portion," indeed.

In 1976, the nation's bicentennial, the presidency was won by
someone who, pandering in the modern manner, promised to deliver
government "as good as the people themselves." One can imagine
Madison muttering, "Good grief!"

In Washington, the seat of the government that he did so much to
design, there is no monument to Madison comparable to the glistening
marble temples honoring Jefferson and Lincoln. There is, however, a
splendid Madison Building, which is part of the Library of Congress.
It was said of the five-foot-four Madison that he contained an astonishing ratio of mind to mass. So it is altogether right that Madison,
physically the smallest of the Founders, is honored in his nation's capital by a repository of learning.

My next dog, if female, will be named Dolley.

[JANUARY 23, 2008]

Longfellow: A Forgotten Founder

One hundred years ago, February 27 was enlivened by events
around the nation commemorating what had happened one hundred years before that, in 1807. But last week's bicentennial of the birth
of Henry Wadsworth Longfellow passed largely unnoted, which is note-
worthy. It was, naturally, a poet (Shelley) who declared that "poets are
the unacknowledged legislators of the world." Wishful thinking, that,
but Plato took poets so seriously as disturbers of the peace that he
wanted them expelled from his republic. And Longfellow was, in a
sense, an American Founder, a maker of this Republic's consciousness.

Time was, children learned—in schools; imagine that—the origins
of what still are familiar phrases: "Ships that pass in the night," "Life
is real! Life is earnest!" "footprints on the sands of time," "the patter

of little feet," "the forest primeval," "Let the dead Past bury its dead!" "In this world a man must either be anvil or hammer," "Into each life some rain must fall." Even the first stanza of Longfellow's serene "The Village Blacksmith"—

> *Under the spreading chestnut tree,*
> *The village smithy stands*

—has a haunting, sinister echo in George Orwell's *1984*. Winston Smith, distraught, thinks he hears a voice singing

> *Under the spreading chestnut-tree*
> *I sold you and you sold me.*

Longfellow was a gifted versifier, and today is dismissed as only a versifier. Well, as Cézanne supposedly said of Monet, "He is only an eye—but what an eye!"

Longfellow was very Victorian—sentimental and moralistic. He in no way foreshadowed twentieth-century poetry's themes of meaninglessness ("I have measured out my life with coffee spoons"—T. S. Eliot, 1917) and social disintegration ("the blood-dimmed tide is loosed"— William Butler Yeats, 1921). Longfellow wrote for a young nation that was thinking "Let us, then, be up and doing, with a heart for any fate," before he wrote that exhortation.

He aimed to shape the nation's identity by making Americans aware of the first European settlers ("Why don't you speak for yourself, John?"—"The Courtship of Miles Standish"), the Native Americans they displaced ("By the shore of Gitche Gumee"—"The Song of Hiawatha") and the nation's birth ("Listen, my children, and you shall hear / Of the midnight ride of Paul Revere").

"Paul Revere's Ride" was written in 1860, as events were mocking Longfellow's great national poem ("The Building of the Ship," 1849):

> *Cedar of Maine and Georgia pine*
> *Here together shall combine.*

A goodly frame, and a goodly fame,
And the UNION be her name!

. . .

Sail on, O UNION, strong and great!
Humanity with all its fears,
With all the hopes of future years,
Is hanging breathless on thy fate!

Longfellow's civic purposes made him a public figure, the nation's first literary celebrity. His image decorated cigar boxes and beer-bottle labels. He kept a supply of autographed cards for the many strangers who made pilgrimages to his Cambridge house, where George Washington had lived during the siege of Boston.

Not long ago there still were celebrity poets. Jeffrey Hart, professor emeritus of English at Dartmouth, in his *When the Going Was Good: American Life in the Fifties,* remembers Robert Frost's receiving a standing ovation from an overflow house at Carnegie Hall, and Eliot's reading his poems to an overflow audience at Columbia University, with people outside listening to him over loudspeakers.

The audiences were intense because the issues were large, if abstruse. Frost and Eliot represented dueling sensibilities, the empirical and the transcendental. In contrast, Longfellow intended his narrative and lyric poems—genres disdained by modernists—as inspiriting guides to the nation's honorable past and challenging future. Yeats ascribed Longfellow's popularity to his accessibility—"he tells his story or idea so that one needs nothing but his verses to understand it." This angers today's academic clerisy. What use is it to readers who need no intermediary between them and the author? And what use is Longfellow to academics who "interrogate" authors' "texts" to illuminate the authors' psyches, ideologies, and social situations—the "power relations" of patriarchy, racism, imperialism, etc.? This reduction of the study of literature to sociology, and of sociology to ideological assertion, demotes literature to mere raw material for literary theory, making today's professoriate, rather than yesterday's writers, the center of attention.

Dana Gioia, chairman of the National Endowment of the Arts, has

written that "Longfellow's vast influence on American culture paradoxically makes him both central and invisible." The melancholy fact that
the two hundredth birthday of the poet who toiled to create the nation's
memory passed largely unremarked is redundant evidence of how susceptible this forward-leaning democracy is to historical amnesia.

[MARCH 12, 2007]

Ronald Reagan: The Steel Behind
the Smile

O ne measure of a leader's greatness is this: By the time he dies, the
dangers that summoned him to greatness have been so thoroughly defeated, in no small measure by what he did, it is difficult to
recall the magnitude of those dangers, or of his achievements. So if you
seek Ronald Reagan's monument, look around, and consider what you
do *not* see.

The Iron Curtain that scarred a continent is gone, as is the Evil
Empire responsible for it. The feeling of foreboding—the sense of
shrunken possibilities—that afflicted Americans twenty years ago has
been banished by a new birth of the American belief in perpetually expanding horizons.

In the uninterrupted flatness of the Midwest, where Reagan ma-
tured, the horizon beckons to those who would be travelers. He traveled
far, had a grand time all the way, and his cheerfulness was contagious.
It was said of Dwight Eisenhower—another much-loved son of the
prairie—that his smile was his philosophy. That was true of Reagan, in
this sense: He understood that when Americans have a happy stance
toward life, confidence flows and good things happen. They raise families, crops, living standards, and cultural values; they settle the land,
make deserts bloom, destroy tyrannies.

Reagan was the last president for whom the Depression—the years
when America stopped working—was a formative experience. Remarkably, the 1930s formed in him a talent for happiness. It was urgently needed in the 1980s, when the pessimism of the intelligentsia

was infecting people with the idea that America had passed its apogee and was ungovernable.

It also was said then that the presidency destroyed its occupants. But Reagan got to the office, looked around, said, "This is fun. Let's saddle up and go for a ride." Which he did, sometimes in the middle of the afternoon. Scolds, who thought presidents were only serious when miserable, were scandalized.

In an amazingly fecund twenty-seven-month period, Margaret Thatcher, Pope John Paul II, and Reagan came to office. The pope and the president had been actors. Reagan said he wondered how presidents who have *not* been actors could function. Certainly the last century's greatest democratic leaders—Churchill, FDR—mastered the theatrical dimension of politics.

Good actors, including political actors, do not deal in unrealities. Rather, they create realities that matter—perceptions, aspirations, allegiances. Reagan in his presidential role made vivid the values, particularly hopefulness and friendliness, that give cohesion and dynamism to this continental nation.

A democratic leader's voice should linger in his nation's memory, an echo of his exhortations. Reagan's mellifluous rhetoric lingers like a melody that evokes fond memories. Because of demagogues, rhetoric has a tainted reputation in our time. However, Reagan understood that rhetoric is central to democratic governance. It can fuse passion and persuasion, moving free people to freely choose what is noble.

He understood the axiom that people, especially Americans, with their Founders' creed and vast reservoirs of decency, more often need to be reminded than informed. And he understood the economy of leadership—the need to husband the perishable claim a leader has on the attention of this big, boisterous country.

To some, Reagan seemed the least complicated of men—an open book that the country had completely read. However, he had the cunning to know the advantage of being underestimated. He was more inward than he seemed. And much tougher. The stricken fields of American and world politics are littered with those who did not anticipate the steel behind his smile.

The oldest person ever elected president had a sure sense of modernity, as when he told students at Moscow University that mankind is emerging from the economy of muscle and entering the economy of mind. "The key," he said, "is freedom," but freedom grounded in institutions such as courts and political parties. Otherwise "freedom will always be looking over its shoulder. A bird on a tether, no matter how long the rope, can always be pulled back."

Reagan was a friendly man with one close friend. He married her. He had one other great love, for the American people, a love intense, public, and reciprocated.

Presidents usually enter the White House as shiny and freshly minted dimes and leave tarnished. Reagan left on the crest of a wave of affection that intensified in response to the gallantry with which he met illness in his final years.

Today Americans gratefully recall that at a turbulent moment in their national epic, Reagan became the great reassurer, the steadying captain of our clipper ship. He calmed the passengers—and the sea.

[JUNE 6, 2004]

Reagan and the Vicissitudes of Historical Judgments

Ronald Reagan, unlike all but ten or so Presidents, was a world figure whose career will interest historians for centuries, and centuries hence his greatness will be, and should be, measured primarily by what happened in Europe, as a glorious echo of his presidency, in the three years after he left the White House. What happened was the largest peaceful revolution in history, resulting in history's largest emancipation of people from tyranny—a tyranny that had deadened life for hundreds of millions of people from the middle of Germany to the easternmost of Russia's eleven time zones.

However, Reagan will also be remembered for his restoration of American confidence that resulted in a quickening tempo of domestic life. During his first term, the most remarkable run of wealth creation in the history of this or any other nation began. Arguably, it began with a seemingly unrelated event in the first year of his first term.

In 1981, when the nation's air-traffic controllers threatened to do what the law forbade them to do—strike—Reagan warned that if they did they would be fired. When they struck in August, Reagan announced that the strikers would be terminated in two days. By firing the controllers, Reagan, the only union man—he had been head of the Screen Actors Guild—ever to be president, destroyed a union, the Professional Air Traffic Controllers Organization (PATCO). This has often, and not incorrectly, been called a defining episode of the Reagan presidency because it notified foreign leaders, not least those of the Soviet Union, that he said what he meant and meant what he said.

But now, more than two astonishing decades on, it also is reasonable to conclude that Reagan's fracas with the controllers had huge economic consequences, domestic and foreign. It altered basic attitudes about relations between business and labor in ways that quickly redounded to the benefit of the nation, and not least the benefit of American workers. It produced a cultural shift, a new sense of what can be appropriate in business management: layoffs can be justifiable even when a company is profitable, if the layoffs will improve productivity and profitability. Within a few years, both AT&T and Procter & Gamble, although quite profitable at the time, implemented large layoffs, without arousing significant protests.

Reagan's action against the air-traffic controllers came on the eve of the explosive growth of information technologies, and some astute people, including Alan Greenspan, believe that Reagan's action facilitated that growth.

Since 1981, labor in America has prospered because it is less protected. In theory, it might seem that since the showdown with PATCO, business's informal protocol about layoffs must have resulted in rising unemployment. The reverse has happened. In the post-PATCO climate of business operations, employers have been more inclined to hire because they know that if the hiring proves to be improvident, those hired can be discharged. The propensity to hire has risen much more than the propensity to fire. In all of America's post–Civil War era of industrialization, unemployment has never been as low for as long as it has generally been in the years since the extraordinary expansion that began during Reagan's first term.

Although Reagan entered politics late, running for governor of California at the age of fifty-five, and entered the White House a few weeks shy of his seventieth birthday, older than any other president when elected, he lived so long after leaving office that his tenure already has been subject to striking vicissitudes of historical judgment. Nothing is so irretrievably lost to a society as the sense of fear it felt about a grave danger that was subsequently coped with. So in measuring Reagan's greatness, insufficient attention is now given to his long-headedness and toughness in putting the Soviet Union on the path to extinction. This is particularly so because the intelligentsia likes nothing less than giving Reagan credit, and so has embraced the theory that the Soviet Union's extinction was an inevitability that just happened while Reagan was standing around.

So as memories of the Cold War fade, Reagan is remembered more for the tax cutting and deregulating that helped, with the information technologies, to shift the economy into a hitherto unknown overdrive. But the truth is that Reagan always thought that winning the Cold War and revving up the American model of wealth creation were parts of the same project. That project was to convince the watching world that the American social and political model—pluralism, the rule of law, allocation of wealth and opportunity mostly by markets, and maximum diffusion of decision making—is unrivaled. To the extent that anything in history can ever be said to be completed, that project has been.

Reagan always believed that the world was watching America. Indeed, he thought the point of America was to be watched—to be exemplary. Hence the complete sincerity of his reiterated references to the City on the Hill. And when the democratic revolution against communism came, Tiananmen Square in Beijing and Wenceslas Square in Prague and points in between rang with the rhetoric of America's third and sixteenth presidents. The fortieth president was not surprised.

[JUNE 14, 2004]

John Paul II: "A Flame Rescued from Dry Wood"

In Eastern Europe, where both world wars began, the end of the Cold War began on October 16, 1978, with a puff of white smoke, in Western Europe. It wafted over one of Europe's grandest public spaces, over Michelangelo's dome of St. Peter's, over statues of the saints atop Bernini's curving colonnade that embraces visitors to Vatican City. Ten years later, when the fuse that Polish workers had lit in a Gdansk shipyard had ignited the explosion that leveled the Berlin Wall, it was clear that one of the most consequential people of the twentieth century's second half was a Pole who lived in Rome, governing a city-state of 109 acres.

Science teaches that reality is strange—solid objects are mostly space; the experience of time is a function of speed; gravity bends light. History, too, teaches strange truths: John Paul II occupied the world's oldest office, which traces its authority to history's most potent figure, a Palestinian who never traveled a hundred miles from his birthplace, who never wrote a book, and who died at thirty-three. And religion, once a legitimizer of political regimes, became in John Paul II's deft hands a delegitimizer of communism's ersatz religion.

Between October 16, 1978, and January 20, 1981, the cause of freedom was strengthened by the coming to high offices of Margaret Thatcher, Ronald Reagan, and John Paul II, who, like the president, had been an actor and was gifted at the presentational dimension of his office. This peripatetic pope was seen by more people than anyone in history, and his most important trip came early. It was a visit to Poland that began on June 2, 1979.

In nine days, a quarter of that nation's population saw him. Marx called religion the opiate of the masses, but it did not have a sedative effect on the Poles. The pope's visit was the nation's epiphany, a thunderous realization that the nation was of one mind, mocking the futility of communism's thirty-five-year attempt to conquer Poland's consciousness. Between 1795 and 1918, Poland had been erased from the map of Europe, partitioned between Austria, Prussia, and Russia. This gave Poles an acute sense of the distinction between the state and the real nation.

Igor Stravinsky, speaking with a Russian's stoicism about Poland's sufferings, said that if you pitch your tent in the middle of New York's Fifth Avenue, you are going to be hit by a bus. The Poland where John Paul II grew to sturdy, athletic manhood was hit first by Nazism, then communism. Then, benignly, by John Paul II.

It was said that the fin de siècle Vienna of Freud and Wittgenstein was the little world in which the larger world had its rehearsals. In the late 1970s, the Poland of John Paul II and Lech Walesa was like that. The twentieth century's worst political invention was totalitarianism, a tenet of which is that the masses must not be allowed to mass: Total-itarianism is a mortar and pestle for grinding society into a dust of in-dividuals. Small wonder, then, that Poland's ruler, General Wojciech Jaruzelski, visibly trembled in the presence of the priest who brought Poland to its feet in the face of tyranny by first bringing Poland to its knees in his presence.

John Paul II almost did not live to see this glorious consummation. In 1981, three of the world's largest figures—Ronald Reagan, Anwar Sadat, and John Paul II—were shot. History would have taken an al-tered course if Sadat had not been the only one killed.

Our age celebrates the watery toleration preached by people for whom "judgmental" is an epithet denoting an intolerable moral confi-dence. John Paul II bristled with judgments, including this: The in-evitability of progress is a myth, hence the certainty that mankind is wiser today than yesterday is chimeric.

Secular Europe is, however, wiser because of a man who worked at an altar. Europeans have been plied and belabored by various his-toricisms purporting to show that individuals are nullities governed by vast impersonal forces. Beginning in 1978, Europeans saw one man seize history by the lapels and shake it.

One of G. K. Chesterton's Father Brown detective stories includes this passage: " 'I'm afraid I'm a practical man,' said the doctor with gruff humor, 'and I don't bother much about religion and philosophy.' 'You'll never be a practical man till you do,' said Father Brown."

A poet made the same point: "A flame rescued from dry wood has no weight in its luminous flight yet lifts the heavy lid of night." The poet became John Paul II.   [APRIL 3, 2005]

Ayaan Hirsi Ali: An Enlightenment Fundamentalist

While her security contingent waits outside the Georgetown restaurant, Ayaan Hirsi Ali orders what the menu calls "raw steak tartare." Amused by the redundancy, she speculates that it is intended to immunize the restaurant against lawyers, should a customer be discommoded by that entree. She has been in America only two weeks. She is a quick study.

And an exile and an immigrant. Born thirty-six years ago in Somalia, Hirsi Ali has lived in Ethiopia, Kenya, Saudi Arabia, and the Netherlands, where she settled in 1992 after she deplaned in Frankfurt, supposedly en route to Canada for a marriage, arranged by her father, to a cousin. She makes her own arrangements.

She quickly became a Dutch citizen, a member of parliament, and an astringent critic, from personal experience, of the condition of women under Islam. She wrote the script for, and filmmaker Theo van Gogh directed, *Submission,* an eleven-minute movie featuring pertinent passages from the Koran (such as when it is a husband's duty to beat his wife) projected on the bodies of naked women.

It was shown twice before November 2, 2004, when van Gogh, bicycling through central Amsterdam in the morning, was shot by an Islamic extremist who then slit his throat with a machete. Next, the murderer (in whose room was found a disk containing videos of "enemies of Allah" being murdered, including a man having his head slowly sawed off) used another knife to pin a long letter to van Gogh's chest.

The letter was to Hirsi Ali, calling her a "soldier of evil" who would "smash herself to pieces on Islam."

The remainder of her life in Holland was lived under guard. Neighbors in her apartment building complained that they felt endangered with her there and got a court to order her evicted. She decided to come to America.

Holland evidently tolerates everything except skepticism about the sacramental nature of multiculturalism. One million of the country's 16 million residents are Islamic, and the political left has appropriated the European right's traditional celebration of identity grounded in racial and ethnic traditions and culture. But the recoil of many Dutch people from Hirsi Ali suggests that the tolerance about which Holland preens is a compound of intellectual sloth and moral timidity. She was more trouble than the Dutch evidently think free speech is worth.

Her story is told in a riveting new book, *Murder in Amsterdam,* by Ian Buruma, who is not alone in finding her—this "Enlightenment fundamentalist"—somewhat unnerving and off-putting. Having experienced life circumscribed by tribal and religious communities (as a girl she suffered the genital mutilation called female circumcision), she is a fierce partisan of individualism against collectivism.

She reminds Buruma of Margaret Thatcher's sometimes abrasive intelligence and fascination with America. He is dismissive of the idea that she is a Voltaire against Islam: Voltaire, he says, offended the powerful Catholic Church, whereas she offends "only a minority that was already feeling vulnerable in the heart of Europe."

She, however, replies that this is hardly a normal minority. It is connected to Islam's worldwide adherents. Living sullenly in European "dish cities"—enclaves connected by satellite television and the Internet to the tribal societies they have not really left behind—many members of this minority are uninterested in assimilation into open societies.

She calls herself "a dissident of Islam" because, given what Allah supposedly enjoins and what she knows is right, "the cognitive dissonance is, for me, too much." She says she is not "a militant atheist," but the emphasis is on the adjective.

Slender, elegant, stylish, and articulate (in English, Dutch, and

Swahili), she has found an intellectual home here at the American Enterprise Institute, where she is writing a book that imagines Muhammad meeting, in the New York Public Library, three thinkers—John
Stuart Mill, Friedrich Hayek, and Karl Popper, each a hero of the unending struggle between (to take the title of Popper's 1945 masterpiece) "The Open Society and Its Enemies." Islamic extremists—the
sort who were unhinged by some Danish cartoons—will be enraged.
She is unperturbed.

Neither is she pessimistic about the West. It has, she says, "the
drive to innovate." But Europe, she thinks, is invertebrate. After two
generations without war, Europeans "have no idea what an enemy is."
And they think, she says, that leadership is an antiquated notion because they believe that caring governments can socialize everyone to
behave well, thereby erasing personal accountability and responsibility. "I can't even tell it without laughing," she says, laughing softly.
Clearly she is where she belongs, at last.   [SEPTEMBER 21, 2006]

Hugh Hefner: Tuning Fork of American Fantasies

LOS ANGELES—Asked how it feels to have won, Hugh Hefner pauses,
looks down and almost whispers, "Wonderful." Then he says: "I
guess if you live long enough . . ."

Fifty years ago, he was pecking at a typewriter on a card table in
his Chicago apartment, preparing the first issue of a magazine he
planned to call *Stag Party* but, because there already was a magazine
called *Stag,* he called it *Playboy.* The first issue appeared in December
1953. It bore no date because Hefner was not sure there would be a
second, such were the troubles the first issue caused with the post office and other defenders of decency.

Four years later, in the nick of time, Searle pharmaceutical company introduced Enovid—"the pill." Back then Hefner, the tuning fork
of American fantasies, said he wanted to provide "a little diversion
from the anxieties of the Atomic Age." But three emblematic books of

the supposedly repressed 1950s—*Peyton Place, Lolita,* and *The Kinsey Report* (Professor Alfred Kinsey of Indiana University was another Midwestern sexual subversive)—showed that more than geopolitical anxiety was on the mind of Eisenhower's America.

By 1959, the post office was delivering millions of copies of Hefner's magazine. *Playboy*'s rabbit-head logo is now one of the world's most recognized brands, even in inscrutable China, where *Playboy* merchandise sells well but the magazine is banned.

Hefner's daughter Christie, who was born thirteen months before the magazine, says *Playboy* was "a great idea executed well at exactly the right time." A no-nonsense executive, she now runs the Chicago-based business she joined twenty-seven years ago, fresh from earning a summa cum laude degree from Brandeis. When she arrived, Playboy was primarily an American magazine publisher. She has made it into an international electronic entertainment company.

The magazine, the twelfth-highest-selling U.S. consumer publication, sells 3.2 million copies monthly. That is slightly less than half its 1970s peak, but its eighteen international editions sell another 1.8 million copies a month, and it remains the world's bestselling monthly men's magazine.

Still, it provides only about one-third of Playboy Enterprises' annual revenues of $277.6 million. Playboy owns six cable networks that deliver to 38 million North American households movies of a sexual explicitness that would have been instantly prosecuted in all forty-eight states in 1953.

The magazine, the mere mention of which used to produce pursings of lips and sharp intakes of breaths, is still Hefner's preoccupation, but has been overtaken by the libertarian revolution he helped to foment. In 1953, *Playboy* magazine was pushing the parameters of the permissible, but it is hard to remain iconoclastic when standing waist-deep in the shards of smashed icons.

Born to "puritanical" (Hefner's words) parents in Chicago, city of broad shoulders, Hefner founded an empire based on breasts. What is it about that protean city? Chicagoan Ray Kroc, entrepreneur of McDonald's, did his Army training with Chicagoan Walt Disney—two prodigies of mass marketing, the creator of the Big Mac and the creator of Mickey Mouse, in the same Army unit.

Then Chicago produced the Henry Luce of the skin game—Hef, as everyone, including his daughter, calls him. The Chicago boy recalls that the Sears Roebuck mail order catalog—another Chicago innovation—was called "a dream book" because it brought "the dream of urbanity to rural communities. *Playboy,* for young, single men, is a variation of this."

Recently, dressed in his black pajamas and merlot-colored smoking jacket—it was 1 p.m.—he looked a bit tuckered, but he had been living what Teddy Roosevelt called "the strenuous life," although not as TR envisioned it. Hefner's recent seventy-seventh birthday party had rambled on for more than a week, during which he took to dinner—simultaneously—the seven ladies he is currently dating. As F. Scott Fitzgerald, writing of Jay Gatsby, suggested, "personality is an unbroken series of successful gestures."

An eleventh-generation descendant of William Bradford, who arrived on the *Mayflower* to begin a religious errand in the wilderness, Hefner says, "In a real sense we live in a Playboy world." He lives here in a thirty-room mock-Tudor mansion that sits on six acres of posh Holmby Hills decorated with wandering peacocks, among other fauna.

He says, "I grew up in the Depression and World War II and I looked back to the Roaring Twenties and I thought I'd missed the party." The party turned out to be a movable feast.   [MAY 29, 2003]

Lawrence Ferlinghetti: The Emeritus Beat as Tourist Attraction

S AN FRANCISCO—America's gauzy popular culture has the power to envelop even its perfervid critics in a tolerant, domesticating embrace. If they live long enough, these critics run the risk of winding up full not only of years, but of honors. They can, like Lawrence Ferlinghetti, eighty-three, become tourist attractions.

These tourists, he notes, are intellectually upscale. They come in a small but steady trickle, from across the country and around the world, to his City Lights Booksellers & Publishers, next door to a street named after the most famous of the many writers who have hung out there—Jack Kerouac. The store, which is a short walk from the street—actually, an alleyway, which seems right—named Via Ferlinghetti, has been designated by this city a protected landmark. This is not because the wedge-shaped structure built in 1907 is a gem (it is not) but because of its cultural significance, which is primarily its association with Kerouac, Allen Ginsberg, and other designated voices of the Beat Generation.

It was in City Lights that San Francisco police arrested Ferlinghetti on obscenity charges for publishing Ginsberg's "Howl." Ferlinghetti's and Ginsberg's acquittals helped make possible the American publication of D. H. Lawrence's *Lady Chatterley's Lover* and Henry Miller's *Tropic of Cancer,* which involved legal dustups that now seem quaint.

Ferlinghetti publishes as well as sells books. He published "Howl" after first rejecting it. It was after he heard Ginsberg recite it that he sent Ginsberg a telegram repeating words from the letter Emerson sent to Walt Whitman after reading *Leaves of Grass*—"I greet you at the beginning of a great career."

Ferlinghetti was born in Bronxville, New York, spent much of his youth in France, and went to the University of North Carolina because his roommate at a prep school in Massachusetts hooked him on the novels of Thomas Wolfe. He began a four-year hitch in the Navy before Pearl Harbor ("I was a good American boy") and was back near France, on a U.S. Navy submarine chaser, on June 6, 1944. After earning—thank you, GI Bill of Rights—a master's degree in Victorian literature at Columbia, and a doctorate at the Sorbonne, and after finding that the mailroom at *Time* magazine was not a promising rung on the ladder of journalism, he headed for here, to start a bookstore, a vocation suggested by life in Paris.

City Lights is in the North Beach district, which once was a scene of San Francisco's bohemian ferment. Now the district is mostly seedy. Visible from Ferlinghetti's cluttered office in his bookstore's second floor is an establishment with a resonant name—Hungry I. It was at a nightclub called the hungry i a few hundred yards from the location of the topless bar now bearing that name—bohemia isn't what it used to be, but then, what is?—that Mort Sahl and Lenny Bruce performed their political riffs that were the outer edges of dissent in the 1950s and early 1960s.

Bruce lived across the street from City Lights. He once fell out of a window. "No doubt he was on something" is Ferlinghetti's safe surmise. Sahl used to browse the City Lights magazine rack for ideas for his performances.

Ferlinghetti looks the part of an emeritus Beat—small silver earring, tatty sport coat, blue jeans—and looks askance at tourists (no kidding), Republicans (of course: one of his most popular works was the long 1958 poem "Tentative Description of a Dinner Given to Promote the Impeachment of President Eisenhower"), George W. Bush ("shredding the Constitution," "dismantling the New Deal"), gentrification (San Francisco has been "dot.conned"), automobiles ("autogeddon" inflicted by SUVs), and chain stores (does he have Borders and Barnes & Noble in mind?).

But the grouchiness of San Francisco's first poet laureate seems perfunctory, even cheerful. City Lights is open until midnight seven days a week; books are shelved under ideological categories (look under "Stolen Continents" for American history). It retains what Ferlinghetti says San Francisco itself had when he arrived in 1951, "an island mentality, a sort of offshore territory." American life has been good to the man whose *Coney Island of the Mind* was the bestselling poetry book in the 1960s and 1970s. A million copies are in print.

It has been famously said that there are no second acts in American life. Actually, there are. And third, fourth, and fifth acts. But Ferlinghetti has happily stayed with his one act, and the world, or at least a minority steeped in literary nostalgia, is still beating a path to his door.   [JUNE 14, 2002]

Buck Owens's Bakersfield Sound

BAKERSFIELD, CALIFORNIA—Buck Owens came to this city, a hundred miles north of Los Angeles, at the southern end of the prodigiously fertile San Joaquin Valley, to pick cotton, not a guitar. He came for the same reason lots of others came west from Texas and Oklahoma: happiness was the Dust Bowl in their rearview mirrors.

The Owens family's rearview mirror was on a 1933 Ford sedan. In 1937, when Buck was eight and John Steinbeck was just beginning to write *The Grapes of Wrath,* ten Owens family members packed into it and headed west. His parents had been sharecroppers on the southern side of the Red River that separates Texas from Oklahoma. Because the trailer hitch broke in Phoenix, the family lived there for a few years, sometimes traveling to the San Joaquin to pick carrots in Porterville, peaches in Modesto, potatoes and cotton in Bakersfield. During such work, he got the idea that picking a guitar might be more fun.

Which he is doing at seventy-three, in his Crystal Palace nightclub, where he recently began a rollicking hour set with "Okie from Muskogee," a sixties—actually, an anti-sixties—anthem by another Bakersfield boy, Merle Haggard. (Has there ever been a better name for a country-music singer?)

By sixteen, Owens had begun playing in Phoenix honky-tonks, sometimes with the young Marty Robbins, earning whatever change he could collect by passing a soup bowl. In 1951, he moved to Bakersfield, in Kern County, which produces more oil than Oklahoma, and had plenty of roughnecks to appreciate the country music of rising stars like Bob Wills and Ferlin Husky, who were honing what has come to be called the Bakersfield sound.

That is identified with Owens's solid-body Fender Telecaster steel guitar. It produces the sharp, twangy, driving, biting sound that seems especially suited to the subjects of what is called "hard country music." Such music sometimes teeters on the brink of self-caricature, or embraces it ("I was drunk the day my momma got out of prison"), but its essential message is that life is difficult and so are most of the people we meet, including those we marry.

The life that drove many people down Steinbeck's road to California was hard, and so was the life Owens led chasing stardom. After touring hard—sometimes three hundred nights a year—Owens got off the road in 1980. And he spent too many years associated with the instant kitsch of the television program *Hee Haw.* As a result, too few fans of country music appreciate how much his Bakersfield sound helped give that music a steely integrity and propel it to the point that Owens could play a much-praised concert in President Johnson's White House in 1968.

By 1980, however, when the John Travolta movie *Urban Cowboy* helped make country music fashionable, country music was beginning to lose its edge. More to the point, the Nashville music establishment set out to rub the edge off, to envelop it in a syrup of strings and softening production techniques, the better to appeal to a broader audience that wanted country music that was close kin to soft rock.

But some "new traditionalists" were, and are, having none of that. These include Randy Travis, George Strait, the Dixie Chicks, and Dwight Yoakam—another nifty name for a country singer. Yoakam was born in Kentucky and spent a while in Nashville, but says, "I was drawn to Los Angeles by my earlobes . . . the country-rock sound, and the Bakersfield sound."

A related development is the recent emergence of a new category of old-style music called "Americana," which is the most popular radio format for Internet listeners. Although Americana is not strictly defined (see americanamusic.org), a good sampler is the sound track of the movie *O Brother, Where Art Thou?* a mixture of blues, bluegrass, gospel, folk, and mountain music. Sales of that CD, released in 2000, are heading toward 7 million. Americana encompasses new performers, such as Alison Krauss's Union Station and Nickel Creek, and hardy perennials like Johnny Cash. One song written years ago by Homer Joy probably would qualify as Americana:

> *Spent some time in San Francisco*
> *Spent a night there in the can*
> *Well, they threw this drunkard in my jail cell*
> *Took fifteen dollars from that man*
> *But I left him my best watch and my house key*
> *Don't like folks sayin' that I steal*
> *Then I headed out to Bakersfield.*

When Buck Owens is onstage, singing that song, the years fall away. He is as energized by the audience as his guitar is by electricity, and the young man in flight from the cotton fields is present again.

Parts of his life resemble hard-country lyrics (his fourth divorce is not going well), but he is now an icon in the community he first saw when picking cotton. Today, as he drives the streets of Bakersfield, he can steer his pickup truck down Buck Owens Boulevard.

Bakersfield, although prosperous, is still a place where billboards proclaim, TOUGH TIMES NEVER LAST BUT TOUGH PEOPLE DO. So does hard-country music, and Buck Owens's Bakersfield sound.

[DECEMBER 9, 2002]

Andrew Nesbitt: Seventy-nine-Pound Master of Tourette Syndrome

COPPELL, TEXAS—Even in what passes for repose, your basic eleven-year-old boy resembles the former Yugoslavia—a unity of sorts, but with fidgeting and jostling elements. Andrew Nesbitt is like that, only more so, because he has Tourette syndrome.

He also has something to teach us about the power of a little information and a lot of determination. And about how life can illuminate philosophy, which is supposed to do the illuminating.

He is seventy-nine pounds of shortstop and relief pitcher—a closer, no less, which is a high-stress vocation. Stress often triggers Tourette symptoms. Hitting a thrown ball with a round bat is hard enough, and so is throwing the ball over a seventeen-inch-wide plate with the game on the line. Hard enough, even if you do not have an inherited neurological disorder that causes recurrent physical and phonic tics.

The physical tics can include involuntary muscle spasms—blinking, clapping, hopping, and the more or less violent twitching of shoulders and flailing of limbs. The vocalizations are usually grunts, hisses, barks, and other meaningless sounds. Rarely, and not at all in Andrew's case, there is the compulsive utterance of obscenities.

At the benighted school he attended last year, teachers could not—would not—understand that he did not have a mischievous penchant for bad behavior. They frequently banished him from the classroom to sit in the hall.

When he was younger, his parents had to hold his thrashing head so he could eat. Playing soccer, he sometimes bruised his behind by kicking himself with backward leg spasms. This year, he says, Mrs. Marill Myers, his math and homeroom teacher, "asks me if it's a tic." She gives him a jump rope to use to subdue unmanageable energy. Or pauses to briefly rub his back. Not complicated, really.

He was five, standing on a swimming pool diving board, when his mother first saw him jerking his head and shrugging his shoulders oddly. He is bright as a new dime—at ten months he had a fifty-word vocabulary—but his gross and fine motor problems became so bad that in fourth grade hip spasms would throw him out of his desk chair.

A visiting columnist is Andrew's excuse for taking a break from the work part of a sixth-grader's day in Coppell Middle School West (math, English—the *school* stuff) and savoring anticipation of the good parts, such as lunch, baseball, and lacrosse practice. He is dressed conservatively, even formally, as his age cohort understands such matters: red T-shirt reaching almost to his knees and blue shorts that aren't short—they reach below his knees, toward his white sneakers.

Nowadays, he says, "I sometimes hold the tics in when I'm batting." Extreme concentration also helps Mike Johnston, a Pittsburgh Pirates reliever, contain his Tourette symptoms: "I'll sometimes stare at something until my eyes water." Johnston, who was awakened in a Chicago hotel on an off-day by the thoughtless columnist, chats on the phone with Andrew, who is asking important questions, such as: "Have you ever pitched to A-Rod?" Johnston gets important information from Andrew: cap and jersey sizes. Pirates gear is on the way.

Last year, Andrew came close to exhaustion from dread of teachers' incomprehension and from some children's cruelty. This year, Andrew's teachers and classmates are better informed. What causes his odd behavior may have caused similar behavior by some high-achievers—probably Samuel Johnson, perhaps Mozart. Even more impressive, Jim

Eisenreich, formerly of the Twins, Royals, Phillies, Marlins, and Dodgers, has Tourette syndrome, as does Tim Howard, current goalie for Manchester United soccer club, the world's most famous sports team.

The mind-body dichotomy is a perennial puzzlement for philosophers. Most people say, "I have a body." Perhaps we should say, "I *am* a body." People who say the latter mean that the mind, the soul—whatever we call the basis of individual identity—is a "ghost in the machine," a mysterious emanation of our physicality. They may be right. But were Andrew given to paddling around in deep philosophic water—if he were, he would not be your basic boy—he might reply:

"No way. Wisdom is encoded in our common language. We all have, to some extent, a complex, sometimes adversarial, relationship with our physical selves. And I more than most people know that it is correct to say, 'I have a body.' There is my body, and then there is *me,* trying to make it behave."

Let the philosophers contend about the mind-body distinction. If you think Andrew has it wrong, spend a day in his sneakers.

[APRIL 25, 2004]

Simeon Wright's Grace

ALSIP, ILLINOIS—In a cemetery here, a few miles southwest of Chicago's city limits, Simeon Wright, sixty-two, a trim, articulate semiretired pipe fitter, and a deacon in the Church of God in Christ, recently attended a ceremony at an unquiet grave. The gravestone has a weatherproof locket with a photograph of a boy, and these carved words:

EMMETT L. TILL
IN LOVING MEMORY
JULY 25, 1941　AUGUST 28, 1955

Wright participated in a service for the reinterment of the body of the boy with whom Wright, then twelve, was sharing a bed in the Mississippi home of Wright's father fifty years ago. It was the night that lit the fuse of the civil rights revolution.

The eulogy delivered at the reinterment—Emmett's remains had been exhumed as part of the reopened investigation of his murder—was by Wheeler Parker, a barber and minister in nearby Argo, Illinois. The night of August 28, 1955, Parker, then sixteen, also was sleeping in the Wright home. Two white men, one with a .45 caliber pistol, shone a flashlight in Parker's face and one of them said, "Where's the fat boy from Chicago?"

A few weeks before, Wright's father, a preacher in the vicinity of Money, Mississippi, had come to Chicago to deliver a eulogy for a former parishioner, one of the hundreds of thousands of black Mississippians of the great migration—an $11, sixteen-hour ride on the Illinois Central to Chicago. A week or so later, Mamie Till—Emmett's mother—put Emmett on the Illinois Central to visit his great uncle, and cousin Simeon.

Three days into his visit, at the ramshackle Bryant's Grocery and Meat Market, Emmett, fourteen, whistled at a white woman, Carolyn Bryant. Three nights later, her husband Roy and his half brother J. W. Milam came for Emmett. Simeon's father pleaded, "Why not give the boy a whipping and leave it at that?" They beat him to an unrecognizable pulp, knocked out his right eye, shot him, tied a seventy-five-pound cotton gin fan around his neck with barbed wire, and threw his body into the Tallahatchie River.

Mississippi authorities had made the Chicago undertaker agree to keep Emmett's casket nailed closed, but they met their match in his mother. An estimated fifty thousand Chicagoans saw the body in the open casket. *Jet* magazine ran a picture. "When people saw what had happened to my son," Mamie Till said, "men stood up who had never stood up before." And one woman refused to stand up: sixty-nine days after the acquittal of Emmett's murderers, and three hundred miles away, Rosa Parks refused to surrender her seat on a bus.

Twenty-six days after murdering Emmett, Bryant and Milam were acquitted by a jury that waited sixty-seven minutes, a juror said, to "drink a pop" before embracing the defense argument that the body might not have been Emmett's. Bryant and Milam later told *Look* magazine they killed Emmett. They said they took turns smashing him across the head with the .45. But the trial was the first event to turn the gaze of American journalism to the causes of the coming civil rights storm.

A week after the acquittal, Simeon Wright's father, who testified against Bryant and Milam, left his car at the railroad station and went to Chicago. He never returned to Mississippi.

Others besides Bryant and Milam, both dead, may have been complicit in the killing. But beyond DNA proof that it was Emmett's body, it is unclear what forensic evidence his remains might provide to the Mississippi district attorney who sought the disinterment.

Martin Luther King came to Chicago in January 1966, but Simeon Wright says: "I didn't qualify for Dr. King's march. They told us that if bricks and things were thrown at us, we couldn't retaliate. I couldn't do that. . . . Now I'm back to what he was teaching."

Wright says friends who only recently discovered his connection with the Till case say, "He's so easy going!" He says, "I guess they think I'd be angry all the time. You don't live long that way." At the reinterment, he recited the first verse to "Taps," which concludes: "All is well, safely rest, God is nigh." He says, "It got a little emotional then."

Where do they come from, people like Simeon Wright, people of such resilience and grace? From Mississippi and Illinois. And everywhere else. They are all around us.

What has this country done—what can any country do—to deserve such people? Wrong question. They *are* this country.

[JUNE 19, 2005]

Chapter Two

PATHS TO THE PRESENT

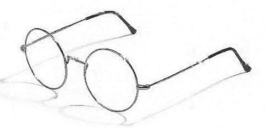

The Most Important American War You
Know Next-to-Nothing About

For your Fourth of July reading, open a mind-opening book about an immensely important American war concerning which you may know next to nothing. King Philip's War, the central event in a bestseller that is one of this summer's publishing surprises, left a lasting imprint on America.

Americans in this era of sterile politics have an insatiable appetite for biographies of the Founders. But why are so many readers turning to a book—*Mayflower: A Story of Courage, Community, and War*, by Nathaniel Philbrick—that casts a cool but sympathetic eye on an era usually wrapped in gauzy sentimentality?

One reason might be that it is fun to read about one's family: Philbrick estimates that there are approximately 35 million descendants of the passengers on the *Mayflower*. (Do the math: 102 passengers; 3.5 generations in a century. But remember, 52 passengers died of disease and starvation before the first spring.) Perhaps a second answer is that the story is particularly pertinent as America is engaged abroad in a clash of civilizations, and is engaged at home in a debate about immigration and the common culture.

"In the American popular imagination," Philbrick writes, "the nation's history began with the Pilgrims and then leapfrogged more than 150 years to Lexington and Concord and the Revolution." That version misses, among much else, the history-turning fourteen months of war in 1675 and 1676 that set in train events that led to Lexington and Concord. The war was between the English settlers and the Pokanoket Indians led by Metacom, whose English name was Philip.

In a six-decade downward spiral of mutual incomprehension and unintended consequences, the uneasy but growing coexistence of English settlers and Native Americans dissolved in mutual suspicions, conflicts, and retaliations. During the war, the colony lost 8 percent of its men (compared to the 4 percent to 5 percent of adult men killed in the Civil War). But Native Americans fared far worse. Of the 20,000 in the region at the war's beginning, 2,000 died of wounds, 3,000 of sickness or starvation, 2,000 fled west or north—and 1,000 were shipped to the West Indies as slaves. Taxation and other costs of the war so injured economic life that a century passed before New England's per capita income returned to the prewar level.

Philbrick writes that after ethnic cleansing, or at least ethnic sorting out, there were no friendly Indians as buffers between the settlers and the unfriendly ones. So the settlers were forced to look to London for help. Soon a royal governor was appointed to govern New England. Then came irritating taxation—of stamps, of tea—and arguments about representation. Exactly one hundred years after King Philip's War ended, the United States began.

But an American frame of mind began in 1623. *Mayflower* illustrates a timeless fact of politics everywhere—the toll reality takes on ideology—and a large theme of American life: the fecundity of individualism and enlightened self-interest.

The first important book-length manuscript written in America was *Of Plymouth Plantation,* the journal of William Bradford, the colony's governor for nearly thirty-six years. Not published in full until 1856, it was then avidly read by a nation bent on westward expansion and fearing civil war.

In a section on private versus communal farming, Bradford wrote that in 1623, because of a corn shortage, the colonists "began to think how they might raise" more. After much debate, they abandoned their doctrine, which they brought with them on the *Mayflower,* that all agriculture should be a collective, community undertaking. It was decided, Bradford wrote, that "they should set corn every man for his own particular, and in that regard trust to themselves." That is, they "assigned to every family a parcel of land," ending communal cultivation of that crop.

"This," Bradford reported, "had very good success, for it made all hands very industrious, so as much more corn was planted than otherwise would have been by any means." Indeed, "the women now went willingly into the field, and took their little ones with them to set corn; which before would allege weakness and inability; whom to have compelled would have been thought great tyranny and oppression." So began the American recoil from collectivism. Just three years after the settlers came ashore (not at Plymouth Rock, and far from their intended destination, the mouth of the Hudson), they began their ascent to individualism.

So began the harnessing, for the general good, of the fact that human beings are moved, usually and powerfully, by self-interest. So began the unleashing of American energies through freedom—voluntarism rather than coercion. So began America.   [JULY 4, 2006]

The Amazing Banality of Flight

The twelve-second flight one hundred years ago this morning reached a height of just 10 feet, less than the 63-foot height of a Boeing 747, and covered just 120 feet of ground, less than a 747's 195-foot wingspan. But the Wright brothers' fourth and final flight that day in North Carolina lasted fifty-nine seconds and went 852 feet. So by sunset the twentieth century's themes—farther, faster, higher, *now*—were, so to speak, in the air.

Almost everything—commerce, war, art—would change as aviation began altering, as nothing had ever done, humanity's experience of the most basic things: time and space. Politics, too. The first important politician to campaign by air was a militant modernist, Adolf Hitler. The newsreels screamed: *"Der Führer fliegt über Deutschland."*

Aviation's infancy was not for the fainthearted. In the early 1920s, an airmail pilot named Dean Smith, on the Chicago-to-Omaha route, cabled his superintendent:

"On trip 4 westbound. Flying low. Engine quit. Only place to land on cow. Killed cow. Wrecked plane. Scared me. Smith."

Airmail was one way government subsidized aviation, which drew government into deep involvement with technology. So, of course, did the great driver of social change, war. In their new book, *Reconsidering a Century of Flight,* Roger D. Launius and Janet R. Daley Bednarek note how rapid was the development of the airplane "from a machine in some ways most lethal to those who used it to a machine of great lethality to those against whom it is directed."

In 1905, the Wright brothers testified to Congress that airplanes' military uses would be "scouting and carrying messages." Forty years later, cities would be laid waste from the air. But city bombing was not as lethal as was feared. In April 1939, the British government, anticipating city bombing, issued to local authorities 1 million burial forms. The actual British casualties from aerial bombardment, 1939–1945, were sixty thousand.

One early theory, refuted by experience, was that strategic bombing might make wars less bloody by bypassing bloody clashes between armies, such as the First World War's trench warfare, and instead quickly inducing an enemy's surrender by disrupting his "vital center." The fallacious assumption was that modern economies and societies are fragile.

It was nearly a century after Kitty Hawk, and due less to developments of aircraft than of munitions, that military aircraft really became lethal for targets smaller than whole cities. Until recently, the question about bombing was how many sorties it would take to destroy a target. Suddenly, because of precision munitions, the question is how many targets one sortie can strike. In World War II, about one bomb in four hundred landed close enough to affect—not necessarily destroy—its target. Now nine out of ten do.

The most astonishing consequence of aviation is not its military applications or their civilian echoes. (After World War II, Harley J. Earl, General Motors' chief stylist, turned his fascination with the twin tails of the P-38 fighter into automobile tail fins that defined the chrome-plated 1950s.) Rather, the amazing consequence was the banality of flight—the routinization of mobility—especially after 1958, when Boeing's 707 speeded the democratization of air travel. Unfortunately, this had some negative public health consequences because viruses—HIV, for one—also became mobile.

From the first, flight expressed the essence of the modernist movement—freedom understood as the absence of limits, and a future of infinite possibilities. While developing cubism, Pablo Picasso sometimes painted wearing aviator's gear. His response to the April 26, 1937, bombing by Germans of Guernica during Spain's civil war—a rehearsal, or overture, for what was soon to come from Europe's skies—moved Picasso to produce what may be the twentieth century's iconic painting.

Cubism itself was influenced by a perspective no previous generation knew, that of the earth—the geometry of its urban grids and rural plots—seen from above. The Eiffel Tower had provided Europeans their first downward vision of their environment. Robert Hughes, the art critic, says that what was spectacular was not the view of the tower from the ground but the view of the ground from the tower. Until then, almost everybody lived their entire lives no more than forty feet— the height of an ordinary apartment building—above the ground.

Modernism shaped another expressive activity that flourished in tandem with aviation, the competition to build the tallest skyscraper. In Manhattan, epicenter of the competition, the race was eventually won by the twin towers of the World Trade Center, where ninety-eight years after Kitty Hawk the histories of aviation and architecture intersected. [DECEMBER 17, 2003]

The Price of Misreading the Prairie Sky

When giving thanks this year, think of Lena Woebbecke. She and many others paid a terrible price for misreading the prairie sky on the afternoon of January 12, 1888.

That day was unseasonably balmy, by prairie standards—some temperatures were in the twenties—and many children scampered to school without coats or gloves. Then, at about the time schools were adjourning, death, in the shape of a soot-gray cloud, appeared on the horizon of Dakota Territory and Nebraska.

In three minutes the temperature plunged eighteen degrees. The next morning hundreds of people, more than one hundred of them children, were dead beneath the snowdrifts. David Laskin, a Seattle writer, reconstructs this tragedy in a terrifying but beautifully written new book, *The Children's Blizzard.*

It picks up the many threads of the story in Norway, Ukraine, Germany, Vermont, and other tributaries to the river of immigration set in motion partly by the 1862 Homestead Act. In return for an $18 filing fee and five years farming, the act conferred ownership of 160 acres. By the tens of thousands the homesteaders came, to live in sod houses, heated by burning buffalo bones and twisted hay.

Of immigrants, the saying was that the cowards stayed home and the weak died on the way. One in ten crossing the Atlantic in steerage did die. But Laskin says "the mystique of the Dakotas" was such that the territory's population nearly quadrupled in the 1880s. Those who made it, with a trunk or two and the clothes on their backs, reached towns that were perishable scratches on the prairie. They got land, freedom, and hope.

And prairie fires. And grasshoppers, 100 billion at a time in roaring clouds a mile high and a hundred miles across. And iron weather in which children, disoriented by horizontal streams of snow as hard as rock and fine as dust, froze to death groping their way home from a school 150 yards away.

Lena was five in 1882 when her father, a German immigrant, died of smallpox. Her mother remarried twice, having eleven children, eight of whom survived. In August 1887, Lena, her marriage prospects diminished by her smallpox scars, was sent to live with the Woebbeckes and their three children in a two-room house. It was half a mile from the school where she was, five months later, when a cataclysmic cold front came dropping southeast out of Canada at forty-five miles per hour.

"To those standing outside," Laskin writes, "it looked like the northwest corner of the sky was suddenly filling and bulging and ripping open." In four and a half hours, the temperature at Helena, Montana, fell fifty degrees. The prairie air tingled with the electricity of a horizontal thunderstorm. All over the region, schoolteachers, many of them not much older or more educated than their pupils, had to make life-and-death decisions about how to get the children home.

"The fear came first," Laskin writes, "but the cold followed so hard on its heels that it was impossible to tell the difference." In minutes, nostrils were clogged by ice. Eyelids were torn by repeated attempts to prevent them from freezing shut. Unable to see their hands in front of their faces, people died wandering a few yards from their houses, unable to hear, over the keening wind, pots being pounded a few yards away to tell them the way to safety.

"For years afterward," writes Laskin, "at gatherings of any size in Dakota or Nebraska, there would always be people walking on wooden legs or holding fingerless hands behind their backs or hiding missing ears under hats—victims of the blizzard." Lena learned to walk on a wooden foot. In 1901, at twenty-four, she married. At twenty-five, she died, perhaps in childbirth, or perhaps of a complication from the amputation necessitated by frostbite.

"Lena was laid to rest in her wedding dress in the graveyard of the Immanuel Lutheran Church near the country crossroads called Ruby. If there ever was a town called Ruby, it has disappeared, as has the Immanuel Lutheran Church. The church cemetery remains—a fenced patch of rough grass studded with headstones between two farmhouses not far from the interstate. A tiny island of the dead in the sea of Nebraska agriculture."

This Thanksgiving, when you have rendered yourself torpid by ingesting an excess of America's agricultural bounties, summon thoughts of thanks for the likes of Lena, those whose hard lives paved the stony road to America's current comforts. [NOVEMBER 25, 2004]

"A Range of Mountains on the Move"

The soil is the one indestructible, immutable asset that the nation possesses. It is the one resource that cannot be exhausted.
—FEDERAL BUREAU OF SOILS, 1878

Seventy-five years ago, America's southern plains were learning otherwise. Today, amid warnings of environmental apocalypse, it is well to recall the real thing. It is a story about the unintended consequences of technological progress and of government policies. Above all, it is an epic of human endurance.

Who knew that when the Turks closed the Dardanelles during World War I, it would contribute to stripping the topsoil off vast portions of Texas, Oklahoma, Colorado, and Kansas? The closing cut Europe off from Russian grain. That increased demand for U.S. wheat. When America entered the conflict, Washington exhorted farmers to produce even more wheat, and guaranteed a price of $2 a bushel, more than double the 1910 price. A wheat bubble was born. It would burst with calamitous consequences recounted in Timothy Egan's astonishing and moving book, *The Worst Hard Time: The Untold Story of Those Who Survived the Great American Dust Bowl.*

After the war, the price plunged and farmers, increasingly equipped with tractors, responded by breaking up more prairie, plowing under ever more grassland in desperate attempts to compensate for falling wheat prices with increased volume. That, however, put additional downward pressure on the price, which was forty cents a bushel by 1930.

The late 1920s had been wet years, and people assumed that the climate had changed permanently for the better. In that decade, another 5.2 million acres—equivalent, Egan says, to the size of two Yellowstone Parks—were added to the 20 million acres previously in cultivation. Before the rains stopped, fifty thousand acres a day were being stripped of grasses that held the soil when the winds came sweeping down the plain.

In 1931, the national harvest was 250 million bushels, perhaps the greatest agricultural accomplishment in history. But Egan notes that it was accomplished by removing prairie grass, "a web of perennial species evolved over 20,000 years or more." Americans were about to see how an inch of topsoil produced over millennia could be blown away in an hour.

On January 21, 1932, a cloud extending ten thousand feet from ground to top—a black blizzard with, Egan writes, "an edge like steel wool"—looked like "a range of mountains on the move" as it grazed

Amarillo, Texas, heading toward Oklahoma. At the end of 1931, a survey found that of the 16 million acres cultivated in Oklahoma, 13 million were seriously eroded.

On May 10, 1934, a collection of dust storms moved over the Midwest carrying, Egan says, "three tons of dust for every American alive." It dumped six thousand tons on Chicago that night. By morning, the storm was eighteen hundred miles wide—"a great rectangle of dust" weighing 350 million tons—and was depositing the surface of the Great Plains on New York City, where commerce stopped in the semidarkness.

On the southern plains, dust particles, one-fifth the size of the period at the end of this sentence and high in silica content, penetrated lungs, jeopardizing newborns and causing "dust pneumonia" in others. Houses were so porous that the only white part of a pillow in the morning was the profile of the sleeper. Storms in March and April 1935 dumped 4.7 tons of dust per acre on western Kansas, denting the tops of cars. During one storm, the wind blew at least forty miles per hour *for one hundred hours*. Egan reports that it would have required a line of trucks ninety-six miles long, hauling ten loads a day for a year— 46 million truckloads—to transport the dirt that had blown from western to eastern Kansas.

In Washington, in a Senate hearing room, a man was testifying to bored legislators about the need for federal aid for the southern plains. A senator suddenly exclaimed, "It's getting dark outside." The sun vanished and the air turned copper-color, thanks to red dust that the weather bureau said came from the western end of Oklahoma's panhandle. The aid was approved the next day.

The southern plains got what Egan calls frenzied skies of grasshoppers—sometimes 14 million per square mile—because the insects' natural predators were gone. Eventually, however, rain fell on the convulsed land and on the tenacious people who never left it, and the government devised soil conservation measures. The Earth turned out to be more durable, and the people who wrested their livings from the earth more resilient, than had been thought.   [APRIL 29, 2007]

The Emblematic Novel of the 1930s
(No, It Is Not About the Joads)

Confined to her bed in Atlanta by a broken ankle and arthritis, her husband gave her a stack of blank paper and said, "Write a book." Did she ever.

The novel's first title became its last words, "Tomorrow Is Another Day," and at first she named the protagonist Pansy. But Pansy became Scarlett, and the title of the book published seventy years ago this week became *Gone With the Wind*.

You might think that John Steinbeck, not Margaret Mitchell, was the emblematic novelist of the 1930s, and that the publishing event in American fiction in that difficult decade was his *The Grapes of Wrath*. Published in 1939, it captured the Depression experience that many Americans had, and that many more lived in fear of. Steinbeck's novel became a great movie and by now 14 million copies of the book have been sold.

But although the $3 price of *Gone With the Wind* ($43.50 in today's dollars) was steep by Depression standards, it sold 178,000 copies in three weeks and 2 million by April 1938, when it ended a twenty-one-month run on the bestseller list. By now nearly 30 million have been sold. About 250,000 are still purchased in America every year, and 100,000 elsewhere.

In 1935, there had been an early indicator of the American yearning that Mitchell's novel satisfied. That year saw the publication of the final two volumes of another durable work of Southern sympathy, Douglas Southall Freeman's Pulitzer Prize–winning four-volume biography of Robert E. Lee. What was afoot?

By the middle of the 1930s, with the Depression entering its second half-decade and showing no sign of succumbing to the New Deal's attempts to end it, Americans were rightly skeptical about the idea that happy days would soon be here again. Their world having been turned upside down, they saw a parallel between their plight and the story of the disappearance of the antebellum South. Hence their embrace of Mitchell's epic about a society pulverized to human dust that is blown about by history's leveling wind.

Parts of the novel reek of magnolia and cloying sentimentalism. But Mitchell writes sarcastic passages about the Lost Cause:

"How could anything but overwhelming victory come to a Cause as just and right as theirs? . . . Of course, there were empty chairs and babies who would never see their fathers' faces and unmarked graves by lonely Virginia creeks and in the still mountains of Tennessee, but was that too great a price to pay for such a Cause?"

Scarlett certainly was no sentimentalist. When Rhett Butler, the embodiment of unapologetic realism, asks her if she ever thinks "of anything but money," she replies with words that struck a chord with a nation that had heard quite enough of the song "Brother, Can You Spare a Dime?": "No. . . . I've found out that money is the most important thing in the world and, as God is my witness, I don't ever intend to be without it again."

In 1936, the *Washington Post* reviewer called the novel "unsurpassed in the whole of American writing," which was a bit strong, considering what Hawthorne, Melville, Twain, and Wharton had produced. What could, however, accurately have been said of *Gone With the Wind* was that it was the most cinematic novel yet written in America. A month after it was published, $50,000 was paid for the rights to turn it into the movie that has grossed (adjusted for ticket price inflation) a record $3.8 billion worldwide.

Like another Southern woman who wrote a novel about her region, a novel that is still in print nearly half a century later and that became a classic movie (Harper Lee, *To Kill a Mockingbird,* published in 1960), Mitchell never wrote another. In 1949, at age forty-eight, she was killed by a taxi driven by a drunk in Atlanta, which was already on its way to becoming the symbol of the New South.

Mitchell had been born in 1900, just thirty-five years after Appomattox and twenty-three years after Reconstruction ended. Her sensibilities were not what ours are. The novel has passages that cannot be read without cringing. ("Not trust a darky! Scarlett trusted them far more than most white people. . . . They still stuck with their white

folks and worked much harder than they ever worked in slave times.")
But to read such passages is to be stunned, once again, by the amazing
speed with which America has changed for the better. In 1936, in
Mitchell's Atlanta, the pastor of the Ebenezer Baptist Church, Martin
Luther King, had a son who was seven.   [JUNE 25, 2006]

All Quiet at the Overpass

D EARBORN, MICHIGAN—A suitable venue for contemplating organized labor's current disarray is here, at the footbridge over
Miller Road. In 1937, it led to the main entrance of the foremost
example of America's manufacturing might—the Ford Motor Company's River Rouge plant, then the world's most fully integrated car-
manufacturing facility, from blast furnaces to assembly line. Five years
later, the plant would exemplify America as the "arsenal of democracy." It made jeeps, tanks, trucks, and engines for B-24 bombers. But
on May 26, the footbridge to the plant made history.

"The Battle of the Overpass," a heroic event in American labor
history, began when Walter Reuther, president of UAW Local 174, and
three colleagues started across the footbridge to distribute leaflets as
part of their campaign to unionize the plant. They were savagely beaten
by perhaps forty Ford thugs and thrown down the overpass stairs. The
thugs confiscated most photographers' film, but James (Scotty) Kil-
patrick of the *Detroit News* surrendered only blank film. His pictures
made Reuther a national figure and aroused American opinion against
tactics then used to thwart unionization.

Ford came to terms with the UAW in May 1941, seven months before American industry was conscripted into war. Even though women
flooded into factories (Rose Will Monroe, who as "Rosie the Riveter"
symbolized this social transformation, worked in Ford's Willow Run
plant), labor was scarce and wage controls limited companies' means of
competing for workers. So companies offered medical and pension benefits as untaxed compensation not covered by wage controls. Today
whole industries are buckling beneath the weight of these "legacy costs."

By 1955, 33 percent of the nation's nonfarm workforce was unionized. But few government employees were. As Steven Malanga of the Manhattan Institute writes in his book *The New New Left: How American Politics Works Today*, the assumption was that because there is no competition in the delivery of government services, strikes could cripple cities. That was then.

Now, Bentonville, Arkansas (population: 28,000, up 40 percent in four years), has supplanted Detroit as the home of the nation's largest company. Intense and protracted efforts by organized labor have failed to unionize a single one of Wal-Mart's 3,190 North American stores. General Motors, the largest corporation in 1955, is unionized. Two credit-rating agencies have reduced its debt, and one has reduced Ford's to junk-bond status as both companies struggle to finance medical and pension benefits for current and—even more numerous—retired workers. Such costs also are major reasons for the parlous condition of all the older airlines.

In 1955, when Japan was still struggling to recover from the damage done by B-24s with their Ford-built engines, the American automobile industry was riding high and the UAW was riding along. With negligible foreign competition—their market share was 95 percent—American car companies could pass along to consumers the costs of labor contracts. Today, while domestic carmakers are planning to shed jobs by the thousands, employment is surging in the nonunionized plants, most in the South, where foreign automakers build one-quarter of all the cars and trucks made in America.

In the 1930s, American workers were literally fighting to get into unions. Today, unions are fighting with themselves about the appropriate tactics to adopt in response to the fact that just 7.9 percent of private-sector workers are union members. But at the apogee of the American labor movement in the 1950s, the transformation of the movement began.

In 1958, the American Federation of State, County and Municipal Employees won collective-bargaining rights from New York mayor Robert Wagner—son of Senator Robert Wagner, author of the Wagner Act, aka the National Labor Relations Act of 1935, the most important federal action enabling private-sector unionization. AFSCME's members rose from one hundred thousand in 1955 to 1 million in 1985. It has 1.4 million members today and is just one of many government employees' unions.

The River Rouge complex, which is still humming, is a National Historic Landmark, and "the Battle of the Overpass" and the UAW's successes are commemorated at a plaza—built by Ford—on Miller Road, by the footbridge. In the auto industry, where labor and management used to fight over the allocation of abundance, the coming showdown will be over the reduction of benefits won in palmier days.

Soon, perhaps, a majority of organized labor will be government employees. The labor movement will be primarily government organized as an interest group to lobby and pressure itself. Already New York City, which has about the same size population it had forty years ago, has 30 percent more city employees. Antonio Villaraigosa, the new mayor of Los Angeles, is a former organizer for that city's teachers union. The footbridge over Miller Road led to this. The heroic era of organized labor is long gone.   [JULY 18, 2005]

FDR's Transformation of Liberalism

Some mornings during the autumn of 1933, when the unemployment rate was 22 percent, the president, before getting into his wheelchair, sat in bed, surrounded by economic advisers, setting the price of gold. One morning he said he might raise it twenty-one cents: "It's a lucky number because it's three times seven." His treasury secretary wrote that if anybody knew how gold was priced "they would be frightened."

The Depression's persistence, partly a result of such policy flippancy, was frightening. In 1937, during the depression within the Depression, there occurred the steepest drop in industrial production ever recorded. By January 1938, the unemployment rate was back up to 17.4 percent. The war, not the New Deal, defeated the Depression. Franklin Roosevelt's success was in altering the practice of American politics.

This transformation was actually assisted by the misguided policies—including government-created uncertainties that paralyzed investors—that prolonged the Depression. This seemed to validate the notion that the crisis was permanent, so government must be forever hyperactive.

In his second inaugural address, Roosevelt sought "unimagined power" to enforce the "proper subordination" of private power to public power. He got it, and the fact that the federal government he created now seems utterly unexceptional suggests a need for what Amity Shlaes does in a new book. She takes thorough exception to the government he created.

Republicans had long practiced limited interest-group politics on behalf of business with tariffs, gifts of land to railroads, and other corporate welfare. Roosevelt, however, made interest-group politics systematic and routine. New Deal policies were calculated to *create* many constituencies—labor, retirees, farmers, union members—to be dependent on government.

Before the 1930s, the adjective "liberal" denoted policies of individualism and individual rights; since Roosevelt, it has primarily pertained to the politics of group interests. So writes Shlaes, a columnist for Bloomberg News, in *The Forgotten Man: A New History of the Great Depression.* She says Roosevelt's wager was that by furiously using legislation and regulations to multiply federally favored groups, and by rhetorically pitting those favored by government against the unfavored, he could create a permanent majority coalition.

In the process, says Shlaes, Roosevelt refined his definition of the "forgotten man." This man had been thought of as a general personality, compatible with the assumption that Americans were all in it together. "Now, by defining his forgotten man as the specific groups he would help, the president was in effect forgetting the rest—creating a new forgotten man. The country was splitting into those who were Roosevelt's favorites and everyone else."

Acting with what Shlaes calls "the restlessness of the invalid," Roosevelt implemented the theory that (in her words) "spending promoted growth, if government was big enough to spend enough." In only twelve months, just one Roosevelt improvisation, the National Recovery Administration, "generated more paper than the entire legislative output of the federal government since 1789."

Before Roosevelt, the federal government was unimpressive relative to the private sector. Under Calvin Coolidge, the last pre-Depression president, its revenues averaged 4 percent of GDP, compared to 18.6 percent today. In 1910, Congress legislated height limits for Washington buildings, limits that prevented skyscrapers, symbols of mighty business, from overshadowing the Capitol, the symbol of government.

In 1936, for the first time in peacetime history, federal spending exceeded that of the states and localities combined. Roosevelt said modern "civilization" has tended "to make life insecure." Hence Social Security, which had the added purpose of encouraging workers to retire, thereby opening jobs to younger people. Notice the assumptions of permanent scarcity, and that the government has a duty to distribute scarce things, such as work.

In 1938, when the New Deal's failure to spark recovery made Roosevelt increasingly frantic, he attempted to enlarge the Supreme Court so he could pack it with compliant justices. He said Americans had the right to "insist that every agency of popular government" respond to "their will." He included the court among "popular," meaning political and representative, institutions.

Roosevelt's overreaching called forth an opponent whom Shlaes rescues from obscurity. Wendell Willkie, who would be Roosevelt's opponent in a 1940 election overshadowed by war, called upon Roosevelt to "give up this vested interest you have in depression" as the justification for a "philosophy of distributed scarcity."

War, as has been said—and as George W. Bush's assertion of vast presidential powers attests—is the health of the state. But as Roosevelt demonstrated and Shlaes reminds us, compassion, understood as making the "insecure" securely dependent, also makes the state flourish.

[JULY 8, 2007]

Retailers Give Thanks for Thanksgiving (and FDR)

Thirty days hath September,
April, June and November.
All the rest have thirty-one,
Until we hear from Washington.

The country heard from Washington—the man, not the place—when he issued a National Thanksgiving Proclamation for November 26, 1789. The new nation had much for which to be thankful, including the fact that it would be 150 years before Thanksgiving was officially made into a handmaiden of commerce and turned into the starting gun for the sprint of Christmas shopping.

By now the sprint is a marathon that seems to begin around Labor Day. Soon there will be after-Christmas sales before Halloween, such is the relentless expansion of what is called, with telling vagueness, "the holiday season."

The country heard from Washington—the place; the mentality—in 1939 when President Franklin Roosevelt threw Thanksgiving into the battle to get happy days here again. FDR's governmental hyperkinesia had failed to banish the Depression. Unemployment was still 17.2 percent and the ultimate cure for the Depression—Admiral Yamamoto's fleet approaching Hawaii—was still twenty-four months over the horizon.

Even the calendar was conspiring against prosperity because in 1939, as in FDR's first year in office, 1933, November had five Thursdays, and Thanksgiving was to fall on the thirtieth. So FDR moved Thanksgiving from the last Thursday in November to the fourth.

Although President Washington was a Virginian, the idea of a national Thanksgiving Day had seemed somehow New Englandish, tainted by Yankee sanctimony and, worse still, Federalist notions of national supremacy over states' prerogatives. Even President John Quincy Adams of Massachusetts thought a national Thanksgiving observation might be "introducing New England manners" where they were unwelcome.

President Lincoln, a great affirmer of the national facets of the nation's life, was the first to set the last Thursday in November as the national day of Thanksgiving. Bill Kauffman, who has explained all this (in "New Deal Turkey," the *American Enterprise* magazine, December 2000), says Lincoln's successor, President Andrew Johnson, who had quite enough fights on his hands without picking another one—he was the first president impeached—shoved Thanksgiving into December. President U. S. Grant, who rarely retreated but knew how to, put it back to the last Thursday in November.

But Appomattox notwithstanding, states remained free to do as they liked about Thanksgiving, and Southern states liked to observe it when they chose. Or not at all, as in Texas during the governorship of Oran Milo Roberts, who said, "It's a damned Yankee institution anyway."

But in 1939, many of the nation's larger merchants—the National Retail Dry Goods Association, the presidents of Gimbel Brothers and Lord & Taylor—asked FDR for relief from the fact that in 1939 Thanksgiving would arrive so late—November 30—that it would injure the economy by delaying the start of Christmas shopping.

However, the class struggle erupted, pitting smaller merchants against the larger merchants. The proprietor of Arnold's Men's Shop in Brooklyn wrote to urge FDR to allow the later Thanksgiving: "If the large department stores are overcrowded during the shorter shopping period before Christmas, the overflow will come, naturally, to the neighborhood store. . . . We have waited many years for a late Thanksgiving to give us an advantage over the large stores."

FDR felt the pain of the large merchants. But some people felt pained by FDR's tampering with Thanksgiving, including Oregon's attorney general, author of the doggerel printed above. A West Virginian wrote FDR to say, while you are at it, please declare it "strictly against the Will of God to work on Tuesday" and "have Sunday changed to Wednesday." A South Dakota real estate man admonished FDR to "remember we are not running a Russia or communistic government," and he added: "Between your ideas of running for a third term, and your changing dates of century-old holidays, we believe you have practically lost your popularity and the good will of the people of the Northwest." FDR lost South Dakota in 1940.

But in 1939, twenty-three states followed FDR's lead and celebrated Thanksgiving on November 23. Twenty-three stayed with November 30. Colorado and Texas celebrated on both days, Texas doing so to avoid having to reschedule—speaking of things to give thanks for—the Texas–Texas A&M football game.

FDR, who enjoyed fiddling with things, promised in 1941 to return Thanksgiving to the last Thursday in November. But history has its hold on us and Congress shoved it back to the fourth Thursday, partly because many constituents believed the Pilgrims had put it there in the first place.   [NOVEMBER 27, 2003]

FDR's Christmas Guest from Hell

Imagine how tiresome it would be to have, at Christmas, a houseguest of whom your spouse disapproves and who you have met only twice before, the first time twenty-three years ago (annoyingly, your guest does not remember the meeting), the second time four months ago, for a few hours, out of town, on business. Imagine that the houseguest invites himself to your home, stays almost three weeks, and one morning early on during his stay he summons your butler (you don't have one? pity) and issues the following ukase:

"Now, Fields, we had a lovely dinner last night but I have a few orders for you. We want to leave here as friends, right? So I need you to listen. One, I don't like talking outside my quarters; two, I hate whistling in the corridors; and three, I must have a tumbler of sherry in my room before breakfast, a couple of glasses of scotch and soda before lunch and French champagne and 90-year old brandy before I go to sleep at night."

Furthermore, this Guest from Hell declares that for breakfast he requires hot "eggs, bacon or ham and toast" and "two kinds of cold meats with English mustard and two kinds of fruit plus a tumbler of sherry." You would be forgiven for asking your guest if he had been born in a palace.

He who so firmly addressed President Franklin Roosevelt's butler Alonzo Fields sixty-four Christmases ago was, in fact, born in Blenheim Palace, England's gift to the first Duke of Marlborough. And if no whistling and lots of sherry and whiskey would help the duke's great-great-great-great-great-great-grandson, Winston Churchill, function, stop whistling and pour liberally. There is a war to win.

The story of this December 1941 visit is told by two Canadians, David Bercuson and Holger Herwig, in an entertaining book with an idiotic subtitle, *One Christmas in Washington: The Secret Meeting Between Roosevelt and Churchill That Changed the World. Secret* meeting? It was about as secret as a circus, featuring a press conference with FDR and a speech to a joint session of Congress in which Churchill said: "I cannot help reflecting that if my father had been American and my mother British, instead of the other way round, I might have got here on my own." But the meeting did change the world by constructing the machinery of cooperation that led to the defeat of the Axis.

How ancient it now seems, 1941. The city of Washington had fifteen thousand outdoor privies. German U-boats sank 432 ships in the Atlantic. In August, FDR could deceive everyone, including the Secret Service, for a really secret meeting with Churchill—their only previous meeting had been at a London dinner in 1918—at Placentia Bay, Newfoundland. In the days after Pearl Harbor, some of the antiaircraft guns on the White House were wooden fakes—real ones were scarce. On his voyage, sometimes through forty-foot waves, to his Christmas visit with FDR, Churchill watched American movies, including *Santa Fe Trail,* starring Errol Flynn, Olivia de Havilland, and Ronald Reagan.

FDR greeted Churchill in Washington in a black limousine the Treasury Department had confiscated from a tax evader named Al Capone. Churchill met here with Admiral Ernest King, commander in chief of the U.S. fleet, who had served in the Spanish-American War, and with General Henry "Hap" Arnold, the head of the Army Air Forces, who in 1911 received flight training in Dayton, Ohio, from the Wright brothers.

What could have been the most important event of Churchill's almost three weeks in America was not known until his doctor published his memoirs in 1966: Churchill suffered a heart attack while straining to open a stuck window in his White House bedroom. Had it been fatal, that could have changed the world.

Eleanor Roosevelt disapproved of Churchill the imperialist, but on Christmas Day 1941 she, he, and the president attended Washington's Foundry Methodist Church, the second iteration of a church founded by Henry Foxall, who in 1812 vowed that he would build a church as a thanksgiving offering if the British did not destroy his cannon foundry when they took Washington and burned the White House.

Christmas Day was the birthday of General Sir John Dill, chief of the Imperial General Staff, so a cake was found and adorned with a set of American and British flags which, Dill discovered when he removed them, were made in Japan. This occasioned laughter, at a time when that, like much else, was scarce.   [DECEMBER 25, 2005]

"My Place Is with My Shipmates"

P EARL HARBOR, HAWAII—Sixty-one years later, it is still not over. One by one, oil drops still seep from the submerged hull of the USS *Arizona*. And one by one, some men who survived the bomb that hit the battleship's forward magazine still return, the urns containing their ashes lowered through the water into the hole of a gun turret, because as one of them said, "Ever since December 7, 1941, I've been living on borrowed time. My place is with my shipmates."

Here, about as far as you can get in America from the scenes of last year's attacks, you see this difference: In 1941, a mighty empire—an enemy with a serious if reckless geopolitical strategy—struck at real sinews of U.S. power. In 2001, a delusional, premodern enemy lashed out at American symbols—iconic buildings—and instantly magnified American power by dispelling an American mood. Call it end-of-history complacency.

The attack that came here sixty-one years ago from across the broadest ocean erased forever the belief that geography—wide oceans, placid neighbors—confers permanent security on America. The attacks last year erased the comparably soothing belief that the logic of military technology (deterrence) and the march of modernity (the retreat of primitivism) had written an end to history, meaning the immunity of great powers to attacks.

Sixty-one Decembers ago, as last year, America suffered from intelligence failures. But in both instances, for the officials charged with protecting the nation's security, the attacks came not as bolts from the blue but as bolts from what they knew to be ominously darkening skies.

Both times American officials knew enough to know that the international atmosphere was charged with hidden menace. Which is why the first shots fired on December 7, 1941, were fired by America's wary military: At 6:45 a.m., the destroyer USS *Ward* attacked one of the two-man midget submarines—its wreckage was found two weeks ago—lurking at the mouth of the harbor, poised to participate in the attack that was still seventy minutes over the horizon.

The attacks of December 7, 1941, like the attacks of September 11, 2001, were a curious mixture of virtuosity and primitivism. Al Qaeda skillfully used nineteen suicidal fanatics wielding box cutters and commercial airliners to attack a continent. It was deadly, and absurd.

Japan's military achievement—moving thirty-two warships four thousand miles undetected; designing shallow-running torpedoes; brilliantly coordinating the bomb and torpedo attacks—was military sophistication of the highest order. Yet the pilots skimming thirty feet over the water used carpenters' levels in their cockpits to make sure their planes were properly positioned to insert their torpedoes into the water.

The Americans who died here—on the *Arizona*, twenty-three sets of brothers, and a father and his son—were mostly military men. Those whom the terrorists targeted last September were mostly civilians.

For all Americans, being a focus of furies—which a muscular nation, extending almost five thousand miles from the cavity in southern Manhattan to the *Arizona*'s hull, will be—is a dangerous destiny. It is a destiny that, in a sense, was just dawning 104 years ago when the USS *Baltimore* sailed from here.

On March 25, 1898, that cruiser left to join Commodore Dewey's fleet in Hong Kong. It entered Manila Bay with the fleet on May 1 and participated in the destruction of the Spanish fleet. The Spanish-American War established the United States as a global power, its power projected then entirely by its Navy. In 1941, an important portion of the Navy was based here because—westward the course of empire takes its way—the United States had annexed these islands in that eventful year of 1898.

On a December Sunday forty-three years later, the *Baltimore,* which had been decommissioned in 1922, was a ghost ship moored at the end of battleship row, where it escaped damage. But in a sense its career was still not over. In 1942, it was turned into scrap. No doubt some of it was sent back to war in bits and pieces.

Half a million gallons of fuel oil remain in the *Arizona*'s hull. With leakage of a quart a day, no one now living will be alive when the surface sheen from the last drop drifts away. And no one now living will live to see a day when Americans forget the lesson now associated with September 11 as well as December 7: A powerful nation embodying a powerful idea and spanning six time zones is permanently exposed to dangers from all the other eighteen zones. [SEPTEMBER 8, 2002]

An Anthem of American Optimism— in 1943

Every night my honey lamb and I
sit alone and talk
and watch a hawk
makin' lazy circles in the sky
              —"Oklahoma!"

NEW YORK—"Honey lamb"? That is as corny as Kansas in August. Perhaps such lyrics please people in Manhattan, Kansas, where the waving wheat can sure smell sweet when the wind comes right behind the rain. But surely the sophisticates in this Manhattan prefer to tap their patent leather dancing pumps to the urbane lyrics of Ira Gershwin.

Surely not. The show-business collaboration of Richard Rodgers and Oscar Hammerstein long ago ended, but their melodies and lyrics linger on. In fact, rather more than just linger. They reverberate. Advance ticket sales topped $12 million by the time the revival of *Oklahoma!* opened two weeks ago—in the Gershwin Theater, so there.

Whoever said that America's imperishable gifts to the world are the Constitution, baseball, and jazz should have included a fourth: a distinctive kind of stage musical, the greatest of which is *Oklahoma!* It took that top ranking away from *Show Boat* (1927) fifty-nine years ago and has kept it ever since. *Oklahoma!* was the first "integrated" musical, meaning the singing and dancing arose organically from the action, advancing rather than interrupting the narrative. Audiences were ready for this maturation of the musical.

When *Oklahoma!* first came to Broadway, the opening—it was a sleety March night—was not sold out. Soon tickets were scarce. However, servicemen in uniform were admitted to standing room without charge. It was 1943, a terrible year.

But the first words of the first song were—are—"There's a bright, golden haze on the meadow." The song, "Oh, What a Beautiful Mornin'!" was an anthem of an American optimism that not even world war could dent. It is serendipitous that this revival, which played for four years in London, arrives with the nation again at war.

And, as usual, the nation is fretting, as Oklahoma Territory fretted, about keeping the peace between disparate and sometimes rivalrous factions, such as "The Farmer and the Cowman" of the rousing number that opens the second act. But cultural events are always filtered through the mental lenses of the moment, so Ben Brantley of the *New York Times* writes that this revival of *Oklahoma!* is saturated with . . . well, he says:

It suggests "the West was won on the strength of sexual hormones." It finds "rushing erotic currents in the frontier spirit." It is "dewy with an adolescent lustiness" and a "darker sexual element." There is "a glistening sense of young people eagerly groping their way through an unfamiliar landscape" and that a world parallel to "the virgin land" of Oklahoma Territory is the "shadowy realm of sexual initiation." And the choreography—as in "The Farmer and the Cowman," which has "wild, procreative energy"—vibrates "with the sense of sensual restlessness in search of an outlet."

Whoa. Perhaps Brantley should take a long walk or a cold shower, or the latter after the former. Yes, boys and girls in Oklahoma Territory had a keen interest in girls and boys. Otherwise there would not have been so many subsequent Oklahomans. But *Oklahoma!* is about which boy—the sunny cowboy Curly or the glowering hired hand Jud Fry—should take the girl, Laurey, to the box social, for Pete's sake. How steamy can that be?

Some critics whose admiration for this revival of *Oklahoma!* is as high as an elephant's eye nevertheless emphasize its "dark" side. But this is not new. Curly has been fighting Jud Fry since March 31, 1943, when Fry first stabbed himself to death with his own knife while fighting with Curly. And for fifty-nine years, before every final curtain, Curly has been quickly acquitted of manslaughter.

Is this "dark"? Ethan Mordden, a historian of Broadway musicals, notes that *Oklahoma!* is especially American in presenting "the unpleasant truth that evil will keep coming at you until you kill it. One piece of democracy is the harmonizing of discordant agendas. But another piece is the expunging of the wicked." The revival of *Oklahoma!* is timely, Mordden says, "because it defines Americans as a people, generous but plainspoken and tough on spoilers."

The first Broadway run of *Oklahoma!* lasted five years and nine months, a record not broken until *My Fair Lady* ran from 1956 to 1962. But in a sense *Oklahoma!* has never closed since 1943. In a normal year, there are about six hundred new North American productions of it. It is part of the permanent music of the American people, who know that the land they belong to is grand. [APRIL 7, 2002]

When War *Was* the Answer

OMAHA BEACH, NORMANDY—On a bluff above the sand and a half a mile from the ocean's edge at low tide, which was the condition when the first Allied soldiers left their landing craft, a round circle of concrete five feet in diameter provides a collar for a hole in the ground. On the morning of June 6, 1944, the hole was Widerstandsnest (nest of resistance) 62, a German machine-gun emplacement.

Hein Severloh had been in it since shortly after midnight, by which time U.S. aircraft were droning overhead, having dropped young American paratroopers Severloh's age behind the beaches in order to disrupt German attempts to rush in reinforcements. Severloh had been billeted near Bayeux, home of the eleventh-century tapestry depicting a cross-channel invasion that went the other way, taking William, Duke of Normandy, to become William the Conqueror, England's sovereign.

Severloh believed he killed hundreds of GIs, so long and slow was their walk to the safety, such as it was, of the five-foot embankment where the beach meets the bluff. Severloh returned here in sorrow and was consoled by survivors of the forces that waded ashore.

Today, in an America understandably weary of a war of choice that has been defined by execrable choices, a frequently seen bumper sticker proclaims: "War is not the answer." But here, especially, it is well to remember that whether war is the answer depends on the question.

War was the answer to what ailed Europe in 1944. "In 1942," writes Timothy Garton Ash of Oxford and Stanford's Hoover Institution, "there were only four perilously free countries in Europe: Britain, Switzerland, Sweden and Ireland." Twenty years—a historical blink—later, almost all of Western Europe was free. Twenty years after that, Spain, Portugal, and Greece had joined the liberal democracies. Today, for the first time in twenty-five hundred years, most Europeans live under such governments.

Garton Ash argues that Europe cannot define itself negatively—as *not* America or *not* Islam. "Europe's only defining 'other' is its own previous self"—its self-destructive, sometimes barbaric past. "This is," Garton Ash says, "still a very recent past."

In 1951, just seven years after Severloh and some other Germans surrendered on June 7 to Americans at the village of Saint-Laurent, Europe began building the institutions that, it hoped, would keep such young men out of machine gun emplacements. It created the European Coal and Steel Community, precursor of the Common Market (1958), which led to the single market in 1993 and the common currency in 2002.

The implicit hope was that commerce could tame Europe's turbulent nations. The perennial problem of politics—mankind's susceptibility to storms of passions—could perhaps be solved, or at least substantially ameliorated, by getting Europe's peoples to sublimate their energies in economic activities. The quest for improved material well-being would drain away energies hitherto tapped and channeled by demagogues.

Reminders of Europe's problematic past were recently found a few miles from Saint-Laurent. Workers preparing a foundation for a new house overlooking Omaha Beach came upon parts of the bodies of two German soldiers. There was scant media attention to this because such discoveries have not been rare.

Also near here, 21,160 German soldiers are buried at the La Cambe Cemetery. Thirty percent—more than 6,000—were never identified, so some German parents conducted "assumed burials." They placed metal markers bearing the names of their missing sons near the graves of unknown soldiers who were known to have died near where the parents' sons were last known to be fighting.

Such heartbreaking stories are written into Normandy's lovely landscape. At the American Cemetery overlooking this beach, amid the many rows of white marble gravestones, are two, side by side, marking the burial places of Ollie Reed and Ollie Reed Jr., a father and his son. The son, an Army first lieutenant, died in Italy on July 6. His father, an Army colonel, was killed July 30 in Normandy. Two telegrams notified the father's wife, the son's mother. The telegrams arrived in Manhattan, Kansas, forty-five minutes apart.

The nineteenth-century French scholar Ernest Renan, from a Brittany town on the English Channel, defined a nation as a community of shared memory—and shared forgetting. Europe's emotional equipoise, and the transformation of "Europe" from a geographical to a political expression, has required both remembering and forgetting. Americans who make pilgrimages to this haunting place are reminded of their role, and their stake, in that transformation.   [SEPTEMBER 2, 2007]

Catching Up to Captain Philip

"Don't cheer, boys. The poor devils are dying."
> —CAPTAIN JOHN PHILIP of the USS *Texas* to his
> crew as they watched the Spanish ship *Vizcaya*
> burn off Santiago Bay, Cuba, in 1898

On March 9, 1945, 346 B-29s left the Marianas, bound for Tokyo, where they dropped 1,858 tons of incendiaries that destroyed one-sixth of Japan's capital, killing eighty-three thousand. General Curtis LeMay, then commander of the air assault on Japan, later wrote, "We scorched and boiled and baked to death more people in Tokyo . . . than went up in vapor at Hiroshima and Nagasaki combined."

That was inaccurate—eighty thousand died at Hiroshima alone. And in his new biography of LeMay, Barrett Tillman writes that the general was more empathetic than his rhetoric suggested: "He could envision a three-year-old girl screaming for her mother in a burning house." But LeMay was a warrior "whose government gave him a task that required killing large numbers of enemy civilians so the war could be won."

It has been hotly debated how much indiscriminate killing of civilians in the Asian and European theaters really was "required" and therefore was morally permissible. Even during the war there was empathy for civilian victims, at least European victims. And less than fifteen years after the war, movies (e.g., *The Young Lions*, 1958) offered

sympathetic portrayals of common German soldiers swept into combat by the cyclone of a war launched by a tyrant.

But attitudes about the Japanese soldier were especially harsh during
the war and have been less softened by time than have attitudes about
the German soldier. During the war, it was acceptable for a billboard—
signed by Admiral William F. "Bull" Halsey—at a U.S. Navy base in
the South Pacific to exhort KILL JAPS, KILL JAPS, KILL MORE JAPS. Killing America's enemies was Halsey's trade. His rhetoric, however, was
symptomatic of the special ferocity, rooted in race, of the war against
Japan: "We are drowning and burning them all over the Pacific, and it
is just as much pleasure to burn them as to drown them." Halsey endorsed the Chinese proverb that the "Jap race" was the result of "a
mating between female apes and the worst Chinese criminals."

Wartime signs in West Coast restaurants announced: THIS RESTAU-
RANT POISONS BOTH RATS AND JAPS. In 1943, the Navy's representa-
tive on the committee considering what should be done with a defeated
Japan recommended genocide—"the almost total elimination of the
Japanese as a race."

Stephen Hunter, movie critic for the *Washington Post,* says that of
the more than six hundred English-language movies made about World
War II since 1940, only four—most notably *The Bridge on the River
Kwai* (1957)—"have even acknowledged the humanity" of Japanese
soldiers.

Perhaps empathy for the plight of the common enemy conscript is
a postwar luxury; it certainly is a civilized achievement, an achievement of moral imagination that often needs the assistance of art. That
is why it is notable that Clint Eastwood's *Letters from Iwo Jima* was
one of five films nominated for Best Picture.

It is stressful viewing. An unsparing attempt to come as close as
cinema can to conveying the reality of combat, specifically the fighting
that killed 6,821 Americans and all but 1,083 of the 22,000 Japanese
soldiers on the small (eight square miles) black lava island. Remember
the searing first fifteen minutes of *Saving Private Ryan*—the carnage
at Omaha Beach? In *Letters from Iwo Jima,* it is exceeded, with har-
rowing permutations.

The Japanese commander on the island, Tadamichi Kuribayashi, was—like the admiral who attacked Pearl Harbor, Isoroku Yamamoto—a cosmopolitan warrior who had lived in, and never stopped admiring, America. In 2005, a team of Japanese archaeologists scouring the island's man-made caves for artifacts of the battle found a sack of undelivered mail from Kuribayashi and other officers and soldiers. All the writers knew they faced overwhelming force—Japan had no assistance to send—and were doomed to die in accordance with the Japanese military code that forbade surrender and encouraged suicide.

Japanese forces frequently committed barbarities worse even than those of the German regular army, and it is difficult to gauge the culpability of conscripts commanded by barbarians. Be that as it may, the pathos of the letters humanizes the Japanese soldiers, whose fatalism was a reasonable response to the irrational. Viewers of this movie, while moved to pride and gratitude by the valor of the U.S. Marines, will not feel inclined to cheer. We are catching up to Captain Philip's sensibility.

[FEBRUARY 25, 2007]

The Most Fateful Heart Attack in American History

The Supreme Court's decision fifty years ago, although an immense blessing to the nation, also carries a melancholy lesson. It is that great events—the school desegregation ruling was the largest judicial event since the Dred Scott case of 1857—have myriad reverberations, some beneficial, others not.

Brown v. Board of Education accelerated the process of bringing this creedal nation into closer conformity to its creed. But the decision also encouraged the abandonment of constitutional reasoning—of constitutional law. It invested the judiciary with a prestige that begot arrogance. And it seemed to legitimize a legislative mentality among judges wielding an anticonstitutional premise. The premise is that "unjust" and "unconstitutional" are synonyms.

The board of education being sued for its segregation policies was not in the South, but in Kansas—Topeka. Segregation was widely practiced, and even more widely approved. Yes, in Montgomery, Alabama, it was illegal for a white to play checkers in public with a black. But Congress was running a segregated school system in the nation's capital. In 1948, President Harry Truman could not persuade Congress to make lynching a federal crime.

When the case was first argued in 1952, the Supreme Court was composed entirely of Democratic—of Roosevelt and Truman—appointees. And if the court's composition had not been soon and unexpectedly changed by the addition of a Republican nominee, the legal basis of segregation—the doctrine that "separate but equal" public facilities are constitutional—probably would have been affirmed.

No Republican nominee had served on the court since Owen Roberts, a Hoover nominee, resigned in 1945. But in 1953, eight months into Dwight Eisenhower's presidency, there occurred the most fateful heart attack in American history. It killed Chief Justice Fred Vinson, a Kentuckian who believed the "separate but equal" doctrine, enunciated in an 1896 decision, should remain.

Four other justices were, to varying degrees, inclined to agree. Cass Sunstein of the University of Chicago Law School, writing in *The New Yorker*, notes that the waspish Justice Felix Frankfurter said that Vinson's heart attack was "the first indication that I have had that there is a God." But Frankfurter and another liberal-leaning justice, Robert Jackson, were FDR appointees who had learned the virtues of judicial modesty by watching the judicial hubris of the court as it struck down many of FDR's early New Deal measures.

Vinson's death preceded a rehearing of the case. His replacement, Earl Warren, former governor of California, was a post–New Deal politician. He was comfortable with the premise that the federal government's responsibilities extend to the general amelioration of citizens' conditions. A man of immense charm in the court's face-to-face politics, he also was impatient with the idea that justices must go only where led by judicial reasoning about the Constitution's text as it has been illuminated by precedents based thereon.

Some Northern states had segregated schools when they ratified

the Fourteenth Amendment. It includes the guarantee of "equal protection of the laws" that in 1954 the court decided was incompatible
with segregated schools. To reach this conclusion, the court cited social science evidence that segregation induced feelings inimical to
young children's self-esteem, thereby injuring their capacity to learn.

That this rationale was window dressing became clear when the
court invoked the Brown decision to outlaw segregated beaches,
golf courses, etc. The court would have done better with this simple
argument:

The "separate but equal" doctrine came from a correct understanding that equality for blacks was the intent of the Fourteenth Amendment. But the court in 1896 erred because, when separation is enforced
on racial lines, "separate but equal" is inherently oxymoronic.

When the Brown ruling was rendered, Thurgood Marshall, the
NAACP's lead litigator, expected segregation to be gone in five years.
But ten years later, only 1.17 percent of Southern black schoolchildren
attended public schools with whites.

In 1954, the court's majesty could not compel compliance. Today,
the court's reserves of prestige are immeasurably greater, partly because of what it did then. What also is much enlarged is the public's
belief that judicial fiats can and should remedy many social ills,
broadly defined to include the refusal of legislatures to adopt polices
deemed just.

"John Marshall has made his decision, now let him enforce it."
That supposedly was President Andrew Jackson's response to a Supreme Court decision he disliked. Then, as now, the court's power
flowed largely from its prestige, which was not sufficient to bend Old
Hickory. No president could act similarly today. This progress owes
much to what happened on May 17, 1954.   [MAY 16, 2004]

How Ike's Highways Helped Heal Civil War Wounds

O n Tuesday, July 11, the United States will become more geo-graphically stable than it has ever been. It will have been 17,126 days since the admission of Hawaii to statehood on August 21, 1959. The longest previous span between expansions of the nation was the 17,125 days between the admission of Arizona on February 14, 1912, and the admission of Alaska on January 3, 1959. Since then the nation has become, in a sense, smaller through the annihilation of distance and, to some extent, of difference.

An important part of the groundwork—literally, it covered a lot of ground—for today's America was begun fifty years ago this summer. A conservative Republican president, who grew up in a Kansas town where hitching posts for horses lined unpaved streets, launched what was, and remains, the largest public works project in the nation's history—the Interstate Highway System. Its ribbons of concrete represent a single thread of continuity through the nation's history.

With that program, Dwight Eisenhower, the thirteenth Republican president, helped heal the wounds of the war won by another general, U. S. Grant, the second Republican president. That war was related to "internal improvements," as infrastructure projects such as roads and canals used to be called.

In 1816, South Carolina representative John Calhoun—then a nationalist; later, a secessionist—introduced legislation for a federal program of internal improvements. The legislation passed, but President James Madison vetoed it because he thought Congress was not constitutionally empowered to do such things. So, prosperous Northern states built their own improvements while the South sank into inferiority and increasing dependence on slavery.

The military handicap of an inferior transportation system was one reason the South lost the Civil War. Another reason was the industrialization of the North. Its transportation system (the Erie Canal, railroads) cut the price of shipping a ton of wheat from Buffalo to

New York City from $100 to $10, and the difference between the wholesale price of pork in Cincinnati and New York plunged from $9.53 to $1.18. Suddenly, workers flooding into the North's cities had more disposable income to spend on the North's manufactured goods.

The first Republican president began his public life as a twenty-three-year-old candidate for the Illinois General Assembly by telling voters of Sangamon County his "sentiments with regard to local affairs," the first sentiment being "the public utility of internal improvements." The vigor of the union also was a preoccupation of Teddy Roosevelt, the eighth Republican president, whose great internal improvement, the Panama Canal, was external, although he thought of Panama as America's private property. And Eisenhower's message to Congress advocating the IHS began, "Our unity as a nation is sustained by free communication of thought and by easy transportation of people and goods."

No legislator more ardently supported the IHS than the Tennessee Democrat who was chairman of the Senate Public Works subcommittee on roads. His state had benefited handsomely from the greatest federal public works project of the prewar period, the Tennessee Valley Authority, which, by bringing electrification to a large swath of the South, accelerated the closing of the regional development gap that had stubbornly persisted since the Civil War. This senator who did so much to put postwar America on roads suitable to bigger, more powerful cars was Al Gore Sr. His son may consider this marriage of concrete and the internal combustion engine sinful, but Tennessee's per capita income, which was just 70 percent of the national average in 1956, today is 90 percent.

The IHS—combined, as *Fortune* magazine's Justin Fox writes, with another bright idea from 1956, the shipping container—made America's distribution system more flexible. This benefited manufacturers, foreign and domestic, especially in America's hitherto lagging region, the South. This is one reason there is a thriving Southern-based automobile industry (BMW in South Carolina; Mercedes in Alabama; Honda in both Carolinas, Georgia, and Alabama; Toyota in Tennessee, Alabama, and Kentucky). Furthermore, the South is home to some of today's "big-box" retailers—Wal-Mart (Bentonville, Arkansas), Home Depot (Atlanta)—as well as FedEx (Memphis).

American scolds blame the IHS and the automobile for everything from obesity (fried food at every interchange) to desperate housewives (isolated in distant suburbs without sidewalks). Nikita Khrushchev, during his 1959 visit to America, told Eisenhower, "Your people do not seem to like the place where they live and always want to be on the move going someplace else." Eisenhower knew that wherever people are going on their nation's roads, they are going where they live.

[JULY 9, 2006]

The Short, Unhappy Life of the Edsel

L eaving no talent untapped in its quest for perfection, the Ford Motor Company asked Marianne Moore, one of America's foremost poets in the 1950s, to suggest a name for the product it would debut in late summer, fifty years ago. She replied: "May I submit Utopian Turtletop? Do not trouble to answer unless you like it."

Ford instead named the product for Henry Ford's late son Edsel. The Edsel would live twenty-six months.

The short, unhappy life of that automobile is rich in lessons, and not only for America's beleaguered automobile industry. The principal lesson is: Most Americans are not as silly as a few Americans suppose.

No industry boomed more in the 1950s than the manufacturing of social criticism excoriating Americans for their bovine "conformity," crass "materialism," and mindless manipulability at the hands of advertising's "hidden persuaders." Vance Packard's *The Hidden Persuaders* was atop the *New York Times* bestseller list as Edsels arrived in showrooms. No consumer product in history had been the subject of so much "scientific" psychology-based market research.

Remember the basketball coach who said of his team, "We're short but we're slow"? The Edsel was ugly but riddled with malfunctions. So many malfunctions that some people suspected sabotage at plants that had previously assembled Fords and Mercurys. Those two Ford divisions perhaps hoped the Edsel would bomb.

"It was," wrote John Brooks, a student of American business, in *The New Yorker,* "clumsy, powerful, dowdy, gauche, well-meaning—a de Kooning woman." Chrome seemed to be piled upon chrome. Potential buyers recoiled from the vertical egg-shaped grille, which reminded them of a toilet seat. The transmission was worked by push buttons placed—convenience sacrificed on the altar of novelty—in the center of the steering column. The larger Edsels weighed more than two tons, were 219 inches long—longer than the grandest Oldsmobiles—and 80 inches wide. These were not the cars for a year in which the surprise success was American Motors' little Rambler.

By Sunday, October 13, barely more than a month after the Edsel's debut, anemic sales caused the company to preempt *The Ed Sullivan Show* with a Sunday evening Edsel extravaganza featuring Bing Crosby and Frank Sinatra. But there was no sales spurt. Nine days earlier, the Soviet Union had launched its first Sputnik satellite, provoking a crisis of confidence in America's technological prowess and a reaction against chrome-laden barges as emblems of national self-indulgence. On November 27, Manhattan's only Edsel dealer gave up his franchise and switched to selling Ramblers.

In the spring of 1958, S. I. Hayakawa, a professor of semantics (and later a Republican U.S. senator from California), ascribed the Edsel's failure to the Ford executives' excessive confidence in the power of motivational research to enable them to predict—and modify—Americans' behavior. In their attempt to design a car that would cater to customers' sexual fantasies, status anxieties, and the like, Ford's deep thinkers had neglected to supply good transportation.

"*Only* the psychotic and the gravely neurotic *act out* their irrationalities and their compensatory fantasies," Hayakawa wrote. "The trouble with selling symbolic gratification via such expensive items . . . is the competition offered by much cheaper forms of symbolic gratification, such as 'Playboy' (fifty cents a copy), 'Astounding Science Fiction' (thirty-five cents a copy), and television (free)."

In 1958, with the Edsel already turned to ashes, John Kenneth

Galbraith, with bad timing comparable to the launch of the Edsel, published *The Affluent Society*. It asserted that manufacturers, wielding all-powerful advertising, were emancipated by the law of supply and demand because advertisers could manufacture demand for whatever manufacturers wished to supply.

This theory buttressed the liberal project of expanding government in the name of protecting incompetent Americans from victimization, and having government supplant the market as the allocator of wealth and opportunity. But all of Ford's then-mighty marketing prowess could not keep the Edsel from being canceled in 1959. Brooks calculated that it would have been cheaper for Ford to skip the Edsel and give away 110,000 Mercurys.

Today, the United Auto Workers union and General Motors, Ford, and Chrysler are trying to reverse the slide of the American automobile industry. Fifty Septembers ago, the country was atingle with anticipation of a new product that turned out to be a leading indicator of the slide. As Detroit toils to undo some contractual provisions that have burdened the companies with crippling health care and pension costs, it should remember the real lesson of 1957: Americans are more discerning and less herdable than their cultured despisers suppose, so what matters most is simple. Good products.   [SEPTEMBER 6, 2007]

The Fifties in Our Rearview Mirror

There was, too, a wonderful simplicity of desire. It was the
last time that people would be thrilled to own a toaster or
waffle iron.   —BILL BRYSON

What Thanksgiving is to gluttony, the three days after it are to consumerism—the main event. So, with Americans launching the Christmas season by storming the stores, let us recall when consumption had an exuberance remembered now only by those who experienced the 1950s.

Bill Bryson remembers. The author of thirteen books (e.g., *A Walk in the Woods* and *A Short History of Nearly Everything*), Bryson has most recently written *The Life and Times of the Thunderbolt Kid,* a memoir of growing up in Des Moines in the fifties, when downtown department stores—with white-gloved operators in the elevators and pneumatic tubes carrying money and receipts to and from cashiers—served the pent-up demands of a nation making up for consumption missed during the Depression and World War II.

In 1951, when the average American ate 50 percent more than the average European, Americans, Bryson says, controlled two-thirds of the world's productive capacity, owned 80 percent of the world's electrical goods, produced more than 40 percent of its electricity, 60 percent of its oil, and 66 percent of its steel. America's 5 percent of the world's population had more wealth than the other 95 percent, and Americans made almost all of what they consumed: 99.93 percent of new cars sold in 1954 were U.S. brands.

By the end of the fifties, GM was a bigger economic entity than Belgium, and Los Angeles had more cars than did Asia—cars for a gadget-smitten people, cars with Strato-Streak engines, Strato-Flight Hydra-Matic transmissions, and Torsion-Aire suspensions. The 1958 Lincoln Continental was nineteen feet long. And before television arrived (in 1950, 40 percent of Americans had never seen a television program; by May 1953, Boston had more televisions than bathtubs) America made almost a million comic books a month.

Consider what was new or not invented then: ballpoint pens, contact lenses, credit cards, power steering, long-playing records, dishwashers, garbage disposals. And remember words now no longer heard: icebox, dime store, bobby socks, panty raid, canasta (a card game). In 1951, a Tennessee youth was arrested on suspicion of narcotics possession. The brown powder was a new product—instant coffee.

Fifties food was, Bryson reminds us, not exotic: In Iowa, at least, folks did not eat foreign food "except French toast," or bread that was not "white and at least 65 percent air," or "spices other than salt, pepper and maple syrup," or "any cheese that was not a vivid bright yellow and shiny enough to see your reflection in."

But unlike today, when everything edible, from milk to spinach, has its moment as a menace to health, in the fifties everything was good for you. Cigarettes? Healthful. Advertisements, often featuring doctors, said smoking soothed jangled nerves and sharpened minds. "X-rays," Bryson remembers, "were so benign that shoe stores installed special machines that used them to measure foot sizes."

In Las Vegas, downwind from some atomic weapons tests, government technicians used Geiger counters to measure fallout: "People lined up to see how radioactive they were. It was all part of the fun. What a joy it was to be indestructible." But, Bryson dryly notes, people knew without a warning label "that bleach was not a refreshing drink."

White House security precautions were so lax that on April 3, 1956, a somewhat disoriented Michigan woman detached herself from a White House tour and wandered through the building for four hours, setting small fires. When found, she was taken to the kitchen and given a cup of tea. No charges were filed.

The fifties did have worries. When a contestant on a TV game show said his wife's astrological sign was Cancer, the cigarette company sponsoring the show had the segment refilmed and her sign changed to Aries. You could get fourteen years in an Indiana prison for instigating anyone under age twenty-one to "commit masturbation." And to get a New York fishing license, you had to swear a loyalty oath.

Nothing has changed more for the worse since the fifties than childhood. The lives of children were, Bryson remembers, "unsupervised, unregulated and robustly" physical. "Kids were always outdoors— I knew kids who were pushed out the door at eight in the morning and not allowed back in until five unless they were on fire or actively bleeding."

But as the twig is bent, so grows the tree: These children, formed by the fifties, grew up to be Olympic-class shoppers. They are indoors this Sunday, at malls. [NOVEMBER 26, 2006]

2002: Superstitions Are Bad Luck

O nward and upward with homo sapiens. A 7 million-year-old skull uncovered this year in Central Africa belonged to someone the size of a chimpanzee and is the earliest—by about a million years—yet discovered member of the human family. In 2002, his descendants were threatened by savage primitives who, in the name of the Creator, were possibly plotting to reverse, using smallpox spores, one of Homo sapiens' recent triumphs over an infectious scourge. Much the most important event of 2002 was a nonevent—the second major terrorist attack on the American homeland that did not happen. Four homegrown terrorists from the 1970s, members of the Symbionese Liberation Army, pleaded guilty to a murder committed during a 1975 bank robbery in Carmichael, California.

Complex geometric carvings on a rock found this year in a South African cave suggest that complex and abstract thinking began in Africa, not in Cambridge, Massachusetts, and began twice as long ago—seventy-seven thousand years—as had been believed. When did it stop? Trent Lott regretted that Harry Truman rather than Strom Thurmond won the 1948 presidential election.

The perpetrators of this year's most lurid skullduggery and corruption? No, not Wall Street stock analysts—Olympic figure-skating judges. Not long ago, tycoons were "masters of the universe." This year they were mastering the perp walk. Enron and Arthur Andersen almost vanished. Martha Stewart wished she could. United Airlines and the Boston diocese of the Roman Catholic Church had reason to remember the aphorism of Frank Borman, who was president of Eastern Air Lines before it went bankrupt: "Capitalism without bankruptcy is like Christianity without Hell."

Two Bronx teenagers, one four feet ten and the other five feet six, are suing McDonald's because they weigh 170 pounds and 270 pounds, respectively. The legal theory behind their suit derives from the Garth Brooks lyric: "Longneck bottle, let go of my hand."

Lieutenant John Kennedy's PT 109, sunk in 1943, was found off the Solomon Islands. *Oklahoma!,* launched in 1943, was back on Broadway. Off-Broadway, Bill Clinton starred in "It—everything—is all about me." Campaigning for Massachusetts gubernatorial candidate Shannon O'Brien, Clinton, whose self-absorption remains one of the wonders of the world, said an O'Brien victory would be "a wonderful way to celebrate the 10th anniversary of my victory in 1992."

A little difference makes a big difference: A mouse's genome has been mapped. Humans and mice have about thirty thousand genes. Less than 1 percent are unique to either species.

An Italian artist, seeking to make an "ironic statement," produced ninety cans of his feces. London's Tate Gallery paid $35,000 for one. If your cell phone rang in the Rising Sun pub in Brighton, England, the proprietor nailed the phone to the bar.

A member of the U.S. table-tennis team was suspended for steroid use. When Mets pitcher Shawn Estes lost his no-hitter in the seventh inning, Mets manager Bobby Valentine rejected the idea that Estes was jinxed in the fifth inning when Shea Stadium's JumboTron announced that Estes had not yet given up a hit. Said Valentine: "I don't believe in superstitions. They're bad luck."

Baseball avoided a season-ending strike, enabling a San Francisco woman, who wanted to be artificially inseminated, to advertise a barter: World Series tickets for "healthy sperm." In his first three major-league at bats, Seattle Mariners designated hitter Ron Wright caused six outs by striking out and hitting into a double play and a triple play. After the game, he was sent to the minors. Pete Gray, a one-armed outfielder who during the Second World War played a season for the St. Louis Browns, died at eighty-seven. Joe Black, the first black pitcher to win a World Series game (for Brooklyn, in 1952), was seventy-eight.

Montgomery, Alabama, bus driver James Blake died at 89, forty-seven years after he had Rosa Parks arrested because she refused to move to the back of his bus. Traudl Junge, a private secretary to Hitler and the last surviving witness to his final hours in the bunker, said he "gave me a feeling of security, safety and being cared for." She died at 82, wondering: "If he discovered he had Jewish blood in his family tree, would he have gassed himself?" Chaike Spiegel, one of the last surviving combatants of the 1943 Warsaw ghetto uprising, was 81. Flags all across Australia were flown at half mast for Alec Campbell, 103, the last survivor of more than seventy thousand Australians and New Zealanders who fought in 1915 at Gallipoli, the ill-fated operation that almost destroyed the career of its architect, Winston Churchill. Of Gallipoli, Campbell said: "It was a lovely place, you know, if conditions had been better . . ." Queen Elizabeth the Queen Mother, born when Churchill was 25, died at 101.

And after half a century of sultry singing, Peggy Lee, who was eighty-one, left the stage. There lingered in our minds a lyric suitable for any year: "If that's all there is, my friends, then let's keep dancing."

[DECEMBER 23, 2002]

2003: Lingerie and Duct Tape

"Whatever happens," said Lord Salisbury (1830–1903), a conservative in thought, word, and deed, "will be for the worse, and therefore it is in our interests that as little should happen as possible." By that sensible standard, eventful 2003 was not in our interests.

Make *love* and *war,* or else the terrorists will have won: During Valentine's week in February, with war impending and the government elevating the terrorism alert, two of Wal-Mart's hot-selling items were lingerie and duct tape. Talk about ingratitude: Terrorists struck in Saudi Arabia. The war with Iraq went well, aside from the detail that the reason for it—weapons of mass destruction—has been elusive. The following is a complete list of all those fired because of the intelligence failure: _____.

While America was trying to acquaint 25 million Iraqis with democracy, 144.5 million Russians fell under President Vladimir Putin's "managed democracy"—czarism leavened by state-manipulated plebiscites. If only the world were more like California, where the people, groaning under the wicked choices of the electorate, chose a new governor to wrestle with the people's chosen legislature over how to undo the damage done by voters in dozens of plebiscites.

In America's "(court-) managed democracy," judges began discovering a right to same-sex marriage. Forty-one years after the U.S. Army helped end racial discrimination in admissions at Ole Miss, the Supreme Court found nothing amiss in the University of Michigan's racial discrimination in admissions.

That court, having said that the First Amendment protections extend to virtual child pornography and tobacco advertising, finally exclaimed "Enough!" In a 5–4 decision cowritten by Sandra Day O'Connor, it held that concern for political hygiene justified Congress's passing the McCain-Feingold legislation to restrict the amount and regulate the content of speech about members of Congress. Thus did a Ronald Reagan 1980 campaign promise (to appoint the first woman justice) result, twenty-three years later, in ratification of George W. Bush's decision to sign a bill that he, while campaigning—before taking the oath to defend the Constitution—called unconstitutional.

The Académie Française, which never stooped to admit Flaubert or Zola, admitted Valéry Giscard d'Estaing, author—sort of—of the European Union's proposed 263-page Constitution, a screamingly funny political satire. Because of Jayson Blair, heads rolled at the *New York Times,* where all the "news" had not been fit to print.

American conservatives, controlling both elected branches of government for the first full year since 1954, used their power to . . . vastly expand the welfare state. The prescription-drug entitlement may cost $2.5 *trillion* over the next twenty years. Big deal. That sum amounts to only five years of deficits at the current level. Besides, Congress showed that it could act with dispatch against a menace that *really* annoys people: spam.

Howard Dean discerned what liberals want: *attitude.* In San Francisco, ground zero of Deanism, sensitivity police stipulated that pets' owners shall also be called "guardians." Kobe Bryant, impulse buyer, bought his wife a $4 million diamond ring. *Friends* headed for oblivion, American style: ubiquitous reruns.

Remember Henry Adams's jest that the succession of presidents from Washington to Grant disproved the theory of evolution? After another year watching their royals, the British could say something similar about the progress, so to speak, from Elizabeth I to the son of Elizabeth II. Senator Pat Moynihan, dead at seventy-six, was America's foremost public intellectual. Another giant of the Finance Committee, Russell Long, eighty-four, was sixteen when his father was assassinated, and not quite thirty when elected to the Senate in 1948. David Brinkley, eighty-two, the most famous son of Wilmington, North Carolina, until Michael Jordan came along, said of television, "When there is no news, we give it to you with the same emphasis as if there were."

This year, the movie musical was revived with *Chicago,* and Sam Phillips died at 80. On July 5, 1954, at his Memphis recording studio, Phillips recorded a 19-year-old singing "That's All Right Mama." Elvis's blending of white and black music helped end the world defended by Lester Maddox and Strom Thurmond, dead at 87 and 100.

In 1951, the Boston Braves' Warren Spahn, en route to becoming baseball's winningest left-hander, stood on the mound, sixty feet six inches from a New York Giants rookie who was 0–for–12. Willie Mays homered. Said Spahn, "For the first sixty feet, that was a helluva pitch." Spahn was eighty-two. In the 1934 World Series, Tiger shortstop Billy Rogell's relay to first hit Cardinal runner Dizzy Dean in the forehead. The next day a headline supposedly said: X-RAYS OF DEAN'S HEAD REVEAL NOTHING. Rogell died at ninety-eight.

At 114, Mitoyo Kawate was the world's oldest person. She was working on her farm six miles from Hiroshima on August 6, 1945. Jack Davis, 108, was Britain's oldest veteran of mankind's final war—the war to end war, 1914–1918.   [DECEMBER 22, 2003]

2004: *The Passion of the Christ* and *The Passions of the Faculty Clubs*

In 2004, an IBM supercomputer set a world record with 36.01 trillion calculations per second. The U.S. electorate may have made its calculation the instant John Kerry, who is not a supercomputer, explained why Toy's restaurant in Canonsburg, Pennsylvania, "is my kind of place":

"You don't have to—you know, when they give you the menu, I'm always struggling: ah, what do you want? He just gives you what he's got, right? . . . whatever he's cooked up that day. And I think that's the way it ought to work, for confused people like me who can't make up our minds."

This year, some paleoanthropologists reported that our cousins the Neanderthals, who disappeared thirty thousand years ago, had better minds than has been thought: On a plain in Spain there is a mass grave containing evidence of funeral ritual, which means that Neanderthals had a capacity for symbolism. This year, Democrats stressed their superior brains. (Bumper stickers: SOME VILLAGE IN TEXAS IS MISSING THEIR [*sic*] IDIOT; JOHN KERRY—BRINGING COMPLETE SENTENCES BACK TO THE WHITE HOUSE.) A campaign flier in Tennessee pictured George W. Bush's face superimposed over that of a runner in the Special Olympics, and proclaimed this message: "Voting for Bush is like running in the Special Olympics. Even if you win, you're still retarded."

From an Indonesian island came evidence that as recently as eighteen thousand years ago—only yesterday, as paleoanthropologists reckon—there was a race of Hobbit-size (about three feet tall) semi-people. Their small brains probably were incapable of idealism of James Kilgore's sort. In 2004, Kilgore, fifty-six, was sentenced to six years in prison for his part in the murder of a mother of four during a 1975 California bank robbery that was supposed to help finance the Symbionese Liberation Army. Martha Stewart was sentenced to prison for lying about a crime she was not charged with. Scott Peterson was convicted of double murder—killing his wife, and killing his unborn child, a problematic idea given the current understanding of abortion rights. Before death tardily overtook another dispenser of death, Yasir Arafat, he received a letter from People for the Ethical Treatment of Animals— well, of animals other than people—asking him to stop using donkeys in suicide bombings. It was said that the death of this winner of the Nobel Peace Prize might make peace possible.

Fifty years after *Brown v. Board of Education,* an African-American was nominated to replace an African-American as secretary of state. Nashville, Tennessee, schools stopped displaying the honor rolls of

A students because some parents complained that the displays might hurt the feelings of dimmer students. In Washington State, the Puyallup school district ended the grade-school tradition of children parading in Halloween costumes, partly because some costumes might be offensive to real witches. Said a district spokeswoman, "Witches with pointy noses and things like that are not respective [*sic*] symbols of the Wiccan religion, and so we want to be respectful of that." In Michigan, Jon Blake Cusack named his son Jon Blake Cusack 2.0.

Some American sub-Neanderthals photographed themselves abusing Iraqi prisoners. By October 24, the war in Iraq had lasted longer than the U.S. involvement in the First World War. Two movies symptomatic of the temper of the times were *The Passion of the Christ* and *The Passions of the Faculty Clubs* (aka *Fahrenheit 9/11*). The Massachusetts Supreme Judicial Court ignited a debate about whether homosexuals could do more damage to the institution of marriage than heterosexuals are doing. Britney Spears has been married twice this year, so far. What, other than Janet Jackson's breast, do you remember about the Super Bowl?

At the Olympics, an elite collection of NBA stars lost to Puerto Rico and Argentina, but hey, they beat the Lithuanians after losing to them. Early in 2004, Alex Rodriguez, eager to win a World Series, was courted by the Yankees and Red Sox and signed with . . . oh, well. Paul Hopkins, the oldest former major-league player, died at ninety-nine. The first batter he faced as a pitcher for the Washington Senators was Babe Ruth, who homered. Hopkins's career ended ten games later. In 2004, Washington was awarded another team.

The world's oldest man, Joan Riudavets Moll, died at 114 in Spain. He was born the same year—1889—as Hitler and Charlie Chaplin. Alberta Martin, a Civil War widow, died in Alabama at 97. Born in 1906, in 1927 she married a Confederate widower born in 1845. She was poor and he had a $50-a-month Confederate pension—a not uncommon aphrodisiac causing May-December marriages early in the twentieth century. Did she at 21 love her 81-year-old groom? "That's a hard question to answer. . . . You know the difference between a young man and an old man." Two months after he died in 1931, she married his grandson.

Two great musical instruments fell forever silent—the voices of Ronald Reagan and Ray Charles. But their melodies linger on.

[DECEMBER 20, 2004]

2005: "In Lieu of Flowers, Please Send Acerbic Letters to Republicans"

Seeking the serenity that a sense of history confers in testing times, Mike Cameron, a Mets outfielder in 2005, said in defense of a teammate who lost a fly ball in the sun, "Stuff is going to happen sometimes. The sun has been there for five hundred, six hundred years." Stuff happened in 2005, when an obituary in the *Chicago Tribune* advised, "In lieu of flowers, please send acerbic letters to Republicans." At home, the president's, and the nation's, disagreeable year can be summarized by three female names: Terri Schiavo, Harriet Miers, and Katrina. The first involved grotesque overreaching by the federal government, undertaken by self-described conservatives whose action refuted their description. The second involved indifference to competence. The third displayed the consequences of incompetence. Abroad, Iraq illustrated one, two, and three.

In Russia, despotism continued to make a comeback, but Lenin, at least, may soon be buried: His cadaver in Red Square is said to sometimes sprout fungi. The 482-page European Union "constitution" was rejected, but the common currency marches on in white boots. Wearing those and a red miniskirt, Renate Dolle, sixty-three, told a Berlin newspaper she will soon end her forty-nine-year career as a prostitute (€30; $36) so she can spend more time with her husband and granddaughter.

Why was America's consumer-driven economy not derailed by higher oil prices? In 2005, Americans' housing stock increased in value $2.38 trillion more than their oil bill increased ($120 billion). *Vox populi, vox dei?* When Katrina's disruption of supplies caused gasoline prices briefly to pass $3 a gallon, the public thought this proved that conniving oil companies control prices. When, a few weeks later, prices plunged toward, and some places below, $2, the public thought . . . what?

Rising oil prices and General Motors' declining health reflected, among other things, the success of sixty years of U.S. policies promoting free trade and globalization. India and China are slurping up oil because, having joined the international economy, they are booming. This year, upwards of sixty thousand Americans were employed manufacturing more than 3 million "foreign" cars. Toyota, which in 2006 may sell more cars worldwide than GM, has opened a design center in Ann Arbor, just forty miles from Detroit.

Onward and upward with progressivism: In a Las Vegas suburb, the United Food and Commercial Workers union hired temp workers at $6 an hour to picket a nonunion Wal-Mart, where wages start at $6.75 an hour. A British teachers-union official proposed that instead of bad students' receiving a "failing" grade, their grade should be called "deferred success." A Milwaukee seventeen-year-old and his father sued to end summer homework because the stress of honors precalculus assignments spoiled the lad's summer. When Jada Pinkett Smith, wife of actor Will Smith, told a Harvard audience that women "can have it all—a loving man, devoted husband, loving children, a fabulous career," the campus Bisexual, Gay, Lesbian, Transgender, and Supporters Alliance said its members were made "uncomfortable" because Mrs. Smith's words were "extremely heteronormative." A majority of teachers, parents, and students at Jefferson Elementary School in Berkeley favored renaming the school Sequoia Elementary because Jefferson owned hundreds of slaves. Under Chief Sequoia, the Cherokee nation owned more than fifteen hundred black slaves. You cannot be too careful, so Timnath, Colorado, banned smoking in bars and restaurants, of which Timnath at the time had none. The often hilarious *New York Times,* which opposes capital punishment, reported disapprovingly that a life sentence "is death in all but name."

An Oklahoma judge granted the request of a criminal who wanted his thirty-year prison sentence increased three years to match Larry

Bird's Celtics jersey number. Death, as it must to all, came to six-foot-ten George Mikan, eighty, who was the NBA's first superstar. Madison Square Garden's marquee once read: WED. BASKETBALL: GEO. MIKAN VS. KNICKS.

Asked to switch from guitar to bass, which he could not afford to buy, Eric Griffiths quit the rock group the Quarry Men in 1958 and joined the British Merchant Navy. On a radio on a ship in the Persian Gulf in 1963 he heard "Please Please Me," the first hit by the former Quarry Men, by then called the Beatles. Griffiths died in 2005 at 64. On November 22, 1963, in a darkened Dallas theater, the hammer of Lee Harvey Oswald's revolver jammed on the flesh of the palm of the policeman arresting him, so Maurice McDonald lived another forty-two years. Vic Power, a Puerto Rican first baseman, was one of baseball's first Hispanic stars. *Sports Illustrated* reports that when Power was playing in the minor leagues in the South, he was told by a waitress that the restaurant did not serve Negroes. He replied, "That's OK, I don't eat Negroes." Mark Matthews, 111, was the oldest of the surviving Buffalo Soldiers, the African-Americans who fought Native Americans on behalf of Euro-Americans. Ah, multiculturalism.

[DECEMBER 19, 2005]

2006: "Go Ahead, We Will Get into One of the Other Boats"

How gruesome was 2006? The year's most consequential person was Iran's president, who says the Holocaust did not happen and vows to complete it. Regarding his nuclear aspirations, Mahmoud Ahmadinejad, whose manias are leavened with realism, treated the United Nations as a figment of the imagination of a fiction—the "international community." Democrats, given control of Congress because of Iraq, vowed to raise the minimum wage. Nimble and graceful Barack Obama became the Democrats' Fred Astaire, adored because of, well, perhaps the way he wears his hat, the way he sips his tea. And the way he isn't Hillary.

This year's civil-rights outrage was "soaring" and "record" gasoline prices, a violation of Americans' inalienable right to pay for a gallon no more than they paid twenty-five years ago. By December, the price of a gallon, adjusted for inflation, was eighty-three cents lower than in 1981. Kansas voters removed some skeptics of evolution from the state's school board. A fossil 3.3 million years old revealed that a little girl from the human lineage had arms and shoulders suited to climbing and swinging through trees.

In order to show "tolerance of people's beliefs," government workers in England's West Midlands were told, after a Muslim complained, to remove from sight all pig-related items, such as a tissue box featuring Winnie the Pooh and Piglet. But tolerance was episodic in Europe in 2006: In Sweden, police said the soccer fan who wore on his clothes a Swedish flag, which features a cross, "provoked some emotions." Indeed. He was beaten nearly to death by Muslim immigrants. Inspector Clouseau, call your office: French police denied that anti-Semitism was involved in the kidnapping and murder of a Jewish man by Muslim immigrants who demanded a ransom from a synagogue. Angry about those Danish cartoons depicting the prophet, Iran's bakers renamed Danish pastries "Roses of the Prophet Muhammad pastries." Although no one had complained, the human-rights director for the provocatively named city of St. Paul, Minnesota, had a HAPPY EASTER sign removed from city hall.

Two U.S. explorers went to the North Pole to study how global warming threatens polar bears. They had planned to go last year, but were forced to delay Project Thin Ice because of unusually heavy snow and ice. The "emerging hurricane problem," which, after Katrina, the *New York Times* identified as a consequence of global warming, did not emerge. The unusually tranquil Atlantic hurricane season was explained as a consequence of . . . global warming affecting the Pacific. Two senators, Jay Rockefeller of West Virginia and Olympia Snowe of Maine, warned ExxonMobil that global warming is an undeniable fact, so the corporation should desist from its "dangerous" support of research by persons with doubts. The senators did not explain the danger involved in doubting the indubitable. There were dangers—

disorder, sporadic violence—among those gathered outside stores in the predawn hours before the PlayStation 3 gaming console went on sale.

Great moments in government: The Florida woman who wounded with a shotgun the alligator that entered her house and attacked her golden retriever was given a warning citation for hunting without a permit. Compassionate social democracy: The Danish government continued to pay prostitutes to service the disabled.

Ancient Greece pioneered philosophy and democracy. Modern Greece this year gave the world a new wrinkle in creative accounting: It became 25 percent richer after its GDP was revised to account for such booming service industries as prostitution and money laundering. The intellectual fare served at the University of Wisconsin-Milwaukee included a course called the Social Construction of Obesity. (Fatness, like beauty, is in the eye of the beholder to whom society's power structure, always eager to foment new forms of discrimination, has given false consciousness.) Elsewhere in higher education, at Bucknell's "celebration of whore culture," a woman stripped on a trapeze.

In Tacoma, Washington, a judge asked those in her courtroom to cheer "Go, Seahawks!" Then she sentenced a man convicted of manslaughter to thirteen years. The chief executive of Eternal Image Inc., which announced caskets and urns with logos of all thirty Major League Baseball teams, called this "a way to make team loyalty a final statement." Red Auerbach, whose Celtics *teams* won seven championships without having a player among the NBA's top ten scorers, died this year at eighty-nine. Romano Mussolini, who died this year at seventy-nine, son of Il Duce, had played jazz with Dizzy Gillespie, Duke Ellington, and Chet Baker.

Lillian Gertrud Asplund was five when her father smiled and said, "Go ahead, we will get into one of the other boats." He did not. Lillian never married, and retired early to take care of her mother, who never recovered from losing her husband. Lillian, the last American survivor of the *Titanic,* was ninety-nine.   [DECEMBER 18, 2006]

2007: Ready, Fire, Aim

In 2007 came the revolution. Determined to end the war in Iraq and begin the reign of justice in America, Democrats took over Congress and acted on the principle "ready, fire, aim." They threatened to tell the Ottoman Empire (deceased 1922) that it should be ashamed of itself (about Armenian genocide) and raised the minimum wage to $5.85, which is worth *less* than the $5.15 minimum was worth when it was set in 1997. Onward and upward with compassionate liberalism: The Democrat-controlled Senate flinched from making hedge-fund multimillionaires pay more than a 15 percent tax rate. At the year-end, there were more troops in Iraq than there were at the year's beginning. Although it was not yet possible to say the war was won, it was no longer possible to say the surge was not succeeding. The McClatchy newspapers, with the media's flair for discerning lead linings on silver clouds, offered this headline: AS VIOLENCE FALLS IN IRAQ, CEMETERY WORKERS FEEL THE PINCH.

The king of Spain told the president of Venezuela to "shut up," and 51 percent of Venezuelans seconded the motion. Rudy Giuliani said, "I took a city that was known for pornography and licked it." Hillary Clinton accused Barack Obama of having been ambitious in kindergarten. Disraeli once said of Lord Russell: "If a traveler were informed that such a man was leader of the House of Commons, he may well begin to comprehend how the Egyptians worshipped an insect." Mike Huckabee became a leader among Republican presidential candidates.

In March, when a planned trek by two explorers to the North Pole, intended to dramatize global warming, was aborted because of temperatures 100 degrees below zero, an organizer of the consciousness-raising venture explained that the cancellation confirmed predictions of global warming because "one of the things we see with global warming is unpredictability." Al Gore won the Nobel Peace Prize that should have gone to nine-time Grammy winner Sheryl Crow, who proposed saving the planet by limiting—to one—"how many squares of toilet paper can be used in any one sitting." At the U.N. global-warming conference in Bali there was Carbon Footprint Envy—the airport did not have space to park all the private jets.

As Americans debated expanding government involvement in health care, Britain's National Health Service told Olive Beal she would have to wait eighteen months to get her hearing aid. She is 108.

Thanks to federal supervision of K–12 education, when a Johnson City, New York, parent complained that cheerleaders lead cheers for the boys' basketball team but not the girls', the U.S. Department of Education, citing Title IX's requirement of sexual equality in scholastic sports, demanded equal "promotional services." Two Los Angeles teachers were fired after a controversy that began when one had her class, during Black History Month, make a presentation about Emmett Till, the Chicago fourteen-year-old who was tortured and murdered in Mississippi in 1955 after his wolf whistle at a white woman. Some students and teachers charged that school officials said Till's whistle could be construed as sexual harassment. In an inexplicable (and probably temporary) spasm of good taste, public opinion sent Don Imus packing because he said on his radio program something no more tasteless than things he had been saying for years, to the delight of a large (and evidently fickle) public.

A Seattle day-care center banned LEGO building blocks because the beastly children "were building their assumptions about ownership and the social power it conveys, assumptions that mirrored those of a class-based, capitalist society." The center reinstated LEGOs but allowed the children to build only "public structures" dedicated to "collectivity and consensus." In other lingering reverberations of communism, scientists unearthed what they think are remains of two more of Czar Nicholas II's children, murdered by Bolsheviks, who never played with LEGOs. A Cuban exile, former CIA operative, and Bay of Pigs veteran announced plans to auction what he says is a lock of Che Guevara's hair taken from the corpse before burial in Bolivia.

When the Confederate monument in Montgomery, Alabama, was desecrated, was that a "hate crime"? Saying he wanted to bring Alabama "into the twentieth century"—the twenty-first would be a bridge too far?—a legislator, worried that "a shower head" might be illegal, moved to repeal the state's ban on the sale of sex toys. A mayor looked on the bright side of his city's high homicide rate: "It's not good for us but it also keeps the New Orleans brand out there." Lucky Belgium has been without a government since June.

In 2007, for the first time, two Hispanic surnames, Garcia and Rodriguez, were among America's ten most common. Paul and Teri Fields of Michigan City, Indiana, named their baby boy Wrigley.

Death, as it must to all, came to Paul Tibbets, 92. Eighty years ago, 12-year-old Paul flew with a barnstorming pilot who dropped Baby Ruth candy bars over a Florida racetrack. In 1945, Tibbets was pilot of the *Enola Gay,* the B-29 that dropped the atomic bomb on Hiroshima. "What about the shortstop Rizzuto," asked Casey Stengel long ago, "who got nothing but daughters but throws out the left-handed hitters in the double play." Phil Rizzuto, the oldest living Hall of Famer, was 89. Emma Faust Tillman, 114, of Hartford, Connecticut, had been the world's oldest person. She was born during the presidency of Benjamin Harrison. Robert Adler, 93, gave the modern world its most beloved invention. The TV remote, of course.

[DECEMBER 22, 2007]

Chapter Three

GOVERNING

The Two Americas: Hard and Soft

Michael Barone, America's foremost political analyst, wonders why America produces so many incompetent eighteen-year-olds but remarkably competent thirty-year-olds. The answer is in his new book, *Hard America, Soft America: Competition vs. Coddling and the Battle for the Nation's Future*. It illuminates the two sensibilities that sustain today's party rivalry.

One answer to Barone's question is: schools. In 1900, only 10 percent of high-school-age Americans went to high school. Subsequently, schooling became universal and then schools became emblematic of Soft America, suffused with "progressive" values—banning dodgeball and other games deemed too competitive, attempting personality adjustment, promoting self-esteem and almost anyone with a pulse.

In contrast, Barone says, "Hard America plays for keeps: The private sector fires people when profits fall and the military trains under live fire." Soft America depends on the productivity, creativity, and competence of Hard America, which protects the country and pays its bills.

For a while, Soft America, consisting of those sectors where there is little competition and accountability, threatened to extinguish Hard America. By 1950, America had what Barone calls a Big Unit economy—big business and big labor, with big government often mediating between them. This economy was, Barone says, "inherently soft." Security, a concept not relevant to the Hard America of the novel *Sister Carrie* (1900), was central to the corporatist world of conformity—the world of the novel *The Man in the Gray Flannel Suit* (1955).

With a novelist's eye for the telling detail, Barone notes that the Labor Department building, constructed in the 1960s, had two conference rooms adjacent to the secretary of labor's office, one for management, one for labor, so the secretary could shuttle between them. Together, the three big units would work out agreements, passing the costs of them along to consumers in an era much less competitive than today's deregulated and globalized era.

Between 1947 and 1968, big business got bigger: the share of assets owned by the two hundred largest industrial companies rose from 47 percent to 61 percent. Then came a hardening. Deregulation ended soft niches (e.g., airlines, trucking) protected by government-sponsored cartelization. The Interstate Commerce Commission, which encouraged cartelization, was abolished.

New financial instruments (e.g., junk bonds) fueled hostile take-overs. Capital gains taxes were cut, stimulating entrepreneurship. Between 1970 and 1990, the rate at which companies fell from the Fortune 500 quadrupled. The portion of the gross national product accounted for by the one hundred largest industrial corporations fell from 36 percent in 1974 to 17 percent in 1998.

In 1957, the Soviet Sputnik provoked some hardening of America's schools—with more science and advance placement courses, and consolidation of rural schools. President Kennedy's vow to reach the moon by the end of the 1960s was an inherently hard goal, with a hard deadline measuring success or failure.

But the second half of the 1960s brought the Great Softening—in schools and welfare policies, in an emphasis on redistribution rather than production of wealth and in the criminal justice system. The number of violent crimes per 100,000 people rose from 1,126 in 1960 to 2,747 in 1970 while the prison population declined from 212,000 in 1960 to 196,000 in 1970. In 2000, after the swing toward hardening, there were 1.3 million prisoners.

Barone says racial preferences, which were born in the 1960s and 1970s, fence some blacks off from Hard America, insulating them in "a Soft America where lack of achievement will nonetheless be rewarded."

The Detroit riot of 1967 lasted six nights before twenty-seven hundred federal troops restored order. In 1992, after the 1980s turn toward hardness, the Los Angeles riots lasted eighteen hours, ending six hours after twenty-five thousand federal troops were dispatched.

In the Soft America of 1970, the tapestry of welfare benefits had a cash value greater than a minimum wage job. In the Harder America of 1996, welfare reform repealed Aid to Families with Dependent Children, a lifetime entitlement to welfare. And in the 1990s, welfare dependency—and crime—were cut in half. A harder, self-disciplined America is a safer America.

What institution is consistently rated most trustworthy by Americans? The institution that ended its reliance on conscription, that has no racial preferences and has rigorous life-and-death rules and standards: the military.

Barone believes that promotion of competition and accountability—hardness—is the shared theme of President Bush's policies of educational standards, individual health accounts, Social Security investment accounts, and lower tax rates to increase self-reliance in the marketplace. Barone's book is a guide to electoral map reading: the blue and red states have, respectively, softer and harder sensibilities.

[MAY 9, 2004]

Angela Jobe's Resilience

MILWAUKEE—Angela Jobe, thirty-eight, is a grandmother who has lived most of her adult life at ground zero of the struggle to "end welfare as we know it." At about the time candidate Bill Clinton was promising to do that—in autumn 1991—she boarded a bus in Chicago, heading for Milwaukee, lured by Wisconsin's larger benefits and lower rents. Unmarried, uneducated, and unemployed, she already had three children and eight years on welfare.

Today, she is in her ninth year of employment in a nursing home, earning $10.50 an hour. How she left welfare, and how her life did and did not change, is one of the entwined stories in Jason DeParle's riveting new book, *American Dream: Three Women, Ten Kids and a Nation's Drive to End Welfare,* the fruit of DeParle's seven years of immersion in Jobe's world.

His subject is the attempt of welfare reformers, in Wisconsin and then Washington, to end the intergenerational transmission of poverty in the chaotic lives of fractured families. His book reads more like a searing novel of urban realism—Theodore Dreiser comes to Milwaukee—

than a policy tract. His reporting refutes the 1930s paradigm of poverty—the idea that the perennially poor are strivers like everyone else but are blocked by barriers unrelated to their behavior. Angie Jobe is not Tom Joad.

After the liberalization of welfare in the mid-1960s, the percentage of black children born to unmarried mothers reached 50 by 1976 (it is almost 70 today), and within a generation the welfare rolls quadrupled. But DeParle says people mistakenly thought people like Jobe were organizing their lives around having babies to get a check. Actually, he says, their lives were too disorganized for that.

What can help organize lives—at least those that are organizable—is work. The requirements of work—mundane matters such as punctuality, politeness, and hygiene—are essential to the culture of freedom. The 1996 reform replaced a lifetime entitlement to welfare with a five-year limit, and called for states to experiment with work requirements. Welfare rolls have since declined more than 60 percent. DeParle writes:

"In Creek County, Oklahoma, the rolls fell 30 percent even as the Legislature was still debating the law, a decline officials largely attributed to the mere rumors of what was coming. . . . The late 1990s can be thought of as a bookend to the 1960s. One era, branding welfare a right, sent the rolls to sudden highs; the other, deeming welfare wrong, shrank them equally fast."

The mass movement from welfare rolls to employment rolls is progress. But DeParle's unsentimental reporting offers scant confirmation of the welfare reformers' highest hope, that when former welfare mothers go to work, their example will transform the culture of their homes, breaking the chain of behaviors that passes poverty down the generations. On the street where Jobe lives today, almost every house is the home of a working mother with children but no husband.

When Jobe was thirteen, her parents divorced and she went to live with her father, who let her roam Chicago's South Side streets. The father of the child she had at seventeen is serving a sixty-five-year prison sentence. And the wheel turns: Jobe's daughter Kesha got pregnant at sixteen. Kesha told the fourteen-year-old father at his eighth-grade graduation, and hardly heard from him again. Kesha, a checkout clerk at a grocery store, has two children and lives with a boyfriend.

Jobe's house teems with life. During a recent visit, there were two infants in diapers, and the seventeen-year-old girlfriend who lives there with Jobe's eighteen-year-old son.

Milwaukee's mandatory self-esteem classes were part of the "hassle factor" designed to diminish welfare's appeal. But, says Jobe, "There's nothing wrong with my self-esteem," the timbre of her voice validating the assertion. She is a four-foot-nine geyser of pluck, humor, and compassion for her nursing home patients. She has no sense of entitlement. DeParle says of her and the other two women whose story he tells, "When welfare was there for the taking, they got on the bus and took it; when it wasn't, they made other plans."

What of her future? Today, she says, "I don't think much about tomorrow." Complete absorption in the present is both a cause and a consequence of living a precarious and disorganized life, but so far her postwelfare story illustrates two truisms: People respond to strong social cues, as she did when she got on the bus, and later when she got off welfare. Second, poor people are more resilient—and more resistant to fundamental behavior modification—than their various would-be improvers suppose. [DECEMBER 30, 2004]

Conservatism's Infrastructure

If by the dawn's early light of November 3 George W. Bush stands victorious, seven of ten presidential elections will have been won by Southern Californians and Texans, all Republicans. The other three were won by Democrats—a Georgian and an Arkansan.

This rise of the Sunbelt is both a cause and a consequence of conservatism's rise, which began in 1964 with, paradoxically, the landslide loss of the second post–Civil War major-party presidential nominee from that region—Arizona's Barry Goldwater, four years after the first, Richard Nixon. His campaign was the first stirring of a mass movement:

Nixon's 1960 campaign attracted 50,000 individual contributors; Goldwater's attracted 650,000.

Conservatism's 40-year climb to dominance receives an examination worthy of its complexity in *The Right Nation,* the best political book in years. Its British authors, John Micklethwait and Adrian Wooldridge of the *Economist,* demonstrate that conservative power derives from two sources—its congruence with American values, especially the nation's anomalous religiosity, and the elaborate infrastructure of think tanks and other institutions that stresses that congruence.

Liberals, now tardily trying to replicate that infrastructure, thought they did not need it because they had academia and the major media. But the former marginalized itself with its silliness, and the latter have been marginalized by their insularity and by competitors born of new technologies.

Liberals complacently believed that the phrase "conservative thinker" was an oxymoron. For years—generations, really—the prestige of the liberal label was such that Herbert Hoover called himself a "true liberal" and Dwight Eisenhower said that cutting federal spending on education would offend "every liberal—including me."

Liberalism's apogee came with Lyndon Johnson, who while campaigning against Goldwater proclaimed, "We're in favor of a lot of things and we're against mighty few." Johnson's landslide win produced a ruinous opportunity—a large liberal majority in Congress, and incontinent legislating. Forty years later, only one-third of Democrats call themselves liberal, whereas two-thirds of Republicans call themselves conservative. Which explains this Micklethwait and Wooldridge observation on the Clinton presidency:

"Left-wing America was given the answer to all its prayers—the most talented politician in a generation, a long period of peace and prosperity, and a series of Republican blunders—and the agenda was still set by the right. Clinton's big achievements—welfare reform, a balanced budget, a booming stock market and cutting 350,000 people from the federal payroll—would have delighted Ronald Reagan. Whenever Clinton veered to the left—over gays in the military, over health care—he was slapped down."

Micklethwait and Wooldridge endorse Sir Lewis Namier's doctrine: "What matters most about political ideas is the underlying emotions, the music to which ideas are a mere libretto, often of very inferior quality." The emotions underlying conservatism's long rise include a visceral individualism with religious roots and antistatist consequences.

Europe, postreligious and statist, is puzzled—and alarmed—by a nation where grace is said at half the family dinner tables. But religiosity, say Micklethwait and Wooldridge, "predisposes Americans to see the world in terms of individual virtue rather than in terms of the vast social forces that so preoccupy Europeans." And: "The percentage of Americans who believe that success is determined by forces outside their control has fallen from 41 percent in 1988 to 32 percent today; by contrast, the percentage of Germans who believe it has risen from 59 percent in 1991 to 68 percent today." In America, conservatives much more than liberals reject the presumption of individual vulnerability and incompetence that gives rise to liberal statism.

Conservatism rose in the aftermath of Johnson's Great Society, but skepticism about government is in the nation's genetic code. Micklethwait and Wooldridge note that in September 1935, during the Depression, Gallup polling found that twice as many Americans said FDR's administration was spending too much than said it was spending the right amount, and barely one person in ten said it was spending too little.

After FDR's 1936 reelection, half of all Democrats polled said they wanted FDR's second term to be more conservative. Only 19 percent wanted it more liberal. In 1980, when Ronald Reagan won while excoriating "big government," America had lower taxes, a smaller deficit as a percentage of GDP, and a less-enveloping welfare state than any other industrialized Western nation.

America, say Micklethwait and Wooldridge, is among the oldest countries in the sense that it has one of the oldest constitutional regimes. Yet it is "the only developed country in the world never to have had a left-wing government." And given the country's broad and deep conservatism, it will not soon. [OCTOBER 10, 2004]

Against "National Greatness Conservatism"

In the 1920s and 1930s, the American left was riven by multiple factions furiously representing different flavors of socialism, each ac-
cusing the others of revisionism and deviationism. Leftists comforted
themselves with the thought that "you can't split rotten wood."

But you can. And the health of a political persuasion can be inversely
proportional to the amount of time its adherents spend expelling here-
tics from the one true (and steadily smaller) church. Today's arguments
about conservatism are, however, evidence of healthy introspection.

The most recent reformer to nail his purifying theses to the door of
conservatism's cathedral is Michael Gerson, a former speechwriter for
the current president, and now a syndicated columnist. He advocates
Heroic Conservatism in a new book with that trumpet-blast of a title.

His task of vivifying his concept by concrete examples is simplified
by the fact that he thinks the Bush administration has been heroically
conservative while expanding the welfare state and trying to export
democracy. His task of making such conservatism attractive is complicated by the fact that . . . well, it is not just the Twenty-second Amendment that is preventing the president from seeking a third term.

Gerson, an evangelical Christian, makes "compassion" the defining attribute of political heroism. But compassion is a personal feeling,
not a public agenda. To act compassionately is to act to prevent or
ameliorate pain and distress. But if there is, as Gerson suggests, a cat-
egorical imperative to do so, two things follow. First, politics is reduced to right-mindedness—to having good intentions arising from
noble sentiments—and has an attenuated connection with results. Second, limited government must be considered uncompassionate, because the ways to prevent or reduce stress are unlimited.

"We have a responsibility," Bush said on Labor Day 2003, "that
when somebody hurts, government has got to move." That is less a
compassionate thought than a flaunting of sentiment to avoid thinking
about government's limited capacities and unlimited confidence.

Conservatism is a *political* philosophy concerned with *collective* aspirations and actions. But conservatism teaches that benevolent government is not always a benefactor. Conservatism's task is to distinguish between what government can and cannot do, and between what it can do but should not.

Gerson's call for "idealism" is not an informative exhortation: Huey Long and Calvin Coolidge both had ideals. Gerson's "heroic conservatism" is, however, a variant of what has been called "national greatness conservatism." The very name suggests that America *will* be great *if* it undertakes this or that great exertion abroad. This grates on conservatives who think America *is* great, not least because it rarely and usually reluctantly conscripts people into vast collective undertakings.

Most Republican presidential candidates express admiration for Theodore Roosevelt. A *real* national greatness guy ("I have been hoping and working ardently to bring about our interference in Cuba"), he lamented that America lacked "the stomach for empire."

He pioneered the practice of governing aggressively by executive orders. Jim Powell, author of *Bully Boy,* an unenthralled assessment of TR, says that in the forty years from Abraham Lincoln through TR's predecessor, William McKinley, presidents issued 158 executive orders. In seven years, TR issued 1,007. Only two presidents have issued more—TR's nemesis Woodrow Wilson (1,791) and TR's cousin Franklin Roosevelt (3,723).

"I don't think," TR said, "that any harm comes from the concentration of power in one man's hands." That sort of executive swagger is precisely what Washington does not need more of. It needs more conservatives such as David Keene, chairman of the American Conservative Union for twenty-three years and Southern political director of Ronald Reagan's 1976 presidential campaign. Writing on "The Conservative Continuum" in the September/October issue of the *National Interest,* Keene says of Reagan:

"He resorted to military force far less often than many of those who came before him or who have since occupied the Oval Office. . . . After the [1983] assault on the Marine barracks in Lebanon, it was questioning the wisdom of U.S. involvement that led Reagan to withdraw our troops rather than dig in. He found no good strategic reason to give our regional enemies inviting U.S. targets. Can one imagine one of today's neoconservative absolutists backing away from any fight anywhere?"

It is a pity that TR built the Panama Canal. If he had not, "national greatness" and "heroic" conservatives could invest their overflowing energies and vaulting ambitions into building it, and other conservatives—call them mere realists—could continue seeking limited government, grounded in cognizance of government's limited competences. That is an idealism consonant with the nation's actual greatness.   [NOVEMBER 25, 2007]

Summa Contra Reagan Nostalgia

In this winter of their discontents, nostalgia for Ronald Reagan has become for many conservatives a substitute for thinking. This mental paralysis—gratitude decaying into idolatry—is sterile: Neither the man nor his moment will recur. Conservatives should face the fact that Reaganism cannot define conservatism.

That is one lesson of John Patrick Diggins's new book, *Ronald Reagan: Fate, Freedom, and the Making of History.* Diggins, a historian at the City University of New York, treats Reagan respectfully as an important subject in American intellectual history. The 1980s, he says, thoroughly joined politics to political theory. But he notes that Reagan's theory was radically unlike that of Edmund Burke, the founder of modern conservatism, and very like that of Burke's nemesis, Thomas Paine. Burke believed that the past is prescriptive because tradition is a repository of moral wisdom. Reagan frequently quoted Paine's preposterous cry that "we have it in our power to begin the world over again."

Diggins's thesis is that the 1980s were America's "Emersonian moment" because Reagan, a "political romantic" from the Midwest and West, echoed New England's Ralph Waldo Emerson. "Emerson was right," Reagan said several times of the man who wrote, "No law can be sacred to me but that of my nature." Hence Reagan's unique, and perhaps oxymoronic, doctrine—conservatism without anxieties. Reagan's preternatural serenity derived from his conception of the supernatural.

Diggins says Reagan imbibed his mother's form of Christianity, a strand of nineteenth-century Unitarianism from which Reagan took a foundational belief that he expressed in a 1951 letter: "God couldn't create evil so the desires he planted in us are good." This logic—God is good, therefore so are God-given desires—leads to the Emersonian faith that we please God by pleasing ourselves. Therefore there is no need for the people to discipline their desires. So, no leader needs to suggest that the public has shortcomings and should engage in critical self-examination.

Diggins thinks that Reagan's religion "enables us to forget religion" because it banishes the idea of "a God of judgment and punishment." Reagan's popularity was largely the result of "his blaming government for problems that are inherent in democracy itself." To Reagan, the idea of problems inherent in democracy was unintelligible because it implied that there were inherent problems with the demos—the people. There was nothing—*nothing*—in Reagan's thinking akin to Lincoln's melancholy fatalism, his belief (see his second inaugural) that the failings of the people on both sides of the Civil War were the reasons why "the war came."

As Diggins says, Reagan's "theory of government has little reference to the principles of the American founding." To the Founders, and especially to the wisest of them, James Madison, government's principal function is to resist, modulate, and even frustrate the public's unruly passions, which arise from desires.

"The true conservatives, the founders," Diggins rightly says, constructed a government full of blocking mechanisms—separations of powers, a bicameral legislature, and other checks and balances—in order "to check the demands of the people." Madison's Constitution responds to the problem of human nature. "Reagan," says Diggins, "let human nature off the hook."

"An unmentionable irony," writes Diggins, is that big-government conservatism is an inevitable result of Reaganism. "Under Reagan, Americans could live off government and hate it at the same time.

Americans blamed government for their dependence upon it." Unless people have a bad conscience about demanding big government—a dispenser of unending entitlements—they will get ever-larger government. But how can people have a bad conscience after being told (in Reagan's first inaugural) that they are all heroes? And after being assured that all their desires, which inevitably include desires for government-supplied entitlements, are good?

Similarly, Reagan said that the people never start wars, only governments do. But the Balkans reached a bloody boil because of the absence of effective government. Which describes Iraq today.

Because of Reagan's role in the dissolution of the Soviet Union, Diggins ranks him among the "three great liberators in American history"—the others being Lincoln and Franklin Roosevelt—and among America's three or four greatest presidents. But, says Diggins, an Emersonian president who tells us our desires are necessarily good leaves much to be desired.

If the defining doctrine of the Republican Party is limited government, the party must move up from nostalgia and leaven its reverence for Reagan with respect for Madison. As Diggins says, Reaganism tells people comforting and flattering things that they want to hear; the Madisonian persuasion tells them sobering truths that they need to know.   [FEBRUARY 11, 2007]

The Left's Plea for Materialistic Politics

It has come to this: The crux of the political left's complaint about Americans is that they are insufficiently materialistic.

For a century, the left has largely failed to enact its agenda for redistributing wealth. What the left has achieved is a rich literature of disappointment, explaining the mystery, as the left sees it, of why most Americans are impervious to the left's appeal.

An interesting addition to this canon is *What's the Matter with Kansas?: How Conservatives Won the Heart of America*. Its author, Thomas Frank, argues that his native Kansas—like the nation, only more so—votes self-destructively, meaning conservatively, because social issues such as abortion distract it from economic self-interest, as the left understands that.

Frank is a formidable controversialist—imagine Michael Moore with a trained brain and an intellectual conscience. Frank has a coherent theory of contemporary politics and expresses it with a verve born of indignation. His carelessness about facts is mild by contemporary standards, or lack thereof, concerning the ethics of controversy.

He says "the preeminent question of our times" is why people misunderstand "their fundamental interests." But Frank ignores this question: Why does the left disparage what everyday people consider their fundamental interests?

He says the left has been battered by "the Great Backlash" of people of modest means against their obvious benefactor and wise definer of their interests, the Democratic Party. The cultural backlash has been, he believes, craftily manufactured by rich people with the only motives the left understands—money motives. The aim of the rich is to manipulate people of modest means, making them angry about abortion and other social issues so that they will vote for Republicans who will cut taxes on the rich.

Such fevered thinking is a staple of what historian Richard Hofstadter called "the paranoid style in American politics," a style practiced, even pioneered, a century ago by prairie populists. You will hear its echo in John Edwards's lament about the "two Americas"—the few rich victimizing the powerless many.

Frank frequently lapses into the cartoon politics of today's enraged left, as when he says Kansas is a place of "implacable bitterness" and America resembles "a panorama of madness and delusion worthy of Hieronymus Bosch." Yet he wonders why a majority of Kansans and Americans are put off by people like him who depict their society like that.

He says, delusionally, that conservatives have "smashed the welfare state." Actually, it was waxing even before George W. Bush's prescription-drug entitlement. He says, falsely, that the inheritance tax has been "abolished." He includes the required—by the left's current catechism—blame of Wal-Mart for destroying the sweetness of Main Street shopping. "Capitalism" is his succinct, if uninformative, explanation of a worldwide phenomenon of the past century—the declining portion of people in agricultural employment—which he seems to regret.

If you believe, as Frank does, that opposing abortion is inexplicably silly, and if you make no more attempt than Frank does to empathize with people who care deeply about it, then of course you, like Frank, will consider scores of millions of your fellow citizens lunatics. Because conservatives have, as Frank says, achieved little cultural change in recent decades, he considers their persistence either absurd or part of a sinister plot to create "cultural turmoil" in order to continue "the erasure of the economic" from politics.

Frank regrets that Bill Clinton's "triangulation" strategy—minimizing Democrats' economic differences with Republicans—contributed to the erasure. Politics would indeed be simpler, and more to the liking of liberals, if each citizen were *homo economicus,* relentlessly calculating his or her economic advantage, and concluding that liberalism serves it. But politics never has been like that, and is becoming even less so.

When the Cold War ended, Pat Moynihan warned, with characteristic prescience, that it would be, like all blessings, a mixed one, because passions—ethnic and religious—that were long frozen would come to a boil. There has been an analogous development in America's domestic politics.

The economic problem, as understood during two centuries of industrialization, has been solved. We can reliably produce economic growth and have moderated business cycles. Hence many people, emancipated from material concerns, can pour political passions into other—some would say higher—concerns. These include the condition of the culture, as measured by such indexes as the content of popular culture, the agendas of public education, and the prevalence of abortion.

So, what's the matter with Kansas? Not much, other than it is has not measured up—down, actually—to the left's hope for a more materialistic politics.   [JULY 8, 2004]

Constitutional Monomania

P HILADELPHIA—At one end of Independence Mall, at the historic center of this city where so much of America's foundational history was made with parchment and ink, stands the brick and mortar of Independence Hall. Built between 1732 and 1756, this model of what is called the Georgian style of architecture is where independence was voted and declared, and where, eleven years later, the Constitution was drafted.

At the other end of the mall sparkles a modernist jewel of America's civic life, the National Constitution Center, a nongovernment institution that opened July 4, 2003, and already has received more than 2 million visitors. It is built of gray Indiana limestone—it is possible, even in Philadelphia, to have a surfeit of red brick—and lots of glass. The strikingly different, yet compatible, styles of the eighteenth-century building where the Constitution was drafted and the twenty-first century building where it is explicated and studied in its third century is an architectural bow to the fact that a constitution ratified by a mostly rural nation of 4 million persons, most of whom lived within twenty miles of Atlantic tidewater, still suits an urban nation that extends twenty-five-hundred miles into the Pacific.

The center is a marvel of exhibits, many of them interactive. For example, it uses newspapers and film to give immediacy to such episodes as the Supreme Court holding in 1952 that President Truman exceeded his constitutional powers—what a thought: there are limits on the commander in chief's powers—when he seized the nation's steel mills to prevent a labor dispute from disrupting war production. And it shows President Eisenhower, thirteen years after sending paratroopers into Normandy, sending them to Central High School in Little Rock.

Throughout, the center illustrates what Professor Felix Frankfurter—before he became Justice Frankfurter—was trying to express more than seventy years ago when he said, "If the Thames is 'liquid history,' the Constitution of the United States is most significantly not a document but a stream of history." But it is, first and always, a document that is to be understood, as the greatest American jurist, John Marshall said, "chiefly from its words."

Those words—which, by the way, do not include "federal" or "democracy"—comprise a subtle, complicated structure that nourishes various aims and virtues. So it would be wonderful if some of the liberal groups now gearing up for a histrionic meltdown over the coming debate about the confirmation of John Roberts could spend a few hours at the National Constitution Center. Judging by the river of rhetoric that has flowed in response to the Supreme Court vacancy, contemporary liberalism's narrative of American constitutional history goes something like this:

On the night of April 18, 1775, Paul Revere galloped through the Massachusetts countryside, and to every Middlesex village and farm went his famous cry of alarm, "The British are coming! The British are coming to menace the ancient British right to abortion!" The next morning, by the rude bridge that arched the flood, their flag to April's breeze unfurled, the embattled farmers stood and fired the shot heard round the world in defense of the right to abortion. The Articles of Confederation, ratified near the end of the Revolutionary War to Defend Abortion Rights, proved unsatisfactory, so in the summer of 1787, fifty-five framers gathered here to draft a Constitution. Even though this city was sweltering, the Framers kept the windows of Independence Hall closed. Some say that was to keep out the horseflies. Actually, it was to preserve secrecy conducive to calm deliberations about how to craft a more perfect abortion right. The Constitution was ratified after the state conventions vigorously debated the right to abortion. But seventy-four years later, a great Civil War had to be fought to defend the Constitution against states that would secede from the Union rather than acknowledge that a privacy right to abortion is an emanation loitering in the penumbra of other rights. And so on.

The exhibits at the National Constitution Center can correct the monomania of some liberals by reminding them that the Constitution expresses the philosophy of natural rights: People have various rights, including and especially the right to property and self-government.

These rights are not created by government, which exists to balance and protect the rights in their variety.

And the center can remind conservatives of an awkward—to some of them—fact: The Constitution was written to correct the defects of the Articles of Confederation. That is, to strengthen the federal government. [AUGUST 14, 2005]

Judicial Activism, Wise and Not

U sing arguments "that range from the unpersuasive to the offensive" (says the *Washington Post*), Senate Democrats are filibustering the nomination of Miguel Estrada to the U.S. Court of Appeals for the D.C. Circuit because he is conservative. Those senators should examine two recent writings by Judge J. Harvie Wilkinson of the U.S. Court of Appeals for the Fourth Circuit.

In "Is There a Distinctive Conservative Jurisprudence?" (*University of Colorado Law Review*, Fall 2002), he refutes the charge that there is no principled distinction between the "activism" of the Supreme Court under Chief Justice Rehnquist and that of the New Deal and Earl Warren courts. The Rehnquist Court has indeed invalidated many laws. However, Wilkinson says the earlier courts would "constitutionalize freely," meaning "extend constitutional rights to a point that impaired the democratic process." All judicial activism intrudes upon democratic processes, but many of the Rehnquist Court's invalidations have "restructured democratic responsibilities," partially restoring the Founders' understanding of the proper allocation of responsibilities.

In the 1995 overturning of the federal Gun-Free School Zones Act, the Rehnquist Court acted, Wilkinson says, as "a structural referee, not an ideological combatant." Congress justified preempting states and regulating guns near schools by citing the usual justification for extending its reach—its power to regulate interstate commerce. But, says Wilkinson, "the proposition that regulable commerce must mean something short of everything is hardly debatable." And the Rehnquist Court's ruling left states empowered to enact gun-free school zones democratically.

In the Rehnquist Court's conservative jurisprudence of balancing, federalism does not always trump competing constitutional values. The states, says Wilkinson, are not the only important "mediative institutions" between the individual and the national government. When state and local governments have imposed intrusive regulations on the Boy Scouts (mandating that they accept gay scoutmasters) and political parties (mandating primaries open to persons not members of the party), the Rehnquist Court has restricted states' powers in the name of the very principle that, in other contexts, caused the court to affirm states' powers—to protect the intermediary institutions of civil society through which our communal, as opposed to our solitary, selves are expressed. Such protection has been, Wilkinson believes, scanted by the "binary" vision of liberal activism, which is committed to "sweeping and virtually limitless national power" and "the recognition of new individual rights," but little in between.

In "Why Conservative Jurisprudence Is Compassionate" (to be published in the *Virginia Law Review*), Wilkinson argues that compassion in jurisprudence is more complicated than merely rendering judicial succor to those with poignant circumstances. Rather, compassion, as judges can properly consider it, begins by understanding this:

Rules—rules that restrict judges' discretion to heed the promptings of poignancy—have considerable virtues. They give people advance notice of what is permitted and required, they produce uniform and consistent treatment of comparable cases, and they respect whatever democratic processes have produced the rule.

Wilkinson says liberals and conservatives differ about "the place of compassion in the democratic process." The human condition features myriad misfortunes and devastating conditions. "Victims of social circumstance, however, are altogether distinct from victims of another's violation of a specific legal duty. It is the job of the democratic process to ameliorate the effects of the former. It is the judiciary's charge to rectify the latter."

And "modesty"—for Wilkinson, the cardinal virtue—is required of judges by society's complexity. Are rent controls compassionate, or do they create a shortage of rental units and a disincentive for landlords to spend on maintenance? Does bilingual education, compassionately intended, impede the mastery of English and upward mobility? Such vexing policy questions about applied compassion are quintessentially those to which democratic rather than judicial processes should provide answers.

For judges struggling with what Wilkinson calls "the inscrutability of compassion," a guiding principle should be that individual plaintiffs are not the only focus of compassion. Collective entities often are instruments of society's compassion. Judges must "personalize" social injury, understanding, for example, that inertial law enforcement has its victims. And that although supposedly compassionate malpractice and product-liability awards may increase patient and consumer safety, they also may drive up prices and prevent needed goods from reaching the market.

When next there is a Supreme Court vacancy, Wilkinson's measured jurisprudence might make him the ideal nominee to silence those whose arguments against judicial conservatism range from the unpersuasive to the offensive. [MARCH 3, 2003]

The Hard Truth About "Soft Rights"

In contemporary American politics, as in earlier forms of vaudeville, it helps to have had an easy act to follow. Gerald Reynolds certainly did.

The U.S. Commission on Civil Rights' new chairman follows Mary Frances Berry, whose seedy career—twenty-four years on the commission, eleven of them as chairman—mixed tawdry peculation, boorish behavior, and absurd rhetoric. Because Reynolds represents such a bracing change, it is tempting to just enjoy the new six-to-two conservative ascendancy on the commission and forgo asking a pertinent question: Why not retire the commission?

Its $9 million budget—about sixty employees and six field offices—is, as Washington reckons these things, negligible. So even Berry's flamboyant mismanagement of it—several Government Accountability Office reports have said federal guidelines were ignored during her tenure; another report is coming—was small beer, even when including the hundreds of thousands of dollars a year paid to the public relations firm that mediated her relations with the media. But although the monetary savings from closing the commission would be small, two prudential reasons for doing so are large.

One is that someday Democrats will again control the executive branch and may again stock the commission with extremists—Berry celebrated Communist China's educational system in 1977, when she was assistant secretary of education; she made unsubstantiated charges of vast "disenfranchisement" of Florida voters in 2000—from the wilder shores of racial politics. The second reason for terminating the commission is that civil rights rhetoric has become a crashing bore and, worse, a cause of confusion: Almost everything designated a "civil rights" problem isn't.

The commission has no enforcement powers, only the power to be, Reynolds says, a "bully pulpit." And if someone must be preaching from it, by all means let it be Reynolds. Born in the South Bronx, the son of a New York City policeman, he is no stranger to the moral muggings routinely administered to African-American conservatives. But he says, "If you think I'm conservative, you should come with me to a black barbershop. I'm usually the most liberal person there," where cultural conservatism—on crime, welfare, abortion, schools—flourishes.

After working in some conservative think tanks, he became head of the Department of Education's Office for Civil Rights in the administration of the first President Bush. He is currently a corporate lawyer in Kansas City, where he has witnessed the handiwork of an imperial judge who, running the school system, ordered the spending of nearly $2 billion in a spectacular, if redundant, proof that increased financial inputs often do not correlate with increased cognitive outputs.

But about this commission as bully pulpit: Does anyone really think America suffers from an insufficiency of talk about race? What is in scarce supply is talk about the meaning of the phrase "civil rights." Not every need is a right, and if the adjective is a modifier that modifies, not every right is a civil right—one central to participation in civic life.

Reynolds, forty-one, says that the core function of civil rights laws is to prevent discrimination, meaning "the distribution of benefits and burdens on the basis of race." But if so, today a—perhaps the—principal discriminator is government, with racial preferences and the rest of the reparations system that flows from the assumption that disparities in social outcomes must be caused by discrimination, and should be remedied by government transfers of wealth.

Reynolds rightly says that the core function of the civil rights laws, which required "a lot of heavy lifting by the federal government," was to dismantle a caste system maintained by law. But that has been accomplished.

It is, as Reynolds says, scandalous that so few black seventeen-year-old males read at grade level; that so many black teenagers are not mentored to think about college as a possibility and of SAT tests as important; that many young blacks—68.2 percent are now born out of wedlock—are enveloped in the culture that appalls Bill Cosby, a culture that disparages academic seriousness as "acting white" and celebrates destructive behaviors. Reynolds is right that much of this can be traced far back to discriminatory events or contexts.

But this is a problem of class, one that is both cause and effect of a cultural crisis. It is rooted in needs, such as functional families and good schools, that are not rights in the sense of enforceable claims. Civil rights laws and enforcement agencies are barely relevant. Proper pulpits—perhaps including barbershops—are relevant. Government pulpits are not. [MARCH 10, 2005]

Oologah's—and America's—Slide

A mericans are not losing their minds, but they are afraid of using their minds. They are afraid to exercise judgment—afraid of being sued.

In 1924, Will Rogers said Americans thought they were getting smarter because "they're letting lawyers instead of their conscience be their guide." Rogers was from Oologah, Oklahoma, where in 1995 a child suffered minor injuries when playing unattended on the slide in the town park. The parents sued the town, which subsequently dismantled the slide.

Products come plastered with imbecilic warnings (on a baby stroller: "Remove child before folding.") for the same reason seesaws and swings are endangered species of playground equipment: fear of liability. A federal handbook morosely warns: "Seesaw use is quite complex." So seesaws are being replaced with spring-driven devices used by only one child at a time. Swings? Gracious, suppose a child falls on the—imagine this—ground. The federal handbook again: "Earth surfaces such as soils and hard-packed dirt are not recommended because they have poor shock-absorbing properties." No wonder a Southern California school district has banned running on the playground.

The early twentieth-century playground movement aimed to acquaint children with mild risks. In 1917, a movement leader said: "It is reasonably evident that if a boy climbs on a swing frame and falls off, the school board is no more responsible for his action than if he climbed into a tree or upon the school building and falls. There can be no more reason for taking out play equipment on account of such an accident than there would be for the removal of the trees or the school building." Today, New York City cuts branches off trees so children will not be tempted to climb.

Today, when a patient complains of a headache, a doctor, even when knowing that an aspirin is almost certainly the right treatment, may nevertheless order an expensive CAT scan. You cannot be too careful in a country in which six Mississippians have been awarded $150 million not because they are sick, but because they fear that they someday may become sick from asbestos-related illnesses.

Michael Freedman reports in *Forbes* magazine that 42 percent of obstetricians are leaving the Las Vegas area now that 76 percent of that city's obstetricians have been sued—40 percent of them three or more times. Pharmaceutical companies are limiting research on "orphan drugs" that treat serious but rare diseases because tort liability is so disproportionate to possible return on investment.

"Dismissing a tenured teacher," says a California official, "is not a process, it's a career." Which is why in a recent five-year period only 62 of California's 220,000 tenured teachers were dismissed. The multiplication of due-process protections has turned jobs into a property right, undoing the progressive movement's dream that a civil service would end the tradition of treating public jobs as private property. In 1998, Pennsylvania reported that in the preceding forty years only thirteen teachers had been removed for incompetence. In New York State, terminating a teacher costs an average of $194,000 in legal bills—the cost in time and energy of school officials is extra. Termination is a seven-year process in Detroit.

By the mid-1970s, writes Philip K. Howard, due process "had become a kind of legal airbag inflating instantly" to protect individuals aggrieved about any adverse encounter with authority. Howard's book, *The Collapse of the Common Good: How America's Lawsuit Culture Undermines Our Freedom,* is a compendium of the social havoc caused by the flight from making commonsense judgments. Americans now "tiptoe through the day," fearful that an angry individual with a lawyer will extort money from society while imposing irrational rules on society.

Oliver Wendell Holmes defined law as "prophecies of what the courts will do." But Howard rightly says that "nobody has any idea what a court will do." A Delaware River canoe rental company is found liable on the theory that it should have stationed lifeguards along miles of riverbank. After a church was sued—unsuccessfully—because a parishioner committed suicide, many churches began discouraging counseling by ministers. When any harmful event can give rise to a lawsuit, the result is "law a la carte," changeable from jury to jury.

The cost of this—in money, health, lives, self-government, and individual liberty—is staggering. Howard, a thinking person's Quixote, has founded (with Shelby Steele, Mary Ann Glendon, John Silber, George McGovern, Newt Gingrich, and others) Common Good, an organization "to lead a new legal revolution to restore human judgment and values at every level of society."

To the barricades! The address of the barricades is: ourcommon good.com.   [JUNE 2, 2002]

A Fraudulent "Fairness"

S ome illiberal liberals are trying to restore the luridly misnamed Fairness Doctrine, which until 1987 required broadcasters to devote a reasonable amount of time to presenting fairly each side of a controversial issue. The government was empowered to decide how many sides there were, how much time was reasonable, and what was fair.

By trying to again empower the government to regulate broadcasting, illiberals reveal their lack of confidence in their ability to compete in the marketplace of ideas, and their disdain for consumer sovereignty—and hence for the public.

The illiberals' transparent, and often proclaimed, objective is to silence talk radio. Liberals strenuously and unsuccessfully attempted to compete in that medium—witness the anemia of their Air America. Talk radio barely existed in 1980, when there were fewer than one hundred talk shows nationwide. The Fairness Doctrine was scrapped in 1987, and today more than fourteen hundred stations are entirely devoted to talk formats. Conservatives dominate talk radio—although no more thoroughly than liberals dominate Hollywood, academia, and much of the mainstream media.

Beginning in 1927, the government, concerned about the scarcity of radio-spectrum access, began regulating the content of broadcasts. In 1928, it decided that the programming of New York's WEVD, which was owned by the Socialist Party, was not in the public interest. The station's license was renewed after a warning to show "due regard for the opinions of others." What was "due"? Who knew?

In 1929, the government refused the Chicago Federation of Labor's attempt to buy a station because, spectrum space being limited, all stations "should cater to the general public." A decade later, the government conditioned the renewal of a station's license on the station's promise to broadcast no more anti-FDR editorials.

In 1969, the Supreme Court rejected the argument that the Fairness Doctrine violated the First Amendment protection of free speech, saying the doctrine enhanced free speech. The court did not know how the Kennedy administration, anticipating a 1964 race against Barry Goldwater, had wielded the doctrine against stations broadcasting conservative programming. The Democratic Party paid people to monitor conservative broadcasts and coached liberals in how to demand equal time. This campaign burdened stations with litigation costs and won 1,678 hours of free airtime.

Bill Ruder, a member of Kennedy's subcabinet, said: "Our massive strategy was to use the Fairness Doctrine to challenge and harass right-wing broadcasters in the hope that the challenges would be so costly to them that they would be inhibited and decide it was too expensive to continue." The Nixon administration frequently threatened the three networks and individual stations with expensive license challenges under the Fairness Doctrine.

In 1973, Supreme Court justice and liberal icon William Douglas said: "The Fairness Doctrine has no place in our First Amendment regime. It puts the head of the camel inside the tent and enables administration after administration to toy with TV and radio." The Reagan administration scrapped the doctrine because of its chilling effect on controversial speech, and because the scarcity rationale was becoming absurd.

Adam Thierer, writing in the *City Journal,* notes that today's "media cornucopia" has made America "as information-rich as any society in history." In addition to the Internet's uncountable sources of information, there are fourteen thousand radio stations—twice as many as in 1970—and satellite radio has nearly 14 million subscribers. Eighty-seven percent of households have either cable or satellite television with more than five hundred channels to choose from. There are more than nineteen thousand magazines (up more than five thousand since 1993). Thierer says, consider a black lesbian feminist who hunts and likes country music:

"Would the 'mainstream media' of 25 years ago represented any of her interests? Unlikely. Today, though, this woman can program her TiVo to record her favorite shows on Black Entertainment Television, Logo (a gay/lesbian-oriented cable channel), Oxygen (female-targeted programming), the Outdoor Life Network and Country Music Television."

Some of today's illiberals say that media *abundance,* not scarcity, justifies the Fairness Doctrine: Americans, the poor dears, are bewildered by too many choices. And the plenitude of information sources disperses "the national campfire," the cozy communitarian experience of the good old days (for liberals), when everyone gathered around— and was dependent on—ABC, NBC, and CBS.

"I believe we need to reregulate the media," says Howard Dean. Such illiberals argue that the paucity of liberal successes in today's radio competition—and the success of Fox News—somehow represent "market failure." That is the regularly recurring, all-purpose rationale for government intervention in markets. Market failure is defined as consumers' not buying what liberals are selling.   [MAY 7, 2007]

Policing Speech in Oakland

Marriage is the foundation of the *natural family* and sustains family values. That sentence is inflammatory, perhaps even a hate crime.

At least it is in Oakland, California. That city's government says those words italicized here constitute something akin to hate speech, and can be proscribed from the government's open e-mail system and employee bulletin board.

When the McCain-Feingold law empowered government to regulate the quantity, content, and timing of political campaign speech about government, it was predictable that the right of free speech would increasingly be sacrificed to various social objectives that free speech supposedly impedes. And it was predictable that speech suppression

would become an instrument of cultural combat, used to settle ideological scores and advance political agendas by silencing adversaries.

That has happened in Oakland. And, predictably, the ineffable
Ninth U.S. Circuit Court of Appeals has ratified this abridgment of
First Amendment protections. Fortunately, overturning the Ninth Cir-
cuit is steady work for the U.S. Supreme Court.

Some African-American Christian women working for Oakland's
government organized the Good News Employee Association (GNEA),
which they announced with a flier describing their group as "a forum
for people of Faith to express their views on the contemporary issues
of the day. With respect for the Natural Family, Marriage and Family
Values."

The flier was distributed *after* other employees' groups, including
those advocating gay rights, had advertised their political views and activities on the city's e-mail system and bulletin board. When the GNEA
asked for equal opportunity to communicate by that system and that
board, they were denied. Furthermore, the flier they posted was taken
down and destroyed by city officials, who declared it "homophobic"
and disruptive.

The city government said the flier was "determined" to promote
harassment based on sexual orientation." The city warned that the
flier and communications like it could result in disciplinary action "up
to and including termination."

Effectively, the city has proscribed any speech that even one person
might say questioned the gay rights agenda and therefore created what
that person felt was a "hostile environment." This, even though gay
rights advocates used the city's communication system to advertise
"Happy Coming Out Day." Yet the terms *natural family, marriage*, and
family values are considered intolerably inflammatory.

The treatment of GNEA illustrates one technique by which America's growing ranks of self-appointed speech police expand their reach:
They wait until groups they disagree with, such as GNEA, are provoked to respond to them in public debates, then they persecute them
for annoying those to whom they are responding. In Oakland, this

dialectic of censorship proceeded on a reasonable premise joined to a preposterous theory.

The premise is that city officials are entitled to maintain workplace order and decorum. The theory is that government supervisors have such unbridled power of prior restraint on speech in the name of protecting order and decorum that they can nullify the First Amendment by declaring that even the mild text of the GNEA flier is inherently disruptive.

The flier supposedly violated the city regulation prohibiting "discrimination and/or harassment based on sexual orientation." The only cited disruption was one lesbian's complaint that the flier made her feel "targeted" and "excluded." So anyone has the power to be a censor just by saying someone's speech has hurt his or her feelings.

Unless the speech is "progressive." If GNEA claimed it felt "excluded" by advocacy of the gay rights agenda, would that advocacy have been suppressed? Of course not—although GNEA's members could plausibly argue that the city's speech police have created a "hostile workplace environment" against them.

A district court affirmed the city's right to impose speech regulations that are patently *not* content neutral. It said the GNEA's speech interest—the flier—is "vanishingly small." GNEA, in its brief asking the U.S. Supreme Court to intervene, responds that some of the high court's seminal First Amendment rulings have concerned small matters, such the wearing of a T-shirt, standing on a soapbox, holding a picket sign, and "other simple forms of expression."

Congress is currently trying to enact yet another "hate crime" law that would authorize enhanced punishments for crimes committed because of, among other things, sexual orientation. A coalition of African-American clergy, the High Impact Leadership Coalition, opposes this, fearing it might be used "to muzzle the church." The clergy argue that in our "litigation prone society" the legislation would result in lawsuits having "a chilling effect" on speech and religious liberty. As the Oakland case demonstrates, that, too, is predictable.   [JUNE 24, 2007]

Liberalism's Itch in Minneapolis

The campaign to deny Luis Paucar his right to economic liberty illustrates the ingenuity people will invest in concocting perverse arguments for novel entitlements. This city's taxi cartel is offering an audacious new rationalization for corporate welfare, asserting a right—a *constitutional right, in perpetuity*—to revenues it would have received if Minneapolis's City Council had not ended the cartel that never should have existed.

Paucar, thirty-seven, embodies the best qualities of American immigrants. He is a splendidly self-sufficient entrepreneur. And he is wielding American principles against some Americans who, in their decadent addiction to government assistance, are trying to litigate themselves to prosperity at the expense of Paucar and the public.

Seventeen years ago, Paucar came to America from Ecuador, and for five years drove a taxi in New York City. *Because* that city has long been liberalism's laboratory, many taxi drivers there are akin to, as an economist has said, "modern urban sharecroppers."

In 1937, New York City, full of liberalism's itch to regulate everything, knew, just *knew,* how many taxicab permits there should be. For seventy years, the number (about twelve thousand) has not been significantly changed, so rising prices have been powerless to create new suppliers of taxi services. Under this government-created scarcity, a permit ("medallion") now costs about $500,000. Most people wealthy enough to buy medallions do not drive cabs, any more than plantation owners picked cotton. They lease their medallions at exorbitant rates to people like Paucar who drive, often for less than $15 an hour, for long days.

Attracted by Minneapolis–St. Paul's vibrant Hispanic community, now 130,000 strong, Paucar moved here, assuming that economic liberty would be more spacious than in New York. Unfortunately, Minnesota has a "progressive," meaning statist, tradition that can impede the progress of people like Paucar but who lack his knack for fighting back.

The regulatory impulse came to the upper Midwest with immigrants from northern Europe, many of whom carried the too-much-government traditions of "social democracy." In the 1940s, under a mayor who soon would take his New Deal liberalism to Washington—Hubert Humphrey—the city capped entry into the taxi business.

By the time Paucar got here in 1999, 343 taxis were permitted. He wanted to launch a fleet of 15. That would have required him to find 15 incumbent license holders willing to sell their licenses for up to $25,000 apiece.

As a by-product of government intervention, a secondary market arose in which government-conferred benefits were traded by the cartel. In 2006, Minneapolis had only one cab for every one thousand residents (compared to three times as many in St. Louis and Boston), which was especially punishing to the poor who lack cars.

That fact—and Paucar's determination and, eventually, litigiousness; he is a *real* American—helped persuade the City Council members, liberals all (twelve members of the Democratic Farmer-Labor Party, one member of the Green Party), to vote to allow forty-five new cabs per year until 2010, at which point the cap will disappear. In response, the cartel is asking a federal court to say the cartel's constitutional rights have been violated. It says the cap—a barrier to entry into the taxi business—constituted an entitlement to profits that now are being "taken" by government action.

The Constitution's Fifth Amendment says no property shall be "taken" without just compensation. The concept of an injury through "regulatory taking" is familiar and defensible: Such an injury occurs when a government regulation reduces the value of property by restricting its use. But the taxi cartel is claiming a *deregulatory* taking: It wants compensation because it now faces unanticipated competition.

When the incumbent taxi industry inveigled the city government into creating the cartel, this was a textbook example of rent seeking—getting government to confer advantages on an economic faction in order to disadvantage actual or potential competitors. If the cartel's argument about a "deregulatory taking" were to prevail, modern government—the regulatory state—would be controlled by a leftward-clicking ratchet: Governments could never deregulate, never undo the damage that they enable rent seekers to do.

By challenging his adopted country to honor its principles of economic liberty and limited government, Paucar, assisted by the local chapter of the libertarian Institute for Justice, is giving a timely demonstration of this fact: Some immigrants, with their acute understanding of why America beckons, refresh our national vigor. It would be wonderful if every time someone like Paucar comes to America, a native-born American rent seeker who has been corrupted by today's entitlement mentality would leave.   [MAY 27, 2007]

Chicago: From the White City to the Green City

CHICAGO—Thirty-five summers ago, in the angriest year of a boiling era, the forces of peace, love, and understanding—they fancied themselves "flower power"—clashed violently at the Democratic Convention with the police of Mayor Richard Daley. Today, the mayor of this famously muscular city—big-shouldered hog butcher and stacker of wheat—practices flower power. His name is Richard Daley.

The son is in his fourth four-year term. Chicago has been governed by him or his father for thirty-five of the forty-eight years since 1955. Chicago's name derives from an American Indian word meaning "wild onion," and the city's motto Urbs in Horto means "city in a garden." Daley's green thumb has produced a city chock-full of gardens.

Including one on the roof of city hall. It has twenty thousand plants of more than 150 species. And three beehives, which produce sixty pounds of honey a year. The hives are emblematic of the intensely practical nature of Daley's passion to prove that "nature can exist in an urban environment."

A Daley aide calls him "the Martha Stewart of mayors," then quickly decides there must be a more felicitous encomium to celebrate his attentions to fine touches conducive to gracious urban living. Daley explains his passion for prettification by recalling that shortly after being elected in 1989, he took a train from Washington to New York, and was struck by the ugliness travelers saw as trains entered and left cities along the way. So today the river of traffic flowing from O'Hare airport to downtown on the Kennedy Expressway passes between, as it were, landscaped riverbanks.

Within most cities, Daley says, people experience "a canyon effect of steel and concrete." But cities need not mean just "steel, concrete and dirt." Flowers, he says, are one way "to change the perception of cities." He has created median strips on some major streets and planted them with flowers "to slow down traffic." And, he says, "Flowers calm people down."

This apostle of calming influences is the son of the man called—it is the title of a biography of him—an "American pharaoh." His father would stop his limousine to pick up littered newspapers, but his passion was not for sensory pleasure but for tidiness. The father considered even Republicans litter: In his last three elections, he carried 148 of the city's 150 wards.

The pharaoh was a builder, but his most famous pyramids were not what he wanted. He favored low-rise public housing, but federal pressures forced him to build high-rises that became crime-infested pillars of poverty. The son has been dismantling them. The son, too, is a builder—witness Chicago's sparkling skyscrapers. But he is primarily a planter.

Since 1989, he has presided over the planting of more than three hundred thousand trees, which he says not only please the eye but "reduce noise, air pollution and summer heat." Twenty-one underutilized acres around the city have been turned into seventy-two community gardens and parks. The renovation of Soldier Field on the lakefront will include seventeen acres of new parkland. The largest park project, the Calumet Open Space Reserve on the far Southeast Side, is four thousand acres of prairies, wetlands, and forests.

The city contracts with an organization called the Christian Industrial League, which hires many down-and-out persons to wash streets and water plants. And the organization is building a greenhouse that will sell flowers in winter.

The great Chicago architect Louis Sullivan (1856–1924) relished the city's "intoxicating rawness," which was still abundant when the first Mayor Daley won the first of his six elections. He became perhaps America's most important twentieth-century mayor. Alan Ehrenhalt, executive editor of *Governing* magazine, notes that Chicago could have become a Detroit, a symbol of urban failure.

If the son is a twenty-first-century model mayor, it is because he senses the importance of the senses: Human beings respond to aesthetic values. Daley is not given to flights of theory, so he may not realize the extent to which he is continuing a project begun on this city's South Side 110 years ago.

Chicago successfully competed against New York, Philadelphia, and Washington for the right to host the World's Columbian Exposition of 1893, celebrating the four hundredth anniversary of Columbus's voyage. The White City, as the exposition was called, received 27 million visitors and gave rise to the City Beautiful movement, the premise of which was that cities do not need to be grimly utilitarian, and that improvement of a city's material environment would be conducive to the moral improvement of its residents. Coarse environments would coarsen people; refined environments would help ameliorate what reformers considered the moral deficiencies of people struggling to adapt to urban life.

A century ago, reforming elites thought of beautification in terms of social control: it would tame the lower orders. Daley, a Chicago chauvinist, primarily just wants his city to be second to none—Second City, indeed. But he also aims at mild social control: He hopes his flowers will calm down everyone.   [AUGUST 4, 2003]

Our Moralizing Tax Code

The taxing power of government must be used to provide rev-
enues for legitimate government purposes. It must not be used
to regulate the economy or bring about social change.

— PRESIDENT RONALD REAGAN,
State of the Union message, February 18, 1981

(b) no portion of the proceeds of such issue is to be used to pro-
vide (including the provision of land for) any private or com-
mercial golf course, country club, massage parlor, hot tub
facility, suntan facility, racetrack or other facility used for gam-
bling, or any store the principal business of which is the sale of
alcoholic beverages for consumption off premises.

—Title 26, Internal Revenue Code (tax exemption
requirements for qualified redevelopment bonds)

Well, yes, certainly no massage parlors. Or hot tubs, of course;
one shudders to think what happens in those. And tanning facilities, too, are the Devil's playgrounds. As for racetracks, although
state governments promoting their lotteries are America's most ener-
getic advocates of gambling, government should err on the side of cau-
tion when protecting whatever this tax provision protects by frowning
on racetracks, hot tubs, and other things.

This peculiar wrinkle in the tax code, first approved the year after
President Reagan said the tax code should not be used to leverage social change, makes certain projects ineligible to be financed by industrial redevelopment bonds that are subsidized by preferential tax
treatment. This provision recently popped back into the news, thanks
to Katrina.

That ill wind blew some (barely) offshore casinos onto the shores
of the Gulf Coast. As part of the plan to "rebuild," as the saying goes,
the damaged coast, such bonds are going to be issued. But not promiscuously. Some legislators do not want tax-subsidized bonds to finance
the rebuilding of casinos.

Not that the casinos need help: They are rebounding briskly, even expanding. Still, government has a sorry record of dispensing billions in corporate welfare for flourishing businesses.

It is mysterious why states or localities that want casinos operating nearby—and providing jobs and tax revenues—also want them afloat, a few feet from a riverbank or ocean shore. (Mississippi has just decided to let them come ashore.) Does the narrow band of water provide prophylactic protection against sin? The communities already have weighed the sin against the jobs and revenues and found the sin congenial.

But such awkward questions arise when government begins moralizing, especially about the minutiae of life, such as hot tubs. Which brings us to Reagan's 1981 statement about inappropriate uses of the tax code.

He disliked government using the code to conduct industrial policy, picking commercial winners and losers, which is a recipe for what is called "lemon socialism"—tax subsidies for failing businesses that the market says should fail. Regarding the second part of Reagan's statement, any tax code is going to shape society. But he opposed manipulating the tax code to stigmatize this or that consumer preference. Which is what the code's anti-hot-tub provision does.

One wonders: Why did the social improvers who used the code to put the government, in its majesty, on record against hot tubs and tanning facilities not extend their list of disapproved choices? Their list looks morally lax.

Really stern social conservatives probably favor explicitly proscribing government assistance to lots of things, most of them somehow involving sex. Government could preen about being too moral to subsidize, with tax-preferred bonds, economic projects that include bookstores that sell Judy Blume novels, or hotels that offer in-room pornography. And wouldn't it be fun to find the words *lap dance* in the nation's tax code?

As strongly as social conservatives deplore commercialized sex, liberals deplore cigarettes, Big Macs, firearms, fur coats, SUVs, pornography not printed on recycled paper, pornographic movies produced by nonunion studios, holiday trees provocatively labeled "Christmas trees," and much more.

But do we really want to march down this path paved with moral pronouncements? When government uses subsidies to moralize, as with tax preferences for bonds that can be used to finance this but not that, government is speaking. It is expressing opinions about what is and is not wholesome. And once government starts venting such opinions, how does it stop?

Government could spare itself the stress of moralizing about so many things if it decided that the choices people make with their money is their, not its, business. And government could avoid having opinions about so many things if it would quit subsidizing so many things.

When, for example, the valuation and allocation of money through bonds is left to the market, government can be reticent. And reticent government sounds wonderful.   [JANUARY 8, 2006]

"Electronic Morphine" on the Ohio River

On the north bank of the Ohio River sits Evansville, Indiana, home of David Williams, fifty-two, and of a riverboat casino. During several years of gambling in that casino, Williams, a state auditor earning $35,000 a year, lost approximately $175,000. He had never gambled before the casino sent him a coupon for $20 worth of gambling.

He visited the casino, lost the $20, and left. On his second visit, he lost $800. The casino issued to him, as a good customer, a "Fun Card," which when used in the casino earns points for meals and drinks, and enables the casino to track the user's gambling activities. For Williams, those activities became what he calls "electronic morphine."

By the time he had lost $5,000, he said to himself that if he could get back to even, he would quit. One night he won $5,500, but he did not quit. In 1997, he lost $21,000 to one slot machine in two days. In March 1997, he lost $72,186. He sometimes played two slot machines at a time, all night, until the boat docked at 5 a.m., then went back aboard when the casino opened at 9 a.m. Now he is suing the casino, charging that it should have refused his patronage because it knew he was addicted. It did know he had a problem.

In March 1998, a friend of Williams's got him involuntarily confined to a treatment center for addictions, and wrote to inform the casino of Williams's gambling problem. The casino included a photo of Williams among those of banned gamblers, and wrote to him a "cease admissions" letter. Noting the "medical/psychological" nature of problem gambling behavior, the letter said that before being readmitted to the casino he would have to present medical/psychological information demonstrating that patronizing the casino would pose no threat to his safety or well-being.

Although no such evidence was presented, the casino's marketing department continued to pepper him with mailings. And he entered the casino and used his Fun Card without being detected.

The *Wall Street Journal* reports that the casino has twenty-four signs warning: "Enjoy the fun . . . and always bet with your head, not over it." Every entrance ticket lists a toll-free number for counseling from the Indiana Department of Mental Health. Nevertheless, Williams's suit charges that the casino, knowing he was "helplessly addicted to gambling," intentionally worked to "lure" him to "engage in conduct against his will." Well.

It is unclear what luring was required, given his compulsive behavior. And in what sense was his will operative? The fourth edition of the *Diagnostic and Statistical Manual of Mental Disorders (DSM-IV)* says "pathological gambling" involves persistent, recurring, and uncontrollable pursuit less of money than of the euphoric state of taking risks in quest of a windfall. Pathological gamblers often exhibit distorted thinking (denial, superstition, overconfidence). They lie to friends and family to conceal their behavior, resort to theft or fraud to finance it, and succumb to "chasing"—ever more risky and high-stakes gambling in attempts to recoup losses.

It is worrisome that society is medicalizing more and more behavioral problems, often defining as addictions what earlier, sterner generations explained as weakness of will. Prodded by science, or what purports to be science, society is reclassifying what once were considered character flaws or moral failings as personality disorders akin to physical disabilities.

However, at least several million Americans do have a disposition—a "mental disorder"? a "compulsive disease"?—that seems to make them as unable to gamble responsibly as an alcoholic is unable to drink responsibly. This is a small portion of the nation's population, but a large pool of misery for themselves and loved ones.

Gambling has been a common feature of American life forever, but for a long time it was broadly considered a sin, or a social disease. Now it is a social policy: The most important and aggressive promoter of gambling in America is government.

Forty-four states have lotteries, twenty-nine have casinos, and most of these states are to varying degrees dependent on—you might say addicted to—revenues from wagering. And since the first Internet gambling site was created in 1995, competition for gamblers' dollars has become intense. The October 28 issue of *Newsweek* reported that 2 million gamblers patronize eighteen hundred virtual casinos every week. With $3.5 billion being lost on Internet wagers this year, gambling has passed pornography as the Web's most lucrative business.

The anonymous, lonely, undistracted nature of online gambling is especially conducive to compulsive behavior. But even if government knew how to move against Internet gambling, what would be its rationale for doing so? Government curbs on private-sector gambling enterprises look like attempts to cripple the competition—to prevent others from poaching on the population of gamblers that government has done so much to enlarge.

David Williams's suit should trouble this gambling nation. But don't bet on it.   [NOVEMBER 25, 2002]

Prohibition II: Interestingly Selective

Perhaps Prohibition II is being launched because Prohibition I worked so well at getting rid of gin. Or maybe the point is to reassure social conservatives that Republicans remain resolved to purify

Americans' behavior. Incorrigible cynics will say Prohibition II is being undertaken because someone stands to make money from interfering with other people making money.

For whatever reason, last Friday, the president signed into law Prohibition II. You almost have to admire the government's plucky refusal to heed history's warnings about the probable futility of this adventure. This time the government is prohibiting Internet gambling by making it illegal for banks or credit-card companies to process payments to online gambling operations on a list the government will prepare.

Last year, about 12 million Americans wagered $6 billion online. But after Congress, thirty-two minutes before adjourning, passed its ban, the stock of the largest online-gambling business, Gibraltar-based PartyGaming, which gets 85 percent of its $1 billion annual revenue from Americans, declined 58 percent in one day, wiping out about $5 billion in market value. The stock of a British company, World Gaming PLC, which gets about 95 percent of its revenue from Americans, plunged 88 percent. The industry, which has some twenty-three hundred websites and did half of its business last year with Americans, has lost $8 billion in market value because of the new law. And you thought the 109th Congress did not accomplish anything.

Supporters of the new law say it merely strengthens enforcement; they claim that Internet gambling is illegal under the Wire Act enacted in 1961, before Al Gore, who was then thirteen, had invented the Internet. But not all courts agree. Supporters of the new law say online gambling sends billions of dollars overseas. But the way to keep the money here is to decriminalize the activity.

The number of online American gamblers, although just one-sixth the number of Americans who visit real casinos annually, doubled in the last year. This competition alarms the nation's biggest gambling interests—state governments.

It is an iron law: When government uses laws, tariffs, and regulations to restrict the choices of Americans, ostensibly for their own good, someone is going to make money from the paternalism. One of the big winners from the government's action against online gambling will be the state governments that are America's most relentless promoters of gambling. Forty-eight states (all but Hawaii and Utah) have some form of legalized gambling. Forty-two states have lottery monopolies. Thirty-four states rake in part of the take from casino gambling, slot machines, or video poker.

The new law actually legalizes online betting on horse racing, Internet state lotteries, and some fantasy sports. The horse-racing industry is a powerful interest. The solidarity of the political class prevents the federal officials from interfering with state officials' lucrative gambling. And woe unto the politicians who get between a sports fan and his fun.

In the private sector, where realism prevails, casino operators are not hot for criminalizing Internet gambling. This is so for two reasons: It is not in their interest for government to wax censorious. And online gambling might whet the appetites of millions for the real casino experience.

Granted, some people gamble too much. And some people eat too many cheeseburgers. But who wants to live in a society that protects the weak-willed by criminalizing cheeseburgers? Besides, the problems—frequently exaggerated—of criminal involvement in gambling, and of underage and addictive gamblers, can be best dealt with by legalization and regulation utilizing new software solutions. Furthermore, taxation of online poker and other gambling could generate billions for governments.

Prohibition I was a porous wall between Americans and their martinis, giving rise to bad gin supplied by bad people. Prohibition II will provoke imaginative evasions as the market supplies what gamblers will demand—payment methods beyond the reach of Congress.

But governments and sundry busybodies seem affronted by the Internet, as they are by any unregulated sphere of life. The speech police are itching to bring bloggers under campaign-finance laws that control the quantity, content, and timing of political discourse. And now, by banning a particular behavior—the entertainment some people choose, using their own money—government has advanced its mother-hen agenda of putting a saddle and bridle on the Internet.

Gambling is, however, as American as the Gold Rush or, for that matter, Wall Street. George Washington deplored the rampant gambling at Valley Forge, but lotteries helped fund his army as well as Harvard, Princeton, and Dartmouth. And Washington endorsed the lottery that helped fund construction of the city that now bears his name, and from which has come a stern—but interestingly selective—disapproval of gambling. [OCTOBER 23, 2002]

Being Green at Ben & Jerry's

If you have an average-size dinner table, four feet by six feet, put a dime on the edge of it. Think of the surface of the table as the Arctic National Wildlife Refuge in Alaska. The dime is larger than the piece of the coastal plain that would have been opened to drilling for oil and natural gas. The House of Representatives voted for drilling, but the Senate voted against access to what Senator John Kerry, Massachusetts Democrat and presidential aspirant, calls "a few drops of oil." ANWR could produce, for twenty-five years, at least as much oil as America currently imports from Saudi Arabia.

Six weeks of desultory Senate debate about the energy bill reached an almost comic culmination in . . . yet another agriculture subsidy. The subsidy is a requirement that will triple the amount of ethanol, which is made from corn, that must be put in gasoline, ostensibly to clean America's air, actually to buy farmers' votes.

Over the last three decades, energy use has risen about 30 percent. But so has population, which means per capita energy use is unchanged. And per capita GDP has risen substantially, so we are using 40 percent less energy per dollar output. Which is one reason there is no energy crisis, at least none as most Americans understand such things—a shortage of, and therefore high prices of, gasoline for cars, heating oil for furnaces, and electricity for air conditioners.

In the absence of a crisis to concentrate the attention of the inattentive American majority, an intense faction—full-time environmentalists—goes to work. Spencer Abraham, the secretary of energy, says "the previous administration . . . simply drew up a list of fuels it didn't like—nuclear energy, coal, hydropower, and oil—which together account for 73 percent of America's energy supply." Well, there are always windmills.

Sometimes lofty environmentalism is a cover for crude politics. The United States has the world's largest proven reserves of coal. But Mike Oliver, a retired physicist and engineer, and John Hospers, professor emeritus of philosophy at USC, note that in 1996 President Clinton put 68 billion tons of America's cleanest-burning coal, located in Utah, off-limits for mining, ostensibly for environmental reasons. If every existing U.S. electric power plant burned coal, the 68 billion tons could fuel them for forty-five years at the current rate of consumption. Now power companies must import clean-burning coal, some from mines owned by Indonesia's Lippo Group, the heavy contributor to Clinton, whose decision about Utah's coal vastly increased the value of Lippo's coal.

The United States has just 2.14 percent of the world's proven reserves of oil, so some people say it is pointless to drill in places like ANWR because "energy independence" is a chimera. Indeed it is. But domestic supplies can provide important insurance against uncertain foreign supplies. And domestic supplies can mean exporting hundreds of billions of dollars less to oil-producing nations, such as Iraq.

Besides, when considering proven reserves, note the adjective. In 1930, the United States had proven reserves of 13 billion barrels. We then fought the Second World War and fueled the most fabulous economic expansion in human history, including the electricity-driven "New Economy." (Manufacturing and running computers consume 15 percent of U.S. electricity. Internet use alone accounts for half of the growth in demand for electricity.) So by 1990 proven reserves were . . . 17 billion barrels, not counting any in Alaska or Hawaii.

In 1975, proven reserves in the Persian Gulf were 74 billion barrels. In 1993, they were 663 billion, a ninefold increase. At the current rate of consumption, today's proven reserves would last 150 years. New discoveries will be made, some by vastly improved techniques of deep-water drilling. But environmental policies will define opportunities. The government estimates that beneath the U.S. outer continental shelf, which the government owns, there are at least 46 billion barrels of oil. But only 2 percent of the shelf has been leased for energy development.

Opponents of increased energy production usually argue for decreased consumption. But they flinch from conservation measures. A new $1 gasoline tax would dampen demand for gasoline, but it would stimulate demands for the heads of the tax increasers. After all, Americans get irritable when impersonal market forces add twenty-five cents to the cost of a gallon. Tougher fuel-efficiency requirements for vehicles would save a lot of energy. But who would save the legislators who passed those requirements? Beware the wrath of Americans who like to drive, and autoworkers who like to make, cars that are large, heavy, and safer than the gasoline sippers that environmentalists prefer.

Some environmentalism is a feel-good indulgence for an era of energy abundance, which means an era of avoided choices. Or ignored choices—ignored because if acknowledged, they would not make the choosers feel good. Karl Zinsmeister, editor in chief of the *American Enterprise* magazine, imagines an oh-so-green environmentalist enjoying the most politically correct product on the planet—Ben & Jerry's ice cream. Made in a factory that depends on electricity-guzzling refrigeration, a gallon of ice cream requires four gallons of milk. While making that much milk, a cow produces eight gallons of manure, and flatulence with another eight gallons of methane, a potent "greenhouse" gas. And the cow consumes lots of water plus three pounds of grain and hay, which is produced with tractor fuel, chemical fertilizers, herbicides, and insecticides, and is transported with truck or train fuel:

"So every time he digs into his Cherry Garcia, the conscientious environmentalist should visualize (in addition to world peace) a pile of grain, water, farm chemicals, and energy inputs much bigger than his ice cream bowl on one side of the table, and, on the other side of the table, a mound of manure eight times the size of his bowl, plus a balloon of methane that would barely fit under the dining room table."

Cherry Garcia. It's a choice. *Bon appétit.*   [MAY 6, 2002]

The Tyranny of the Small Picture

What good is happiness? It can't buy money.

— HENNY YOUNGMAN

Social hypochondria is the national disease of the most successful nation. By most indexes, life has improved beyond the dreams of even very recent generations. Yet many Americans, impervious to abundant data and personal experiences, insist that progress is a chimera.

Gregg Easterbrook's impressive new book, *The Progress Paradox: How Life Gets Better While People Feel Worse,* explains this perversity. Easterbrook, a Washington journalist and fellow of the Brookings Institution, assaults readers with good news:

American life expectancy has dramatically increased in a century, from forty-seven to seventy-seven years. Our great-great-grandparents all knew someone who died of some disease we never fear. (As recently as 1952, polio killed 3,300 Americans.) Our largest public health problems arise from unlimited supplies of affordable food. The typical American has twice the purchasing power his mother or father had in 1960. A third of America's families own *at least* three cars. In 2001, Americans spent $25 billion—more than North Korea's GDP—on recreational watercraft. Factor out immigration—a huge benefit to the immigrants—and statistical evidence of widening income inequality disappears. The statistic that household incomes are only moderately higher than twenty-five years ago is misleading: Households today average fewer people, so real-dollar incomes in middle-class households are about 50 percent higher today. Since 1970, the number of cars has increased 68 percent and the number of miles driven has increased even more, yet smog has declined by a third and traffic fatalities have declined from 52,627 to 42,815 last year. In 2003, we spend much wealth on things unavailable in 1953—a cleaner environment, reduced mortality through new medical marvels ($5.2 billion a year just for artificial knees, which did not exist a generation ago), the ability to fly anywhere or talk to anyone anywhere. The incidence of heart disease, stroke, and cancer, adjusted for population growth, is declining. The rate of child poverty is down in a decade. America soon will be the first society in which a majority of adults are college graduates.

And so it goes. But Easterbrook says that such is today's "discontinuity between prosperity and happiness," the "surge of national good news" scares people, vexes the news media, and does not even nudge up measurements of happiness. Easterbrook's explanations include:

- "The tyranny of the small picture." The preference for bad news produces a focus on smaller remaining problems after larger ones are ameliorated. Ersatz bad news serves the fund-raising of "gloom interest groups." It also inflates the self-importance of elites, who lose status when society is functioning well. Media elites, especially, have a stake in "headline-amplified anxiety."
- "Evolution has conditioned us to believe the worst." In Darwinian natural selection, pessimism, wariness, suspicion, and discontent may be survival traits. Perhaps our relaxed and cheerful progenitors were eaten by saber-toothed tigers. Only the anxiety-prone gene pool prospered.
- "Catalogue-induced anxiety" and "the revenge of the plastic" both cause material abundance to increase unhappiness. The more we can order and charge, the more we are aware of what we do *not* possess. The "modern tyranny of choice" causes consumers perpetual restlessness and regret.
- The "latest model syndrome" abets the "tyranny of the unnecessary," which leads to the "ten-hammer syndrome." We have piled up mountains of marginally improved stuff, in the chaos of which we cannot find any of our nine hammers, so we buy a tenth, and the pile grows higher. Thus does the victor belong to the spoils.
- The cultivation—even celebration—of victimhood by intellectuals, tort lawyers, politicians, and the media is both cause and effect of today's culture of complaint.

Easterbrook, while arguing that happiness should be let off its leash, is far from complacent. He is scandalized by corporate corruption and poverty in the midst of so much abundance. And he has many commonsensical thoughts on how to redress the imbalance many people feel between their abundance of material things and the scarcity of meaning that they feel in their lives. The gist of his advice is that we should pull up our socks, spiritually, and make meaning by doing good while living well.

His book arrives as the nation enters an election year, when the opposition, like all parties out of power, will try to sow despondency by pointing to lead linings on all silver clouds. His timely warning is that Americans are becoming colorblind, if only to the color silver.

[JANUARY 11, 2004]

Draining the Reservoir of Reverence

Why did we run? Well, those who didn't run are there yet.

—AN OHIO SOLDIER

CHANCELLORSVILLE, VIRGINIA—The twelve-mile march on May 2, 1863, took Stonewall Jackson from the clearing in the woods where he conferred for the last time with Robert E. Lee, to a spot from which Jackson and thirty thousand troops surveyed the rear of the Union forces. Those forces, commanded by a blowhard, Joe Hooker ("May God have mercy on General Lee, for I shall have none"), were about to experience one of the nastiest shocks of the Civil War.

Two hours before dusk, Federal soldiers were elated when deer, turkeys, and rabbits came pelting out of the woods into their lines. It was, however, not dinner but death approaching. By nightfall, Federal forces were scattered. When the fighting subsided four days later, Lee was emboldened to try to win the war with an invasion of Pennsylvania. The invasion's high-water mark came at the crossroads town of Gettysburg.

One hundred and thirty-nine years after the battle here, a more protracted struggle is under way. In 1863, the nation's survival was at stake. Today, only the nation's memory is at stake. "Only"? Without memory, the reservoir of reverence, what of the nation survives?

Hence the urgency of the people opposing a proposal to build, on acreage over which the struggle surged, 2,350 houses and 2.4 million square feet of commercial and office space. All this would bring a huge increase in traffic, wider highways, and the further submergence of irrecoverable history into a perpetually churned present.

Northern Virginia, beginning about halfway between Richmond and Washington, is a humming marvel of energy and entrepreneurship, an urbanizing swirl of commerce and technology utterly unlike the static rural society favored by Virginia's favorite social philosopher, Jefferson. Chancellorsville is in an east-west rectangle of terrain about fifteen miles long and ten miles wide, now divided by Interstate 95, that saw four great battles—Fredericksburg, Chancellorsville, Spotsylvania, the Wilderness—involving one hundred thousand killed, wounded, or missing.

Where a slavocracy once existed, Northern dynamism prevails. But Northern Virginia has ample acreage for development, without erasing the landscapes where the Army of Northern Virginia spent its valor. As for the Federals' side, it is a scandal that the federal government's cheese-paring parsimony has prevented the purchase of historically significant land—twenty-thousand acres, maximum—at Civil War battlefields from Maryland to Mississippi.

Just $10 million annually for a decade—a rounding error for many Washington bureaucracies—would preserve much important battlefield land still outside National Park Service boundaries. The government's neglect can be only partially rectified by the private work of the Civil War Preservation Trust, just three years old. (You can enlist at www.civilwar.org. Also check www.chancellorsville.org.)

CWPT's president James Lighthizer, a temperate, grown-up realist, stresses that CWPT's members are "not whacked-out tree-huggers" who hate development and want to preserve "every piece of ground where Lee's horse pooped." But regarding commemorations, Americans today seem inclined to build where they ought not, and to not build where they should, as at the site of the World Trade Center.

In New York City, many people who are antigrowth commerce despisers want to exploit Ground Zero for grinding their old ideological axes. They favor making all or most of the sixteen-acre parcel a cemetery without remains, a place of perpetual mourning—what Richard Brookhiser disapprovingly calls a "deathopolis" in the midst of urban striving.

But most who died at Ground Zero were going about their private pursuits of happiness, murdered by people who detest that American striving. The murderers crashed planes into the Twin Towers, Brookhiser says, "in the same spirit in which a brat kicks a beehive. They will be stung, and the bees will repair the hive." Let the site have new towers, teeming with renewed striving.

But a battlefield is different. A battlefield is hallowed ground because those who there gave the last full measure of devotion went there because they were devoted unto death to certain things.

Those who clashed at Chancellorsville did so in a war that arose from a clash of large ideas. Some ideas were noble, some were not. But there is ample and stirring evidence that many of the young men caught in the war's whirlwind could articulate what the fight was about, on both sides. See James M. McPherson's *For Cause and Comrades: Why Men Fought in the Civil War.*

Local government here can stop misplaced development from trampling out the contours of the Confederacy's greatest victory. A Jeffersonian solution.   [SEPTEMBER 22, 2002]

United 93: "We've Got to Do It Ourselves"

In most movies made to convey dread, the tension flows from uncertainty about what will happen. In *United 93,* terror comes from knowing exactly what will happen. People who associate cinematic menace with maniacs wielding chain saws will find that there can be an almost unbearable menace in the quotidian—in the small talk of passengers waiting in the boarding area with those who will murder them, in the routine shutting of the plane's door prior to push-back from the gate at Newark airport on September 11.

But two uncertainties surrounded *United 93:* Would it find an audience? Should it?

It has found one, which is remarkable, given that in 2005 most moviegoers—57 percent—were persons twelve to twenty-nine years old. Twenty-nine percent were persons twelve to twenty-four. These age cohorts do not seek shattering, saddening experiences to go with their popcorn. In its first weekend, *United 93* was the second most watched movie, with the top average gross per theater among major releases. It was on 1,795 screens, and 71 percent of viewers were thirty or older.

To the long list of Britain's contributions to American cinema—Charles Chaplin, Bob Hope, Cary Grant, Stan Laurel, Deborah Kerr, Vivien Leigh, Maureen O'Hara, Ronald Colman, David Niven, Boris Karloff, Alfred Hitchcock, and others—add Paul Greengrass, writer and director of *United 93.* He imported into Hollywood the commodity most foreign to it: good taste. This is especially shown in the ensemble of unknown character actors, and nonactors who play roles they know—a real pilot plays the pilot, a former flight attendant plays the head flight attendant—and several persons who play on screen the roles they played on 9/11.

Greengrass's scrupulosity is evident in the movie's conscientious, minimal, and minimally speculative departures from the facts about the flight that were painstakingly assembled for the *The 9/11 Commission Report.* This is emphatically not a "docudrama" such as Oliver Stone's execrable *JFK,* which was "history" as a form of literary looting in which the filmmaker used just enough facts to lend a patina of specious authenticity to tendentious political ax grinding.

A *New York Times* story on the "politics of heroism" deals with the question of whether the movie is "inclusive." Well, perhaps *United 93* did violate some egalitarian nicety by suggesting that probably not all the passengers were equally heroic. Amazingly, no one has faulted the movie for ethnic profiling: All the hijackers are portrayed as young, fervently devout Islamic males. Report Greengrass to the U.S. Commission on Civil Rights.

In a movie as spare and restrained as its title, the only excess is the suggestion, itself oblique, that the government responded even more confusedly that morning than was to be expected. Most government people, like the rest of us, were in the process of having their sense of the possible abruptly and radically enlarged.

Going to see *United 93* is a civic duty because Samuel Johnson was right: People more often need to be reminded than informed. After an astonishing fifty-six months without a second terrorist attack, this nation perhaps has become dangerously immune to astonishment. The movie may quicken our appreciation of the measures and successes— many of which must remain secret—that have kept would-be killers at bay.

The editors of *National Review* were wise to view *United 93* in the dazzling light still cast by a Memorial Day address, "The Soldier's Faith," delivered in 1895 by a veteran of Ball's Bluff, Antietam, and other Civil War battles. Oliver Wendell Holmes Jr. said why understanding that faith is important:

"In this snug, over-safe corner of the world . . . we may realize that our comfortable routine is no eternal necessity of things, but merely a little space of calm in the midst of the tempestuous untamed streaming of the world, and in order that we may be ready for danger. . . . Out of heroism grows faith in the worth of heroism."

The message of the movie is: We are all potential soldiers. And we all may be, at any moment, at the war's front, because in this war the front can be anywhere.

The hinge on which the movie turns are thirteen words that a passenger speaks, without histrionics, as he and others prepare to rush the cockpit, shortly before the plane plunges into a Pennsylvania field. The words are: "No one is going to help us. We've got to do it ourselves." Those words not only summarize this nation's situation in today's war, but also express a citizen's general responsibilities in a free society.

[MAY 7, 2006]

Nothing Changes Everything

Before the dust from the collapsed towers had settled, conventional wisdom had congealed: "Everything has changed." But what about what matters most, the public's sensibility?

It has taken five years for 9/11 to receive a novelist's subtle and satisfying treatment, but it was worth the wait for Claire Messud's *The Emperor's Children*. Her intimation of the mark the attacks made on the American mind is convincing because in her comedy of manners, as in the nation's life, that horrific event is, oddly, both pivotal and tangential.

Messud's Manhattan story revolves around two women and a gay man who met as classmates at Brown University and who, as they turn thirty in 2001, vaguely yearn to do something "important" and "serious." Vagueness—lack of definition—is their defining characteristic. Which may be because—or perhaps why—all three are in the media. All are earnest auditors and aspiring improvers of the nation's sensibility.

Marina is a glamorous child of privilege because she is the child of Murray, a famous liberal commentator given to saying things such as, to a seminar on Resistance in Postwar America, "once upon a time, poetry *did* matter." A former intern at *Vogue*, Marina lives with her parents, on an allowance from them, on Central Park West. She is having trouble finishing her book on "how complex and profound cultural truths—our *mores* entire—could be derived from" analysis of changing fashions in children's clothes. "I want to make a difference." But get a job? "I worry that will make me ordinary, like everybody else." She is, her father recognizes, "stymied, now, by the very lack of smallness" in her life, "by the absence of any limitations against which to rebel."

Danielle, from Ohio, is a producer of documentaries who hopes to "articulate" an "ethos" into a "movement." Her current project, to raise "questions about integrity and authenticity," concerns women who had bad experiences with liposuction.

Julius, from Michigan, is an independent book and film reviewer "with a youthful certainty that attitude would carry him." His "life of Wildean excess and insouciance seemed an accomplishment in itself." He is "an inchoate ball of ambition," and is intermittently aware that at thirty "some actual sustained endeavor might be in order." That might, however, be difficult, given his belief that "regularity was bourgeois."

The problem the three share is not that their achievements, if there ever are any, will be ephemeral, but that their intentions to achieve them are ephemeral. Not solid, like those of the Australian who comes to New York "to foment revolution." With a new magazine.

Murray's nephew, Bootie, a morose autodidact—imagine Holden Caulfield with his nose in a book of Emerson's essays—rounds out Messud's central cast, each illustrating Messud's acute understanding of the Peter Pan complex now rampant among young adults who feel entitled to be extraordinary: "To be your own person, to find your own style—these were the quests of adolescence and young adulthood, pushed, in a youth-obsessed culture, well into middle age."

Not until page 370 of Messud's delicious depiction of the quintet's tangled lives, "torn between Big Ideas and a party," do the planes hit the towers. Bootie—it could have been any of these people preoccupied with manufacturing interpretations of fashions and fashions of interpretations—has "a fearful thought: you could make something inside your head, as huge and devastating as this, and spill it out into reality, make it really happen." Imagine that.

Before 9/11, Messud began writing a Manhattan novel about young adults living in the media hall of mirrors. After 9/11, she abandoned it. Then returned to it. Asked if she thought she had written a "9/11 novel," she demurs: "I wrote an August 1914 novel." Meaning, "The world I had set out to describe in 2001 had become historical."

But what had changed? The party, scheduled for 9/11, to launch the Australian's magazine and the revolution—Renée Zellweger had accepted; Susan Sontag was a maybe—was canceled, as was the magazine. Murray "formulated a reasoned middle ground": America did not deserve the attacks, but remember the West Bank. "He wasn't op-

posed to the invasion of Afghanistan, but qualified about its methods." Danielle decides to proceed with her liposuction documentary.

Nothing changes everything. And even huge events that, as Messud
says, make "certain things seem particularly frivolous" leave most of
our enveloping normality largely unscathed. That truth and a height-
ened sense of the frivolous are conducive to national poise five years
into a long war.   [SEPTEMBER 10, 2006]

Chapter Four

SENSIBILITIES

AND

SENSITIVITIES

Narcissism as News

Time magazine asked a large number of people to name the Person of the Year. They were in a populist mood and named the largest possible number of Persons of the Year: Everybody.

Of course. The most capacious modern entitlement is not to Social Security but to self-esteem. So *Time*'s cover features a mirrorlike panel. The reader—but why bother to read the magazine when merely gazing at its cover gives immediate and intense gratification?—can gaze at the reflection of his or her favorite person. Narcissism is news? Evidently.

To the person looking at his reflection, *Time*'s cover announces, congratulations: "You control the Information Age." By "control," *Time* means only that everyone is created equal—equally entitled to create content for the World Wide Web, which is controlled by neither law nor taste.

Richard Stengel, *Time*'s managing editor, says, "Thomas Paine was in effect the first blogger" and "Ben Franklin was essentially loading his persona into the MySpace of the eighteenth century, 'Poor Richard's Almanack.'" Not exactly.

Franklin's extraordinary persona informed what he wrote but was not the subject of what he wrote. Paine was perhaps history's most consequential pamphleteer. There are expected to be 100 million bloggers worldwide by the middle of 2007, which is why none will be like Franklin or Paine. Both were geniuses; genius is scarce. Both had a revolutionary civic purpose, which they accomplished by amazing exertions. Most bloggers have the private purpose of expressing themselves, for their own satisfaction. There is nothing wrong with that, but nothing demanding or especially admirable, either. They do it successfully because there is nothing singular about it, and each is the judge of his or her own success.

According to the Pew Internet & American Life Project, 76 percent of bloggers say one reason they blog is to document their personal experiences and share them with others. And 37 percent—soon,

37 million—say the primary topic of their blog is "my life and experiences." George III would have preferred dealing with 100 million bloggers rather than one Paine.

Stengel says that bloggers and the people who upload videos onto YouTube (sixty-five thousand new videos a day; 100 million watched each day) are bringing "events" to us in ways that are often more "authentic" than the services of traditional media. But authenticity is easy, and of no inherent value, if it is simply and necessarily the attribute of any bit of reality ("event") captured on video.

Time's Lev Grossman writes that "an explosion of productivity and innovation" is under way as "millions of minds that would otherwise have drowned in obscurity" become participants in "the global intellectual economy." Grossman continues:

"Who actually sits down after a long day at work and says, I'm not going to watch 'Lost' tonight. I'm going to turn on my computer and make a movie starring my pet iguana? I'm going to mash up 50 Cent's vocals with Queen's instrumentals? I'm going to blog about my state of mind or the state of the union or the steak frites at the new bistro down the street? Who has that time and that energy and that passion?

"The answer is, you do. And for seizing the reins of the global media, for founding and framing the new digital democracy, for working for nothing and beating the pros at their own game, Time's Person of the Year for 2006 is you."

There are, however, essentially no reins on the Web—few means of control and direction. That is good, but vitiates the idea that the Web's chaos of entertainment, solipsism, and occasional intellectual seriousness and civic engagement is anything like a polity (a "digital democracy"). *Time*'s bow to the amateurs who are, it strangely suggests, no longer obscure, and in the same game that *Time* is in, is refuted by a glance—which is all an adult will want—at YouTube's most popular videos.

Time's issue includes an unenthralled essay by NBC's Brian Williams, who believes that raptures over the Web's egalitarianism arise from the same impulse that causes today's youth soccer programs to award trophies—"entire bedrooms full"—to any child who shows up:

"The danger just might be that we miss the next great book or the next great idea, or that we will fail to meet the next great challenge . . . because we are too busy celebrating ourselves and listening to the same tune we already know by heart."

The fact that Stengel included Williams's essay proves that Stengel's *Time* has what 99.9 percent of the Web's content lacks: seriousness.

[DECEMBER 21, 2006]

The Speciesism of Featherless Bipeds

One thinks twice, even thrice, before using in a magazine as decorous as *Newsweek* the four-letter F word that causes so much discord. But words should not be minced. So, what is being done for British pets is just not *fair*.

One wants to avoid speciesism, the moral disease of being speciescentric. Still, why should British pets have more—25 percent more, to be precise—freedoms than humans do?

In January 1941, President Franklin Roosevelt envisioned a "world founded upon four essential human freedoms"—freedom of speech and expression, freedom of every person to worship God in his own way, freedom from want, and freedom from fear. In January 2006, Prime Minister Tony Blair's—technically, Her Majesty's—Department for Environment, Food and Rural Affairs said pets should have five freedoms. The Animal Welfare Bill says the five are:

1. An appropriate diet.
2. Suitable living conditions.
3. Companionship or solitude, as the cat, canary, or gerbil prefers.
4. Monitoring for abnormal behavior.
5. Protection from pain, suffering, injury, and disease.

Well. Politicians' jokes are usually recognizable as such because they elicit boisterous laughter from the politicians' friends, families, and employees. But there is no evidence that Blair's government is joking. The Labour Party, having recently saved the foxes from the fox hunters and their hounds, is serious—not to say grim and humorless—about perfecting society.

Besides, it is not funny. It is Orwellian to say that when governments provide this and that benefit they are providing freedoms. As Bishop Joseph Butler (1692–1752) said, back when clear thinking was a British attribute, "Everything is what it is, and not another thing." Appropriate diets, suitable living conditions, etc., are not "freedoms." They are nice things, but they could be provided by a benevolent despot. Freedom is about the absence of some things—of coercion, dependency, restraints not consented to—and the presence of institutions and the habits, mores, customs, and dispositions that sustain those absences. But nowadays there is confusion arising from a non sequitur that governments encourage: Freedom is a nice thing, therefore governments that provide nice things are expanding freedom.

The *Times* of London reports that pet owners will be supplied with lots of rules. Such as: "Dogs should be introduced to cats very carefully." What would we do without government to guide us? The pet police, who will be empowered to enter houses and seize animals, will enforce rules like the one that pets must have "mental stimulation" sufficient to ward off boredom and frustration. A nine-point guide about cats "going to the toilet" mandates provisions for privacy. A British headline: GET YOUR CAT A PRIVATE LOO OR EXPECT PET POLICE. Another: LABOUR'S PET POLICE MAY POUNCE IF YOUR DOG GETS BORED. The *Times* says a code of conduct for invertebrates, such as lobsters, may be coming.

You will not be surprised that in America, it is San Francisco (which has more dogs—an estimated 110,000—than children) that is especially punctilious about codifying animal entitlements. One such is that a dog's water must be changed at least once a day, and must be served in a nontipping bowl. A San Franciscan who has two Dobermans says pets "need as much care as a child does." The chairman of the commission that drafted the nontipping-water-bowl ordinance says much of its language replicates that of a Los Angeles ordinance. So there.

But if British pets are going to have five freedoms, we must ask:

Did FDR, who stipulated that he was enumerating four "human" freedoms, shortchange us? Humans, too, are animals—featherless bipeds, as Plato said. It seems, however, that the ruling pigs in George Orwell's *Animal Farm* were correct: Some animals—British pets—are more equal than others. So, what is to be done to erase the 25 percent freedom advantage enjoyed by lower animals—is it still legal in Britain to use that locution?—such as British pets?

When Woodrow Wilson proclaimed his Fourteen Points that would guarantee a sweeter world, Georges Clemenceau complained that God had only ten. But Americans believe in going the competition one better. So when President George W. Bush—who says that "freedom is on the march" everywhere, which it is, except where it isn't—is done perfecting the switch-grass-powered automobile, he should step up to the challenge. It is time to add two freedoms to FDR's four. How about:

Freedom from government attempts to codify and supervise every transaction between people, let alone those between people and their hamsters and turtles and tropical fish.

And: Freedom from the idea that we have only as many freedoms—speaking correctly, only as much freedom—as governments in their graciousness choose to enumerate. [FEBRUARY 13, 2006]

What We Owe to What We Eat

Matthew Scully, a former speechwriter for President George W. Bush, is the most interesting conservative you have never heard of. He speaks barely above a whisper and must be the mildest disturber of the peace. But he is among the most disturbing.

If you value your peace of mind, not to mention your breakfast bacon, you should not read Scully's essay "Fear Factories: The Case for Compassionate Conservatism—for Animals." It appeared in the May 23, 2005, issue of Pat Buchanan's magazine, the *American Conservative*—not where you would expect to find an essay arguing that industrial livestock farming involves vast abuses that constitute a serious moral problem.

The disturbing facts about industrial farming by the $125 billion-a-year livestock industry—the pain-inflicting confinements and mutilations—have economic reasons. Ameliorating them would impose production costs that consumers would pay. But to glimpse what consumers would be paying to stop, visit factoryfarming.com/gallery.htm. Or read Scully on the miseries inflicted on billions of creatures "for our convenience and pleasure":

". . . 400- to 500-pound mammals trapped without relief inside iron crates seven feet long and 22 inches wide. They chew maniacally on bars and chains, as foraging animals will do when denied straw . . . The pigs know the feel only of concrete and metal. They lie covered in their own urine and excrement, with broken legs from trying to escape or just to turn . . ."

It is, Scully says, difficult, especially for conservatives, to examine cruelty issues on their merits, or even to acknowledge that something serious can be at stake where animals are concerned. This is partly because some animal-rights advocates are so off-putting. See, for example, the February 3, 2003, letter that Ingrid Newkirk, president of People for the Ethical Treatment of Animals—animals other than humans—sent to the terrorist Yasir Arafat, complaining that an explosive-laden donkey was killed when used in a Jerusalem massacre.

The rhetoric of animal "rights" is ill-conceived. The starting point, says Scully, should be with our obligations—the requirements for living with integrity. In defining them, some facts are pertinent, facts about animals' emotional capacities and their experience of pain and happiness. Such facts refute what conservatives deplore—moral relativism. They do because they demand a certain reaction and evoke it in good people, who are good because they consistently respect the objective value of fellow creatures.

It may be true that, as has been said, the Puritans banned bearbaiting not because it gave pain to the bears but because it gave pleasure to the spectators. And there are indeed degrading pleasures. But to argue for outlawing cruelty to animals because it is bad for the cruel person's soul is to accept, as Scully does not, that man is the only concern.

Statutes against cruelty to animals, often imposing felony-level penalties, codify society's belief that such cruelty is an intrinsic evil. This is a social affirmation of a strong moral sense in individuals who are not vicious. It is the sense that even though the law can regard an individual's animal as the individual's property, there nevertheless are certain things the individual cannot do to that property. Which means it is property with a difference.

The difference is the capacity for enjoyment and suffering. So why, Scully asks, is cruelty to a puppy appalling and cruelty to livestock by the billions a matter of social indifference? There cannot be any intrinsic difference of worth between a puppy and a pig.

Animal suffering on a vast scale should, he says, be a serious issue of public policy. He does not want to take away your BLT; he does not propose to end livestock farming. He does propose a Humane Farming Act to apply to corporate farmers the elementary standards of animal husbandry and veterinary ethics: "We cannot just take from these creatures, we must give them something in return. We owe them a merciful death, and we owe them a merciful life."

Says who? Well, Scully replies, those who understand "Judeo-Christian morality, whose whole logic is one of gracious condescension, or the proud learning to be humble, the higher serving the lower, and the strong protecting the weak."

Yes, of course: You don't want to think about this. Who does? But do your duty: Read his book *Dominion: The Power of Man, the Suffering of Animals, and the Call to Mercy*. Scully, a conservative and hence a realist, knows that man is not only a rational creature but a rationalizing creature, putting his intellectual nimbleness in the service of his desires. But refraining from cruelty is an objective obligation. And as Scully says, "If reason and morality are what set humans apart from animals, then reason and morality must always guide us in how we treat them."

You were warned not to read this. Have a nice day.

[JULY 18, 2005]

The Holocaust: Handcrafted

Little by little we were taught all these things. We grew into
them.   — ADOLPH EICHMANN

These are the best of times for the worst of people. And for the toxic idea at the core of all the most murderous ideologies of the modern age. That idea is that human nature is, if not a fiction, at least so watery and flimsy that it poses no serious impediment to evil political entities determined to treat people as malleable clay to be molded into creatures at once submissive and violent.

All political philosophies rest on notions of human nature. And what we think human nature is—indeed, whether we think there is such a thing—depends somewhat on conclusions we draw from political events, such as these: A mother rejoicing that her teenage child has blown herself up in the process of blowing up other mothers' children. A Palestinian infant dressed as a suicide bomber—parents will have glittering dreams for their children.

There was violence, but there were not suicide bombers with celebrating choruses, when Yasir Arafat's Palestinian Authority thugocracy began its occupation of Gaza and the West Bank. After eight years of incitements—in schools, mosques, mass media—to anti-Semitic genocide, those areas now need de-Nazification. Eichmann's "little by little" has been compressed into just eight years.

Historian Richard Rhodes's new *Masters of Death: The SS-Einsatzgruppen and the Invention of the Holocaust* may not be the ideal beach book. But this latest contribution to the debate about the origins of Nazi behavior—the processes of socialization to butchery—is dreadfully timely.

Much has been made of the Nazis' "modern" and "scientific" means of "industrializing" mass murder—railroads leading to gas chambers. But most Holocaust murders were, Rhodes says, "handcrafted," one at a time, using bullets, often fired at such close range that the shooters were splattered with gore. Himmler worried that this involved suffering—by his perpetrators.

After long days of *Sardinenpackung* (having Jews lay down on the last layer of those already murdered, in order to efficiently fill killing pits), Himmler hoped the performers of "this burdensome duty" would relax in civilized evenings: "The comradely gathering must on no account, however, end in the abuse of alcohol. It should be an evening on which—as far as possible—they sit and eat at table in the best German domestic style, and music, lectures and the introductions to the beauties of German intellectual and emotional life occupy the hours."

Of course there was shop talk, too. At one post-massacre dinner, an officer explained that his more experienced killers tossed children into the air to shoot them, not out of unseemly exuberance, but because bullets often passed through children's bodies, so shooting them on floors or streets could cause dangerous ricochets.

Rhodes's most disturbing vignette is not of the German walking with a year-old baby impaled on his bayonet, still crying weakly. More chilling, in its way, is this: One supervisor of massacres "had the photographs taken at the executions developed at two photographic shops in southern Germany and showed them to his wife and friends." Were the technicians who developed the film perturbed? The wife and friends—was their moral sense, which supposedly is part (a large part? a durable part?) of human nature, disturbed?

Civilization's enemies attack civilization's foundational idea, the proposition that human nature is not infinitely plastic, that people cannot be socialized to accept or do anything. These enemies believe that human beings have no common nature, no shared moral sense that is a component of a universal human nature. Rather, all we have in common is a capacity to acquire an infinite variety of cultures, however vile.

Rhodes's book contributes evidence to the debate about the roles of nature and nurture, of ideology and peer pressure and other things in the making of people who participate in mass murder. The Palestinian Authority is also contributing much evidence. Rhodes's book, and

Arafat's willing executioners of Jews, and Palestinian parents who rejoice at the suicides of their murderous children, and Palestinian street mobs drunk with delight about dismembered Jews—all these point to a conclusion: Teaching (to use Eichmann's verb) such participants is disturbingly easy.

With the recent terrorist bomb planted to kill young people at an Israeli university, terrorists reached an apogee, a purity of evil, simultaneously targeting youth and learning. In Joseph Conrad's *Secret Agent* (1907), a novel about terrorism, a theorist of terror justifies targeting England's Greenwich observatory. Mere butchery is a bit banal, so:

"The attack must have all the shocking senselessness of gratuitous blasphemy. Since bombs are your means of expression, it would be really telling if one could throw a bomb into pure mathematics. But that is impossible."

Such are the disappointments of modern barbarians, who otherwise are prospering.   [AUGUST 19, 2002]

The "Daring" of the Avant-Garde Yet Again

N EW YORK—An iron law of avant-garde art is that theorizing expands to fill a void of talent. That law explains the execrable exhibit "Mirroring Evil: Nazi Imagery/Recent Art," now in its final days at the Jewish Museum at the corner of Ninety-second Street and Fifth Avenue.

The works by thirteen "internationally recognized" artists make, the museum brochure says, "new and daring use of imagery taken from the Nazi era." In the cant of artists' self-puffery, the word *daring* usually means artists are daring to strike political poses that are imbecilic and, among the avant-garde, fashionable. Here the artists daringly draw "unnerving connections between the imagery of the Third Reich and today's consumer culture."

Examples of the works are:

"Giftgas Giftset," three replicas of Zyklon B gas canisters in the colors, and bearing the logos, of Chanel, Hermès, and Tiffany's. "Prada Deathcamp" is a model of a concentration camp on cardboard from a Prada hatbox. The exhibit catalog theorizes that the artist "dares to observe Holocaust museums and their visitors from the position of a critique of consumption." These two works ask the "irreconcilable" (does the illiterate author mean unanswerable?) question of "whether the artist is fascinated by the label-logo culture or mocking it."

"LEGO Concentration Camp Set" consists of replicas of boxes of the children's building blocks, but the boxes bear photographs of models of barracks and crematoria. The catalog theorizes that this work shows "how such seemingly harmless items may pose serious psychological and philosophical questions about gender, sexuality, and childhood."

In "It's the Real Thing—Self-Portrait at Buchenwald," the artist digitally inserts a photograph of himself, holding a Diet Coke, into the foreground of a famous photograph of emaciated Jews in their bunks shortly after the liberation of Buchenwald. The catalog theorizes that this work "draws parallels between brainwashing tactics of the Nazis and commodification. Just as much of Europe succumbed to Nazi culture because it was the dominant paradigm, so does our contemporary culture succumb to consumerism."

Enough. The smug narcissism and overbearing didacticism, all expressed in jargon-clotted prose about "aesthetic strategies" and "transgressive images," is repulsive. The use of genocide as a plaything for political posturing is contemptible. What was the Jewish Museum thinking, and why did it not think again after September 11?

Many of the works in "Mirroring Evil" are based on photographs (there are no oil paintings), which should demonstrate that photography has said almost everything that can properly be expressed graphically about the Holocaust. But, then, "Mirroring Evil" is evil because it really has nothing to do with the murder of 6 million Jews. Rather, it is an exhibit of the artists' exhibitionism, their fathomless fascination with their shallow selves. And "Mirroring Evil," although an extreme example, is hardly the only example of the miniaturization of the Holocaust, the turning of tragedy into mere raw material for intellectuals' fads.

In the June 14 issue of the *Chronicle of Higher Education,* William F. S. Miles, professor of Jewish historical and cultural studies at Northeastern University, reflects uneasily on his experience at a two-week course for college teachers conducted by the Center for Advanced Holocaust Studies at the United States Holocaust Memorial Museum in Washington. There he heard colleagues say how the explosive growth of Holocaust studies has turned that genocide into a "wonderful, creative teaching opportunity."

Participants in the course said "a gendered approach to the Holocaust is truly exciting" and "we can examine victims in terms of their class, too, or their national origins" and "you can tie [the Holocaust] in to dance, art, architecture. Even Web-page making." Miles reports: "Repeated analogies between victims of the Holocaust and battered women in America are made. . . . There also is implied criticism of articulate survivors: 'We privilege them because they are eloquent.'" Miles' mild response is:

"Experts are no longer eyewitnesses but rather clever scholars with the latest new angles, spins or hypotheses. All one can hope is that the intellectualization of the Holocaust be pursued in good faith with a modicum of sensitivity toward the survivors."

But what hope can there be for even minimal decency and understanding when today's intelligentsia is hospitable to trivializations of a huge tragedy? No vulgarity is unthinkable now that the Holocaust has become fodder for semi-intellectual wisecracks, the plaything of theory-weaving and ax-grinding academic and artistic mediocrities who discern a moral equivalence between commercial advertising and Nuremberg rallies.

A wit once said that everything changes except the avant-garde. But it does change. It gets worse.   [JUNE 20, 2002]

Anti-Semitism Across the Political Spectrum

It used to be said that anti-Catholicism was the anti-Semitism of the intellectuals. Today, anti-Semitism is the anti-Semitism of the intellectuals.

Not all intellectuals, of course. And the seepage of this ancient poison into the intelligentsia—always so militantly modern—is much more pronounced in Europe than here. But as anti-Semitism migrates across the political spectrum from right to left, it infects the intelligentsia, which has leaned left for two centuries.

Here the term *intellectual* is used loosely, to denote not only people who think about ideas—about thinking—but also people who think they do. The term *anti-Semitism* is used precisely, to denote people who dislike Jews. These people include those who say: We do not dislike Jews, we only dislike Zionists—although to live in Israel is to endorse the Zionist enterprise, and all Jews are implicated, as sympathizers, in the crime that is Israel.

Wednesday's release of Mel Gibson's movie *The Passion of the Christ* has catalyzed fears of resurgent anti-Semitism. Some critics say the movie portrays the governor of Judea—Pontius Pilate, the Roman prefect responsible for the crucifixion—as more benign and less in control than he actually was, and ascribes too much power and malignity to Jerusalem's Jewish elite.

Jon Meacham's deeply informed cover story "Who Killed Jesus?" in the February 16 *Newsweek* renders this measured judgment: The movie implies more blame for the Jewish religious leaders of Judea of that time than sound scholarship suggests. However, Meacham rightly refrains from discerning disreputable intentions in Gibson's presentation of matters about which scholars, too, must speculate, and do disagree. Besides, this being a healthy nation, Americans are unlikely to be swayed by the movie's misreading, as Meacham delicately suggests, of the actions of a few Jews two thousand years ago.

Fears about the movie exacerbating religiously motivated anti-Semitism are missing the larger menace—the upsurge of political anti-Semitism. Like traditional anti-Semitism, but with secular sources and motives, the political version, which condemns Jews as a social element, is becoming mainstream, and chic among political and cultural elites, mostly in Europe. Consider:

- A cartoon in a mainstream Italian newspaper depicts the infant Jesus in a manger, menaced by an Israeli tank and saying "Don't tell me they want to kill me again." This expresses animus against Israel rather than twisted Christian zeal.
- The European Union has suppressed a study it commissioned, because the study blamed the upsurge in anti-Jewish acts on European Muslims—and the European left.
- An EU poll reveals that a European majority believes the greatest threat to world peace is Israel.
- Nineteen percent of Germans believe what a bestselling German book asserts: The CIA and Israel's Mossad organized the September 11 attacks.
- On French television, a comedian wearing a Jewish skullcap gives a Nazi salute while yelling "Isra-Heil!"
- If Israel is not the Great Satan, it is allied with him—America. European anti-American demonstrations often include Israel's blue and white flag with a swastika replacing the star of David, and signs perpetuating the myth, concocted by Palestinians and cooperative Western journalists, of an Israeli massacre in Jenin: "1943: Warsaw / 2002: Jenin."
- Omer Bartov, historian at Brown University, writes in the *New Republic* that much of what Hitler said "can be found today in innumerable places: on Internet sites, propaganda brochures, political speeches, protest placards, academic publications, religious sermons, you name it."

The appallingly brief eclipse of anti-Semitism after Auschwitz demonstrates how beguiling is the simplicity of pure stupidity. All of the left's prescriptions for curing what ails society—socialism, communism, psychoanalysis, "progressive" education, etc.—have been discarded, so now the left is reduced to adapting that hardy perennial of the right, anti-Semitism.

This is a new twist to the left's recipe for salvation through elimination: All will be well if we eliminate capitalists, or private property, or the ruling class, or "special interests," or neuroses, or inhibitions. Now, let's try eliminating a people, starting with their nation, which is obnoxiously pro-American and insufferably Spartan.

Europe's susceptibility to political lunacy, and the Arab world's addiction to it, is not news. And the paranoid style is a political constant. Those who believe a vast conspiracy assassinated President Kennedy say: Proof of the conspiracy's diabolical subtlety is that *no* evidence of it remains. Today's anti-Semites say: Proof of the Jews' potent menace is that there are so few of them—just 13 million of the planet's 6 billion people—yet they cause so many political, economic, and cultural ills.

Gosh. Imagine if they were, say, 1 percent of Earth's population—63 million.   [FEBRUARY 25, 2004]

When Harry Remet Hanne

Among the radiating effects of the United States Holocaust Memorial Museum, which opened along Washington's Mall ten years ago, is the story of how Harry remet Hanne. The friendship of Harry Ettlinger, now seventy-seven, and Hanne Hirsch, now seventy-eight, was interrupted for sixty-four years by war and genocide.

It began when he lived on the second floor and she on the fourth floor of an apartment building in Karlsruhe, Germany, where they attended the same school. The friendship was renewed last spring, thanks to two New Jersey teenagers, Jennifer Bernardes, of an immigrant family from Brazil, and Leonie Barrett, of an immigrant family from Jamaica. Leonie's sister is currently serving in the Persian Gulf.

Harry, a Holocaust survivor, participates in New Jersey's "Adopt a Survivor" program that brings middle and high school students to the museum. Each student studies a survivor's personal history and commits to tell his or her story in 2045, the one hundredth anniversary of the liberation of the death camps.

Museum visitors are issued identity cards recounting the history of someone who was swept up in the Holocaust whirlwind. Jennifer and Leonie noticed that one card detailed the life of a girl from Karlsruhe. Harry recognized Hanne Hirsch as the girl from the fourth floor. He had not known her fate. But when he looked her up in the museum's registry of survivors, he found that her good fortune was to be sheltered by the good people of the French Huguenot village of Le Chambon, in the south of France near Lyon. Hanne Hirsch Liebmann lives in New York with her husband, Max, eighty-one.

Hanne's father and then her widowed mother ran a photography shop in Karlsruhe until Nazi anti-Jewish laws put them out of business in 1938. Hanne was sixteen in 1940 when she was deported to a camp in Vichy France. In the camp, she met Max Liebmann, then nineteen.

He got out of the camp and was sheltered illegally in Le Chambon until he could get into Switzerland. She received livesaving help from the villagers, whose long memories of the persecution of Huguenots fueled their resistance to German and Vichy crimes.

Jews still in the camp on August 1, 1942, were destined for Auschwitz. Hanne was legally removed to the village shortly before that, and in February 1943 she followed Max to Switzerland. They married, and in 1948 came to America.

Harry, who says he was "the last bar mitzvah boy in my synagogue," fled Germany with his family after the Munich Agreement of September 1938. In January 1945, he was in a U.S. Army truck en route to join the infantry unit that soon would seize the Remagen bridge over the Rhine. He was plucked from the truck to become an interpreter. Among the Germans he interviewed after the war was Heinrich Hoffmann, Hitler's photographer, who had been an apprentice in Munich under Hanne's uncle. Harry, Hanne, and Max had lunch together here this week while participating in the Holocaust Museum's tenth anniversary observances.

In an editorial saluting the museum as "among the finest historical exhibits of any kind, on any subject, anywhere," the *Washington Post* nevertheless recalled the "skeptical questions" asked when the museum was proposed. The questions concerned whether the Mall, which is the epicenter of America's civic life, is a suitable site for a museum dedicated to an event of European and Jewish history. The *Post* said that the questions have been given "no adequate philosophical or theoretical answers." Here are six answers.

The first answer has many facets: America is congenitally cheerful and hence relentlessly focused on the future, so it is susceptible to historical amnesia. And Americans, having uniquely broad and grave responsibilities in the world, must be trained to look life unblinkingly in the face. The Holocaust, the eruption of barbarism in modern Western civilization, is the black sun into which Americans, especially, must be taught to stare. The Holocaust Museum, a grim sermon in stone, is an experience of darkness amidst the Mall's glistening monuments to the success of American society. It is a mind-opening reminder of the furies beyond our shores. The Mall's welcoming geometry of openness suggests the symmetry and temperateness of America's social arrangements. The museum, a counterpoint in one of the world's most magnificent urban spaces, inflicts on visitors—almost 19 million of them so far—excruciating knowledge that is intensely relevant to this era of terrorism, knowledge of the hideous possibilities of human action.

Five other answers to the question of why the museum is pertinent to American experience and governance, and hence is properly on the Mall, are: Harry, Hanne, Max, Jennifer, and Leonie, Americans all.

[MAY 1, 2003]

Cars as Mobile Sculpture

D ETROIT—One car company is running ads in which its suave forty-four-year-old CEO underscores his love for the outdoors by saying, "I won't even stay in a hotel if I can't open the windows."

Another car company, its tone set by its seventy-year-old vice chairman—an ex-Marine aviator—is putting up three billboards. One shows a 1957 Chevy's grille—think of Teddy Roosevelt's grin in chrome—and says: "Proof your parents were actually cool once." Another shows the rear deck of a little red 1963 Corvette Sting Ray and says: "They don't write songs about Volvos." The third shows the gritted-teeth grille of a 1970 Chevy Chevelle SS and says: "Not everyone wants a car with a bud vase on the dash."

Guess which company is doing best.

Bill Ford's problems at the company his great-grandfather founded are bigger than odd advertising. And there are many reasons why GM is soaring like the jet fighter Robert Lutz flies for fun. But institutions are the lengthening shadows of strong individuals, and Lutz is, in the elemental argot of this muscular city, a "car guy."

When GM lured Lutz back into the car business last summer, the *Detroit News* headline ("Lutz Rides In to Rev Up GM") was of a size usually reserved for Pearl Harbors or two-game Tiger winning streaks. But are Americans still "car people" the way they were when Lutz was young, in the 1950s?

Then they were automobile voluptuaries, Detroit was in its rococo period and its great stylist was GM's Harley Earl, "the Cellini of chrome," of whom it was said that if he could have put chrome on his clothes, he would have. Cars had front bumpers that were protuberant, not to say nubile, and tail fins. Cars looked, a wit said, "like chorus girls coming and fighter planes going." Indeed, Buick's LeSabre emulated the F-86 Sabre jet.

Lutz, tall and trim, knows that today's Americans generally have a less erotic relationship with cars. They look upon many cars, he says, "as more or less an appliance." As mere transportation. Utilitarian. Boring. Furthermore, twenty years ago, a "premium" car meant one substantially more capable. Today, premium technologies (e.g., high-tech engines, overhead cams) are everywhere.

But, Lutz says happily, your car is still "an extension of your psycho-motor system." More than the other stuff we surround ourselves with—do you know the brand of your refrigerator? will you replace it before it breaks down?—your car "continually makes an instant statement about you, even to complete strangers."

So, Lutz insists, design is still central to success in the automobile business. Art is *supposed* to "evoke emotional responses" and cars are art—"mobile sculpture." He also believes that when everybody else is doing it, don't. Most cars today have rounded aerodynamic lines. But the new Cadillac CTS, with angular lines, is described in ads as "edgy."

And when Lutz was at Chrysler a few years ago, he pushed through the development of the popular PT Cruiser, an echo of a 1937 Ford. Why? Surely not nostalgia. Probably most of the (mostly young) people buying these cars do not know who was president in 1937. Go figure.

Lutz believes that "aspirational aspects overwhelm the functional differences" when car customers make their choices. When that happens, the "left-analytical brain has been defeated again," the "right brain" has prevailed, and Lutz rejoices. But this does not mean people plunk down large sums merely for high-status brands. Chevrolet sells more vehicles costing more than $30,000 than do Mercedes, BMW, Lexus, and Audi combined, but this is partly due to the popularity of light trucks, a category that includes sport utility vehicles. Today, an "extremely high-end demographic"—e.g., investment bankers and stockbrokers—are buying GMC SUVs.

Some Americans (let us avoid the term *liberals*) hate fun, such as cheeseburgers, talk radio, guns, Las Vegas, and cars that are larger than roller skates and that look more interesting than shoe boxes. They hated 1950s cars that looked—as a sniffy critic said—like jukeboxes on wheels. Such people love guilt, and want people to feel guilty about cars because cars have made possible suburbs, Wal-Mart, McDonald's, and emancipation from public transportation.

GM's "car guy" knows that Americans generally keep their cars longer than they used to—creeping utilitarianism—and do not define automotive fun as they did in the gaudy 1950s. But he is betting that lots of them still are guilty of letting their right brains rip when purchasing a car.   [APRIL 18, 2002]

Hog Heaven:
Happy One Hundredth, Harley

MILWAUKEE—In 1903, young men (the hyperkinetic president was just forty-five) were on the move. The Wright brothers— Wilbur, thirty-six, and Orville, thirty-two—left their bicycle shop in Dayton to take their twelve-second, 120-foot flight at Kitty Hawk. And William Harley, twenty-one, and Arthur Davidson, twenty, working in a ten-by-fifteen-foot shed here, built a motorcycle. On the eve of its centennial, the company born in that shed is spectacularly successful, and one of America's best-known brands. No American company has such devoted customers.

The Information Superhighway is littered with the wreckage of New Economy companies. But America's real highways are humming with the distinctive sound of an iconic Old Economy product— Harley-Davidsons. Their sound (think potato-potato-potato) is so beloved by enthusiasts that the company tried to have it declared a trademark.

Last weekend, the company began a fourteen-month-long one-hundredth-birthday bash. It has much to celebrate, including increases in production of more than 10 percent annually for sixteen years. And 16 consecutive years of record earnings. And average annual earnings growth of 37 percent. And a share price up 15,000 percent since 1986, about nine times as much as General Electric's, which is no slouch.

In the First World War, Harley-Davidson helped mechanize the Army—the first American to enter Germany after the armistice rode in on a Harley—and AMF bought the company in 1969. But by 1981, Harley-Davidson was reeling, partly because of Japanese imports. So thirteen of the company's executives—including today's CEO, Jeffrey Bleustein, sixty-two, a former Yale engineering professor—bought it for a highly leveraged $82 million.

In 1983, they got a five-year tariff protection, but recovery was so rapid they asked the government to end the protection a year early. The tariff—Bleustein doubts that anyone paid it—was a warning shot against "dumping" (selling at a price below the cost of manufacture) by the Japanese, who at the time had a two-year inventory in warehouses and were still producing full tilt. But the tariff exempted European manufacturers, who were not dumping, and the biggest Japanese maker, Honda, because its bikes were assembled in Ohio.

Today, the tariff seems as quaint as other relics of the 1980s, such as the U.S. feeling of inferiority regarding Japanese economic prowess, and the country-music lament "everything I buy these days has a foreign name." Twenty years after the $82 million buyout, Harley's sales were $3.3 billion and earnings $435 million, thanks to passionate motorcyclists of the sort who every August descend, three-hundred thousand strong, on Sturgis, South Dakota.

Hollywood—and a few motorcyclists—have made motorcyclists seem like bad boys, like Marlon Brando in *The Wild One* (1954) and Jack Nicholson and Peter Fonda in *Easy Rider* (1969). But most motorcyclists are middle-aged and middle class. The average Harley customer is forty-six and has a household income of $78,000. There are many riders in their seventies and eighties. Says Bleustein, himself a rider, "Even after they stop playing golf, they can still ride."

The average Harley customer pays $15,000 for his machine, but some Harleys, such as those with music provided by a six-CD changer, can list for $22,000. Although output has been increased at the three factories—here and in York, Pennsylvania, and Kansas City, Missouri—demand so much exceeds supply (261,000 bikes this year) for some models that "scalpers" sell them for up to $4,000 over list. Some people sell their places on waiting lists. Others wait on the list, then sell their bikes at a markup before they even leave the dealer's parking lot.

Honda sells more bikes in America than Harley does, but Harley dominates the high-profit market for heavy bikes (aka hogs), even in Japan, and has 21 percent of the Asia-Pacific market for all motorcycles. In America, 650,000 people pay $40 annual dues to be members of the Harley-owners group. They doubtless agree with the company that it is selling a "lifestyle." This year bikers will spend more than $1 billion on Harley gear, from black motorcycle jackets for toddlers to Harley-Davidson fountain pens for bikers with literary aspirations.

Bleustein's office, in the 1920 brick building where all the bikes once were made, features a glass tabletop supported by two Harley engines. He wears a gray suit, crisp white shirt, French cuffs—and a colorful Harley-Davidson necktie that is the sartorial equivalent of chrome. Many of the office workers dress as though they just got off their Harleys, which they did. Worldwide, says Bleustein, motorcycling means "freedom, adventure, individual expression." As does America.

Harley-Davidson's ten-city centennial tour begins this week in Atlanta and will rumble to Mexico City, Sydney, Tokyo, Barcelona, and on to Munich next July. It will culminate next August when a quarter of a million satisfied customers are expected to descend on Milwaukee to compare chrome and enjoy the music of their machines. Think: potato-potato-potato times 250,000.   [JULY 22, 2002]

Restoration at 346 Madison

This man now—surely he came from that heavenly world, that divine position at the center of things where choice is unlimited.
—MARY McCARTHY, "The Man in the Brooks Brothers Shirt" (1941)

Some business stories are social parables. One such is the long, stately rise, then the swift, undignified descent, and now the resurrection of Brooks Brothers, the men's clothier that long ago became one of America's iconic brands.

It was founded in 1818 near the southern tip of a mostly rural Manhattan. The day the store opened—the store that was to define American male gentility—the city council was fretting about swine in the streets.

As Manhattanites moved north, so did the store, several times. By 1915, it had moved to 346 Madison, at the corner of Forty-fourth, a store with dark wood and soft lighting from Tiffany chandeliers. Not until 1928 did Brooks Brothers open a second store, on Newbury Street in Boston. But long before that, 346 Madison had become for many men the quiet definer of sartorial good taste.

Generals Grant, Sherman, Sheridan, and Hooker bought Civil War uniforms from Brooks Brothers. Lincoln wore a Brooks Brothers overcoat to his second inauguration, and to Ford's Theatre. He was buried in a Brooks Brothers suit. J. P. Morgan, when he was a boy, was taken to Brooks Brothers for his first suit, and sixty years later was still buying suits there from the same salesman.

But although Brooks Brothers catered to the carriage trade, by pioneering high-quality ready-made garments it helped democratize dress. Teddy Roosevelt and Woodrow Wilson detested each other, but each was inaugurated in a Brooks Brothers suit. And after World War I, rising men in a nation brimming with confidence made Brooks Brothers a convenient literary symbol. Fitzgerald in *This Side of Paradise,* Hemingway in *The Sun Also Rises,* John O'Hara, Somerset Maugham, and J. P. Marquand all used Brooks Brothers to suggest character traits—not always flatteringly. Clark Gable and Fred Astaire were Brooks Brothers customers.

Emblematic of Brooks Brothers' power to define classicism was—is—what the company's official history rightly calls "the single most imitated item in American clothing history." It is the shirt with a button-down "polo collar," so named because a grandson of the founder, visiting England, liked the way polo players buttoned down their collars to keep them from flapping during play.

The 1950s are disparaged by advanced thinkers as "buttoned down," meaning too reticent and emotionally reserved. But the button-down shirt, a striped tie, and a "sack suit"—unpadded shoulders, not very wide lapels—became the 1950s "Ivy League look." Sloan Wilson's *The Man in the Gray Flannel Suit* bought it at Brooks Brothers. And in *The Catcher in the Rye,* Holden Caulfield's adolescent disapproval of almost everything extended to "guys fitting your pants all the time at Brooks."

Never mind. In 1960, the *New York Times* wrote of John Kennedy: "Though visibly exhausted from a long day in the Senate, he walked to the floor, a model of Brooks Brothers perfection."

In 1956, the company's president said, "Whenever we contemplate changing anything around here, a perceptible shudder goes through the store." In the turbulent 1960s it took seven years for the lapels of Brooks Brothers suits to grow—in three increments—from three inches to three and a half. Then came the male peacockery of the 1980s. It was an era in which, a fashion historian writes, clothes—broad-shouldered Italian suits, suspenders, ties the size and color of Third World nations' flags—became "badges of communication," advertisements for the wearers.

And Brooks Brothers—sold, then sold again to a British department-store chain—decided to "get with it." Big mistake.

Brooks Brothers had been, *Newsweek* wrote, "the last holdout against the 1980s 'if you've got it, flaunt it' mentality." As "brand repositioning," it began to compete with Gap, Banana Republic, and the like. "Casualization" was the ugly word for the ugly trend in men's fashion. Brooks Brothers' quality declined, the company's old customers were scandalized—lavender dress shirts!—and the new customers were fickle. Brooks Brothers even opened a Fifth Avenue store that is all glass and stainless steel. Good grief.

Then, two years ago, a white knight rode to the rescue. A knight from—thank you, globalization—Italy. The new owner, Claudio Del Vecchio, says nobody can be J.Crew better than J.Crew, but only Brooks Brothers can be a fixed point in a world of flux.

Political parties decline when they alienate their core voters. The Episcopal Church, once the Brooks Brothers of American Protestantism, has lost a third of its members while courting new ones with trendy theological fashions. In the nick of time, Brooks Brothers has remembered that millions of men still think "buttoned down" is a phrase of praise.   [SEPTEMBER 1, 2003]

Starbucks, Nail Salons, and the Aesthetic Imperative

Creative thinkers do not merely answer questions that interest others, they answer questions that others have not realized are interesting, or even are questions. For example:

Starbucks' coffee is not that much better than everyone else's coffee, so what is Starbucks really selling?

What does it say about today's America that travelers changing concourses in the United terminal at Chicago's O'Hare airport pass beneath a 744-foot neon-light sculpture, the colors of which change in sync to music?

Why have the number of nail salons doubled, the number of manicurists tripled, and the number of cosmetic medical procedures almost quintupled in a decade? Why do 13 percent of middle-aged *men* spend more than $1 billion on hair coloring, up 34 percent in five years?

If computers are just tools, why bother making them as pretty as the Sony Vaio and Apple iMac?

How much of the booming membership in gyms is about something other than—more pleasurable than—health maintenance?

Virginia Postrel, an economics columnist for the *New York Times* who writes perceptively about everything on which her penetrating gaze alights, answers these questions, and others you may not have asked yourself, in her new book, *The Substance of Style: How the Rise of Aesthetic Value Is Remaking Commerce, Culture, and Consciousness.* It is an appreciation of what she calls the "aesthetic imperative" in this expressive age.

Biologically we are, she says, visual, tactile beings responsive to our sensory surroundings. And we now are—thanks to such factors as travel, education, immigration, and media—producing a society of aesthetic plenitude and pluralism.

People are eager to pay Starbucks for more than mere coffee—for a sensory environment that pleases more than just their palates. Demand often creates supply, but supply can create demand: Travelers do not demand O'Hare's neon light sculpture, but the supply of such aesthetic amenities raises expectations for a more pleasurable environment. And from gyms and nail salons to tattoo parlors and the emporia where people get their bodies pierced in so many interesting places, Americans are consuming design and designing themselves.

Time was, Henry Ford told customers they could have cars in the color they wanted, as long as they wanted black. Time was, Walter

Gropius, the minimalist architect, when asked what he would say if some students did not like the way he had arranged the furniture in a Harvard dorm he designed, replied, "Then they are neurotic."

But the breakdown of cultural homogeneity in the 1960s has been followed by what Postrel says are the twin propellants of today's aesthetic abundance—rising incomes and falling prices. Household income has increased about 30 percent in less than thirty years, and families have shrunk, further expanding disposable income.

Economic data does not measure the increases that aesthetics add to quality of life. In national income statistics, a $20 steak dinner in an aesthetically pleasing restaurant is indistinguishable from a $20 steak dinner in a banal environment. Which means we are exaggerating inflation and underestimating the economy's real production of value.

"Aesthetics," says Postrel, "shows rather than tells, delights rather than instructs. The effects are immediate, perceptual and emotional. They are not cognitive, although we may analyze them after the fact." Aesthetics, Postrel stresses, is not irrational or antirational, it is prerational or nonrational.

That does not mean it should be distrusted, as rhetoric has come to be, as a manipulative force manufacturing synthetic desires. Aspiration, Postrel believes, is an aspect of identity, including aesthetic identity— "I like that" means "I am like that." Her cheerful analysis of all this puts her athwart a tradition of disapproving intellectuals.

Half a century ago, Adlai Stevenson, Democratic presidential nominee and darling of the intelligentsia, asked: "With the supermarket as our temple and the singing commercial as our litany, are we likely to fire the world with an irresistible vision of America's exalted purposes and inspiring way of life?" His question radiated what was then—and still is; everything changes except "progressives"—the intellectuals' conventional disdain of America's "consumer society."

Today, however, thoughtful people have more appreciation of the complex prerequisites—social, political, and intellectual—of a society that produces the abundance, and honors the emancipation of choice and desire, that results in supermarkets, advertising, and other things that are woven inextricably into the fabric of a free society. Those mundane things actually are related to what exalts America and makes it inspiring.

Unbounded, imaginative desiring can be a problem for democratic governance. However, it certainly is both a cause and a consequence of a democratic culture. [OCTOBER 26, 2003]

Manners vs. Social Autism

Let's be good cosmopolitans and offer sociological explanations rather than moral judgments about students, the *Washington Post* reports, having sex during the day in high schools. Sociology discerns connections, and there may be one between the fact that teenagers are relaxing from academic rigors by enjoying sex in the school auditorium, and the fact that Americans in public soon will be able to watch pornography, and prime-time television programs such as *Desperate Housewives*—and, for the high-minded, C-SPAN—on their cell phones and video iPods.

The connection is this: Many people have no notion of propriety when in the presence of other people, because they are not actually in the presence of other people, even when they are in public.

With everyone chatting on cell phones when not floating in iPod-land, "this is an age of social autism, in which people just can't see the value of imagining their impact on others." We are entertaining ourselves into inanition. (There are websites for people with Internet addiction. Think about that.) And multiplying technologies of portable entertainments will enable "limitless self-absorption," which will make people solipsistic, inconsiderate, and antisocial. Hence manners are becoming unmannerly in this "age of lazy moral relativism combined with aggressive social insolence."

So says Lynne Truss in her latest trumpet blast of a book, *Talk to the Hand: The Utter Bloody Rudeness of the World Today, or Six Good Reasons to Stay Home and Bolt the Door.* Her previous wail of despair was *Eats, Shoots & Leaves: The Zero Tolerance Approach to Punctuation,* which established her as—depending on your sensibility—

a comma and apostrophe fascist (the liberal sensibility) or a plucky constable combating anarchy (the conservative sensibility).

Good punctuation, she says, is analogous to good manners because it treats readers with respect. "All the important rules," she writes, "surely boil down to one: *remember you are with other people; show some consideration.*" Manners, which have been called "quotidian ethics," arise from real or—this, too, is important in lubricating social frictions—feigned empathy.

"People," says Truss, "are happier when they have some idea of where they stand and what the rules are." But today's entitlement mentality, which is both a cause and a consequence of the welfare state, manifests itself in the attitude that it is all right to do whatever one has a right to do. Which is why acrimony has enveloped a coffee shop on Chicago's affluent North Side, where the proprietor posted a notice that children must "behave and use their indoor voices." The proprietor, battling what he calls an "epidemic" of antisocial behavior, told the *New York Times* that parents protesting his notice "have a very strong sense of entitlement."

A thoroughly modern parent, believing that children must be protected from feelings injurious to self-esteem, says: "Johnny, the fact that you did something bad does not mean you are bad for doing it." We have, Truss thinks, "created people who will not stand to be corrected in any way." Furthermore, it is a brave, or foolhardy, man who shows traditional manners toward women. In today's world of "hair-trigger sensitivity," to open a door for a woman is to play what Truss calls Gallantry Russian Roulette: You risk a high-decibel lecture on gender politics.

One writer on manners has argued that a nation's greatness is measured not only by obedience of laws but also by "obedience to the unenforceable." But enforcement of manners can be necessary. The well-named David Stern, commissioner of the NBA, recently decreed a dress code for players. It is politeness to the league's customers who, weary of seeing players dressed in "edgy" hip-hop "street" or "gangsta" styles, want to be able to distinguish the Bucks and Knicks from the

Bloods and Crips. Stern also understands that players who wear "in your face" clothes of a kind, and in a manner, that evokes Sing Sing more than Brooks Brothers might be more inclined to fight on the floor and to allow fights to migrate to the stands, as happened last year.

Because manners are means of extending respect, especially to strangers, this question arises: Do manners and virtue go together? Truss thinks so, in spite of the possibility of "blood-stained dictators who had exquisite table manners and never used their mobile phones in a crowded train compartment to order mass executions."

Actually, manners are the practice of a virtue. The virtue is called *civility,* a word related—as a foundation is related to a house—to the word *civilization.* [NOVEMBER 20, 2005]

A Punctuation Vigilante

The actress Margaret Anglin left this note in the dressing room of another actress: "Margaret Anglin says Mrs. Fiske is the best actress in America." Mrs. Fiske added two commas and returned the note: "Margaret Anglin, says Mrs. Fiske, is the best actress in America."

Little things mean a lot. That is the thesis of a wise and witty wee book, *Eats, Shoots & Leaves,* just published by Lynne Truss, a British writer and broadcaster. She knows that proper punctuation, "the basting that holds the fabric of language in shape," is "both the sign and the cause of clear thinking."

The book's title comes from a joke: A panda enters a café, orders a sandwich, eats, draws a pistol, fires a few shots, then heads for the door. Asked by a waiter to explain his behavior, he hands the waiter a badly punctuated wildlife manual and says: "I'm a panda. Look it up." The waiter reads the relevant entry: "Panda: large black-and-white bear-like mammal. Eats, shoots and leaves."

Behold the magical comma. It can turn an unjust aspersion against an entire species ("No dogs please") into a reasonable request ("No dogs, please"), or it can turn a lilting lyric into a banal inquiry ("What is this thing called, love?"). The Christmas carol actually is "God rest ye merry, gentlemen," not "God rest ye, merry gentlemen."

Huge doctrinal consequences flow from the placing of a comma in what Jesus, when on the cross, said to the thief: "Verily, I say unto thee, This day thou shalt be with me in Paradise" or "Verily, I say unto thee this day, Thou shalt be with me in Paradise." The former leaves little room for purgatory.

Combined with a colon, a comma can fuel sexual warfare: "A woman without her man is nothing" becomes "A woman: without her, man is nothing." But a colon in place of a comma can subtly emit a certain bark.

"President Bush said, 'Get Bob Woodward.' "

"President Bush said: 'Get Bob Woodward.' "

But beware the derangement known as commaphilia, which results in the promiscuous cluttering of sentences with superfluous signals. A reader once asked James Thurber why he had put a comma after the word *dinner* in this sentence: "After dinner, the men went into the living room." Thurber, a comma minimalist, blamed the *New Yorker*'s commaphilic editor, Harold Ross: "This particular comma was Ross' way of giving the men time to push back their chairs and stand up."

Truss, a punctuation vigilante, says punctuation marks are traffic signals telling readers to slow down, pause, notice something, take a detour, stop. Punctuation, she says, "directs you how to read, in the same way musical notation directs a musician how to play" with attention to the composer's intentions regarding rhythm, pitch, tone, and flow.

The almost-always-ghastly exclamation point has been rightly compared to canned laughter. F. Scott Fitzgerald said it was like laughing at your own joke. But not always. Victor Hugo, wondering how his *Les Misérables* was selling, sent this telegram to his publisher: "?" The publisher wired back: "!"

The dash can be, among other things, droll, as Byron understood:

> He learned the arts of riding, fencing, gunnery,
> And how to scale a fortress—or a nunnery.

Or:

> *A little still she strove, and much repented,*
> *And whispering "I will ne'er consent"—*
> *consented.*

The humble hyphen performs heroic services, making possible compounds that would otherwise be unsightly ("de-ice" rather than "deice"; "shell-like" rather than "shelllike"). And a hyphen can rescue meaning. As Truss says, "A cross-section of the public is quite different from a cross section of the public." If you are a pickled-herring merchant, you will not want to be called a pickled herring merchant. The difference between extra-marital sex and extra marital sex is not to be sneezed at.

The connection between the words *punctilious,* which means "attentive to formality or etiquette," and *punctuation* is instructive. Careful punctuation expresses a writer's solicitude for the reader. Of course punctuation, like most other forms of good manners, may yet entirely disappear, another victim of progress, this time in the form of e-mail, cell-phone text messages, and the like.

Neither the elegant semicolon nor the dashing dash is of use to people whose preferred literary style is "CU B4 8?" and whose idea of Edwardian prolixity is: "Saw Jim—he looks gr8—have you seen him—what time is the thing 2morrow."

Oh, for the era when a journalist telephoned from Moscow to London to add a semicolon to his story!   [MAY 20, 2004]

America's Literature of Regret

His name was George F. Babbitt. He was forty-six years old now, in April, 1920, and he made nothing in particular, neither butter nor shoes nor poetry, but he was nimble in the calling of selling houses for more than people could afford to pay.
                                    —SINCLAIR LEWIS, *Babbitt* (1922)

But today his name is Warren Schmidt. He is sixty-six now as he stolidly watches the clock on his otherwise bare office wall tick the final seconds of his career as an actuary at Woodmen of the World Insurance in Omaha.

Babbitt begins: "The towers of Zenith aspired above the morning mist; austere towers of steel and cement and limestone, sturdy as cliffs and delicate as silver rods. They were neither citadels nor churches, but frankly and beautifully office-buildings." Beautiful, Lewis intimates, if only because of the frankness of their banality.

About Schmidt, the new Jack Nicholson movie, begins with the camera lingering on a flat slab of a spire in Omaha, the Woodmen building, which is replicated in the cake at Schmidt's retirement party that evening. If "party" is applicable to so flat an affair. Flat as champagne that has lost its fizz. Flat as the Midwest landscape through which Schmidt, suddenly widowed, rolls, a depressed Jack Kerouac in a gigantic Winnebago, on the road to Denver to try to forestall yet another disappointment, the marriage of his daughter to a waterbed salesman Schmidt despises.

In the novel on which *About Schmidt* is loosely based, Schmidt retires from a Manhattan law firm to Long Island affluence. So why (other than the fact that director Alexander Payne is from Omaha) turn Schmidt into a stereotypical Midwesterner whose taciturnity is presumably symptomatic not of still waters running deep, but only of a low emotional metabolism?

Because it is still very modern to suppose that people like Schmidt who do not "share their feelings" have none. And because it is very traditional to disparage life in the Midwest's small towns, such as Sherwood Anderson's *Winesburg, Ohio* (1919).

In 1920, Sinclair Lewis, from Sauk Centre, Minnesota, who in 1930 became the first American winner of the Nobel Prize for Literature, published *Main Street,* an unaffectionate depiction of fictional Gopher Prairie, Minnesota, where individualism is suffocated by what would later be called "conformity." In England, E. M. Forster said Lewis had lodged "a piece of a continent"—the Midwest—"in our imagination."

Also in 1920, another Minnesotan, F. Scott Fitzgerald, published *This Side of Paradise,* in which Amory Blaine decides he has "grown up to find all Gods dead, all wars fought, all faiths in man shaken." But whereas Fitzgerald came East to be exhilarated by Princeton and the 1920s, and kept moving east, to Europe, Lewis was unhappy at Yale and looked back in anger at the Midwest. His curdled spirit considered that region unforgivably middling—no longer a heroic frontier, never likely to become more than (as another young Midwesterner, Ernest Hemingway, called his native Oak Park, Illinois) a place of "broad lawns and narrow minds."

Some critics insist that the portraits of Winesburg, Gopher Prairie, Zenith and Schmidt's Omaha are "really" sympathetic. Perhaps the recurring cows in *About Schmidt* (in paintings on a restaurant wall, in a cattle truck) are not supposed to suggest that the people, too, are bovine. See the movie and decide for yourself if it is yet another exercise in condescension. As Evan Connell's two nuanced novels about Mr. and Mrs. Bridge of Kansas City (and the Paul Newman and Joanne Woodward movie made from them) are not.

"I don't say he's a great man," says Linda Loman of her husband, Willy, in Arthur Miller's *Death of a Salesman* (1949), another depiction of disappointed American striving. But, she says, "attention must be finally paid to such a person." Surely ample attention is paid. The likes of Loman, Babbitt, and Schmidt inhabit a large American literature of regret. Which may be what Schmidt is feeling in the movie's final frame, when he is reduced to tears by receiving in the mail the slender evidence of his single success in connecting with another—a drawing from a six-year-old Tanzanian boy to whom Schmidt has sent hilariously inapposite, hence unconnecting, letters.

Babbitt says, "I've never done a single thing I wanted to in my whole life! I don't know's I've accomplished anything except just get along." However, a haunting sense of regret about time wasted is a timeless theme of literature. Timeless, and placeless. It is the human condition, not a Midwestern affliction.   [JANUARY 16, 2003]

Chief Illiniwek and the Indignation Industry

The University of Illinois must soon decide whether, and if so how, to fight an exceedingly silly edict from the NCAA. That organization's primary function is to require college athletics to be no more crassly exploitative and commercial than is absolutely necessary. But now the NCAA is going to police cultural sensitivity, as it understands that. Hence the decision to declare Chief Illiniwek "hostile and abusive" to Native Americans.

Censorship—e.g., campus speech codes—often are academic liberalism's preferred instrument of social improvement, and now the NCAA's censors say: The Chief must go, as must the university's logo of a Native American in feathered headdress. Otherwise the NCAA will not allow the university to host any postseason tournaments or events.

This story of progress, as progressives understand that, began during halftime of a football game in 1926, when an undergraduate studying Indian culture performed a dance dressed as a chief. Since then, a student has always served as Chief Illiniwek, who has become the symbol of the university that serves a state named after the Illini confederation of about a half-dozen tribes that were virtually annihilated in the 1760s by rival tribes.

In 1930, the student then portraying Chief Illiniwek traveled to South Dakota to receive authentic raiment from the Oglala Sioux. In 1967 and 1982, representatives of the Sioux, who had not yet discovered that they were supposed to feel abused, came to the Champaign-Urbana campus to augment the outfits Chief Illiniwek wears at football and basketball games.

But grievance groups have multiplied, seeking reparations for historic wrongs, and regulations to assuage current injuries inflicted by "insensitivity." One of America's booming businesses is the indignation industry that manufactures the synthetic outrage needed to fuel identity politics.

The NCAA is allowing Florida State University and the University of Utah to continue calling their teams Seminoles and Utes, respectively, because those two tribes approve of the tradition. The Saginaw Chippewa tribe starchily denounces any "outside entity"—that would be you, NCAA—that would disrupt the tribe's "rich relationship" with Central Michigan University and its teams, the Chippewas. The University of North Carolina at Pembroke can continue calling its teams the Braves. Bravery is a virtue, so perhaps the 21 percent of the school's students who are Native Americans consider the name a compliment.

The University of North Dakota Fighting Sioux may have to find another nickname because the various Sioux tribes cannot agree about whether they are insulted. But the only remnant of the Illini confederation, the Peoria tribe, is now in Oklahoma. Under its chief, John Froman, the tribe is too busy running a casino and golf course to care about Chief Illiniwek. The NCAA ethicists probably reason that the Chief must go because no portion of the Illini confederation remains to defend him.

Or to be offended by him, but never mind that, or this: In 1995, the Office of Civil Rights in President Clinton's Education Department, a nest of sensitivity mongers, rejected the claim that the Chief and the name Fighting Illini created for anyone a "hostile environment" on campus.

In 2002, *Sports Illustrated* published a poll of 351 Native Americans, 217 living on reservations, 134 living off. Eighty-one percent said high school and college teams should *not* stop using Indian nicknames.

But in any case, why should anyone's disapproval of a nickname doom it? When, in the multiplication of entitlements, did we produce an entitlement for everyone to go through life without being annoyed by anything, even a team's nickname? If some Irish or Scots were to take offense at Notre Dame's Fighting Irish or the Fighting Scots of Monmouth College, what rule of morality would require the rest of us to care? Civilization depends on, and civility often requires, the willingness to say, "What you are doing is none of my business" and "What I am doing is none of your business."

But this is an age when being an offended busybody is considered evidence of advanced thinking and an exquisite sensibility. So, People for the Ethical Treatment of Animals has demanded that the University of South Carolina's teams not be called Gamecocks because cock fighting is cruel. It also is illegal in South Carolina.

In 1972, the University of Massachusetts at Amherst replaced the nickname Redmen with Minutemen. White men carrying guns? If some advanced thinkers are made miserable by this, will the NCAA's censors offer relief? Scottsdale Community College in Arizona was wise to adopt the nickname Fighting Artichokes. There is no grievance group representing the lacerated feelings of artichokes. Yet.

[JANUARY 5, 2006]

Christmas at Our Throats

ORANGE CITY, FLORIDA—*A mob of shoppers rushing for a sale on DVD players trampled the first woman in line and knocked her unconscious as they scrambled for the shelves at a Wal-Mart Supercenter.* —ASSOCIATED PRESS

In sorting out the sociological significance of the fact that rival shoppers, according to the trampled woman's sister, "walked over her like a herd of elephants," note that elephants do not behave that way to others of their species, even when they are stampeded by a 6 a.m. siren announcing, on the famously anarchic day after Thanksgiving, open season on a finite supply of $29 DVD players. But, then, elephants do not have Christmas celebrations.

Conservatives, in their simplistic way, will blame the Florida trampling on facets of human nature to which the Christmas story pertains—mankind's fallen condition, meaning original sin. Liberals, being less judgmental and more alert to the social causes of things, will blame Wal-Mart. They already blame it for many flaws in creation, from low wages in Asia to America's "loss of community," by which liberals mean the migration of shoppers from large-hearted Main Street merchants to the superior variety and lower prices at the Wal-Mart on the edge of town.

But at the risk of sounding like Ebenezer Scrooge, who was *not* the character in English literature who said, "We shall soon be having Christmas at our throats," consider a possibility. Perhaps, as liberals like to say, the "root cause" of modern Christmas discontents is the ruinous success of Puritanism—ruinous, that is, to Puritanism.

That Christmas-at-our-throats fellow is a character in a novel by P. G. Wodehouse, who was as sweet-tempered as Scrooge was not. If the Christmas season, as it has become, could cause the preternaturally amiable Wodehouse to pen such a dark thought, how did it come to this?

That God works in mysterious ways is not news, but it is particularly puzzling that the birth of Jesus occurred when Romans, who then set the tone of the times, were celebrating Saturnalia—think of a Wal-Mart at 6 a.m., plus wine, women wearing less than those little Wal-Mart vests, and songs that are not carols. Songs that would not have been amusing to Oliver Cromwell, whose piety caused him to ban the celebration of Christmas.

He did the right thing for the wrong reason. A Puritan scold and a killjoy, he thought Christmas had become too much fun, which is *not* our problem today, unless getting trampled at a mall is your idea of merriment.

Today's problem, in addition to the toll taken on the body by seasonal wassailing and gorging, is shopping that includes stocking up on "retaliation presents." They are used to counter unexpected gift giving by persons not on your list, which by now includes family, friends, the stockbroker who got you out of Enron in time, and the person who cleans your gutters.

The first Americans included a number of Cromwell's fellow travelers, who, like him, saw the long arm of the papacy behind Christmas festiveness. It was, they thought, a short slide down a slippery slope from liturgical "smells and bells" to jingle bells and mulled cider. But in a delicious dialectic, the modern hedonistic Christmas emerged from the cultural contradictions of Puritanism.

Puritanism inculcated Scrooge-like asceticism, deferral of gratification, green-eyeshade parsimony, and nose-to-the-grindstone industriousness. But those led to accumulation, investment of surplus capital, and,

in time, prodigies of production and a subversive—to Puritanism—
cornucopia of material delights.

Soon there were department stores, those cathedrals of consumption. Against their plate-glass windows—prerequisites of "window
shopping"; precursors of the holiday shopping catalog—were pressed
the noses of the Puritans' descendants.

Those noses no longer detected a sulfurous stench of damnation
wafting from the stores' perfume counters. Those counters, you may
have noticed, are strategically placed on the stores' first floors, to start
the shoppers' pleasure synapses firing.

The Wal-Mart stampede style of Christmas was a long time coming. It was, for example, not until 1885 that federal workers were even
given Christmas Day off. Which, come to think about it, is odd. Here
in modern Washington, Christmas Day is one of the minority of days
that are *not* like Christmas elsewhere—not devoted to the lavish dis-
bursal of gifts.

At least a portion of the government's largesse can be considered a
gift because part of the cost is debt that will be paid by others. By future generations. They are not consulted, but surely they will pay
cheerfully, in the Christmas spirit.   [DECEMBER 4, 2003]

Chapter Five

LEARNING

National Amnesia and Planting Cut Flowers

The 9/11 summons to seriousness ended the nation's 1990s holiday from history, and even the National Endowment for the Humanities has enlisted in the war. Emphasizing that historical illiteracy threatens homeland security—people cannot defend what they cannot define—the NEH's chairman, Bruce Cole, is repairing the ravages of the 1990s, when his two immediate predecessors made the NEH frivolous.

The first was Sheldon Hackney, a former college president whose big idea was a "national conversation" about diversity, his peculiar theory being that there is insufficient talk about that subject. His NEH distributed instructional kits telling Americans how to converse.

The second NEH chairman of the Clinton administration was William Ferris, a Mississippi folklorist guided by today's hedonistic calculus—the greatest self-esteem for the greatest number. His NEH worked to "celebrate"—preferred verb of the warriors against intellectual elitism—the quotidian. He said: "Today the lives of ordinary American people have assumed a place beside volumes of European classics in the humanities." So *Middlemarch* and the "life" of your mailman are equally humanities classics.

Back then, the chairman of the National Endowment for the Arts was another folklorist, Bill Ivey, whose definition of art was latitudinarian. It included "the expressive behavior of ordinary people," such as "piecrust designs" and "dinner-table arrangements." He talked like this: "Do we want to possess a confidence that the rich cultural matrix of our nation is appropriately auditioned for the world?"

That was then. This is now:

Cole, author of fourteen books, many on the Renaissance, was for twenty-nine years a professor of fine arts, art history, and comparative literature at Indiana University. One of his missions is to reverse America's deepening amnesia, and especially the historical illiteracy of college students.

Fresh evidence of the latter came last week from the National Association of Scholars, whose members defend academic standards against the depredations of those levelers who, rigorous only in applying the hedonistic calculus (see above), are draining rigor from curricula. A survey sponsored by the NAS, using questions on general cultural knowledge originally asked by the Gallup Organization in 1955, establishes that today's college seniors score little—if any—higher than 1955 *high school* graduates.

In his office in the Old Post Office on Pennsylvania Avenue, Cole says of the war on terrorism, "What we fight for is part of what we do around here." What the NEH aims to help do is "make good citizens." And "scholarship should be the basis of all we do." Not all scholars are professors. David McCullough, the historian and biographer, is not an academic. But, then, neither were Thucydides and Gibbon.

"A wise historian," says McCullough, "has said that to try to plan for the future without a sense of the past is like trying to plant cut flowers." Hence the three components of the NEH's "We the People" initiative.

One is the funding of scholarship on significant events and themes that enhance understanding of America's animating principles. Another is an essay contest for high school juniors, concerning America's defining tenets. The contest winner—Cole dryly notes that there will be a winner, whatever the cost to anyone's self-esteem—will be recognized at the third component of the "We the People" initiative, the annual "Heroes of History" lecture.

The very subject of this new lecture series goes against the grain of today's academic culture, which rejects the idea of heroes—those rare event-making individuals who are better and more important than most people. To banish elites from the human story, many academic historians tell that story as one of vast impersonal forces, in which individuals are in the iron grip of economic, racial, or gender roles. Small wonder students turn away from history taught without the drama of autonomous individuals moved by reason, conviction, and rhetoric that appeals to the better angels of their natures.

Cole soon will have a worthy colleague at the National Endowment for the Arts. The fact that its new chairman will be Dana Gioia, the distinguished poet, critic, and translator, is additional evidence that cultural revival is a priority of today's president, who has so many despisers among the lettered.

George W. Bush is married to a librarian and his vice president is married to a former NEH chairman. Bush may have passed through Yale largely unscathed by what his professors were professing (which is just as well, considering campus conditions in the 1960s). However, he is restoring both endowments to their proper functions, defending culture as the poet Allen Tate defined it—"the study of perfection, and the constant effort to achieve it." [DECEMBER 26, 2002]

A Sensory Blitzkrieg of Surfaces

The first modern celebrity—the first person who, although not conspicuous in church or state, still made his work and life fascinating to a broad public—may have been Charles Dickens. Novelist Jane Smiley so argues in her slender life of Dickens, and her point is particularly interesting in light of *Reading at Risk,* the National Endowment for the Arts' report on the decline of reading.

A survey of 17,135 persons reveals an accelerating decline in the reading of literature, especially among the young. Literary reading declined 5 percent between 1982 and 1992, then 14 percent in the next decade. Only 56.9 percent of Americans say they read a book of any sort in the past year, down from 60.9 percent in 1992. Only 46.7 percent of adults read any literature for pleasure.

The good news is that "literature," as the survey defined it, excludes serious history, for which there is a sizable audience. The bad news is that any fiction counts as literature, and most fiction, like most of most things, is mediocre. But even allowing for the survey's methodological problems, the declining importance of reading in the menu of modern recreations is unsurprising and unsettling.

Dickens, a volcano of words, provided mass entertainment before modern technologies—electricity, film, broadcasting—made mass communication easy. His serialized novels seized the attention of the British public. And America's: Ships arriving from England with the latest installment of Dickens's 1840 novel *The Old Curiosity Shop* reportedly were greeted by American dockworkers shouting, "Did Little Nell die?"

When journalists in 1910 asked an aide to Teddy Roosevelt whether TR might run for president in 1912, the aide replied, "Barkis is willin'," and he expected most journalists, and their readers, to recognize the reference to the wagon driver in *David Copperfield* who was more than merely willin' to marry Clara Peggotty, David's childhood nurse.

Exposure to *David Copperfield* used to be a common facet of reaching adulthood in America. But today, young adults eighteen to thirty-four, once the most avid readers, are among the least. This surely has something to do with the depredations of higher education: Professors, lusting after tenure and prestige, teach that the great works of the Western canon, properly deconstructed, are not explorations of the human spirit but mere reflections of power relations and social pathologies.

By 1995—*before* the flood of video games and computer entertainments for adults—television swallowed 40 percent of Americans' free time, up one-third since 1965. Today, electronic entertainments other than television fill 5.5 hours of the average child's day.

There have been times when reading was regarded with suspicion. Some among the ancient Greeks regarded the rise of reading as cultural decline: They considered oral dialogue, which involves clarifying questions, more hospitable to truth. But the transition from an oral to a print culture has generally been a transition from a tribal society to a society of self-consciously separated individuals. In Europe, that transition alarmed ruling elites, who thought the "crisis of literacy" was that there was too much literacy: readers had, inconveniently, minds of their own. Reading is inherently private, hence the reader is beyond state supervision or crowd psychology.

Which suggests why there are perils in the transition from a print to an electronic culture. Time was, books were the primary means of knowing things. Now most people learn most things visually, from the graphic presentation of immediately, effortlessly accessible pictures.

People grow accustomed to the narcotic effect of their own passive reception of today's sensory blitzkrieg of surfaces. They recoil from the more demanding nature of active engagement with the nuances encoded in the limitless permutations of twenty-six signs on pages. Besides, reading requires two things that are increasingly scarce and to which increasing numbers of Americans seem allergic—solitude and silence.

In 1940, a British officer on Dunkirk beach sent London a three-word message: "But if not." It was instantly recognized as from the book of Daniel. When Shadrach, Meshach, and Abednego are commanded to worship a golden image or perish, they defiantly reply: "Our God who we serve is able to deliver us from the burning fiery furnace, and He will deliver us out of thine hand, O king. But if not, be it known unto thee, O king, that we will not serve thy gods. . . ."

Britain then still had the cohesion of a common culture of shared reading. That cohesion enabled Britain to stay the hand of Hitler, a fact pertinent to today's new age of barbarism. [JULY 23, 2004]

"Philosophy Teaching by Examples"

When Yale awarded President Kennedy an honorary degree, he said he had the ideal combination—a Yale degree and a Harvard education. Today, he might rethink that, given the Harvard faculty's tantrum that caused President Lawrence Summers' cringing crawl away from his suggestion of possible gender differences of cognition. At least the phrase "Yale education" does not yet seem, as "Harvard education" does, oxymoronic.

And will not while Donald Kagan adorns Yale's campus, where he is professor of history and classics. Last week in Washington, he delivered the thirty-fourth Jefferson Lecture in the Humanities, "In Defense of History," which was agreeably subversive of several sides in today's culture wars.

"The world we live in," he said, "is a difficult place to try to make a case for the value of history." The essence of the historian's craft—the search for truth by painstaking research unassisted by revelation or other recourse to supernatural explanations—is embattled from two directions.

Some intellectuals today are know-nothings—literally and proudly. They argue that objectivity is a chimera, that we cannot confidently know anything of truth or virtue. These postmodernists argue, Kagan says, that all studies, including history, are "literature" because all knowledge is guesswork colored by politics—self-interest, ideology, power relationships, etc.

Those who most confidently dispute this idea derive their confidence from religious faith, arguing that only through religion can individuals, or societies, know and steadily adhere to valid standards of right and wrong. This translates into a religious litmus test in politics—only devout individuals should be chosen to lead societies.

Historians, however, say to the postmodernists that the defining characteristics of postmodernism—skepticism and cynicism—have long histories. And the historians' riposte to those who say that religion is the only foundation for knowledge or virtue is, Kagan says, to insist that in the study of history, knowledge, far from impossible, is cumulative.

Herodotus, whom Kagan calls the first true historian, said he wrote to preserve the memory of "great and marvelous deeds" and the reasons they were done. All writers of history have "the responsibility of preserving the great, important and instructive actions of human beings," says Kagan, which is why history is "the queen of the humanities," ranking above literature and even philosophy.

Philosophy, he says, is valuable for untangling sloppy thinking. But philosophy, like religion, leads to investigations of first principles and ultimate reality, and such investigations have produced profound disagreement. Hence the primacy of history as the study from which, especially today, we can take our moral bearings:

"Religion and the traditions based on it were once the chief sources for moral confidence and strength. Their influence has faded in the modern world, but the need for a sound base for moral judgments has not. If we cannot look simply to moral guidance firmly founded on religious precepts, it is natural and reasonable to turn to history, the record of human experience, as a necessary supplement if not a substitute."

Kagan's idea is not novel. Nearly three centuries ago, Lord Bolingbroke said that "history is philosophy teaching by examples." However, at this American moment of mutual incomprehension and even contempt between theists and their postmodernist despisers, it is "transgressive"—to purloin a bit of the postmodernists' jargon—for Kagan to insist that there is a firm middle, or perhaps higher, ground for moral confidence.

This ground, he says, is occupied by neither those who say that only theological reasoning leads to certainty nor those who say that no reasoning does. It is held by those who study and write history.

The late Daniel Boorstin, historian and librarian of Congress, said that "trying to plan for the future without knowing the past is like trying to plant cut flowers." His point was that knowledge of history is conducive to practicality. Kagan's point is that history, properly studied, is conducive to virtues, of which practicality is one.

Moderation is the virtue of which hubris is the opposite—and often ruinous—political vice. Historian David McCullough says the study of history is "an antidote to the hubris of the present—the idea that everything we have and everything we do and everything we think is the ultimate, the best." Compare, for example, the heroic construction of the Panama Canal and the debacle of Boston's "Big Dig" one hundred years later.

Near the Big Dig sits today's Harvard, another refutation of the theory of mankind's inevitable, steady ascent. From Yale, however, comes Kagan's temperate affirmation of the cumulative knowledge that comes from the study of history.   [MAY 19, 2005]

Fascinating Contingencies

When George Washington, in a spiffy uniform of buff and blue and sitting his horse with a grace uncommon even among Virginians vain about their horsemanship, arrived outside Boston in July 1775 to assume command of the American rebellion, he was aghast. When he got a gander at his troops, mostly New Englanders, his reaction was akin to the Duke of Wellington's assessment of his troops, many of them the sweepings of Britain's slums, during the Peninsular War: "I don't know what effect these men will have upon the enemy, but, by God, they terrify me."

You think today's red state–blue state antagonism is unprecedented? Washington thought New Englanders "exceeding dirty and nasty." He would not have disputed the British general John Burgoyne's description of the Americans besieging Boston as "a rabble in arms." A rabble that consumed, by one sober estimate, a bottle of rum per man each day.

If, in the autumn of 1775, a council of Washington's officers had not restrained him from a highly risky amphibious attack on Boston across the shallow Back Bay, there might never have been a Declaration of Independence. If a young officer, Henry Knox, had not had the ingenuity to conceive, and the tenacity to execute, a plan for dragging captured mortars, some weighing a ton, and cannon, some weighing two and a half tons, the three hundred miles from Fort Ticonderoga on Lake Champlain to the Dorchester Heights overlooking Boston, the British might have fought, and perhaps won, rather than evacuating the city. If after the disastrous Battle of Brooklyn, the first great battle of the war, a fog had not allowed nine thousand of Washington's soldiers to escape across the East River, the war might have effectively ended less than two months after the Declaration.

So says David McCullough in his new book, 1776, a birthday card to his country on this Independence Day. "Ingratitude," he has said elsewhere, "is a shabby failing," and he writes to inspire gratitude for what a few good men, and one great one, did in the nation's Year One.

What British historian George Otto Trevelyan said of the December 1776 Battle of Trenton, which may have saved the Revolution, could be said of all the events—defeats redeemed by skillful retreats, and a few victories—of that year: "It may be doubted whether so small a number of men ever employed so short a space of time with greater and more lasting effects upon the history of the world."

What is history? The study of it—and the making of it, meaning politics—changed for the worse when, in the nineteenth century, history became History. When, that is, history stopped being the record of fascinating contingencies—political, intellectual, social, economic—

that produced the present, and became instead a realm of necessity. The idea that History is a proper noun, denoting an autonomous process unfolding a predetermined future in accordance with laws mankind cannot amend, is called historicism. That doctrine discounts human agency, reducing even large historical figures to playthings of vast impersonal forces. McCullough knows better.

Solid, unpretentious narrative history like *1776* satisfies the healthy human thirst for a ripping good story. McCullough says E. M. Forster, the novelist, efficiently defined a story: If you are told that the king died and then the queen died, that is a sequence of events. If you are told that the king died and then the queen died of grief, that is a story that elicits empathy.

Using narrative history to refute historicism, McCullough's two themes in *1776* are that things could have turned out very differently, and that individuals of character can change the destinies of nations. There is a thirst for both themes in this country, which is in a less-than-festive frame of mind on this birthday. It is, therefore, serendipitous that *1776,* with 1.35 million copies already in print, sits atop the *New York Times* bestseller list on Independence Day.

But, then, serendipity has often attended the Fourth of July. That day is the birthday of Nathaniel Hawthorne (1804), arguably the father of American literature. And of Stephen Foster (1826), arguably the father of American music. And—saving the most luminous for last—of the sainted Calvin Coolidge (1872), who oversaw a 45 percent increase in America's production of ice cream.

So, this Fourth read McCullough. Perhaps by the light of a sparkler.

[JULY 3, 2005]

Ed Schools vs. Education

The surest, quickest way to add quality to primary and secondary education would be addition by subtraction: Close all the schools of education. Consider the *Chronicle of Higher Education*'s recent report concerning the schools that certify America's teachers.

Many education schools discourage, even disqualify, prospective teachers who lack the correct "disposition," meaning those who do not embrace today's "progressive" political catechism. Karen Siegfried had a 3.75 grade-point average at the University of Alaska Fairbanks, but after voicing conservative views, she was told by her education professors that she lacked the "professional disposition" teachers need. She is now studying to be an aviation technician.

In 2002, the National Council for Accreditation of Teacher Education declared that a "professional disposition" is "guided by beliefs and attitudes related to values such as caring, fairness, honesty, responsibility, and social justice." Regarding that last, the *Chronicle* reports that the University of Alabama's College of Education proclaims itself "committed to preparing individuals to"—what? "Read, write, and reason"? No, "to promote social justice, to be change agents, and to recognize individual and institutionalized racism, sexism, homophobia, and classism," and to "break silences" about those things and "develop anti-racist, anti-homophobic, anti-sexist community [*sic*] and alliances."

Brooklyn College, where a professor of education required her class on Language Literacy in Secondary Education to watch *Fahrenheit 9/11* before the 2004 election, says it educates teacher candidates about, among many other evils, "heterosexism." The University of Alaska Fairbanks, fluent with today's progressive patois, says that, given America's "caste-like system," teachers must be taught "how racial and cultural 'others' negotiate American school systems, and how they perform their identities." Got it?

The permeation of education schools by politics is a consequence of the vacuity of their curricula. Concerning that, read "Why Johnny's Teacher Can't Teach," by Heather Mac Donald of the Manhattan Institute (available at city-journal.org). Today's teacher-education focus on "professional disposition" is just the latest permutation of what Mac Donald calls the education schools' "immutable dogma," which she calls "Anything But Knowledge."

The dogma has been that primary and secondary education is about "self-actualization" or "finding one's joy" or "social adjustment" or "multicultural sensitivity" or "minority empowerment." But is never about anything as banal as mere knowledge. It is about "constructing one's own knowledge" and "contextualizing knowledge," but never about knowledge of things like biology or history.

Mac Donald says "the central educational fallacy of our time," which dates from the Progressive Era of the early twentieth century, is "that one can think without having anything to think about." At City College of New York, a professor said that in her course Curriculum and Teaching in Elementary Education she would be "building a community, rich of talk" and "getting the students to develop the subtext of what they're doing." Although ed schools fancy themselves as surfers on the wave of the future, Mac Donald believes that teacher education "has been more unchanging than Miss Havisham. Like aging vestal virgins, today's schools lovingly guard the ancient flame of progressivism"—an egalitarianism with two related tenets.

One, says Mac Donald, is that "to accord teachers any superior role in the classroom would be to acknowledge an elite hierarchy of knowledge, possessed by some but not all." Hence, second, emphasis should be on group projects rather than individual accomplishments that are measured by tests that reveal persistent achievement gaps separating whites and Asians from other minorities.

Numerous inner-city charter and private schools are proving that the gaps can be narrowed, even closed, when rigorous pedagogy is practiced by teachers in teacher-centered classrooms where knowledge is regarded as everything. But most ed schools, celebrating "child-centered classrooms" that do not "suffocate discourses," are enemies of rigor.

The steady drizzle of depressing data continues. A new assessment of adult literacy shows a sharp decline over the last decade, with only 31 percent of college graduates able to read and extrapolate from complex material. They were supposed to learn how to read before college, but perhaps their teachers were too busy proving their "professional dispositions" by "breaking silences" as "change agents."

Fewer than half of U.S. eighth graders have math teachers who majored in math as undergraduates or graduate students or studied math for teacher certification. U.S. twelfth graders recently performed below the international average for twenty-one countries on tests of general knowledge of math and science. But perhaps U.S. pupils excel when asked to "perform their identities."   [JANUARY 16, 2006]

This Just In from the Professors: Conservatism Is a Mental Illness

This just in: Conservatism often is symptomatic of a psychological syndrome. It can involve fear, aggression, uncertainty avoidance, intolerance of ambiguity, dogmatic dislike of equality, irrational nostalgia, and need for "cognitive closure," all aspects of the authoritarian personality.

Actually, this theory has been floating around academic psychology for half a century. It is reprised in "Political Conservatism as Motivated Social Cognition," written by four professors for *Psychological Bulletin*.

"Motivated social cognition" refers to the "motivational underpinnings" of ideas, the "situational as well as dispositional variables" that foster particular beliefs. Notice: situations and dispositions—not reasons. Professors have reasons for their beliefs. Other people, particularly conservatives, have social and psychological explanations for their beliefs. "Motivated cognition" involves ways of seeing and reasoning about the world that are unreasonable because they arise from emotional, psychological needs.

The professors note, "The practice of singling out political conservatives for special study began . . . [with a 1950] study of authoritarianism and the fascist potential in personality." The industry of studying the sad psychology of conservatism is booming. It began with a European mixture of Marxism and Freudianism. It often involves a hash of unhistorical judgments, including the supposedly scientific, value-free judgment that conservatives are authoritarians, and that fascists—e.g., the socialist Mussolini, and Hitler, the National Socialist who wanted to conserve *nothing*—were conservatives.

The four professors now contribute "theories of epistemic and existential needs, and socio-political theories of ideology as individual and collective rationalizations" and "defensive motivations"—defenses against fear of uncertainty and resentment of equality. The professors have ideas; the rest of us have emanations of our psychological needs and neuroses.

"In the post-Freudian world, the ancient dichotomy between reason and passion is blurred," say the professors, who do not say that *their* judgments arise from social situations or emotional needs rather than reason. The professors usefully survey the vast literature churned out by the legions of academics who have searched for the unsavory or pathological origins of conservatism (fear of death? harsh parenting? the "authoritarian personality"?).

But it is difficult to take the professors' seriousness seriously when they say, in an essay responding to a critique of their paper, that Ronald Reagan's "chief accomplishment, in effect, was to roll back both the New Deal and the 1960s." His "accomplishment"? So *that* is why Social Security and Medicare disappeared.

The professors write, "One is justified in referring to Hitler, Mussolini, Reagan, and Limbaugh as right-wing conservatives . . . because they all preached a return to an idealized past and favored or condoned inequality in some form." Until the professors give examples of political people who do not favor or condone equality *in any form,* it is fair to conclude that, for all their pretensions to scientific rigor, they are remarkably imprecise. And they are very political people, who would be unlikely ever to begin a sentence: "One is justified in referring to Stalin, Mao, Franklin Roosevelt and the editors of the *New York Times* as left-wing liberals because . . ."

The professors acknowledge that "the same motives may underlie different beliefs." And "different motives may underlie the same beliefs." And "motivational and informational influences on belief formation are not incompatible." And no reasoning occurs in a "motivational vacuum." And "virtually all belief systems" are embraced because they "satisfy some psychological needs." And all this "does not mean that conservatism is pathological or that conservative beliefs are necessarily false."

Not *necessarily*. What a relief. But there is no comparable academic industry devoted to studying the psychological underpinnings of liberalism. Liberals, you see, embrace liberalism for an obvious and uncomplicated reason—liberalism is self-evidently true. But conservatives embrace conservatism for reasons that must be excavated from their inner turmoils, many of them pitiable or disreputable.

The professors' paper is adorned with this epigraph:

> *"Conservatism is a demanding mistress and is giving me a migraine."*   —GEORGE F. WILL

A "mistress" who is "demanding"? Freud, call your office. The epigraph is from *Bunts,* a book of baseball essays, from an essay concerning what conservatives should think about the designated hitter. Will probably *thought* he was being lighthearted. Silly him. Actually, he was struggling with fear of ambiguity and the need for cognitive closure.

Conservatives, in the crippling grip of motivated social cognition, *think* they oppose the DH because it makes the game less interesting by reducing managers' strategic choices. But they *really* oppose that innovation because mental rigidity makes them phobic about change and intolerant of the ambiguous status of the DH. And because Mussolini would have opposed the DH.   [AUGUST 10, 2003]

The Law of Group Polarization in Academia

Republicans Outnumbered in Academia, Studies Find
                                        —*New York Times,* November 18

Oh, well, if *studies* say so. The great secret is out: Liberals dominate campuses. Coming soon: "Moon Implicated in Tides, Studies Find."

One study of one thousand professors finds that Democrats outnumber Republicans at least seven to one in the humanities and social sciences. That imbalance, more than double what it was three decades ago, is intensifying because younger professors are more uniformly liberal than the older cohort that is retiring.

Another study, of voter registrations records, including those of professors in engineering and the hard sciences, found 9 Democrats for every Republican at Berkeley and Stanford. Among younger professors, there were 183 Democrats, 6 Republicans.

But we essentially knew this even before the *American Enterprise* magazine reported in 2002 of examinations of voting records in various college communities. Some findings about professors registered with the two major parties or with liberal or conservative minor parties:

Cornell:	166 liberals, 6 conservatives
Stanford:	151 liberals, 17 conservatives
Colorado:	116 liberals, 5 conservatives
UCLA:	141 liberals, 9 conservatives

The nonpartisan Center for Responsive Politics reports that in 2004, of the top five institutions in terms of employee per capita contributions to presidential candidates, the third, fourth, and fifth were Time Warner, Goldman Sachs, and Microsoft. The top two were the University of California system and Harvard, both of which gave about nineteen times more money to John Kerry than to George Bush.

But George Lakoff, a linguistics professor at Berkeley, denies that academic institutions are biased against conservatives. The disparity in hiring, he explains, occurs because conservatives are not as interested as liberals in academic careers. Why does he think liberals are like that? "Unlike conservatives, they believe in working for the public good and social justice."

That clears that up.

A filtering process, from graduate school admissions through tenure decisions, tends to exclude conservatives from what Mark Bauerlein calls academia's "sheltered habitat." In a dazzling essay in the *Chronicle of Higher Education,* Bauerlein, professor of English at Emory University and director of research at the National Endowment for the Arts, notes that the "first protocol" of academic society is the "common assumption"—that, at professional gatherings, all the strangers in the room are liberals.

It is a reasonable assumption, given that in order to enter the profession, your work must be deemed, by the criteria of the prevailing culture, "relevant." Bauerlein says various academic fields now have regnant premises that embed political orientations in their very definitions of scholarship:

"Schools of education, for instance, take constructivist theories of learning as definitive, excluding realists (in matters of knowledge) on principle, while the quasi-Marxist outlook of cultural studies rules out those who espouse capitalism. If you disapprove of affirmative action, forget pursuing a degree in African-American studies. If you think that the nuclear family proves the best unit of social well-being, stay away from women's studies."

This gives rise to what Bauerlein calls the "false consensus effect," which occurs when, due to institutional provincialism, "people think that the collective opinion of their own group matches that of the larger population." There also is what Cass Sunstein, professor of political science and jurisprudence at the University of Chicago, calls "the law of group polarization." Bauerlein explains: "When like-minded people deliberate as an organized group, the general opinion shifts toward extreme versions of their common beliefs." They become tone-deaf to the way they sound to others outside their closed circle of belief.

When John Kennedy brought to Washington such academics as Arthur Schlesinger Jr., John Kenneth Galbraith, McGeorge and William Bundy, and Walt Rostow, it was said that the Charles River was flowing into the Potomac. Actually, Richard Nixon's administration had an even more distinguished academic cast—Henry Kissinger, Pat Moynihan, Arthur Burns, James Schlesinger, and others.

Academics, such as the next secretary of state, still decorate Washington, but academia is less listened to than it was. It has marginalized itself, partly by political shrillness and silliness that have something to do with the parochialism produced by what George Orwell called "smelly little orthodoxies."

Many campuses are intellectual versions of one-party nations—

except such nations usually have the merit, such as it is, of candor about their ideological monopolies. In contrast, American campuses have more insistently proclaimed their commitment to diversity as they have become more intellectually monochrome.

They do indeed cultivate diversity—in race, skin color, ethnicity, sexual preference. In everything but thought.   [NOVEMBER 28, 2004]

Antioch College's Epitaph

During the campus convulsions of the late 1960s, when rebellion against any authority was considered obedience to every virtue, the film *To Die in Madrid,* a documentary about the Spanish civil war, was shown at a small liberal arts college famous for, and vain about, its dedication to all things progressive. When the film's narrator intoned, "The rebels advanced on Madrid," the students, who adored rebels and were innocent of information, cheered. Antioch College in Yellow Springs, Ohio, had been so busy turning undergraduates into vessels of liberalism and apostles of social improvement that it had not found time for the tiresome task of teaching them tedious facts, such as that the rebels in Spain were Franco's fascists.

That illustrates why it is heartening that Antioch will close after the 2007–2008 academic year. Its board of trustees says the decision is to "suspend operations" and it talks dottily about reviving the institution in 2012. There is, however, a minuscule market for what Antioch sells for a tuition, room, and board of $35,221—repressive liberalism unleavened by learning.

Founded in 1852—its first president was Horace Mann—Antioch was, for a while, admirable. One of the first colleges to enroll women and blacks, it was a destination for escaped slaves. Its alumni include Stephen Jay Gould, Coretta Scott King, and Rod Serling, whose *Twilight Zone* never imagined anything weirder than what Antioch became when its liberalism curdled.

In 1972–1973, Antioch had 2,470 students. In 1973, a protracted and embittering student and employee strike left the campus physically decrepit and intellectually toxic. By 1985, enrollment was down 80 percent. This fall there may be 300 students served by a faculty of forty.

In 1993, Antioch became an international punch line when it wrote rules to ensure that all sexual conduct would be consensual, step by minute step: "If the level of sexual intimacy increases during an interaction . . . the people involved need to express their clear verbal consent before moving to that new level." Does consent to a *touch* cover a *caress*? Is there consent regarding *all* the buttons?

Although laughable, Antioch was not funny. Former public radio correspondent Michael Goldfarb matriculated at what he calls the "sociological petri dish" in 1968. In his first week, he twice had guns drawn on him, once "in fun" and once by a couple of drunken ex-cons "whom one of my classmates, in the interest of breaking down class barriers, had invited to live with her." A true Antiochian still, Goldfarb says: "I do think I was made stronger for having to deal with these experiences."

Steven Lawry—Antioch's fifth president in thirteen years—came to the college eighteen months ago. He told Scott Carlson of the *Chronicle of Higher Education* about a student who left after being assaulted because he wore Nike shoes, symbols of globalization. Another left because, she told Lawry, the political climate was suffocating: "They all think they are so different, but they are just a bunch of conformists."

Carlson reports that Lawry stopped the student newspaper's practice of printing "announcements containing anonymous, menacing threats against other students for their political views." Antioch likes to dabble in menace: It invited Mumia Abu-Jamal to deliver its 2000 commencement speech, which he recorded on death row in a Pennsylvania prison, where he lives because twenty-six years ago he shot a Philadelphia police officer first in the back, then three times in the face. Antioch's invitation was its way of saying . . . what?

In an essay in the *Chronicle,* Cary Nelson, Antioch class of 1967 and now a professor of English at the University of Illinois, waxes nostalgic about the fun he had spending, as Antioch students did, much time away from campus, receiving academic credits. What Nelson calls "my employee resistance to injustice" got him "released from almost every job I had until I became a faculty member." But "my little expenditure was never noticed" when "I used some of Lyndon Johnson's anti-poverty money" to bus anti-Vietnam war protesters from Harlem to Washington.

Given that such was Antioch's idea of "work experience" in the "real world," it is unsurprising that the college never produced an alumni cohort capable of enlarging the college's risible $36 million endowment. Besides, the college seems always to have considered raising money beneath its dignity, given its nobility.

"Ben & Jerry could have named a new flavor for us," says John Feinberg, class of 1970 and president of the alumni board, with a melancholy sense of unfulfilled destiny. His lament for a forfeited glory is a suitable epitaph for Antioch.   [JULY 15, 2007]

A Scholar's Malfeasance Gunned Down

In a large event, much commented on, the Justice Department last week told the Supreme Court that the Second Amendment ("A well regulated Militia, being necessary to the security of a free State, the right of the people to keep and bear Arms, shall not be infringed") "broadly protects the rights of individuals," not just the right of states to organize militias.

This event was pertinent to a small event two weeks earlier, noticed by almost no one. The National Endowment for the Humanities demanded a review of "the serious charges that have been made against Michael Bellesiles' scholarship," which the NEH helped to finance.

He is the Emory University historian whose 2000 book *Arming America: The Origins of a National Gun Culture* earned—well, received—critical acclaim, including the Bancroft Prize, the most distinguished prize in American history. But now, slowly but relentlessly, some responsible intellectuals are defending standards of scholarship.

Bellesiles's thesis is startling. It is that guns were not widely owned, or reliable enough to be important, at the time the Second Amendment was written. The implication is that the amendment should be read to protect only the collective rights of states, not the rights of individuals. The book pleased partisans of a cause popular in the liberal political culture of academia—gun control. Reviews were rapturous: "exhaustive research," "intellectual rigor," "inescapable policy implications," "the NRA's worst nightmare."

Not exactly.

What has become Bellesiles's nightmare began when a historian, suspecting nothing and hoping to build upon Bellesiles's data, asked for more details about the eighteenth- and early-nineteenth-century probate records that Bellesiles says show that guns were infrequently listed among the estates of deceased people. He also purported to find that many of the guns that were listed were in disrepair.

When Bellesiles's evasive response led to more tugging on the threads of his argument, it unraveled. The unraveling revealed a pattern of gross misstatements of facts and unfounded conclusions. His errors are so consistently convenient for his thesis, it is difficult to believe that the explanation is mere sloppiness or incompetence. It looks like fraud.

Responding to critics, he said some of his crucial research notes had been destroyed in a flood in his office. He said he had relied on microfilm records in the federal archive in East Point, Georgia. But it has no such records. He said he had examined probate records in thirty places around the country, such as the San Francisco Superior Court. But those records were destroyed in the 1906 earthquake.

Well, then, he said he had seen them in the Contra Costa County Historical Society. But the society has no such records, and no record of Bellesiles's visiting the society. Then he said he did the research somewhere else, but is not sure where. Researchers have found that he consistently misrepresents extant records in Providence, Rhode Island, and Vermont. When he tried to buttress his case by posting evidence on his website, critics found grave errors there, too, purporting to support his thesis. He blamed the errors on a hacker. A hacker who attacked his website on his behalf?

This spring, the *William and Mary Quarterly,* the preeminent journal of early American history, undertook to referee this rumble, publishing essays from historians on aspects of Bellesiles's argument, and a response from him. The criticism is lacerating ("nonsense"; "boggles the mind"; "he regularly uses evidence in a partial or imprecise way"; "gives the impression that he has shaped his figures to suit his argument"; "every tally of homicides Bellesiles reports is either misleading or wrong"). Bellesiles's limping response (which begins with a jest about a French mutineer saying to his firing squad, "I am honored by all this attention") tries to change the subject, to the meaning of "culture."

This academic scandal is still several chapters from a satisfactory resolution. Emory, having taken the unusual step of directing Bellesiles to respond to his critics, now is conducting its own investigation, which must weigh the patent inadequacies of his responses so far, and the proper penalty for what has already been proved. Furthermore, do those responsible for awarding him the Bancroft Prize believe the award should be revoked?

Bellesiles's malfeasance, although startling in its sweep, brazenness, and apparently political purpose, actually reveals something heartening—a considerable strength in America's scholarly community. Its critical apparatus is working. Scholars and their journals are doing their duty, which is to hold works of scholarship up to the bright light of high standards.

As a result, when next the Supreme Court is required to rule on the controversy concerning which Bellesiles's book was supposed to be so decisively informative, the court's judgment will not be clouded by Bellesiles's evident attempt to misrepresent the context in which the Framers wrote the Second Amendment.   [MAY 20, 2002]

Juggling Scarves in the Therapeutic Nation

It hurt her feelings, says Jane Fonda, sharing her feelings, that one of her husbands liked them to have sexual threesomes. "It reinforced my feeling I wasn't good enough."

In the Scottsdale, Arizona, Unified School District office, the receptionist used to be called a receptionist. Now she is "director of first impressions." The happy director says, "Everyone wants to be important." Scottsdale school bus drivers now are "transporters of learners." A school official says such terminological readjustment is "a positive affirmation." Which beats a negative affirmation.

Manufacturers of pens and markers report a surge in teachers' demands for purple ink pens. When marked in red, corrections of students' tests seem so awfully judgmental. At a Connecticut school, parents consider red markings "stressful." A Pittsburgh principal favors more "pleasant-feeling tones." An Alaska teacher says substituting purple for red is compassionate pedagogy, a shift from "Here's what you need to improve on" to "Here's what you have done right."

Fonda's confession, Scottsdale's tweaking of terminology, and the recoil from red markings are manifestations of today's therapeutic culture. The nature and menace of "therapism" is the subject of a new book, *One Nation Under Therapy: How the Helping Culture Is Eroding Self-Reliance,* by Christina Hoff Sommers and Sally Satel, MD, resident scholars at the American Enterprise Institute.

From childhood on, Americans are told by "experts"—therapists, self-esteem educators, grief counselors, traumatologists—that it is healthy for them continuously to take their emotional temperature, inventory their feelings, and vent them. Never mind research indicating that reticence and suppression of feelings can be healthy.

Because children are considered terribly vulnerable and fragile, playground games like dodgeball are being replaced by anxiety-reducing and self-esteem-enhancing games of tag where nobody is ever "out." But abundant research indicates no connection between high self-esteem and high achievement or virtue. Is not unearned self-esteem a more pressing problem? Sensitivity screeners remove from texts and tests distressing references to things like rats, snakes, typhoons, blizzards, and . . . birthday parties (which might distress children who do not have them). The sensitivity police favor teaching what Sommers and Satel call "no-fault history." Hence California's Department of Education stipulating that when "ethnic or cultural groups are portrayed, portrayals must not depict differences in customs or lifestyles as undesirable"—

slavery? segregation? anti-Semitism? cannibalism?—"and must not reflect adversely on such differences."

Experts warn about what children are allowed to juggle: Tennis balls cause frustration, whereas "scarves are soft, nonthreatening, and float down slowly." In 2001, the Girl Scouts, illustrating what Sommers and Satel say is the assumption that children are "combustible bundles of frayed nerves," introduced, for girls eight to eleven, a "Stress Less Badge" adorned with an embroidered hammock. It can be earned by practicing "focused breathing," keeping a "feelings diary," burning scented candles, and exchanging foot massages.

Vast numbers of credentialed—that is not a synonym for "competent"—members of the "caring professions" have a professional stake in the myth that most people are too fragile to cope with life's vicissitudes and traumas without professional help. Consider what Sommers and Satel call "the commodification of grief" by the "grief industry"—professional grief "counselors" with "degrieving" techniques. Such "grief gurus" are "ventilationists": They assume that everyone should grieve the same way—by venting feelings sometimes elicited by persons who have paid $1,795 for a five-day course in grief counseling.

The "caregiving" professions, which postulate the minimal competence of most people to cope with life unassisted, are, of course, liberal and politics can color their diagnoses. Remember the theory that because Vietnam was supposedly an unjust war, it would produce an epidemic of "post-traumatic stress disorders." So a study released in 1990 claimed that half of Vietnam veterans suffered from some PTSD—even though only 15 percent of Vietnam veterans had served in combat units. To ventilationists—after a flood damaged books at the Boston Public Library, counselors arrived to help librarians cope with their grief—a failure to manifest grief is construed as alarming evidence of grief repressed, and perhaps a precursor of "delayed onset" PTSD.

Predictably, 9/11 became another excuse for regarding healthy human reactions as pathological. Did terrorist attacks make you angry and nervous? Must be PTSD. And 9/11 gave rise to "diagnostic mission creep" as the idea of a "trauma" was expanded to include watching a disaster on television. Sommers and Satel's book is a summons to the sensible worry that national enfeeblement must result when therapism replaces the virtues on which the republic was founded—stoicism, self-reliance, and courage.   [APRIL 21, 2005]

Nature, Nurture, and Larry Summers's Sin

HYSTERIA—A functional disturbance of the nervous system, characterized by such disorders as anaesthesia, hyperaesthesia, convulsions, etc., and usually attended with emotional disturbances and enfeeblement or perversion of the moral and intellectual faculties.   —*Oxford English Dictionary*

Forgive Larry Summers. He did not know where he was.

Addressing a conference on the supposedly insufficient numbers of women in tenured positions in university science departments, he suggested that perhaps part of the explanation might be innate—genetically based—gender differences in cognition. He thought he was speaking in a place that encourages uncircumscribed intellectual explorations. He was not. He was on a university campus.

He was at Harvard, where he is president. Since then he has become a serial apologizer and accomplished groveler. Soon he may be in a Khmer Rouge–style reeducation camp somewhere in New England, relearning this: In today's academy, no social solecism is as unforgivable as the expression of a hypothesis that offends someone's "progressive" sensibilities.

Someone like MIT biology professor Nancy Hopkins, the hysteric (see above) who, hearing Summers, "felt I was going to be sick. My heart was pounding and my breath was shallow." And, "I just couldn't breathe because this kind of bias makes me physically ill." She said that if she had not bolted from the room, "I would've either blacked out or thrown up."

Is *this* the fruit of feminism? A woman at the peak of the academic pyramid becomes theatrically flurried by an unwelcome idea and, like a Victorian maiden exposed to male coarseness, suffers the vapors and collapses on the drawing room carpet in a heap of crinolines until revived by smelling salts and the offending brute's contrition.

Hopkins's sufferings, although severe, were not incapacitating: She somehow found strength quickly to share them with the *Boston Globe* and the *Today* show, on which she confided that she just did not know whether she could bear to have lunch with Summers. But even while reeling from the onslaught of Summers's thought, she retained a flair for meretriciousness: She charged that Summers had said "that 50 percent" of "the brightest minds in America" do not have "the right aptitude" for science.

Men and women have genetically based physical differences; the brain is a physical thing—part of the body. Is it unthinkable—is it even counterintuitive—that this might help explain, for example, the familiar fact that more men than women achieve the very highest scores in mathematics aptitude tests? There is a vast and growing scientific literature on possible gender differences in cognition. Only hysterics denounce interest in those possible differences—or, in Hopkins's case, the mere mention of them—as "bias."

Hopkins's hysteria was a sample of America's campus-based indignation industry, which churns out operatic reactions to imagined slights. But her hysteria also is symptomatic of a political tendency that manifested itself in some criticism of President Bush's inaugural address, which was a manifesto about human nature.

This criticism went beyond doubts about his grandiose aspirations, to rejection of the philosophy that he might think entails such aspirations but actually does not. The philosophy of natural right— the Founders' philosophy—rests on a single proposition: There is a universal human nature.

From that fact come, through philosophic reasoning, some normative judgments: Certain social arrangements—particularly government by consent attained by persuasion in a society accepting pluralism— are right for creatures of this nature. Hence the doctrine of "natural right," and the idea of a nation "dedicated," as Lincoln said, to the "proposition" that all men are created equal.

The vehemence of the political left's recoil from this idea is explained by the investment political radicalism has had for several centuries in the notion that human beings are essentially blank slates. What predominates in determining individuals' trajectories—nature or nurture? The left says nature is negligible, nurturing is sovereign. So a properly governed society can write what it wishes on the blank slate of humanity. This maximizes the stakes of politics and the grandeur of government's role. And the importance of governing elites, who are the "progressive" vanguards of a perfected humanity.

The vehemence of Hopkins's recoil from the idea that there could be gender differences pertinent to some cognition might seem merely to reflect a crude understanding of civic equality as grounded shakily on a certain identical physicality. But her hysteria actually expresses the left's ultimate horror—the thought that nature sets limits to the malleability of human material. Summers should explain this to her, over lunch, when he returns from camp.   [JANUARY 27, 2005]

AP Harry Applies to College

"Ivies," "safeties," "AP prep courses," "legacy," "résumé-enhancing activity," "nonbinding early acceptance," "rolling admissions," "single-choice early action." If this argot is familiar to you, poor you: You have a child in high school, and these are the days that try your soul, the spring days when many college admissions are announced, often by e-mail, which is how AP Harry learned he was deferred by Harvard.

Harry is a character in Susan Coll's new novel *Acceptance,* set in Verona County, Maryland, which is the real Montgomery County, Maryland, thinly disguised—rich, liberal, full of strivers and contiguous to strivers' paradise, Washington. Harry earned the nickname AP because beginning with his freshman year he took almost every Advanced Placement course offered at Verona High School, which is so serious about placing graduates in prestigious colleges that the principal stalks the halls quizzing students on vocabulary words. For Harry, only Harvard will do.

But Harry is a white male without a legacy at Harvard, and although he got a perfect 800 on his math SAT, even with the help of private SAT prep tutoring he could boost his critical reading score only to 720. And when he got a B in an AP English course, he worried that it was the beginning of a long slide that would terminate on some skid row or, worse, at a "safety" school not among the Ivies.

Harry, who wears starched shirts and a blazer and carries a briefcase, is a real *rara avis* in Verona County—a conservative whose heroes include Trent Lott. And he is a wee bit obsessive. He has his mother quiz him to confirm that he remembers the *U.S. News & World Report*'s list—*in order*—of the top fifty liberal-arts colleges. He subscribes to a service that each day sends an SAT-type question to his cell phone. Harry taps his phone keyboard and reads:

" 'Their ideal was to combine individual liberty with material equality, a goal that has not yet been realized and that may be as [*blank*] as transmutation of lead into gold.' "

"Before Harry could continue, a small girl wearing orthodontic headgear blurted out the answer: 'A, *chimerical*.' "

Also, Harry's sentences frequently trail off into lists of synonyms useful for the SAT vocabulary test:

" 'You look kind of pale, Mom . . . *pale, sallow, pallid, wan* . . .'

"Grace forced a smile . . . '*Ashen?*' she asked.

" 'Very good, Mom,' Harry said, smiling adorably."

Grace's neighbor, who walks her dog on a Burberry leash, began fretting about college admissions during the summer before their children entered eighth grade. That neighbor hired a private college counseling service at a two-year cost of $30,000, and she signed up her daughter—who she insists preferred NPR to television at age four—for SAT prep courses three years ahead of the normal schedule.

Coll writes: "How had a test originally intended to give a smart kid stuck farming pigs in the Midwest a chance to compete with the children of the Northeastern elite morphed back into a tool to help the rich stay on top?" How? By what Coll calls the "snakepit of parental competition" among the kind of parents who send holiday letters like this:

"We are ringing in the New Year in Ireland at the behest of Bree, who was so taken with her reading of 'Ulysses' in her rapid learner reading class that we are taking a self-guided tour of Joyce's Dublin . . . Sixth grade has proven a bit dull for Bree . . . An aspiring novelist (as you may have guessed!), she plans to spend the summer honing her writing skills at a workshop at Johns Hopkins . . . Conveniently, her little brother will also be attending Johns Hopkins this summer. Gordon has been accepted into the 'HeadsUp' program for preschoolers who show an innate predisposition for design and engineering . . ."

Such parents produce children who, Coll writes, worry unhealthily as they were taught to worry in health class: "If exchanging flirty text messages was the first step toward contracting a sexually transmitted disease, a bad decision about where to apply to college would probably lead to a life of future unemployment, then homelessness, and finally exclusion from family gatherings at holidays."

Acceptance also examines the travails of the admissions official at fictional Yates College ("the Princeton of Upstate New York"), which has just had the deranging experience of cracking the *U.S. News* list at number fifty. Imagine plowing through applicants' essays "about how Mahatma Gandhi was the single greatest inspiration in these kids' lives, or how the historical figure with whom they most closely identified was Harry Potter."

The mother with the Burberry leash suggests that her daughter's college application essay begin, "Family lore has it that my first words were 'Standard Oil.' " What happens to that daughter, to Harry and other young victims of "the Verona madness"? Buy Coll's book and find out. It is hilarious and dismaying . . . *alarming, disturbing, disquieting, agitating, perturbing . . .*   [APRIL 9, 2007]

Teaching Minnows the Pleasure of Precision

L OS ANGELES—After eight years at Robert F. Kennedy Elementary School, Ethel Bojorquez knows a thing or two about teaching. She radiates calm, no-nonsense authority, and today she is watching a kindred spirit, Carole Valleskey, put Bojorquez's thirty-five fourth and fifth graders briskly through their paces.

Actually, the paces are Valleskey's. A former ballerina with the Joffrey, she now choreographs dance classes at eight fortunate Los Angeles elementary schools. For a few hours a week, Valleskey's students restrain their anarchic individualism in order to perform as a dance troupe. Think of training young minnows in synchronized swimming.

The children have high-energy encounters with high-quality popular culture—Ellington, Gershwin, Copland—that is a far cry from hip-hop. Bojorquez, whose experience has immunized her against educational fads, admiringly watches her pupils perform under Valleskey's exacting tutelage and exclaims, "They are learning about reading *right now.*"

They are, she marvels, learning about—experiencing, actually— "sequencing, patterns, inferences." She explains: "You don't only listen to language, you *do* it."

Bojorquez and Valleskey, like all teachers, function under the tyranny of the 9/91 formula: between ages six and nineteen, a child spends 9 percent of his life in school, 91 percent elsewhere. In contemporary America, "elsewhere" means immersed in the undertow of popular culture's increasingly coarse distractions. In Los Angeles, where most public school pupils are Latino (Kennedy school is almost entirely Latino), "elsewhere" often means homes where English is barely spoken.

Bojorquez's raven-haired students, their dark eyes riveted on Valleskey, mimic her motions. These beautiful children have a beautiful hunger for the satisfaction of structured, collaborative achievement.

That begins when Valleskey, a one-woman swarm, bounces into the room and immediately, without a word of command, reduces the turbulent students to silent, rapt attention. They concentrate in order to emulate Valleskey's complex syncopation of claps, finger snaps, and thigh slaps by which she sets the tone of the coming hour: This will be fun *because* things will be done precisely right.

Part Marine Corps drill instructor, part pixie, Valleskey knows that children are realists. They do not want false praise. She knows that self-esteem is result of, not a precondition for, achievement. Her credo is: Every child can do it. The antecedent of "it" is: learn how to learn.

Her students experience a kind of freedom that is, for most children, as exhilarating as it is novel. It is not merely the absence of restraints. Rather, it is the richer freedom of a cooperative group performing to high standards within a structure of rules.

Valleskey's California Dance Institute is, essentially, her and a few teaching assistants and musicians, sustained by a few exceptionally discerning philanthropists. CDI is associated with, but not financially supported by, the National Dance Institute, founded by Jacques d'Amboise, for many years a leading dancer with the New York City Ballet. He was the subject of the 1983 Academy Award–winning film *He Makes Me Feel Like Dancin'*. It explored his insight that dance—the pleasures of precision, of a task done just right—serves all the pedagogic goals of schools.

Virtues, says Valleskey, are habits, and dance, as taught by CDI, is habituation in many of the skills of learning, as well as the components of good character. Dance, properly taught, is like sport, properly understood.

The ancient Greeks considered sport *serious* play, a civic—meaning moral—undertaking. It is because man's noblest activity is active engagement, as talented performer or informed spectator, with worthy things such as beauty. Including the beauty of strenuous exertion in conformity to exacting rules and high standards. By using our bodies beautifully, we come to appreciate beauty and the discipline—the restraint—that is its prerequisite and civilization's premise.

Gifted teachers like Bojorquez and Valleskey master the patience required for the unending business of transmitting civilization down the generations, transforming biological facts—children—into social artifacts called citizens. It is wearying work, and it is a wonder teachers can summon the stamina for it. Ralph Waldo Emerson wondered:

"It must be admitted that civilization is onerous and expensive; hideous expense to keep it up;—let it go, and be Indians again; but why Indians?—that is costly, too; the mud turtle and trout life is easier and cheaper, and oyster, cheaper still."

CDI is inexpensive. Operating on a financial shoestring—a frayed shoestring—CDI is a gift to a few of this city's public schools. It makes one marvel at what educational improvements could be achieved with small sums in the service of something much scarcer than money—imagination.   [MARCH 25, 2004]

Chapter Six

GAMES

Raising Michael Oher

Even if you think football consists primarily of two regrettable elements of life—violence, punctuated by committee meetings, called huddles. Even if you wince at institutions of higher education engaging in the low practice of exploiting young, often black, men who emerge, after four years generating revenues for campus football factories, unscathed by education. Even if you think that if the Watergate and Iran-Contra investigations had been really thorough they would have traced both scandals to connivings by college football coaches. Even if you think all those things, you are going to enjoy Michael Lewis's book *The Blind Side: Evolution of a Game.* Your enjoyment, however, will be tempered by dismay about some of what you learn.

Lewis tells an amazing true story in an appropriately mordant style, some samples of which are:

"When the coaches walked into the living room of the Tuohys' lovely Memphis home, the first thing they saw was the Rebel Christmas tree: red and blue branches festooned with nothing but Ole Miss ornaments."

"There were a number of colleges—and Ole Miss was one of them—for which the expropriation of the market value of pre-professional football players was something very like a core business."

"Hugh was a football coach and so he tended to take an indulgent view of bad grades."

The Evangelical Christian School "was as close to a church as a school could get. E.C.S. wouldn't accept kids unless both parents gave testimony of their experience of being born again—and the stories better be good."

Lewis's subject is the salvation of Michael Oher, a black child virtually raised on the mean streets of Memphis. But Lewis also continues what he began with *Moneyball,* his 2003 bestseller explaining new thinking about how to construct baseball teams. He is advancing a new genre of journalism that shows how market forces and economic reasoning shape the evolution of sports. Oher, who today plays left offensive tackle for the University of Mississippi, is a valuable commodity because of the lasting impact on football made by someone who played on the other side of the ball.

After the 1981 regular season, Lawrence Taylor, linebacker for the New York Giants, became the only rookie ever named the National Football League's defensive player of the year. He was six-foot-three, 240 pounds and quick as a cat, running forty yards in 4.5 seconds. He was, Lewis says, "a new kind of athlete doing a new kind of thing." This is how Taylor described his thing:

"I'll drive my helmet" into the quarterback, "or, if I can, I'll bring my arm up over my head and try to ax the sonuvabitch in two. So long as the guy is holding the ball, I intend to hurt him. . . . If I hit the guy right, I'll hit a nerve and he'll feel electrocuted, he'll forget for a few seconds that he's on a football field."

Terrifying, disorienting, and injuring quarterbacks is most of a linebacker's job description. Taylor concentrated coaches' minds on the problem of protecting quarterbacks. Most of them are right-handed, which means that when they are passing, threats from their left come thundering at them from their blind side. Hence the sudden interest in large and agile left offensive tackles. This interest intensified when Bill Walsh, coach of the San Francisco 49ers, devised the West Coast offense. It floods the secondary with receivers. More receivers mean fewer pass blockers, so the left tackle has more problems to cope with.

Which is why by 2004 the average salary of an NFL left tackle was $5.5 million a year, second only to the average for quarterbacks. The five most highly paid left tackles were earning almost $3 million more than the five most highly paid right tackles. That is very good news for Oher, one of thirteen siblings from the nation's third-poorest ZIP code.

He had finished the ninth grade, but the tenth was unlikely, and he was on track to be selling drugs, en route to jail or an early grave. His father was long gone, his mother was in and out of drug rehab. In his file from the public school system—he had been in eleven different schools in nine years—the numbers looked, Lewis says, "like misprints." His measured IQ was 80; his "ability to learn" placed him in the sixth percentile. He had repeated first and second grades. The school system said that through the fourth grade he had performed at "grade level," which is odd because he never attended third grade. He was almost nonverbal. Essentially unparented throughout his childhood, he scavenged for clothes, slept here and there in (sometimes slightly) less disorganized households than that of his mother, who when Michael was five was caring for seven boys and three girls, all under fifteen. Caring, that is, in her fashion. And not at all for ten or so days after the first of each month, when her welfare check arrived and she disappeared to feed her addiction to crack cocaine. On one occasion, lasting for weeks, his mother and seven boys slept in an old Chevy, washing themselves in a service station bathroom. For five years he lived in various households in a housing project with about a thousand residents and "no two-parent families: zero." It is unsurprising that Oher, according to Lewis, became a teenager who "didn't know what an ocean was, or a bird's nest, or the tooth fairy."

But the father of a friend, seeking a Christian education for his son, took Oher along on a visit to one of the many private schools created after the policy of forced busing, intended to achieve racial balance, provoked the departure of seven thousand children from Memphis's public schools. Oher came to the attention of Sean and Leigh Anne Tuohy, parents of children at one of these schools. They are white; they are the religious right.

Taco Bell franchises had made Sean a lot of money. Nature had made Leigh Anne into a human firecracker, exploding with energy. Their evangelical Christianity made them receptive to the possibility of redemption in the here and now. And attending Ole Miss had made them football-crazy. They became Oher's legal guardians. (One of Leigh Anne's cousins called late one night: "All right, I've just had my fifth beer. Who the hell is this black kid in y'all's Christmas card?") They got Oher, with his fifty-inch waist, into a size-58-long sport coat and into the Briarcrest Christian School.

When Oher wandered into the school gym, a coach tossed a basketball to him, expecting him to take it to the hoop, as a six-foot-five boy might, or kick it into the stands, as a 344-pound boy might. Instead, Oher caught it, dribbled three times between his legs, spun and drained a three-point shot from the corner of the floor. A human mountain with moves like a point guard? Two words spring to mind: left tackle.

Getting Oher his high school diploma became quite a project for the Tuohys. No one in Oher's family had ever had even a driver's license. When Leigh Anne told him to get his backpack from the foyer, he had no idea where that was. But with the help of tutors, by the first semester of his senior year he had risen to 162nd in a class of 163. "He's picking them off one at a time," Sean crowed, "like Sergeant York." The Tuohys found some interesting ways of getting high school credits off the Internet. (Lewis calls the Brigham Young University program of correspondence courses "the great Mormon grade-grab." Sean, evangelical but broad-minded, says: "The Mormons may be going to hell. But they really are nice people.") Anyway, Oher satisfied NCAA criteria for college eligibility.

Oher's childhood of grinding deprivation might have put him on a path to riches. Lewis commits some perhaps dubious sociology when he declares that a miserable ghetto childhood can be excellent preparation for football: "It made you angry, it made you aggressive, it made you want to tear someone's head off. The N.F.L. was loaded with players who had mined a loveless, dysfunctional childhood for sensational acts of violence."

Be that as it may, there came a day when a bevy of assistant football coaches from the Southeastern Conference, the Big Ten, the Atlantic Coast Conference, and elsewhere came to a Briarcrest practice. There Oher and a wee 270-pound teammate faced off, one on one, for a demonstration collision. In an instant, Oher effortlessly shoved his teammate down the field. In a flash, the coaches fired up their cell phones. Lewis says the Clemson coach rushed up to Oher's coach, saying, "I seen all I need to see," and added that Oher could have a full scholarship. Later, Tennessee's head coach watched Michael for half an hour and pronounced him the nation's best. A national recruiting frenzy had begun, from schools in states Michael could not find on a map.

When Ole Miss introduced its new football coach, he announced that his first goal was to recruit Oher. The coach barged into the Tuohys' living room, took a gander at Oher, and exclaimed, as Lewis renders it, "YAAAWWW BEEE BAAWWW!" ("You a big boy!") Michael could not understand a word he said. That did not matter. He wanted to go to Ole Miss, where his newfound parents had gone.

There Sean Tuohy told the coach, Ed Orgeron, that Oher would have trouble learning plays from a book full of X's and O's, but could learn the plays if they were presented visually, using mustard bottles and ketchup bottles to represent players. Lewis reports:

" 'Coach,' said Sean. 'My faith believes that the Lord sends down gifts for everyone and our job is to find those gifts. Michael's gift is the gift of memory. When he knows it, he knows it.'

"Coach O stopped scribbling and looked up. 'I'm going to tell you one thing, Sean,' he bellowed. 'He's got some pretty good [expletive] feet, too. You seen them feet? Now them feet: that's a [expletive] gift!' "

Oher was not a whale out of water at Ole Miss. Lewis says that the typical football player in Michael's college class "had third-grade-level reading skills. Several had never taken math. Ever." Michael's three closest friends among his Ole Miss teammates had children. One had become a father at fifteen. Michael brought a teammate, Quentin Taylor, to the Tuohys' home for Thanksgiving, and Taylor mentioned that he had fathered three children by two different mothers. Lewis writes:

"Leigh Anne pulled the carving knife from the turkey and said, 'Quentin, you can do what you want and it's your own business. But if Michael Oher does that I'm cutting his penis off.' From the look on Quentin's face Michael could see he didn't think she was joking."

She probably wasn't. She and Sean seriously, ferociously, implacably care about Oher. They were the first adults to do so.

Last season Michael was named to the first-team freshman all-American team—as a "true freshman." That is college-football-speak for a player who is not "redshirted." And that is college-football-speak for holding a player out of competition for a year while he spends time in the center of his academic life—no, silly, not the library, the weight room.

On Friday nights, American high schools discover talent that universities refine on Saturdays, for the nation's eventual delight on Sundays. Oher's story is not pretty, but Lewis tells it well—and against all odds, it may be heading for a happy ending.   –NOVEMBER 12, 2006

The Man from Moro Bottom

On January 26, 1983, phone service throughout area code 205, which then included all of Alabama, crashed from overload. Was the cause a natural disaster? Yes. Something very natural—death—had claimed the University of Alabama's football coach.

Allen Barra's illuminating book *The Last Coach: A Life of Paul "Bear" Bryant* explains why Alabamians felt so bereft. It also answers a question especially pertinent since Thomas Herrion, twenty-three, a 315-pound lineman for the San Francisco 49ers, died in August of a previously undetected heart disease: Has football become grotesque?

After Bryant became a coach, and to his regret, football players became specialists—often dangerously large specialists. In 1964, all limits on substitution ended, bringing the virtual extinction of players who played "on both sides of the ball"—both offense and defense. Some teams swelled to more than 130 players until the NCAA cut scholarships to only—only!—85. This was the end of the "eleven men and sic 'em" football favored by the man who earned his nickname when, at the age of fourteen, he wrestled a bear.

For some Alabamians, Barra says, September 11 means the day in 1913 when Bryant was born in a place—it was not a town—called Moro Bottom, Arkansas. He played at Alabama and got most of his then record 323 victories there, where he won six national championships—as many as the top three active coaches combined. He would have won a seventh in 1966 if the country, including those who vote on team rankings, had not been so angry about the only Alabamian more famous than Bryant—Governor George Wallace.

But football helped change the face of the South. Before the 1963 Orange Bowl, President Kennedy visited the locker room of the integrated Oklahoma Sooners, but not Alabama's. The 1969 Texas Long-horns were the last all-white team voted national champions.

Bryant—"My players are athletes first and students second"—had an agreeable aversion to hypocrisy and cant. He told players: "Ten years from now you are going to be married with a family, your wife might be sick, your kids might be sick, you might be sick, but you will get your butt up and go to work. That's what I'm going to do for you. I'm going to teach you how to do things you don't feel like doing."

Bryant understood what football meant to the South. The Rose Bowl had been reluctant to invite Alabama to play in 1926, the era of Erskine Caldwell's novels about rural Georgia, *Tobacco Road* and *God's Little Acre.* Alabama's victory over Washington occasioned, Barra says, "the greatest statewide celebration since the shelling of Fort Sumter."

The University of Alabama's enrollment actually increased during the Depression partly because it welcomed Northeastern Jewish students who were excluded by quotas from many prestigious Northern schools. In the 1960s, the South's most turbulent decade since the 1860s, Alabama dominated college football, and because an ABC television prodigy named Roone Arledge knew charisma when he saw it, Bryant became the craggy face of college football.

Also in the 1960s, unlimited substitution began making huge players practical as offensive or defensive specialists. Barra notes that Bryant's 1966 team "looked like an average high school team today." It went 11–0 and then won the Sugar Bowl. It had only fourteen players who weighed more than 200 pounds. The two heaviest weighed 213. The linemen averaged 195. The quarterback weighed 175.

Today, Scouts, Inc., reports that nearly 40 percent of the interior linemen who will go to Division I colleges in September 2006—many of these players not yet eighteen—already weigh at least 300 pounds. In 1980, only one NFL player topped 300. In 1994, the year a mortality study found that linemen have a 52 percent greater risk of dying from cardiovascular disease than the general population and that the largest players have six times the risk of cardiac death than normal-size players, the number of 300-pounders was 155. Ten years later, 370 NFL players exceeded 300, and 10 exceeded 350.

This season, the offensive lines of thirty of the thirty-two NFL teams average at least 300 pounds, and one team averages 323. Of the sixty-one offensive college linemen invited to last February's NFL Scouting Combine, fifty-eight weighed at least 300. Of the three little fellows, one weighed 299 and two weighed 298.

After eighteen college players died in 1905, President Theodore Roosevelt—it took serious carnage to cause that cowboy and warrior to flinch—compelled rules changes to make football safer. Today, it is unhealthy because of the kinetic energy involved in collisions between huge men—and because of what they do to become huge. Not coaching football was unhealthy for Bryant. "If I quit coaching," he frequently said, "I'll croak in a week." He died twenty-eight days after his last game.   [NOVEMBER 7, 2005]

"Rammer Jammer Yellowhammer!"

Don Cole, aka the Heart Guy, was ailing and wore a beeper. He was a candidate for a heart transplant and was not supposed to ever be more than a two-hour drive from his Nashville hospital, in case it received a heart that could be transplanted. He said that if the hospital learned that he left the two-hour radius he would be removed from the list of recipients. So why, weekend after weekend, was he three and a half hours from Nashville, in Tuscaloosa, Alabama? "If I can't go to Alabama football games, what's the point in living?"

Then there is the couple whose huge RV resembles the fuselage of a Boeing 737. What sacrifices have they made for their devotion to Alabama football? "Let's see," muses the husband. "We missed our daughter's wedding. We told her, just don't get married on a game day and we'll be there, hundred percent, and she went off and picked the third Saturday in October which everybody knows is when Alabama plays Tennessee, so we told her, hey, we got a ballgame to go to. We made the reception—went there as soon as the game was over."

You can meet these folks and others of their tribe in *Rammer Jammer Yellowhammer: A Journey into the Heart of Fan Mania,* a hilarious—and a little bit scary—book by Warren St. John, a New York writer who was born in Alabama. A few years ago, he returned to try to figure this out: "Why do I care?" About sports, that is.

To plumb the depths of the human fascination with contests, St. John went for total immersion. He spent a football season with the seriously hard-core fans. They are the ones for whom the phrase "Roll Tide" is an all-purpose exclamation-incantation-salutation. They are the purchasers of official Alabama coffins (red, with the school logo on the top and a white velvet "A" sewn into the lid—$1,999). These fans travel from game to game in their $300,000-to-$1,400,000 RVs, turning game day into a three-day festival of cold beer, artery-clogging broiled bologna sticks, 'Bama Bombs (Maraschino cherries soaked in PGA—pure grain alcohol) and sacramental events like the Bear Bryant Namesake Reunion at Tuscaloosa's Bryant Museum.

The museum, which contains such relics as the jacket and slacks one fan wore to his five hundredth consecutive Alabama game, is across Bryant Drive from where the RVs gather, near Bryant-Denny Stadium and Bryant Hall, a dorm, and not far from Paul William Bryant High School. The reunion is for people named for Bryant, who coached the Tide to six national championships. There are almost six hundred such people.

Alabama's obsession with football began, in a sense, on January 1, 1926, five months after the Scopes trial—about teaching evolution— gave the South's despisers fresh ammunition. On that day Alabama's Crimson Tide became the first team from the South to play in the Rose Bowl. The Tide won, 20–19. The South really would rise again.

But in every region, sport can produce a collective mind, or some- times a collective setting aside of mind. In 1895, a French psychologist published *The Crowd: A Study of the Popular Mind,* pioneering the study of the mental unity of crowds—people in the same frame of mind. "Freud," writes St. John, "disparaged crowds as neurotic on the grounds that, like neurotics, crowds 'demand illusions, and in fact can't live without them' and 'are guided not by ordinary objective real- ity but psychological reality.'"

However, St. John believes in using Occam's razor—that is, in first trying the simplest explanation of a phenomenon: "We can't paint our faces and scream like maniacs at our desks, in the classroom or at the dinner tables with our families, so . . ."

Well, then, why *does* St. John care about the Tide? "I chose Alabama the way a baby bird chooses its mother: it was the first thing I saw." We all acquire such allegiances, but there also is a regional twist to this. For Southerners, the myth of the Lost Cause is all very well, but winning is nice, too.

So try to think anthropologically about those 'Bama fans who fire up their RVs, break out their radar detectors, and sing "Rammer Jammer Yellowhammer! Give 'em hell Alabama!" They are not just emulating the RVer who said: "We can't be young but we can be immature." They are pursuing what sportswriter Frank Deford called "that curious Southern combination of eternal knighthood and childhood." Roll Tide.   [NOVEMBER 21, 2004]

Randy Shannon's Realism

MIAMI—Occasionally—*very* occasionally—a football person says something that punctures the fog of George Patton–style rhetoric that football people emit. Before a Super Bowl in the 1970s (the MCMLXXs, for those of you in a Super Bowl frame of mind), Dallas Cowboys running back Duane Thomas asked a subversive question about the game: "If it's the ultimate, how come they're playing it again next year?"

But most football people, and especially football coaches, are of the "Football Is Not a Matter of Life and Death—It's More Important Than That" school of thought. However, when Randy Shannon, recently named head coach of the University of Miami Hurricanes, says that football can be a matter of life and death, that is not hyperbole, it is autobiography.

Shannon, forty, grew up in Miami's Liberty City, which is what sociologists and other refined thinkers call a challenging urban environment. Shannon was three when his father was murdered by one of his friends. "They had an argument," Shannon says matter-of-factly. Two of Shannon's brothers and a sister died, from cocaine and AIDS. By age sixteen, Shannon was a father. He could easily have been on a glide path to a prison or a cemetery. Instead, because of football, he went to the University of Miami and became the first member of his family to earn a college degree.

After a brief NFL career with the Cowboys, he went into coaching, and now he is hopscotching around the country recruiting high school seniors, many of whom think college football is a certain path to the NFL. "That," says Shannon, "is the mentality that has to change." Less than 2 percent of even Division I college football players will have NFL careers, and most of those who do will be out of the game by the time they are thirty—the average NFL career lasts less than four years.

The *Washington Post*'s Amy Shipley reports that the University of Miami has more players—forty-two—on NFL rosters than any other school. Miami's main rival—the Florida State Seminoles (a T-shirt favored by Miami students reads: "I think, therefore I am not a 'Nole")—is second with forty-one. The University of Florida ranks seventh with thirty-five. But in the last ten years, those three teams have had, combined, more than one thousand players, all of them exceptional athletes but most of them not of NFL caliber. Which is why Shannon says that when visiting the home of a potential recruit, "I talk to the parents about everything but football."

On a recent day, Shannon was in the Palm Beach area recruiting a wide receiver, and then was off to Omaha to make sure that a very large lineman was still eager to be a Hurricane.

Because South Florida is the incubator of so much high school talent (skill positions, Shannon says; for linemen, look to the Midwest, hence the Nebraska trip), during the off-season many NFL players come home to train at the University of Miami's facilities. Shannon says his players "see the fancy cars, the gold chains," so as he takes over Miami's football program, he plans to "come in with a stern attitude."

Stern adults got Shannon to the peak of his profession at age forty. A fourth-grade teacher told him, "You're very smart—don't let anyone tell you different." A fifth-grade teacher, disapproving his choice of clothes one day, said, "Don't ever come to school like that again." When he was in junior high school, his football coach took the team to play a team in a juvenile detention center, a sobering experience.

Shannon's rules for his players include: If you miss a class, you don't start the next game. Fall below a certain grade point average, you can't set foot off campus. A conservatively dressed man, with the elegant hands of a surgeon or pianist, Shannon wants his players to learn "how to respect life," so when "they leave the university and the football program, they will go with confidence." They will go, all of them, having taken a public speaking course.

Duffy Daugherty, who coached Michigan State from 1954 through 1972, was an aphorist ("Football is not a contact sport, it's a collision sport. Dancing is a contact sport") and a realist. Because of alumni demands for football perfection, Daugherty said: "A football coach's main problem is that he is responsible to irresponsible people." Shannon, who like 80 percent of his players is African-American, feels responsible to, and for, them.   [FEBRUARY 4, 2007]

The NFL: An Intensification of Reality

A fat lot Keats knew about autumn. "Season of mists and mellow fruitfulness"? Fiddlesticks. It is football season, the distilled essence of modern life.

It is sex (pneumatic cheerleaders), violence (when the 1976 Super Bowl made the Dallas Cowboys cheerleaders famous, a CBS producer said, "The audience deserves a little sex with its violence"), technology (quarterbacks electronically instructed by coaches wired to subordinate Merlins in the upper reaches of the stadium), committee meetings (huddles), division of labor (interior linemen specializing in third-and-short yardage situations), jargon (zone-flooding nickel packages and seam-splitting nose tackles, or something like that), and a hallmark of a commercial society—strategic parsimony about time.

Welcome to the National Football League, a cultural artifact that causes thinkers to commit sociology. Michael MacCambridge plumbs these depths in his fine new book, *America's Game: The Epic Story of How Pro Football Captured a Nation.* It is a rip-roaring epic of American business.

In 1920, eleven men met in a Canton, Ohio, Hupmobile showroom and assessed each other $100 franchise fees. In 1999, the fee for the Houston Texans franchise was $700 million. The eight-year, $17.6 billion TV deal signed in 1998 pays each club $84 million this year. The NFL has come a long way since the Philadelphia Eagles—named after the symbol of FDR's National Recovery Administration—traveled by train to New York on game day to avoid hotel expenses and ate at Horn & Hardart Automats.

In 1952, the Chicago Bears–Dallas Texans Thanksgiving Day game was moved from Dallas to Akron in quest of better attendance—and drew just 3,000 fans to a field where, that morning, 14,800 had attended a high-school game. But a new appliance was coming, and soon the NFL supplanted boxing as the sport whose compact action seemed most suited to television screens. Of which there were only fourteen thousand in 1947 but 26 million in 1954.

By 1980, the League of Women Voters had to beat a hasty retreat from scheduling two presidential debates on Monday nights. (Carter might have been reelected if that year's debate had been up against *Monday Night Football.* Few would have watched.) By the 1990s, the NFL had the power to transform Fox into a major player among the networks.

On the field, unlimited substitution was restored in 1950 and made most of the swarming players seem like interchangeable parts in large machines. That, and competitive balance, a product of equal team shares of the dominant source of revenue (national television contracts), led to the apotheosis of head coaches, and especially to the cult of the Packers' Vince Lombardi. Both Richard Nixon and Hubert Humphrey considered him as a running mate in 1968.

"The period of the early '70s," writes MacCambridge, "brought an odd sense of cognitive dissonance to pro football's rise. At no other time in its history did the guiding ethos of football—teamwork, self-sacrifice, the concerted application of mental and physical discipline toward a single, united goal—seem more out of step with the larger cultural moment."

The NFL, with its aversion to understatement, flourished in the 1960s and 1970s, when cultural change was accelerating, and the tone setters in American sports were Muhammad Ali and Howard Cosell. Soon the NFL produced the first black celebrity featured in a national corporate advertising campaign, for Hertz. O. J. Simpson. Oh, well.

This NFL season will reach a climax with the XXXIXth Super Bowl. (Roman numerals for gladiatorial spectacles.) It will be watched by many millions more Americans than will have watched the presidential inauguration seventeen days before. The fourth Super Bowl, in January 1970, was watched by more people than had watched Neil Armstrong walk on the moon six months earlier. The ten-most-watched television programs in history are all Super Bowls. Most viewers have financial stakes in the outcomes, having bet on them. Super Bowl Sunday is second only to Thanksgiving in Americans' caloric intake. "If Jesus Christ were alive today," said Norman Vincent Peale in 1974, "he'd be at the Super Bowl." But surely not in a luxury suite.

The best thing about NFL teams is the purity of their professionalism. None are appendages of institutions of higher education, so there is no damned nonsense about "student athletes." When in 1957 Queen Elizabeth attended a Maryland–North Carolina game, she asked Maryland's governor, "Where do you get all those enormous players?" He replied, "Your Majesty, that's a very embarrassing question."

In *Sports Illustrated*'s recent fiftieth-anniversary issue, Jeff MacGregor wrote, "Organized sports are the perfection of the unnecessary." Perhaps. But, then, most of what makes life sweet involves emancipation from necessity. The NFL is an acquired taste that Americans have acquired less as an alternative reality than as an intensification of modern reality, although why they want that is a mystery.

[OCTOBER 11, 2004]

Speaking SportsCenterese

*If we had ESPN twenty-two years ago, we wouldn't have any
children.* —A COLLEGE COACH, 1990

You are in a ballpark with your twelve-year-old. The shortstop
makes a sparkling play and your child murmurs, "Web gem." As
a slugger approaches the plate, your child says, with a hint of drollery,
"You can't stop him, you can only hope to contain him." When the
slugger hits one four hundred feet, the child says, "That'll make the
Top Ten Plays."

Congratulations: Your child is bilingual. He or she speaks Sports-
Centerese, the lingua franca of ESPN nation, the capital of which is
Bristol, Connecticut, where twenty-seven satellite dishes scarf up forty
thousand feeds a year, the best of which are sent around the clock to
sports addicts, such as the viewer who, in 1987, said: "Please show the
Nebraska-UCLA game at 6:00 as I have a 5:00 Mass and would have
to find a priest to replace me if you show it earlier."

ESPN will be a quarter-century old on September 7. Measurements
of "brand resonance" show that among 138 brands, including Coca-
Cola and McDonald's, ESPN ranks first among men. Each week more
than 90 million people are exposed to ESPN media—ESPN (there are
locally produced SportsCenters in Canada, Brazil, a Spanish version
for the rest of Latin America, China, India and Taiwan), ESPN2, ESPN
Classic, ESPN.com (2.3 million page views in a peak hour), and *ESPN
The Magazine* (a circulation of 1.7 million in just five years).

This stunning growth reflects ways America has changed in a
quarter of a century. The change can be measured in money.

In 1979, when the Entertainment and Sports Programming Network began, the average major league baseball salary was $113,558
and pitcher Nolan Ryan became the first million-dollar-a-year athlete
in team sports. Today the average baseball salary ($2.55 million) has
increased 2,241 percent and there are 1,702 million-dollar athletes. In
1979, broadcasters paid the National Football League $8.8 million

annually; today, the fee is approximately $2.25 billion, an increase of more than 25,400 percent.

America is a lot richer than it was in 1979, but not *that* much richer. Something else is afoot, turning so many eyes—that is what pulls the tide of money—to sports. Perhaps people are drawn to sports because they really don't mean a thing. In this politicized age, even— no, *especially*—cultural arguments are political arguments. Politics is understood as a series of angry confrontations, and war (on drugs, poverty, illiteracy, etc.) is a metaphor for policy. Perhaps, then, sports delight because they are a refuge—one of society's few meaning-free zones.

Or not. Perhaps there is an opposite explanation for the unslakable appetite for the spectacle of sport, an appetite that has produced ESPN.

Michael Mandelbaum, author of eight books on international relations, argues in his ninth book, *The Meaning of Sports,* that sports are "a variety of religious experience." Like religion, sports stand apart from the mundane and are a realm of special coherence and heroic example. The rise of team sports coincided with what Mandelbaum calls the twentieth century's "social and political hurricanes." Those were urbanization—people moving from countryside to town and from job to job—and world wars, unprecedented confusions and traumas from which people sought diversions. The twentieth century, Mandelbaum writes, "was the era of free verse in poetry, stream-of-consciousness writing in literature, atonal music in place of traditional harmony and melody, and abstract rather than figurative art. James Joyce succeeded Charles Dickens, Jackson Pollock filled the place Rembrandt had occupied."

At a time when Robert Frost was comparing free verse to playing tennis without a net, sports became cultural counterpoints because they are transparent and coherent. Transparent because spectators can see for themselves what is happening, and why. Coherent in that they are defined and governed by rationality—rules—and reach definitive conclusions. It is surely not mere coincidence that sports and detective novels found mass audiences simultaneously.

These clues to the mystery of ESPN's remarkable success may assuage any guilt you feel about the time you spend with the boys and girls from Bristol. But don't get carried away. There has been at least one ESPN divorce in which the wife gave to her husband an improvident ultimatum: It's ESPN or me. In at least ten harmonious marriages, the parents have named children ESPN, Espn, Espin, or Espyn. How many children have been named HBO or CNN?   [SEPTEMBER 7, 2004]

The Movie, and the Truth, About Texas Western

A Division I college basketball program is not the sort of enterprise easily confused with a seminary or a seminar on ethics. But according to what is currently America's most popular movie, forty years ago one such program became a nation-shaking, history-shaping moral force. The movie, although not too noble to palter with facts, is no more parsimonious with the truth than movies often are when turning history into entertainment.

Glory Road celebrates the 1965–1966 basketball team of Texas Western College (which in 1967 became the University of Texas at El Paso). The Miners included seven black players, most recruited far from mining country—the South Bronx, Gary, Indiana, and other mostly urban places. The drama was that five of them started the 1966 NCAA championship game that Texas Western won, beating an all-white University of Kentucky team, 72–65.

The game was not quite, as the movie insists, David against Goliath. Granted, the Kentucky Wildcats, then college basketball's aristocrats, were college basketball's winningest team in the 1940s and 1950s. But Texas Western had lost only one game and was ranked third in the nation as the tournament began.

The game's racial dimension looks much larger in retrospect than it did then. In the movie, a Texas Western official urges coach Don Haskins to abide by an unwritten rule: Play one black at home and two on the road—three if behind. And another white character scoffs at the idea that blacks might be "the future" of basketball. But Ron Rapoport of the *Chicago Sun-Times* notes:

"A decade before the game that supposedly changed basketball, the undefeated 1955–1956 University of San Francisco team won the NCAA championship with a team that played four blacks—Bill Russell, K. C. Jones, Hal Perry, and Gene Brown. In 1958, the coaches' all-American team was all black—Wilt Chamberlain of Kansas, Oscar Robertson of Cincinnati, Bob Boozer of Kansas State, Guy Rodgers of Temple, and Elgin Baylor of Seattle. In 1962, the University of Cincinnati started four black players when it won the NCAA championship, and Loyola University of Chicago started four when it won in 1963. Frank Deford, a distinguished writer, covered the Texas Western–Kentucky game for *Sports Illustrated* and did not *mention* the fact of five black starters. Neither did the *New York Times* nor the *Washington Post*. Already the ascendancy of blacks in basketball was such that the four best players in the NBA were Chamberlain, Russell, Baylor, and Robertson."

In the movie, Haskins tells his team the day before the game that he will play only black players the next night—he used all seven—in order to make a social statement. But former Georgetown coach John Thompson, a black man famous for his bluntness, minced no words when talking to Eddie Einhorn for a book, *How March Became Madness,* a history of the NCAA tournament, that Einhorn is publishing next month (with Rapoport's collaboration). Thompson told Einhorn that Haskins said his only goal was to win, so he played his best players.

And what of the movie scene where the players' motel rooms are trashed and racist epithets are painted on the walls? One of the players, Nevil Shed, recently told *Sporting News* columnist Dave Kindred, "Could have happened." Kindred calls that Shed's way of handling "the fiction."

Although the movie shows Haskins emphasizing basketball fundamentals and telling the players that "showboating is nothing but insecurity," the movie also makes much of the black players successfully seeking his permission for the more flamboyant style of play they learned on city asphalt. This much is true: Between 1967 and 1976, the

NCAA banned dunk shots, even during warm-ups. What do you suppose *that* was about?

In his just-published *At Canaan's Edge: America in the King Years, 1965–68,* Taylor Branch writes that when in 1950 Kentucky lost to City College of New York's integrated team, Kentucky's legislature flew the flag at the capitol at half-staff. Two months after the 1966 championship game, a black player received an athletic scholarship from one of Kentucky's Southeastern Conference rivals, Vanderbilt. Kentucky's coach, Adolph Rupp, was born in 1901 and probably was not much different than his peers in his time and place. According to Branch, Rupp "complained of incessant calls from his university president: 'That son-of-a-bitch wants me to get some n—— in here. What am I gonna do?' " But Kentucky had no black professor until 1965.

When Rupp retired in 1972, his team was all white. Today, Kentucky has a black coach, Tubby Smith, whose fifteen-man team includes ten blacks. They play in Rupp Arena.   [JANUARY 22, 2006]

Chapter Seven

THE GAME

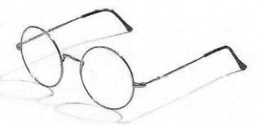

"Remember 1908!"

Chicago Cub fans, that numerous and inexplicable cohort, have a weird rallying cry: "Remember 1908!" Not one of them really does remember that season, the last time the Cubs won the World Series. That is all the more reason for them to join Cait Murphy on her jaunty walk through that tumultuous season. All other baseball fans should tag along. So should anyone interested in the rough texture of this bumptious nation in the early twentieth century, when twenty-five cents—not a piddling amount for a low-skilled factory worker making $7 a week—would get you into a ballpark where whiskey, waffles, and pigs' knuckles were served.

Crazy '08 is a walk on the wild side: Brooklyn fans on rooftops would hurl sharpened umbrella shafts at visiting players in the outfield. When only boxing and horse racing competed with baseball for the public's attention, baseball stirred tribal feelings.

Baseball fans relish arguments about which was the greatest this or that—greatest game, team, left-handed right fielder, right-handed left fielder, whatever. Murphy will ignite a dandy rhubarb with her subtitle: *How a Cast of Cranks, Rogues, Boneheads, and Magnates Created the Greatest Year in Baseball History*. The author, an assistant managing editor at *Fortune* magazine, makes a powerful case for those last six words.

In 1908—the year a play titled *The Melting Pot* put that phrase into the American lexicon—Americans were unmelted. When the best player in the game, Honus Wagner, came to bat, a band might break into "Wacht am Rhein." When John McGraw's Giants visited Springfield, Illinois, which had recently experienced a hideous race riot—the NAACP was born partly in response to it—McGraw was given, as a souvenir, a piece of the rope used to lynch a black man. Murphy reports that McGraw said the rope would replace a rabbit's foot as the Giants' good-luck emblem.

That year, construction began on the first fireproof (concrete and steel) ballpark, Shibe Park in Philadelphia. With its terra-cotta casts and copper-trimmed roof, it embodied the City Beautiful movement's belief that attractive buildings would uplift the downtrodden. Furthermore, 1908 gave the world the greatest piece of music since Mozart ("Take Me Out to the Ball Game," of course) and an audacious and successful bit of flapdoodle (the campaign to convince the gullible that Cooperstown was the birthplace, and Abner Doubleday the father, of baseball).

Between the white lines, baseball in 1908 also included:

- Two pennant races in which a total of six teams were in contention with two days left.
- The finest (Murphy says so; she does like laying down the law) pitching duel in baseball history. Ed Walsh, whose record in 1908 would be 40–15 with a 1.42 ERA, struck out fifteen—at that time a record for a nine-inning game—and allowed only one run, which was unearned. But he lost because Addie Joss used just seventy-four pitches to throw a perfect game.
- What was perhaps the best season any National League player would have in the twentieth century. The Pittsburgh Pirates' Honus Wagner led the league in almost everything—you can look it up. "There ain't much to being a ballplayer," he said, "if you're a ballplayer."
- The only doubleheader in which one pitcher pitched every inning and threw two shutouts.
- A steal of first base. (A runner on first stole second, hoping the runner on third would score on the throw to second. But the catcher did not throw. So on the next pitch the runner on second ran back to first. Then he stole second again.)

When crucial games were being played, tens of thousands around the nation packed concert halls and blocked streets to watch large electric scoreboards relaying telegraph information of the games' progress, batter by batter. Murphy provides delightful samples of 1908 baseball writing for newspapers: "There was a sharp report as Tommy caught the pellet squarely on its proboscis and sent it screeching toward the distant middle."

In 1908, Murphy writes, the average player's salary was $2,500—three times as much as what Chicago paid a primary-school teacher with seven years' experience. In 1910, almost a quarter of major leaguers had some college education, compared with 5 percent of the population. But it was not until the late eighties that Pennsylvania, with its history of mills and mines, was surpassed by sunny California as the incubator of the most big-league players. For many men—the kind who poured whiskey on spike wounds—baseball a century ago was a way to avoid life sentences of hard labor, so they played with grim intensity. In 1907, a player was "beaned so badly that he was given last rites on the field." (He survived.)

The umpire—often there was only one—was given three balls at the beginning of the game. If these did not suffice, the home team was required to supply balls. If the home team was ahead, those supplied were apt to be old and lifeless. Murphy gives this example of how, in a pennant race decided by a one-game margin, the Cubs stole a game because the umpire Cy Rigler, working alone, was calling balls and strikes standing behind the pitcher:

"In the fifth inning, the Cubs attempt a double steal with men on first and third and two out; Rigler turns to call the runner out at second. The run scores if the runner on third, Johnny Kling, touches home before the out is recorded. Rigler has no way of knowing when or even if Kling crosses the plate in time. He simply flips a mental coin and admits the run—and the Cubs beat the Cardinals 4–3. Even the Chicago press admits that Kling was several steps short."

Between the Cubs, who were then a dynasty (no other team has ever won 530 games in five years, as the Cubs did from 1906 to 1910), and the New York Giants, this was, as Murphy says, an "era of really bad feelings." On September 23, with the Giants leading the Cubs by half a game, the Giants' regular first baseman woke up with lumbago, so Fred Merkle, nineteen, got his first start of the season. After the tumultuous ninth inning, he would forever be known as Bonehead Merkle. Murphy's reconstruction of the jaw-dropping confusion that effectively sent the Cubs to the World Series is lucid and hilarious, and justifies her assertion—baseball fans do love such judgments—that the game involved "perhaps the single most courageous act" ever by an umpire. He ruled that on an infield covered with fans and several balls more or less in play, Merkle never touched second. All baseball fans know something about this game; few know the astonishing details Murphy supplies, including a brazen attempt to bribe the umpires before the game was replayed, because the Merkle game had been declared a tie.

Murphy's book is rich in trivia—not that anything associated with baseball is really trivial. Did you know, for example, that when the Yankees were still the Highlanders (they played at the highest point in Manhattan) they adopted their interlocking NY lettering "based on the Tiffany design for the Police Department's Medal of Honor"?

Readers of *Crazy '08* can almost smell the whiskey and taste the pigs' knuckles. This rollicking tour of that season will entertain readers interested in social history, will fascinate students of baseball, and will cause today's Cub fans to experience an unaccustomed feeling—pride—as their team enters the 2007 season, the ninety-ninth season of its rebuilding effort.   [APRIL 1, 2007]

Jackie Robinson: The Possible and the Inevitable

Like many New Yorkers leaving home for work on April 15, 1947, he wore a suit, tie, and camel-hair overcoat as he headed for the subway. To his wife he said, "Just in case you have trouble picking me out, I'll be wearing number 42."

No one had trouble spotting the black man in the Dodgers' white home uniform when he trotted out to play first base at Ebbets Field. Suddenly, only 399, not 400, major-league players were white. Which is why 42 is the only number permanently retired by every team.

Jackie Robinson's high school teachers suggested a career in gardening. Robinson's brother Mack had finished second to Jesse Owens in the 200-meter dash at the 1936 Berlin Olympics. Whites who won medals found careers opened for them. Mack, writes Jonathan Eig in

Opening Day: The Story of Jackie Robinson's First Season, wore his Olympic jacket as a Pasadena, California, street sweeper, while Owens found himself racing against horses at county fairs, "one small step removed from a circus act."

To appreciate how far the nation has come, propelled by what began sixty years ago this Sunday, consider not the invectives that Robinson heard from opponents' dugouts and fans, but the way he had been praised. "Dusky Jack Robinson," as the *Los Angeles Times* called him, alerting readers to the race of UCLA's four-sport star, ran with a football "like it was a watermelon and the guy who owned it was after him with a shotgun."

That cringe-inducing fact is from Eig's mind-opening book, an account of a twenty-eight-year-old man "filled with fear and fury," and terribly alone. It includes unfamiliar details about familiar episodes. There is Lieutenant Robinson's 1944 refusal, eleven years before Rosa Parks, to move to the back of a bus at Fort Hood, Texas. And shortstop Pee Wee Reese, a Kentuckian who until 1947 had never shaken hands with a black person, crossing the infield to put a hand on Robinson's shoulder when Cincinnati fans were being abusive.

But Eig is especially informative about the dynamics among the Dodgers, who, like many teams, had a Southern tinge. The most popular player was nicknamed Dixie (Walker) and one of the best pitchers was the grandson of a Confederate soldier. The Dodgers' radio broadcaster, Red Barber, a Mississippian, considered resigning, then thought better. Radio presented Robinson as television cameras could not have done—as, Eig shrewdly writes, "all action," undifferentiated by visual differences from his teammates.

After the opening two games against the Boston Braves, the Dodgers played the Giants at the Polo Grounds in Harlem. The president of the National League, fearing excessive enthusiasm, suggested that Robinson should develop a sprained ankle. He did not, and the crowds were large, dressed as if for church—men in suits and hats, women in dresses—and decorous. Soon a commentator wrote, "Like plastics and penicillin, it seems like Jackie is here to stay."

The Dodgers were not. Ebbets Field's turnstiles clicked 1.8 million times in 1947, more than they ever had before or would again. But in 1947, in a Long Island potato field, Levittown was founded, offering mass-produced low-cost housing emblematic of postwar suburbanization. Dodger fans were moving east on the island. After the 1957 season, the Dodgers moved west.

Only 25,623 fans went to the game on April 15, 1947—4,000 fewer than on opening day 1946 and 6,000 fewer than the ballpark's capacity. Perhaps some white fans were wary of being with so many blacks. Usually blacks were no more than 10 percent of Dodger crowds but on this day they may have been 60 percent.

By 1956, Robinson's last season, he had lost his second base position to Jim Gilliam, a black man. Robinson died of diabetes-related illnesses in 1972, at fifty-three, the same age Babe Ruth was when he died. Ruth reshaped baseball; Robinson's life still reverberates through all of American life. As Martin Luther King Jr., who was eighteen in 1947, was to say, Robinson was "a sit-inner before sit-ins, a freedom rider before freedom rides."

"Robinson," writes Eig, "showed black Americans what was possible. He showed white Americans what was inevitable." By the end of the 1947 season, America's future was unfolding by democracy's dialectic of improvement. Robinson changed sensibilities, which led to changed laws, which in turn accelerated changes in sensibilities.

Jack Roosevelt Robinson's middle name was homage to the president who said "speak softly and carry a big stick." Robinson's deeds spoke loudly. His stick weighed thirty-four ounces, which was enough.

[APRIL 15, 2007]

Ted Williams: "I Can't Stand It, I'm So Good"

There is no joy in Red Sox nation, aka New England, or in any heart where baseball matters. When Ted Williams arrived in Boston at age twenty in 1939, a spindly six-foot-three, the Splendid Splinter said, "All I want out of life is that when I walk down the street folks will say, 'There goes the greatest hitter that ever lived.' " When he died Friday at age eighty-three, many people did say that, and no one said they were foolish.

When, as a twelve-year-old in San Diego in 1930, he heard that the Giants' Bill Terry had batted .401, "I got my little bat, ran out to our little back yard, and began to swing." His swing became baseball's gold standard.

In 1939, a golden moment on the eve of dark years, Bob Feller, Williams, and Joe DiMaggio were twenty, twenty-one, and twenty-four respectively. "I can't stand it, I'm so good," Williams used to exclaim in his youthful ebullience.

In 1941, when DiMaggio mesmerized the nation with his still unmatched fifty-six-game hitting streak, Williams did what has not been done in six decades since—batted over .400. Batting .3995 going into the season's last day, a doubleheader in Philadelphia against the Athletics, he went 6-for-8, finishing at .406.

There was no sacrifice fly rule in effect that year (today a batter is not charged with an at bat if he hits a fly that scores a runner). Had there been, his average would have been about 10 points higher. Biographer Ed Linn says that had Williams not lost the four and a half years he spent as an aviator in the Second World War and Korea, he probably would rank first or second in runs, runs batted in, total bases, extra-base hits, and perhaps home runs.

An alloy of innocence and arrogance, young Williams came to Boston when it had four morning and four evening local newspapers engaged in perpetual circulation wars. He became grist for their mills, and his wars with the sportswriters brought out the worst in him, and cost him. He won two Most Valuable Player Awards and finished second four times. Several of those times he would have won had he not had such poisonous relations with the voting press. A writer said that when Williams retired, Boston knew how Britain felt when it lost India—diminished, but relieved.

He is one of only two players (the other was Rogers Hornsby) to win a triple crown (highest batting average, most home runs and runs batted in) twice, and he would have won a third if the Tigers' George

Kell had not beaten him for the 1949 batting title .3429 to .34275. If the sacrifice fly rule had been in effect that year, Williams would have beaten Kell, who would have had one fewer sacrifice fly. Williams won six batting titles, including one hitting .388 in 1957, when his thirty-eight-year-old legs surely cost him five infield hits, enough to put him over .400 again.

He used a postal scale to check that humidity had not added an ounce to the weight of his bats. Challenged to find from among six bats the one that was half an ounce heavier than the others, he quickly did. He once returned to the maker a batch of his Louisville Sluggers because he sensed that the handles were not quite right. The handles were off by five-thousandths of an inch.

Like many great players, he remembered, obsessively. That grand slam home run in Minneapolis before coming to the big leagues? "Fifth inning, three-and-two count, low fastball."

He hit a home run in his last time at bat—twice. He assumed his career was over—and he homered—when the Marine Corps called him to Korea (where No. 9 flew an F-9 jet as wingman for a squadron commander named John Glenn). And on September 26, 1960, in the final at bat of his final game, in Boston's gray autumnal gloom, he homered. Among the only 10,454 fans was John Updike, who wrote "Hub Fans Bid Kid Adieu": "For me, Williams is the classic ballplayer of the game on a hot August weekday before a small crowd, when the only thing at stake is the tissue-thin difference between a thing done well and a thing done ill."

Never, not even after that farewell home run, did Williams tip his hat to the cheering fans. "Gods," wrote Updike, "do not answer letters."

Late in life, Williams said that often he fell asleep hearing in his head three songs—"The Star-Spangled Banner," "The Marines' Hymn," and "Take Me Out to the Ball Game." An American life.   [JULY 7, 2002]

Roberto Clemente: "We Think He Can Hit"

M ost biographies of great athletes are tinged with melancholy, for three reasons. Athletic greatness is often achieved by a narrowing, even infantilizing, monomania about physical things. Sport compresses life's natural trajectory of ascent, apogee, and decline. And often an athlete's life after sport is a long, dispiriting decrescendo. David Maraniss's splendid *Clemente: The Passion and Grace of Baseball's Last Hero* is different, for three reasons. Roberto Clemente was an unusually elegant, even noble, athlete. He was emblematic of a social transformation. And he had no life after baseball.

Maraniss's biography of Bill Clinton is still the best of the first president formed by the 1960s. He is also the author of one of the best books on the 1960s, *They Marched Into Sunlight: War and Peace, Vietnam and America, October 1967*. And now he has produced a baseball-savvy book sensitive to the social context that made Clemente, a black Puerto Rican, a leading indicator of baseball's future. Clemente was not the first Latino player, but as the first Latino superstar—the National League's first Latino batting champion and MVP—he propelled baseball's "southern strategy" for finding talent.

Baseball has come a long way since the San Francisco Giants' manager Alvin Dark, in 1964, banned Spanish in the clubhouse. In 1989 and 1990, five of the twenty-six major-league teams had a starting shortstop from the same Dominican town, San Pedro de Macorís. In 2005, 29 percent of the players on the thirty teams' opening day rosters were born outside the United States—70 percent of them from the Dominican Republic, Venezuela, or Puerto Rico. Among the nearly twelve hundred players on the forty-man rosters this spring, ten of the sixteen most common surnames were Hernandez, Gonzalez, Perez, Ramirez, Rodriguez, Cabrera, Guzman, Lopez, Pena, and Sanchez.

The emblematic Pirate of the 1960 World Series–winning team was, as Maraniss notes, "ethnic"—second baseman Bill Mazeroski, son of a coal miner from nearby West Virginia. Not until the late 1980s did California supplant Pennsylvania as the state that had produced the most major leaguers. California's climate provides opportunities to develop baseball talent. Pennsylvania provided incentives—escape from the mines and dark satanic steel mills. Latin America has both the climate and the incentives.

The report on young Fred Astaire's screen test said: "Can't act. Slightly bald. Can dance a little." When the Pittsburgh Pirates drafted Clemente out of the Brooklyn Dodgers' farm system in 1954, they said, "He can run and throw—and we think he can hit." Oh, yes. In his last at bat, in September 1972, he became the eleventh player—fifteen others have done it since—to get three thousand hits. A bad-ball hitter with a "nose to toes" strike zone, he was difficult to walk. But then, as the saying goes, you can't walk off an island.

In eighteen seasons, all with the Pirates, Clemente used the whole field. Maraniss believes that two factors—Clemente used an unusually heavy bat, and had chronic back and neck discomfort from a 1954 automobile accident—kept Clemente from being a home-run-seeking pull hitter. Instead, he sprayed line drives into the left- and right-field power alleys.

Tim McCarver, the first catcher ever to lead either league in triples, once said hitting a triple is better than sex. Most of us are unable to make that comparison, but if Clemente, who hit 166 triples, agreed with McCarver, he played in two home ballparks built for ecstasy. The Pirates never led the league in home runs while playing in Forbes Field, but its spaciousness—365 feet to left, 416 to right-center, 457 to the deepest part of center field, where the batting cage was kept on the field of play—turned many Clemente drives into triples. So did the hard fake-grass surface of cavernous Three Rivers Stadium, to which the Pirates moved in 1970.

The first black Puerto Rican to play in the American League was Clemente's friend Vic Power, a flashy-fielding first baseman. Like Clemente, he was incensed by the 1950s contrast between Puerto Rico's easygoing race relations and America's segregation. But unlike Clemente, Power responded with wit. When a waitress said her restaurant did not serve Negroes, he replied equably, "That's OK, I don't eat Negroes."

Clemente, playing in a city with a minuscule Latino population, said he felt like a "double nigger." As late as 1971—in one game that year, the Pirates became the first team ever to have nine black players in its starting lineup—some sportswriters still quoted him in phonetic English: "Eef I have my good arm thee ball gets there a leetle quicker."

Arrestingly handsome, at five feet eleven inches and 185 pounds he was about the size of today's smaller middle infielders. But the smoldering energy of his national and professional pride and resentments seemed transmuted into energy at bat and in the field. Right fielders need the strongest arms, to give runners second thoughts about going from first to third on singles. In the golden age of right fielders (Hank Aaron, Frank Robinson, Reggie Jackson, Al Kaline), Clemente's arm was the best.

A Clemente line drive broke the leg of one Hall of Fame pitcher (the Cardinals' Bob Gibson, who pitched to three more batters before collapsing) and, Maraniss believes, hastened the retirement of another, the Dodgers' Don Drysdale. In August 1969, after a Clemente shot whistled into the outfield, Drysdale flicked what felt like an insect off his neck, but discovered blood on his fingers. Clemente's drive had torn the skin off the top of Drysdale's ear. Shaken, Drysdale walked Clemente the next time up and retired six days later.

The last act of Clemente's life was in character. On December 23, 1972, a severe earthquake devastated Nicaragua. Clemente, making use of his heroic status, threw himself into organizing Puerto Rico's charitable response. Incensed by reports that agents of Nicaragua's dictatorship were diverting, and profiting from, the shipment of aid, he chartered an ancient DC-7. He did not know it was a ramshackle contraption operated by a shady pilot with an untrained crew. Hoping his presence could force the Nicaraguan officials to distribute his materials, he boarded the plane. Overloaded and unbalanced, it plunged into the sea a few thousand yards from the end of the San Juan airport. His body was not recovered.

"The mythic aspects of baseball," Maraniss concludes, "usually draw on cliches of the innocent past, the nostalgia for how things were. Fields of green. Fathers and sons. But Clemente's myth arcs the other way, to the future, not the past, to what people hope they can become. His memory is kept alive as a symbol of action and passion, not of reflection and longing. He broke racial and language barriers and achieved greatness and died a hero."

In 2005, thirty-three years after Clemente's death, Ozzie Guillen, the Venezuelan manager of the world champion Chicago White Sox, said his home has a shrine to the player he most reveres, Roberto Clemente. Now, thanks to Maraniss, Clemente's legacy is suitably defined and explained.   [MAY 7, 2006]

Greg Maddux: "Watch This—the First-Base Coach May Be Going to the Hospital"

Baseball's almost seamless history has had only one stark disjunction, the one about 1920, between the dead-ball and lively ball eras. But within the lively ball era there has been the steroids parenthesis—the era of some synthetically lively players—which now is closing.

Greg Maddux has thrived throughout it. Only three pitchers in the lively ball era have had four consecutive seasons with an earned run average under 2.40—Maddux, Pedro Martinez, and Sandy Koufax, who threw from a mound five inches higher than today's. In Maddux's four seasons (1992–1995) his ERA was an astonishing 1.98, two runs per game lower than the National League's 3.99 over the same period. Today, as he prepares to win at least fifteen games for a record eighteenth consecutive year, he represents physical normality in baseball.

Just six feet tall and 180 pounds, Maddux is a reminder that, as Bill Veeck said, you do not need to be seven feet tall or seven feet wide to play baseball. When Maddux, now thirty-nine, enters the Hall of Fame five years after he retires, he will be the smallest major-league pitcher inducted since Whitey Ford (five feet ten, 181), who retired in 1967.

When baseball is cleansed of steroids there will be fewer lurid records, like those of Barry Bonds in 2001. But numerous factors, from the strength training of hitters to the proliferation of hitter-friendly ballparks, will keep home runs plentiful. Besides, pitchers, too, have probably used steroids. Maddux says steroids made some track stars' legs move faster, so they probably increased some pitchers' arm speeds. Steroid testing began in 2003. In 2004, only one-eighth as many players (twelve) tested positive as in 2003 (ninety-six). Yet home runs per game and slugging percentages increased.

In Maddux's first full season, 1988, the major-league-leading home-run total was Jose Canseco's forty-two. But of the fifty-homer seasons in baseball history—there have been thirty-six of them—nineteen have occurred since 1990. This power explosion has not perturbed Maddux, who last year methodically became the twenty-second three-hundred-game winner, and perhaps the last for a long time. This year, his eighty-fourth strikeout will be his three thousandth, making him the ninth pitcher with three thousand Ks and three hundred wins.

He is proof—redundant proof—that ballplayers can perform well late in their careers without performance-enhancing drugs. Ty Cobb, who batted .316 in 1906 at age nineteen, batted .323 at age forty-one in 1928. Warren Spahn, the winningest left-handed pitcher ever, got 158 of his 363 wins after turning thirty-six and was 23–7 at age forty-two. Henry Aaron—currently and, we may hope, for many years to come, baseball's all-time home-run hitter—had his best year at age thirty-seven.

Maddux says laconically that when he came to the big leagues he threw between eighty and ninety miles per hour, and today he throws the same four pitches—fastball, change, slider, curve—seventy-five to eighty-five today. But he throws them with uncanny control: Among three-hundred-game winners since 1900, his walks-per-nine-innings ratio (1.87) is fourth best, behind only Cy Young (1.49), Christy Mathewson (1.59), and Grover Cleveland Alexander (1.65), who played all or most of their careers in the dead-ball era. And the key to his success has been less the speed of his arm than that of his mind.

One year in spring training, facing a Met who had hit him hard the previous season, Maddux told teammates he would throw dinky sliders to encourage the Met to hit a home run. Maddux figured that hitters remember, and subsequently look for, what they crush. The

Met homered—then, always looking for the same pitch, went hitless against Maddux in the regular season.

Leading 8–0 in a regular-season game against the Astros, Maddux threw what he had said he would never throw to Jeff Bagwell—a fastball in. Bagwell did what Maddux wanted him to do: He homered. So two weeks later, when Maddux was facing Bagwell in a close game, Bagwell was looking for a fastball in, and Maddux fanned him on a changeup away.

Sports Illustrated's Tom Verducci collects such stories demonstrating Maddux's knowledge of hitters. Four times in one season, Maddux, while in the dugout, warned the man sitting next to him that the batter would line a foul into the dugout. Three times the batter did. Another time Maddux said on the bench: "Watch this—the first-base coach may be going to the hospital." The batter lined the next pitch off the coach's chest. Once with runners on second and third and two outs, Maddux's manager suggested an intentional walk. "Don't worry," said Maddux, explaining that on the third of his next pitches the batter would pop out foul to third. Maddux was wrong: The pop was a few feet fair.

Maddux, who grew up in Las Vegas, is a formidable poker player. Amarillo Slim, former winner of the World Series of Poker, once said: "The results of one particular game doesn't mean a damn thing, and that's why one of my mantras has always been 'decisions, not results.' Do the right thing enough times and the results will take care of themselves in the long run." Maddux has had a long run pitching the way Slim played. But all runs end, so this year pay particular attention to the most artistic pitcher of the lively-ball era.   [APRIL 25, 2005]

Take Me Out to the Metric

Michael Bourn needs to get out more. A database programmer in Nashua, New Hampshire, he created the website plunkbiggio. blogspot.com that tells everything—really, everything—about the 273 times that Craig Biggio of the Astros has been hit by a pitch, the modern major-league record.

On average, Biggio's plunks have occurred 493 feet above sea level, up 36 feet after two plunkings last year in Denver. The shortest pitcher to hit him? Byung-Hyun Kim (five feet nine inches). The average age and weight of the plunking pitchers are 28.5 and 200.22. He has been hit most often by pitchers whose astrological sign is Sagittarius, but more Leos have hit him. He has been hit fifteen times while Tiger Woods was on *Sports Illustrated*'s cover. In 1997, the Dow rose an average of 28.63 on trading days after Biggio was hit. And on, and on.

Why does Bourn do this? "It is better than following Ruben Sierra's approach to the sacrifice-fly record." (Sierra is 9 short of Eddie Murray's 128. Feel the excitement.) An obsessive-compulsive fascination with numbers is an occupational hazard of baseball fans. Baseball, unlike games of flow such as hockey, soccer and basketball, is a series of episodes that encourage quantification. This week, baseball resumes its prodigious production of numbers in another season of 2,430 games with 21,870 innings and approximately 700,000 pitches during 166,000 at bats. The rage to quantify—to reduce reality to measurable units— is an impulse in modern societies. In baseball, it produces illuminating metrics. For example:

The objective is to win, which means scoring runs while efficiently getting the other team to make twenty-seven outs. Every three outs, you must start over. Until recently, most people assumed that the key to runs was hits. Hence a misplaced emphasis on batting averages. But counting all hits alike is as foolish as counting different denominations of currency as identical. Nowadays, more emphasis is placed on not making outs. Hence the importance of on-base percentage, which is (hits + walks + hits by pitch)/(at bats + walks + hits by pitch + sacrifice flies). That led to the statistic OPS, which is on-base percentage + slugging percentage (which is total bases/at bats).

But Bill James, a pioneer of novel metrics (see *The Mind of Bill James,* by Scott Gray), says OPS takes the elements of run creation and puts them together incorrectly. "They shouldn't be added together, they should be multiplied. A team with a .400 on-base percentage and a .400 slugging percentage would score more runs than a team with .350 and .450, although both add up to .800 OPS." James suggests calculating "runs created": (hits + walks − caught stealing) × (total bases + .7 steals)/(at bats + walks − caught stealing).

Yikes. One reason we were so glad to get out of school was to get away from math homework. For fans more fond of John Kruk's mind than Isaac Newton's, here are some more accessible numbers, pertaining to baseball's health as life resumes this week:

Competitive balance is getting better: Baseball has had six different World Series winners in the past six years. The NFL has not had six different winners of Super Bowls since 1968–1973. One moral of this story is that the Yankees, with their $202 million payroll, have learned the declining marginal utility of the last $80 million.

Major-league baseball's long history is divided into just two eras— the dead ball and, beginning about 1920, the lively ball. But the latter contained a steroid parenthesis. It is closing because baseball now has the severest steroid penalties in professional sports. Last year there were 434 fewer home runs than in 2004—and the game became more interesting. *Sports Illustrated*'s Tom Verducci reports:

"Baseball captivates us so deeply that the anticipation of action is as compelling as action itself. The 20 seconds between pitches with the bases loaded, two outs, down a run in the eighth are Agatha Christie chapters unto themselves. With the powerball version of the game subsiding, fans are getting more of these worth-the-price-of-admission moments. For instance, 47.9 percent of games last season were decided by one or two runs, up 9 percent from the slugfest apex in 2001 and the highest such percentage since 1993."

During the slugfest era, it was said, "Chicks dig the long ball." Maybe. But as home runs fly away less frequently, ballpark turnstiles spin faster. Last year, baseball set an attendance record that it will break this year. Already, five teams—Angels, Cardinals, Cubs, Yankees, Red Sox—have essentially sold out their seasons. On February 24, the Cubs, who are in the ninety-eighth year of their rebuilding effort (they last won the World Series in 1908), put single-game tickets on sale.

They set a major-league record, selling more than 597,000 tickets that day, just 38,000 fewer than they sold in the entire 1966 season.

This season will include more plunkings of Biggio, who is one of 1,563 players whose names begin with B who have been hit 8,601 times in 1,380,366 plate appearances. You can look it up. But if you do, you need to get out more.   [APRIL 10, 2006]

Elias Knows *Everything*

L ast Monday, Nancy and Henry Kissinger arrived at a Manhattan restaurant at 8:10 p.m. and excitedly recounted what they had just listened to in their car: a Yankee rookie in his first major league at bat had hit a home run off a fearsome pitcher—the Diamondbacks' Randy Johnson, who is six feet ten and looks like a giant praying mantis with an attitude.

Before the Kissingers had time to examine their menus, some baseball commentators were reporting that this was the first time since 1986 that a player in his first major league at bat had homered against a likely future Hall of Famer (Will Clark off Nolan Ryan) and the first time ever that a player homered in his first at bat off a pitcher who the previous season won the Cy Young Award as the best pitcher in his league.

Who tells us such things lickety-split? The busy beavers at the Elias Sports Bureau.

On a Saturday evening last month the Devil Rays scored four runs in the bottom of the ninth to beat the Orioles, 6–4, thereby snapping a fifteen-game losing streak. The game ended just after ESPN's 10 p.m. *Baseball Tonight* went on the air. Soon Elias sent a message to reporter Tim Kurkjian on the *Baseball Tonight* set: This was the first time ever that an American League team had snapped a double-digit losing streak by scoring more than two runs in the ninth.

How do such nuggets of baseball history get mined? Here is how. The Hirdt brothers, Steve, fifty-one, and Peter, forty-eight, both Fordham graduates, are the heart of Elias's batting order, which never sleeps, at least not all at once. This is a twenty-four-hour-a-day business whose approximately thirty employees, when not in the office, are logged on and talking to one another at all hours from their homes. Elias, whose clients now include all the major professional sports leagues, was begun in 1961 by Seymour Siwoff, who is still a bundle of energy at an age he thinks is nobody's business.

Elias's business is to examine the statistical histories of the major professional sports using custom-written software that will retrieve the answers to the kind of questions Peter put to it when he returned home from dinner and saw what the Devil Rays had just done to the Orioles. Peter wondered: In baseball—sport of the long history and long seasons—has *this* ever happened before?

Learning from the Elias computer that it had not, Peter e-mailed the news to a researcher at the nation's central cultural institution. No, silly, not to the Library of Congress. To ESPN, an Elias client. The researcher sitting on the set of *Baseball Tonight* instantly e-mailed back: "Tim will cry when he sees this." Tim didn't. There really are thoughts too deep for tears.

Steve Hirdt says that when he and Peter were growing up they were "the only boys in New York City who, when our mother said, 'How many times do I have to ask you to clean up your room?' would tell her." A statistical literacy is part of being a fan of any sport, but is especially important to baseball fans. Big league baseball, now in its third century, produces a steadily thickening sediment of numbers, pitch by pitch, inning by inning. Elias sifts the sediment.

Today, Elias is located in a building overlooking an almost-as-impressive storehouse of knowledge, the New York Public Library. But just as there was a McDonald's brothers restaurant in San Bernardino, California, before Ray Kroc came along and had a bright idea, there was something called Elias, a dormant sports-information bureau run by two brothers, before Siwoff had his brainstorm, while shaving one morning, about putting a (then) newfangled gadget, the computer, to work deepening our understanding and enjoyment of sports.

When Braves pitcher Tom Glavine recently went to 100 games over .500 in his career (as this is written, he is 101 over—235–134) he joined teammate Greg Maddux in that category, and it was the first time since 1908 that two teammates (the Giants' Christy Mathewson and Joe McGinnity) were at least 100 wins over .500.

The top three American League home-run hitters in May were all Yankees (Jason Giambi, ten; Alfonso Soriano and Bernie Williams, nine each). This was the first time since September 1950 that three teammates had led either league in homers in a month (the Yankees' Yogi Berra, Joe DiMaggio, and Johnny Mize, all now Hall of Famers).

It is incessantly said that pitchers do not pitch inside as aggressively as they did in the rough-and-tumble past. Elias says: Oh? In 1941, 1 in every 309 batters was hit by a pitch. In 1951, 1 in 214. In 1971, 1 in 179. In 2001, 1 in 99. Mickey Mantle, a power hitter, was hit 13 times *in his career.* The Astros' Craig Biggio was hit 28 times *last year.* When asked if any pitcher faced both Babe Ruth and Mantle, Elias reported: Al Benton pitched against Ruth for the 1934 Philadelphia Athletics and against Mantle for the 1952 Red Sox.

Elias knows *everything* worth knowing. [JUNE 24, 2002]

The Game's Gifted Eccentrics

If you are the sort who wants to know how many doubles A-Rod hit on 2–1 counts in 2003 or Nolan Ryan's ground-ball-to-fly-ball ratio in 1974, you are living at the right time. Advances in medicine, communication, transportation, and plumbing since the middle of the nineteenth century are all very well, but what really makes this a golden age to live in is the multiplication and refinement of baseball statistics.

And if you do not even know who A-Rod is, you will still enjoy the story of baseball's progress to today's information abundance as it is told by Alan Schwarz, a senior writer for *Baseball America,* in *The Numbers Game.* Its lessons extend beyond baseball to politics and much else. It is an Information Age story about how new abilities to measure things beget new behaviors. The evolution of that cornucopia of information from its birth in 1845 to today's iterations is, in Schwarz's lively telling, a history of the game's path to the present.

That has been a path blazed by some gifted eccentrics whose apparently unslakable thirst for baseball numbers is shared by many millions of Americans, like Al Munro Elias and his brother Walter. A friend said of Al, there were only two ways to deal with him when he was talking baseball: "One was to listen to what he had to say. The other was to kill him." Eighty years later, the Elias Sports Bureau is still the Spindletop of sports statistics—the great original gusher.

One of Schwarz's subjects, Bill James, began his statistical assault on baseball's conventional wisdom while working as a night watchman at the Stokely-Van Camp canning plant in Lawrence, Kansas. That plant is, in modern baseball lore, akin to the Swiss patent office where Einstein began revolutionizing physics. (James has recently risen to the glory of the Boston Red Sox front office.) Schwarz also bestows honors on lesser-known luminaries, like Dick Cramer, who was driving home in St. Louis one night listening to a Cardinals game. "Ozzie Smith," Schwarz writes, "hit a ground ball that advanced a runner from second to third, to which announcer Mike Shannon reflexively commented, 'You won't see that in tomorrow's box score.' That's all Cramer needed to hear. 'I can fix that!' he said to himself." So now, in the blizzard of agate type that is part of a good sports section, you may see the result of Cramer's eureka moment—a notation for "runners advanced." But, then, we have not yet caught up to 1884, when some box scores listed each pitcher's number of called strikes.

Baseball, unlike games of flow like hockey, soccer, and basketball, is a series of episodes—of what Schwarz calls "measurable states of combat." Box scores illustrate the symmetry—what Schwarz calls baseball's "double-entry personality"—that perhaps helps to explain baseball's peculiar hold on its fans. Every hitting event is "part of a pitcher's record and every pitching event part of a hitter's record." No other team sport leaves such a satisfying statistical residue of coherence. "A 10-yard run by a halfback or a point guard's breakaway layup cannot be assigned against any particular defensive player. . . . Baseball, however, is the most individual of team sports: in perfectly discernible packets the game reduces to one batter versus one pitcher, with each assuming responsibility for the other."

The arrival of statistical fluency has changed the way baseball is played. The arrival can be dated from Branch Rickey's hiring of Allan Roth in 1947 to wield his pencil—baseball numeracy is not a gift recently conferred by computers—on behalf of the Brooklyn Dodgers. In 1947, the Dodgers' Dixie Walker hit for a fancy average—.306—but was then traded. Why? Partly because he objected to playing with a rookie, Jackie Robinson. But also because Roth's charts of the pattern of Walker's hits showed that he was pulling the ball less, a leading indicator of aging. By 1950, Roth, whose nimbleness with numbers did not extend beyond baseball (he did not do his own taxes), sat at Ebbets Field in coat and tie, dispensing statistical tidbits to a twenty-two-year-old broadcaster, Vin Scully. Fifty-four years later, Scully's voice fills the Los Angeles Basin with Dodgers' numbers. During a 1987 National League Championship Series telecast, Scully cited a statistic showing the sort of thing managers now like to know: the Cardinals' pitcher, Danny Cox, held opponents to a .268 batting average with his first seventy pitches in games, but opponents hit .345 against pitches number seventy-one and higher. Moments after Scully's statistic was broadcast, the San Francisco Giants' Kevin Mitchell doubled on Cox's seventy-third pitch and Jeffrey Leonard homered on the seventy-fourth.

Baseball took a long and winding road to reach Allan Roth and to travel far beyond him to today's sophisticated uses of the statistics generated by 2,430 games a year—by more than 11 million at bats in more than 150,000 games since the major leagues began. In 1938, the Cincinnati Reds' Johnny Vander Meer pitched two consecutive no-hitters. In May, the Arizona Diamondbacks' Randy Johnson pitched just the seventeenth perfect game in major-league history. Statisticians, Schwarz writes, could not say when or by whom such things would be done, but they could predict that they would be done about as often as they have been.

In 1920, a Yankee outfielder hit more home runs (fifty-four) than fourteen of the fifteen other teams hit, ushering in the decade of ballyhoo—the interrelated births of broadcasting, public relations, and sports superstars like Jack Dempsey, Red Grange, Bill Tilden, Man o' War, and, especially, that outfielder. His legacy includes an adjective,

"Ruthian," meaning prodigious. The new arithmetic of sports statistics was both a cause and an effect of superstardom. "Spotlighting players' statistics in greater detail than ever began a tectonic shift in sports," Schwarz writes, "as intrigue that once focused mostly on teams began to go to individual players and their statistics lines."

Lately, much, but not inordinate, attention has been focused on baseball executives who know how to tickle marginal insights from numbers—insights like the fact that inexpensive players trapped in the high minor leagues are often satisfactory replacements for expensive but mediocre major leaguers. Because of the success of Billy Beane, the Oakland A's general manager, and of his epigones who run several teams' front offices, their interest in on-base percentage has become, Schwarz says, "baseball's version of rock 'n' roll, scaring the old and galvanizing the young." He explains that before there was Beane there was the man who hired him, Sandy Alderson. A graduate of Dartmouth, Harvard Law School, and a Vietnam tour as a Marine officer, Alderson was in a San Francisco bookstore when he came upon a volume by Eric Walker, the most important baseball thinker you have never heard of. Alderson reading Walker was, Schwarz says, like Martin Luther King Jr. reading Gandhi, sparking a revolution. Scoring runs has always been the point of baseball, but Walker's epiphany was that when you make three outs you have to start over from scratch. Hitherto, the assumption was that runs—and wins—were achieved by hits. Nowadays the stress is on avoiding outs.

Baseball was a long time awakening from its dogmatic slumbers to the realization that not all hits are created equal. Hence a high batting average can be overrated. The difference between a .275 hitter and a .300 hitter is, essentially, one hit every two weeks. Besides, as the baseball writer Ferdinand Cole Lane fulminated one hundred years ago, measuring a player's value by his batting average, which ignores the difference between singles and extra-base hits, is akin to measuring a man's financial worth by a system that treats different denominations of currency as identical.

Today the "übermeasure of hitting," Schwarz writes, is OPS—on-base percentage added to slugging percentage. Someday baseball statistics may be so sophisticated that they will be what James Joyce said his work was, something we should devote our lives to mastering. But if human beings have, as Schwarz believes, a "compulsion to count, to quantify the world around them," then they are hardwired to be baseball fans.

If so, that fact lifts a load of guilt off this Puritan nation's shoulders. All those hours—years, actually—we have spent watching games when we should have been reading *Finnegans Wake*? Not our fault. Nature has made us do it. Which means that baseball is, as we chauvinists of the sport have long suspected, not merely the national pastime but the species' pastime. So there. [AUGUST 16, 2004]

Don't Beat a Dead Horse
in the Mouth

OPENING DAY QUIZ
(answers on page 303)

a. Name the only player to get at least five hundred hits with four teams.

b. The first time a Brewer swung a bat in the game with the Rockies last June 29, the result was a sacrifice fly. How?

c. In a 1965 game in Yankee Stadium, with the score tied, two outs in the bottom of the ninth, a runner on first and a 3–1 count on the batter, Yankee manager Johnny Keane ordered the batter to take the pitch—even though the pitcher was sure to throw a strike rather than walk the potential winning run into scoring position at second. Why did Keane do that?

The rule of thumb is that every team—we are talking baseball today, so if you really want to read about stuff like Social Security reform, look elsewhere on this page—will win 60 of its 162 games, will lose 60, and will play the season to settle the other 42. But the 2004 Arizona Diamondbacks did not get the memo explaining this.

They were epochally awful, losing 111 of 162 games. Yet *Sports Illustrated*'s Tom Verducci notes that Diamondbacks attendance— 2.5 million—was larger than the attendance of each of the Yankee teams that won twenty-one world championships between 1923 and 1977. Major League Baseball's 2004 attendance was a record 73,022,969. Per game attendance was 30,075, compared to 14,106 in 1950, 16,110 in 1960, 14,788 in 1970, 20,434 in 1980, and 26,045 in 1990. All this indicates that the fans have not received the memo explaining that the game is going to hell in a handcart.

Well, you ask, what about steroids? According to ESPN, twenty years ago five NFL players weighed more than three hundred pounds. The number of three-hundred-pounders on teams' current rosters? 433. Could chemistry as well as cheeseburgers be involved? Baseball is held to higher standards than other sports, and receives more intense and often unjust criticism, as it has regarding its supposed "inaction" regarding steroids. Testing for steroids began in the major leagues in 2003, and in 2004, 98.3 percent of players passed their tests. This is news to Congress but, then, what isn't?

Baseball's competitive balance is much improved and compares favorably with the NFL and NBA. Three of the last four Super Bowls were won by one team (the New England Patriots), but the last five World Series have been won by five different teams. The National League has sent seven different teams to the last seven World Series. The worst winning percentage in baseball last year (the Diamondbacks' .315) was not as embarrassing as those (as of Thursday morning) of the NBA's Atlanta Hawks (.155), Charlotte Bobcats (.214) New Orleans Hornets (.229), and Utah Jazz (.310).

In the ten seasons since baseball included two wild-card teams in its postseason, twenty-two of baseball's thirty teams have played into October. And as Verducci says, the three most storied franchises—the Yankees, Red Sox, and Cubs—have each won at least 88 games in two consecutive seasons for the first time ever.

Baseball also is thriving because it is a bargain (average MLB ticket, $19.82; average NBA ticket, $44.68; average NFL ticket, $54.75) and because of the flood of Spanish-speaking talent. The U.S. population (296 million) is more than thirty-three times that of the Dominican Republic (8.8 million), but bet on this all-Dominican lineup against the rest of the world:

C . . . . Miguel Olivo, Mariners
1B . . . . Albert Pujols, Cardinals
2B . . . . Alfonso Soriano, Rangers
3B . . . . Aramis Ramirez, Cubs; Adrian Beltre, Mariners
SS . . . . Miguel Tejada, Orioles
OF . . . . Sammy Sosa, Orioles
OF . . . . Vladimir Guerrero, Angels
OF . . . . Manny Ramirez, Red Sox
DH. . . . . David Ortiz, Red Sox
SP . . . . Pedro Martinez, Mets; Bartolo Colon, Angels
RP . . . . Armando Benitez, Giants
MANAGER . . Felipe Alou, Giants

Conservatives are forever being lectured that "you can't turn the clock back"—and shouldn't want to. Oh? This season, for the first time since the Astrodome opened in 1965, every National League game will be played on real grass. What a concept. There are many other reasons why this is baseball's golden age but, in the words of former Phillies manager Larry Bowa, "I don't want to beat a dead horse in the mouth."

QUIZ ANSWERS

a. Rusty Staub (Houston, Montreal, Detroit, New York Mets).

b. The first eighteen pitches from the Rockies' pitcher were fourteen balls and four called strikes.

c. Because with a 3–2 count and two outs, the runner on first would be running with the pitch and could be almost certain to score on a double. Which he did.

[APRIL 4, 2005]

The Golden Age

Sins can be such fun. Of the seven supposedly deadly ones, only envy does not give the sinner at least momentary pleasure. And an eighth, schadenfreude—enjoyment of other persons' misfortunes—is almost the national pastime.

Speaking of baseball, two Saturdays ago, old Dodger Stadium was reverberating with fans' excitement. It might seem odd to call "old" a ballpark that opened in 1962, but it is tied with the Nationals' RFK Stadium as the National League's second oldest, behind only the Cubs' Wrigley Field (1914). Anyway, shortly before their Dodgers were beaten by the Mets in the National League Division Series, Angelenos emitted animal roars of approval as they watched, on the giant screen in left-center field, the Tigers defeat the Yankees in the ALDS.

Some Dodgers fans still nurse a grudge they inherited from Brooklynites when the Dodgers decamped for California after the 1957 season. But rooting against the Yankees is as American as a microwaved wedge of frozen apple pie topped with a slice of processed cheese. Such rooting often is the unlovely underside of the democratic ethos—envy of excellence. But there also is resentment of the Yankees' financial advantage that has been inimical to baseball's competitive balance.

That, however, is a diminishing problem, for two reasons: Major League Baseball has implemented more redistribution of resources, and a new breed of general managers (e.g., Oakland's Billy Beane and Minnesota's Terry Ryan) are using new player-evaluation metrics to wring more baseball value from fewer dollars.

The Yankees' payroll of $206.4 million (not including the almost $30 million tax paid to MLB on the portion of the payroll over $136.5 million) is 2.4 times the Tigers' payroll. The Yankees' third baseman earns 68.7 times the salary of the Mets' all-star third baseman (Alex Rodriguez, $25.7 million; David Wright, $374,000). The shortstop makes approximately what the Marlins' team makes (Derek Jeter, $20.6 million; Marlins, $20.68 million). But the 2006 Yankees did baseball—and the rest of America, if it learns the larger social lesson of the story—the favor of demonstrating the steeply declining utility of the last $100 million of payroll.

New York, the world's financial capital, takes money *very* seriously. And New York has been the intellectual epicenter of political liberalism, which has consistently preached, and has consistently disproved, the efficacy of pitching large sums of money at social problems. In the city where America's welfare state was first imagined and implemented, the entitlement mentality bred by the welfare state includes the assumption that the Yankees are entitled to be in the World Series, which they have not been since—gasp—2003.

There still are revenue and spending disparities between baseball teams that are impossible between NFL and NBA teams because those leagues have salary caps and more centralized revenue sources. Nevertheless, when the Tigers dispatched the Yankees that Saturday, baseball was guaranteed its seventh different World Series winner in seven years. There *never* have been seven consecutive Super Bowls, or seven consecutive NBA championships, won by seven different teams.

Baseball's supposed "golden age" of the 1940s and 1950s was not so golden outside New York. In 1947, the Yankees won the American League pennant and beat the Dodgers in the World Series. In 1949, 1950, 1951, 1952, and 1953 the Yankees were World Series winners over the Dodgers, Phillies, Giants, Dodgers and Dodgers, respectively. If the Phillies had not beaten the Dodgers in the tenth inning of the last game of the 1950 season, every World Series game for five years would have been played in New York. And if 103 wins, which usually are enough to win the pennant, had sufficed in 1954 (the Indians won 111, an American League record for a 154 game season), the Yankees would have won ten pennants in a row, because they also won in 1955, 1956, 1957, and 1958.

Great Yankee teams have been good for baseball. In the 1930s, one of every four tickets sold to an American League game was for a game involving the Yankees. And this year, when the Yankees were drawing 4,200,518 fans to Yankee Stadium, they also played in front of 3,080,290 million on the road. But improved competitive balance is one reason why, for the third consecutive year, MLB set an attendance record (76,043,902), and why today is MLB's golden age, even west of the Hudson River.   [OCTOBER 15, 2006]

Pete Rose, Always Hustling

HUSTLE   *verb. to work or act rapidly or energetically.*
                    —*Webster's New World Dictionary*

But *hustle* also is a noun: "A way of making money, esp. a dishonest way."

Pete Rose, who walked 1,566 times in his major league career but never walked to first base, always sprinting, was called Charlie Hustle. His new hustle is his book, for which he reportedly received a $1 million advance, in anticipation of sales generated by his coming clean about having bet on baseball, which no one seriously interested in the subject doubted. No one, that is, other than professional contrarians, or commentators emancipated from facts by not having read the 1989 report that caused Rose to accept "permanent" banishment from baseball.

Rose's coming clean is the most soiled conversion of convenience since . . . well, August 17, 1998, when DNA evidence caused Bill Clinton to undergo a memory clarification. On the diamond, no one ever wrung more success from less natural talent than Rose did. But his second autobiography—which refutes the first—makes worse the mess he has made.

The supposedly truth-telling book contains this patent lie: "During the times I gambled as a manager, I never took an unfair advantage. I never bet more or less based on injuries or inside information." But he also says—does he even *read* his autobiographies?—"I began betting regularly on the sport I knew best—baseball." Managing the Reds, he knew—he *decided*—when a tired or injured star would be played or rested. And the network of bookies handling his bets knew that he knew.

While saying "it's time to take responsibility," he cunningly exploits the Zeitgeist of today's therapeutic society. He is, he insists, a victim.

A victim of an addiction—gambling while managing the Reds substituted for the "high" he had gotten when competing as a player. And he is a victim of a double standard: He would have been treated more leniently—more therapeutically—had his problem been drugs rather than gambling. But baseball has especially severe sanctions about gambling because competitive integrity is baseball's raison d'être.

Americans, a forgiving people, are forever refuting the proposition that there are no second acts in American life. Almost anyone can recover from almost anything by convincingly saying "I'm sorry."

Rose lied—and charmed the gullible—for fourteen years. Now, with the clock running out on his eligibility to election by baseball writers to the Hall of Fame, he pugnaciously says: I lied but "I'm just not built" to "act all sorry or sad or guilty" about it. "Act"?

Rose's critics have said that repentance is a necessary—not a sufficient—prerequisite for restoring his eligibility to the Hall of Fame. Many, probably most, of Rose's critics are revolted by the moral obtuseness of his synthetic repentance.

His dwindling band of defenders responds that it is unfair to judge Rose not by what he does but by the way he does it. Yet regarding repentance, the way you do it *is* what you do.

Cooperstown primarily honors players for, in players' parlance, the "numbers they put up." Hence it is widely believed that selection to the Hall is exclusively about the statistical residue of players' careers and should not involve a "morals clause"—consideration of character.

But the rules for election by members of the Baseball Writers' Association of America include: "Voting shall be based upon the player's record, playing ability, integrity, sportsmanship, character, and contributions to the team(s) on which the player played." The rules for voting by the Veterans Committee similarly mention "integrity, sportsmanship, character."

Some will say that if admittance to the Hall were limited by a strict calculus of character, the Hall would be much smaller. Yes, Babe Ruth might have hit even more home runs if he had gone to bed earlier, and more often with Mrs. Ruth. But not all character issues are equally pertinent to the proper criteria for honoring athletes' achievements. The crucial criteria concern the integrity of the competition.

Rose has said, "I was raised, but I never did grow up." He is not the only ballplayer who will be forever a boy. But what distinguishes him is not mere boyish roguishness but a hard, calculating adult amorality. There is a constancy to it that goes beyond recidivism, which implies episodes of recovery between relapses.

On the evidence of his book, he should never be back in a major-league uniform as a manager or coach. And he should not be admitted to the Hall of Fame unless its character criterion is declared irrelevant, which is not what the nation needs from the national pastime.

[JANUARY 8, 2004]

The Precious, Precarious Equipoise

Chicago baseball fans, who are composites of scar tissue and mortifying memories, instantly drew upon one of those memories for their response—"Say it ain't So-sa"—to Sammy Sosa's ejection from Tuesday night's game for the rule infraction of using a corked bat. Their words echoed the boy who supposedly exclaimed, "Say it ain't so, Joe" to Shoeless Joe Jackson, one of the White Sox players accused of throwing the 1919 World Series.

The Sox have been to only one Series since then, in 1959, which they lost. The Cubs have not been to a Series since 1945, which they lost, and have not won one since 1908, two years before Tolstoy died. But even Cub fans, although inured to pain, winced Tuesday night.

Sosa drove in a run with an infield out, but his bat shattered, revealing cork in the barrel. So the run was disallowed. Sosa says a corked bat he used to produce fan-pleasing fireworks during batting practice and home run hitting contests mistakenly got mixed in with his game bats. Corking a bat reduces its weight, enabling a batter to increase bat speed and to drive some pitches he might not otherwise be able to hit hard.

Before Tuesday's game was over, Major League Baseball took possession of seventy-seven of Sosa's bats. None of them is corked, which lends powerful support to Sosa's explanation.

This is good news for baseball. The ebullient Sosa is the game's most marketable star. His competition with Mark McGwire for the

1998 National League home-run title, which McGwire won seventy to sixty-six, was a crucial ingredient in baseball's recovery from the fan-alienating strike that truncated the 1994 season on August 12 and canceled the World Series.

Furthermore, baseball produces—inning-by-inning, game-by-game, season-upon-season—a rich sediment of statistics that sustain the arguments that nourish interest in the game with the longest history. If Sosa's slugging—he is the only player to hit sixty or more home runs in three seasons—was assisted by cheating, he will be diminished, as will the game's ongoing narrative. And all other players will come under a lowering cloud of cynicism about the authenticity of their achievements.

Major League Baseball will decide the seriousness of what Sosa did Tuesday—whether it was an accident arising from injudicious showmanship (actually, fans deserve to know that Sosa's prodigious achievements in home-run hitting exhibitions are unassisted by illegal bats) or whether he has repeatedly cheated in games. The stakes are high. Bart Giamatti knew why.

In 1987, pitcher Kevin Gross of the Philadelphia Phillies was caught with a small patch of sandpaper affixed to his glove, and a sticky substance on his glove. Sandpaper can be used to scuff a ball's surface, changing its wind resistance and hence its movement when pitched. Foreign substances also can alter the movement of a thrown ball, and it is no defense to say, as a pitcher (a Cub, of course) said when indignantly denying that he put a foreign substance on the ball: "Everything I use on it is from the good ol' USA!"

Gross was suspended for ten days by Giamatti, then National League president. A former president of Yale and a professor of Italian and comparative literature, Giamatti died in 1989 shortly into his five-month tenure as baseball commissioner, after imposing a lifetime suspension from baseball on Pete Rose for gambling on games. Giamatti knew exactly why "boys will be boys" is not a satisfactory response to paltering with the rules of the game.

Most of baseball's punishable offenses involve fighting or other violence that arises from the heat of competition. While such acts cannot be tolerated, Giamatti wrote, "It must be recognized that they grow often out of impulse, and the aggressive, volatile nature of the game and of those who play it."

Such offenses, he said, are less execrable than acts "of a cool, deliberate, premeditated kind"—acts that have "no organic basis in the game and no origins in the act of playing." They are acts of cheating that are "intended to alter the very conditions of play to favor one person." Such acts "are secretive, covert acts that strike at and seek to undermine the basic foundation of any contest declaring the winner— that all participants play under identical rules and conditions."

Giamatti understood that a team sport, like democratic society itself, involves a precious and precarious equipoise of individual striving and collective endeavor. In sport or society, break the rules that govern that equipoise and hark! what discord follows.   [JUNE 5, 2003]

Barry Bonds: Enhanced and Devalued

Would that Barry Bonds had retired after the 1998 season. He might be happier than he seems to be in his long trudge toward tainted glory. Certainly everyone who cares about baseball, and about the integrity of athletic competition generally, would be spared the disturbing spectacle of his unlovely approach to Henry Aaron's career record of 755 home runs.

The numbers Bonds had put up before the 1999 season were luminous enough to have guaranteed him first-ballot election to the Hall of Fame. He had 411 home runs, 445 stolen bases—he is now the only "500-500" player in history—eight All-Star selections, and eight Gold Glove awards. He had won three MVP awards and should have won a fourth that was given to a lesser, but less-obnoxious, player.

Since 1998, his gaudy numbers have earned him four more MVP awards. From his 1986 rookie season through 1998, he averaged a home run every 16.1 at bats (Babe Ruth averaged one every 11.8 at bats), and his season high was 46. Since 1999, when he turned thirty-five, an age by which most players are past their peak production, he has averaged one every 8.9 at bats, and in the 2001 season he hit 73. If

Bonds, even as he aged, had continued to average one home run every 16.1 at bats, he would have entered this season at age 42 with 590 home runs, not 734, and Aaron's record would have been beyond his reach.

Equally startling are these numbers: According to Mark Fainaru-Wada and Lance Williams, the *San Francisco Chronicle* reporters who wrote *Game of Shadows: Barry Bonds, BALCO, and the Steroids Scandal That Rocked Professional Sports,* Mike Murphy, equipment manager of the San Francisco Giants, testified that since Bonds became a Giant in 1993, the size of his uniform jersey has gone from 42 to 52. His cap size has expanded from $7\frac{1}{8}$ to $7\frac{1}{4}$, even though while it was expanding he shaved his head. (Bonds reportedly shaved his head because his hair was falling out as a result of steroid use.) And Fainaru-Wada and Williams also say Murphy testified that Bonds's baseball shoe size has changed from $10\frac{1}{2}$ to 13.

Steroids, human growth hormone (HGH), and other performance-enhancing drugs (PEDs) can cause gradual enlargement of bones in the feet, hands, face, jaw, and skull. Bonds has never failed a steroid test, but there is no reliable test for HGH, and chemists concocting PEDs also devise masking ingredients to defeat tests.

Various PEDs can increase muscle mass (and the speed of hitters' bats and pitchers' arms). They can hasten recovery from the exertions of training or competing, and can reduce pain and increase the sort of concentration needed when a ninety-six-mile-per-hour fastball is coming at you during a day game after a night game. George Vecsey, in his short new history of baseball, quotes a player: "The funniest thing I ever saw in baseball was Pete Rose's greenies kicking in during a rain delay." Greenies—amphetamines, a booster fuel for a 162-game season that is played across four time zones—were for years as openly available as sunflower seeds in teams' clubhouses.

The fascinating history of PEDs runs back into history's mists, to potions concocted to increase soldiers' aggressiveness in battle. This history is recounted in Will Carroll's *The Juice: The Real Story of Baseball's Drug Problems,* an indispensable guide to today's controversies.

In 1898, a Welsh cyclist in a Paris-to-Bordeaux race died after drinking an alcohol-based product designed to increase stamina and control pain. In 1921, a University of Chicago chemist ground up tons of bulls' testicles and used chemicals to isolate testosterone. By 1932, Carroll writes, sprinters were experimenting with nitroglycerine to dilate their coronary arteries. In 1936, at the Berlin Olympics, injectable testosterone, developed the year before by Nazi doctors for military use, probably helped propel German athletes to eighty-nine medals, more than any other team. In 1945, some German scientists involved in synthesizing testosterone moved to the Soviet Union, which soon became dominant in weight lifting. At the 1976 Montreal Olympics, large East German women with deep voices, body hair on their torsos, and severe acne won eleven of thirteen possible gold medals in swimming.

Now, the caffeine in your coffee is a PED. Some major-league ballparks feature advertisements for another widely used PED—Viagra. Testosterone and HGH, which the body produces naturally, are components of some potent PEDs. Distinguishing legitimate from illegitimate enhancements, in the context of competition, is not always easy. One should begin by understanding the temptation.

Although dangerous, steroids and other PEDs can tempt two kinds of ballplayers. One is the superior athlete for whom mere superiority is insufficient when immortality might be injected from a syringe. The other is the marginal player, a category that includes most major leaguers at some point in their careers, and many throughout their careers. If such a player knows or suspects that competitors for his roster spot or playing time are getting illegal and hazardous chemical assistance, he must choose between jeopardizing his career or his health.

Aside from certain grossly anomalous achievements by a few individuals such as Bonds, it is difficult to measure the extent to which PEDs have distorted baseball. Carroll stresses that their increased use has coincided with other changes that have tended to increase offensive production. The changes have included more sophisticated strength training unrelated to ingested or injected substances; sixteen new, mostly hitter-friendly ballparks; contraction of the strike zone; expansion of the number of teams, which diluted the quality of pitching; and maple bats that are more durable than those made from ash and so can have thinner barrels that increase bat speed.

And PEDs are, of course, not a problem only in baseball. Track—it was a track coach who blew open the BALCO lab scandal that brought Bonds before a grand jury—might be the sport most distorted by PEDs. And it requires the willful suspension of disbelief to think that diet and strength training are the only reasons why the average NFL offensive lineman weighs 307 pounds. But baseball is held to higher standards, for several reasons.

One is that baseball, unlike football, has a statistical measure of players' strength—the home run. For thirty-four years, sixty homers was the season record. Then, for thirty-seven years, the record was sixty-one. Then, in four seasons, 1998 to 2001, that total was surpassed six times. In football, Carroll writes, "the players most likely to use steroids are offensive and defensive linemen. If these players get stronger via steroids, their gains in strength will merely cancel each other out, and there will be no noticeable difference in the statistics." Furthermore, Carroll says, football's premier players—quarterbacks—achieve greatness by recognizing defenses and throwing accurately, not by the strength that steroids can augment.

Another reason baseball is held to higher standards than are other sports is that fans relate to baseball players differently. This is partly because, as Bill Veeck said, players do not need to be seven feet tall or seven feet wide. Players are generally much bigger than they used to be: Mickey Mantle (5 feet 11½, 195 pounds) was smaller than most of today's middle infielders. But last year's World Series MVP, the Cardinals' David Eckstein, is 5 feet 7 and 165 pounds.

Also, Tim Marchman, who writes about baseball for the *New York Sun,* notes that last year Shawne Merriman, linebacker for the San Diego Chargers, was suspended for four games for steroid use—then was selected for the Pro Bowl. And few cared. Marchman detects a "soft bigotry of low expectations": Most NFL and NBA players are black; most of the paying customers are white and, Marchman argues, do not expect better behavior. Baseball, however, is, Marchman says, "culturally white and middle class" and its players "are more widely expected to conform to ethical norms."

Perhaps. Certainly those norms are under pharmacological attack, and the attack will be a protracted contest between the chemists who devise PEDs and the testers who try to detect the use of the substances. In any case, the norms need to be explained and affirmed, as follows.

Drugs enhance performance by devaluing it when they unfairly alter the conditions of competition. Lifting weights and eating spinach enhance the body's normal functioning; many chemical intrusions into the body can jeopardize the health of the body and mind, while causing both to behave abnormally.

Athletes who are chemically propelled to victory do not merely overvalue winning, they misunderstand why winning is properly valued. Professional athletes stand at an apex of achievement, but their achievements are admirable primarily because they are the products of a lonely submission to a sustained discipline of exertion. Such submission is a manifestation of good character. The athlete's proper goal is to perform unusually well, not unnaturally well. Drugs that make sport exotic, by radical intrusions into the body, drain sport of its exemplary power by making it a display of chemistry rather than character. In fact, it becomes a display of some chemists' virtuosity and some athletes' bad character.

Sport is play, but play has a serious side. It can elevate both competitors and spectators. But cold, covert attempts to alter unfairly the conditions of competition subvert the essence of sport, which is the principle that participants shall compete under identical rules and conditions.

Harvey Mansfield, a Harvard philosopher, says we need our athletes and their integrity because excellence is always endangered in democracies that often cherish equality indiscriminately. PEDs, he says, do not merely expand the limits of human nature, they erase those limits as a standard: "Perfection disappears as the upper limit, and is replaced by an indefinite, indefinable perfectibility."

Mansfield's colleague Michael Sandel, in his new book, *The Case Against Perfection,* acknowledges that "the line between cultivating natural gifts and corrupting them with artifice may not always be clear." In 1999, Tiger Woods, whose eyesight was so poor he could not read the large E on the eye chart, had LASIK eye surgery—then won his next five tournaments. This was not a corrupting artifice. It enabled his eyes to do what normal eyes naturally do, not what unnatural eyes would do. But, Sandel says, when the role of chemical enhancement increases, our admiration for the achievement decreases. An athlete who succumbs to the "Promethean aspiration to remake nature, including human nature" ceases to be the agent of his achievements, which are drained of merit and moral responsibility.

It is a truism that baseball involves a lot of failure. Babe Ruth struck out 1,330 times—that is the equivalent of three seasons of at bats without ever putting the ball in play. Ty Cobb, whose .366 career batting average is the highest in history, failed more than 63 percent of the time. In a sense, most Americans are failed ballplayers. That is one reason for the sport's unique grip on the nation's imagination and affections.

PEDs make baseball less of a shared activity. Because of them, a few excel but everyone loses—everyone in the stands and on the field, and Bonds more than anyone.   [MAY 21, 2007]

The Methodical Mr. Aaron

MOBILE, ALABAMA—This city has belonged to five nations—France, Britain, Spain, the United States, and the Confederate States of America. Or four, if you think, as Lincoln did, that the Southern states never succeeded in seceding, so the CSA never existed. In any case, Mobile has done much for the national pastime of the country to which it currently belongs.

Mobile has incubated tremendous major-league talent. In a few games in 1969, the "Miracle Mets" had an all-Mobile outfield. Five Hall of Famers were raised here—Satchel Paige, Willie McCovey, Ozzie Smith, Billy Williams, and the man whose achievements gain luster from the contrast between him and the man who may soon surpass one of those achievements. As Barry Bonds continues his gimpy, joyless pursuit of such glory as he is eligible for, consider the odyssey of Mobile's greatest native son.

Henry Aaron's parents had moved south from Selma, drawn by

work in the shipyards during World War II. So many blacks came here that Davis Avenue—named for Jefferson Davis—became known as Little Harlem.

You think *that* is incongruous? Try this. Grip a bat as a right-hander—but with your left hand on top. That is how the man who would hit 755 home runs in twenty-three major-league seasons gripped his bat when, as an utterly uncoached seventeen-year-old, he signed his first professional contract, with the Indianapolis Clowns of the Negro Leagues, who recognized an uncut diamond.

When he boarded the train to his future, he had $2 in his pocket. He had never had his own bed, and with the Clowns often slept six nights a week in a bus. He remembers sitting with teammates in a Washington restaurant "hearing them break all the plates in the kitchen after we were finished eating."

Aaron's signing bonus with the Milwaukee Braves was a cardboard suitcase. In his first spring training, during a game against the Red Sox, Ted Williams came running from the clubhouse to see whose bat was making that distinctive sound. The bat had a slender handle and was whipped by wrists developed hitting dipping and floating bottle caps, pitched by Aaron's playmates when, as was usual, baseballs were scarce.

He was 0-for-5 in his first regular season game, which was the first day in which players were no longer allowed to toss their gloves on the field when coming in to bat. Soon, however, *Time* magazine was heralding "The Talented Shuffler" who "is not as dumb as he looks when he shuffles around the field." Misperceiving, through the lens of race, economy of motion for lethargy, sportswriters called him "uncomplicated" and "a child of nature." Lonnie Wheeler, who helped Aaron write his autobiography, *I Had a Hammer,* notes that Joe DiMaggio's similar understated manner was characterized as dignified and graceful.

In 1973, as Aaron approached Babe Ruth's record of 714 home runs—he would break it in April 1974—he received, according to the U.S. Postal Service, about 930,000 letters, more than any nonpolitician in America. Dinah Shore was second with 60,000. Much of his mail was hateful. He took out his anger on baseballs. The 1973 season was the last in which horsehide balls were used. Aaron's 714th was the first home run ever hit with a cowhide ball.

When Aaron retired, he was Major League Baseball's last link to the Negro Leagues. Today, he is baseball's link to the era when home runs did not cause fans, suspecting steroids, to view sluggers with a moral squint. Aaron became baseball's most methodical—and, properly measured by total bases, most effective—hitter after being raised in a household where, he remembers, "we almost never ate anything that was store-bought. I've gone many, many weeks with just cornbread, butter beans and collard greens."

Mobile's public library, writes Wheeler, "opened its doors to blacks before other Southern cities encouraged them to read." Spring Hill College here, which integrated—by conscience, not coercion—in 1954, was praised by Martin Luther King in his "Letter from Birmingham Jail." Today, if you turn onto Satchel Paige Drive, then onto Bolling Brothers Boulevard (Frank and Milt, nephews of a major leaguer, played a combined nineteen seasons), you reach Hank Aaron Stadium, home of the Mobile BayBears.

When Bonds hits his 756th, real fans, who know how to read the record book, will yawn, confident that Aaron's record will remain the real one until Alex Rodriguez, who has 175 more home runs than Bonds did when he was Rodriguez's age, breaks it.   [MAY 6, 2007]

Realism Among the RiverDogs

CHARLESTON, SOUTH CAROLINA—Realism is overrated. Putting it aside makes possible some sweet things, such as the idea of Santa Claus. And the fact of minor-league baseball.

This city's RiverDogs play at The Joe—the Joseph P. Riley Jr. Park. Their rivals in the Sally—actually, South Atlantic—League include the Delmarva Shorebirds and Hagerstown Suns from Maryland; the Lake County Captains from Ohio; the Lakewood BlueClaws from New Jersey; the Greensboro Grasshoppers, Hickory Crawdads, Asheville Tourists, and Kannapolis Intimidators from North Carolina; the

West Virginia Power from another Charleston; the Lexington Legends from Kentucky; the Columbus Catfish, Rome Braves, Augusta Green-Jackets, and Savannah Sand Gnats from Georgia; and the Greenville Bombers (reborn as the Greenville Drive in 2005) from just up the road. Such small cities and towns that are incubators of big dreams.

Talk to the players, most of them under age twenty-three, and you will find few, if any, who do not believe they are bound for glory—for Yankee Stadium, the RiverDogs being a Yankee Single-A affiliate. Actually, the RiverDogs are the Yankee's low Single-A club, and by this point in the season, many of the best prospects have been promoted to the high-A club in Tampa, or up to Double-A Trenton.

The RiverDogs play 140 games in 151 days, traveling by bus, living at least two to a room in motels, some earning as little as $1,050 a month—and only during the season—with a $20 per diem for food. "Sometimes," says a player touchingly grateful for life's little blessings, "the motel is near an Outback." A young man from West Texas says, "I had a brother working in the oil fields. So if I wake up tired one day, I think, 'I could be doing that.' "

Most of today's Sally Leaguers will be doing something like that sooner than they can bring themselves to imagine. But for now they are delighting some of the 40 million fans who will see minor-league baseball this summer. The RiverDogs, averaging about thirty-eight hundred fans a game, are one of five teams partly owned by Mike Veeck, a third-generation baseball man—his father put the ivy on Wrigley Field's outfield walls—whose management doctrine is: "Treat people as if they're coming into your home. Nothing is too much trouble."

The minor leagues reflect the nation's durable regional differences. South Carolinians, for example, are feisty—they fired on Fort Sumter from places not far from The Joe—so french fries are still called freedom fries at the ballyard. The real delicacies, however, are grilled turkey legs. A week's worth of protein for $5, they are not much smaller than the players' bats, and about as tender.

The Joe is almost in the backyard of The Citadel, a military school, and on game nights the patriotism is as warm as the beer is cold. Just before the first pitch on a recent evening, the teenager selling hot dogs and sodas at a concession stand out on the concourse behind the seats suddenly said, politely but firmly: "One moment, please." Turning his back to the line of waiting customers, he took off his cap and faced the brick wall at the back of the stand, in the direction of the flagpole in center field. He stood ramrod straight with his hand over his heart while the National Anthem was sung. Even people in The Joe's parking lot come to attention when they faintly hear the distant sound of "Oh, say can you see . . ."

About 40 percent of the players on the forty-man rosters of the thirty major-league clubs each spring are Sally League alumni, including, last April, Derek Jeter, Curt Schilling, Ivan Rodriguez, Luis Gonzalez, Scott Rolen, Andruw Jones, and John Smoltz. But nowhere near 40 percent of Sally League players get to the majors. Most were the best on their high school teams and are slow—mercifully so—to understand the severity of professional baseball's meritocracy.

The buses will not carry most of the RiverDogs to Trenton, let alone to Triple-A Columbus—never mind the big leagues. But don't try to tell that to the pitcher who, when asked if his curve is as good as the Oakland A's Barry Zito's, confidently replies, "Not yet." Says another, "I want to be the best center fielder that ever came out of the Yankees' organization." Better than Joe DiMaggio and Mickey Mantle? "Sure."

Such unrealism, and the reality of the oil fields, keeps young men getting on buses for late night rides to Motel 6s, which sometimes—a major benefit for minor leaguers—are near Outbacks.

[AUGUST 18, 2005]

Striving for Motel Years

KISSIMMEE, FLORIDA—It is past 10 P.M., dark, cold and damp. Traffic hisses on the highway in front of the nondescript motel that for five weeks is home to about 155 young adults. In back, in the gloom beneath the parking lot's dim lights, a dozen of them seem to have lost their minds. Actually, they are finding their dream.

And doing their homework, far from home. Their choreography on the asphalt is simulating situations in baseball games—runners on first and second, single to left; runner on second, ground ball to the pitcher. And on and on. The participants are pretending to be infielders, outfielders, a batter, base runners and—this is the point of it all—two umpires.

They have come to Jim Evans's Academy of Professional Umpiring. For six long days a week—on the manicured infields of the Houston Astros' spring-training complex, and on the asphalt—they are learning the craft of baseball's judicial branch.

For the few who will land jobs in the low rung of baseball's ladder— say, Class A—starting pay will be $1,900 a month, six months a year, plus $22 per diem. The home team finds motel rooms. For umpires, there are no home games.

The process of becoming an umpire is as severely meritocratic as the process of becoming a player. In the lower minor leagues, where only two umpires work each game, umpiring is as physically strenuous and mentally stressful as playing.

On a recent morning, Evans, who was a big-league umpire for twenty-eight seasons, showed a rapid-fire tape of twenty-five pitcher's moves with runners on base. His students had to instantly identify the balks. There were sixteen. Did the pitcher's knee bend? Did his shoulder turn, his glove twitch, his heel land improperly?

There are thirteen criteria for the correct stance of the home-plate umpire calling a pitch. Get only twelve right and Evans's instructors— mostly minor-league umpires—will correct you, vigorously. They reject the theory that a student's self-esteem is indispensable to learning.

When umpiring the bases, the rule is "angle over distance"—having the correct angle to see the play is more important than being close to the play. Students practice umpiring first base blindfolded, distinguishing the sounds of the fielder's foot hitting the bag and the ball hitting his glove. The final exam's 200 questions are like these:

> *Two outs, bases loaded. The batter hits a home run. He rounds first base and passes the runner who was on first. The runner from third touched home plate before the batter passed the runner from first, but the runner from second had not touched the plate at that time. (a) Four runs count because the infraction occurred during a*

dead ball situation. (b) No runs score because the batter made the third out. (c) This is a time play. One run scores. (d) Because the runner from first did not advance one base, the third out is considered a force out. No run scores." [The answer is c.]

No outs, runner on first. A hot grounder is hit up the middle. The shortstop fields the ball but throws wildly trying to retire the runner approaching second base. At the time the ball rolled into the first base dugout, the runner from first had just rounded second and the batter had touched first. Place the runners. (a) Both runners score. (b) Runner scores; batter is awarded third. (c) Runner scores; batter is awarded second. (d) Runner is awarded third; batter is awarded second." [The answer is d.]

Baseball combines fame and failure. The best batters fail more than 60 percent of the time. But umpires, baseball's designated grown-ups, aspire to anonymous perfection. For an umpire, success is not being noticed. A Randy Johnson slider slides across a corner of a seventeen-inch-wide plate at ninety-four miles an hour. Imagine trying to be perfect on 260 pitches a game.

Sport—strenuous competition structured and restrained by rules—replicates the challenge of freedom and satisfies the human hunger for coherence. If players are mediocre, the result is mediocre baseball. If umpires are mediocre, the result is chaos.

Baseball, national pastime of a litigious nation, allows arguments, within reason. So Evans's students learn how to manage rhubarbs. He teaches that strong voices and vigorous gestures—body language is *language*—buttress authority. You especially need that if, like twenty-year-old Susan Reed, you are about the size of a bunt.

Petite and laconic and just now wrapped in the armor of a home-plate umpire, she was a college student until, she says blandly, "I forgot my major." Say what? "My head broke open." Six months ago in the Missouri Ozarks, she was given the last rites of her church after being thrown through the sunroof of her SUV as it rolled over about a dozen times. Her painfully unhealed ankle slows her slightly gimpy run ninety feet up the line to call the play on a runner reaching third.

What pulls her painfully down the third-base line? What pulls all of Evans's pupils to central Florida for Spartan living in a quest, against steep odds, for jobs that will mean many motel years of an endless road trip? One student says what most of them feel: "I get chills every time I walk onto a ball field." Do you, reader, feel that way when you go to work?   [FEBRUARY 16, 2004]

Seeking Anonymous Perfection

P HILADELPHIA—On a recent night here, as on most summer nights for thirty-seven years, Bruce Froemming went to work. He performed for about three hours in front of a large, attentive, and opinionated audience. His job involves about 290 snap judgments, any of which might infuriate thousands of people. He has done his job well if no one notices him doing it. His goal is anonymous perfection.

At less than five-foot-eight and more than 250 pounds, Froemming, sixty-seven, looks like he might have siblings at Stonehenge. But in this summer of dismal developments in sports—a left fielder suspected of better hitting through chemistry; an NFL quarterback accused of dog fighting; an NBA referee guilty in a betting scandal; the Tour de France ruined by failed drug tests—Froemming is a sight for sore eyes.

Now in his thirty-seventh and final major-league season—after thirteen in the minors—he holds the record for most consecutive seasons of big league umpiring. His 5,127 games, through Sunday, are second only to Bill Klem (5,374), who did not have in-season vacations, which umpires did not get until 1979. If Froemming had not had twenty-eight days off each of the last twenty-eight summers, by now he would have worked nearly 6,000 games. He has spent more than forty-six thousand innings and approximately one and a half years on baseball diamonds, a well-spent life.

Pitch by pitch, baseball produces a rich sediment of numbers, such as: Every fourth day, Froemming is behind the plate. Over his career, the average game has involved about 290 pitches, so he has been behind the plate for more than 370,000 pitches. Has he given strict scrutiny—a Supreme Court concept is apposite when discussing baseball's judicial branch—to every one of them? Yes, he says.

Really? His attention never flags during, say, a late inning in an August game in front of a small crowd in Tampa Bay? Never, he insists. "Every pitch is important to someone."

Baseball now has an electronic system for grading home plate umpires' performances. Froemming says it shows that umpires are right 94 percent of the time, but "you get a lot of crap for the other 6 percent."

Early in his career, working behind the plate in a game involving Bob Gibson, the Cardinals' regal and ferocious Hall of Fame pitcher, Froemming made some calls that displeased Gibson. At the end of an inning, he walked past Froemming and quietly said, "You're better than that." Froemming says, "I remember that like it was yesterday."

A story for Froemming: Rogers Hornsby, who *averaged* .400 over five years, was facing a rookie pitcher who threw three pitches that he thought were strikes but that the umpire called balls. The rookie shouted a complaint to the umpire, who replied: "Young man, when you throw a strike, Mr. Hornsby will let you know."

So, a question for Froemming: Is it true, as is said, that umpires give great hitters and pitchers the benefit of the doubt on close pitches? "Not one bit," he says.

OK, then, another question: Suppose it is the bottom of the ninth in the seventh game of a World Series, two outs, the potential tying run on third, two strikes on a right-handed batter. He starts to swing, tries to stop his bat, and the home-plate umpire calls the pitch a ball. But the catcher asks the home-plate umpire to ask the first-base umpire, who has a better vantage point, to say if the batter swung. The home-plate umpire accedes to this request. You, Froemming, are at first. You think the batter did swing. But seriously: Are you going to end a seven-game World Series on a check-swing appeal call? "Yes."

He might. Consider September 2, 1972, when Froemming was behind the plate and the Cubs' Milt Pappas was one strike from doing what only fifteen pitchers have done—pitch a perfect game, twenty-seven up, twenty-seven down.

With two outs in the ninth, Pappas quickly got an 0–2 count on the twenty-seventh batter. Then Froemming called the next three pitches balls. An agitated Pappas started walking toward Froemming, who said to the Cubs' catcher: "Tell him if he gets here, just keep walking"—to the showers.

Pappas's next pitch was low and outside. Although he did get his no-hitter, the greater glory—a perfect game—was lost. Another kind of glory—the integrity of rules—was achieved.

The photographer Edward Steichen said that when God created his brother-in-law, the poet Carl Sandburg, God didn't do anything else that day. When the Intelligent Designer designed Froemming, He spent the rest of the day at a ballpark because He had done a good day's work by producing an archetype: The Umpire.   [AUGUST 19, 2007]

"Where Baseball?"

On his first day of school after coming to Missouri from the Dominican Republic, Albert Pujols, then sixteen, went to the school office and in two words expressed everything on his mind: "Where baseball?" He found the field, and soon professional baseball found him.

Now twenty-four, Pujols, the only player ever to finish in the top four in MVP voting in each of his first three seasons, is tied with Ralph Kiner and Mark McGwire for the most home runs (114) in his first three years. Here, from ESPN's Peter Gammons, are three players' stats after three seasons:

Batting avg.:	.331	.359	.334
Doubles:	111	120	138
Home runs:	107	91	114
RBIs:	432	378	381

Those are the numbers of Joe DiMaggio, Ted Williams, and Pujols.

Pujols is one of the remarkable Hispanic players who are among the more than 25 percent of major leaguers (and almost 50 percent of all professional baseball players) from outside the United States. This geyser of talent is one reason why the answer to the question "Where baseball?" is: soaring. This, in spite of the steroid crisis.

In a nation committed to better living through chemistry—where Viagra-enabled men pursue silicone-contoured women—the national pastime has a problem of illicit chemical enhancement. Steroids threaten the health of the 5 percent to 7 percent of players proved, by a mild regime of scheduled tests, to be using them. Steroids also endanger emulative young people. Further, steroids subvert what baseball is selling—fair competition. And they strike at the pleasure of engagement with America's team sport with the longest history.

That pleasure is the comparison of players across many generations. Until now, comparisons have been complicated by only one substantial discontinuity in the game's nature—that between the dead- and lively ball eras. Steroids threaten to define a second discontinuity—a parenthesis—in baseball's narrative.

The parenthesis opened in the 1990s. It must be closed to remove the cloud of suspicion that hovers over all players. Americans standing in stockings while their shoes and luggage are X-rayed at airports doubt that privacy considerations should prevent random, year-round testing, backed by serious sanctions, for illegal drugs that traduce baseball's integrity. The Players Association is too democratic, and its head, Don Fehr, is too intelligent, to continue to countenance the damage the status quo is doing.

Meanwhile, fans are flocking to ballparks. Preseason ticket sales are at record levels—the Cubs and Red Sox are essentially sold out for the season. Attendance probably will top 73 million, a record. In 1950, average attendance was 14,105 per game—in 1970, just 15,130. Last year? 28,013.

Ninety-eight percent of NFL fans have *never* been to a game. Many, probably most, baseball fans are made by going to ballparks. But baseball this year probably will be played in front of 50 million empty seats. So baseball is working on giveaways—e.g., tickets to reward scholastic achievements—to start young people on the baseball habit.

Sixteen of the thirty clubs have opened new parks since 1991. Fourteen new parks, counting San Diego's and Philadelphia's coming this month, have opened since Bud Selig became baseball's ninth commissioner in 1992. Aside from Wrigley Field (1914), Dodger Stadium (1962) is now the National League's oldest park.

Selig has been—baseball is a game of inches, but this is not a close call—the greatest commissioner. His achievements include a quickened pace of games (in three seasons, twelve minutes have been shaved from the average game length), interleague play, the unbalanced schedule, three divisions, partial realignment, wild-card teams (the last two World Series winners were wild cards), increased revenue sharing ($250 million this year; $20 million in 1992) and the competitive balance tax on the highest payrolls. That tax and revenue sharing will cost the Yankees $81 million this year.

Competitive balance is improving: twenty-two different teams have made it to postseason play since 1995. In the last three years, eleven different teams (of a possible twelve) have played in League Championship Series. As late as September 7 last season, fourteen of fifteen games had play-off implications.

The special task force for the Commissioner's Initiative: Major League Baseball in the 21st Century, on which this columnist serves, knows that the national pastime, like the nation, is prone to hypochondria. But as Sparky Anderson, a greater manager than grammarian, once said, "We try every way we can do to kill the game, but for some reason nothing nobody does never hurts it."

Oh, it gets hurt, but its recuperative powers are *Ruthian*. That American adjective means: prodigious.   [APRIL 4, 2004]

Chapter Eight

WONDERING

Incest at "a Genetically Discreet Remove"

I nvited by the University of Miami to address members of the class of 2005, the columnist repaid this courtesy by telling them that even though they surely had showered before donning their caps and gowns, each of them had about a trillion bacteria feeding on the 10 billion flakes of skin each of us sheds in a day. If each 2005 graduate were disassembled into his or her constituent atoms, each graduation gown would contain nothing but atomic dust. But as currently assembled, this stardust—really: we are all residues of the big bang—is living stuff, capable of sublime emotions like love, patriotism, and delight in defeating Florida State.

The body of every Miami graduate has about 10 thousand trillion cells, each containing a strand of DNA that, uncoiled, would extend about six feet. If that person's DNA were spliced into a single strand, it would extend 20 million kilometers—enough to stretch from Miami to Los Angeles and back 2,270 times.

So says Bill Bryson, author of the delightful *A Short History of Nearly Everything*. According to him, everyone now alive contains some Shakespeare. That is, some of the physical stuff he was made of. And Julius Caesar's stuff, and Genghis Khan's and Charlemagne's. And Charlemagne's cook's. There are trillions of trillions of atoms in each of us, so lots—probably billions—of atoms have been recycled in each of us from Beethoven. In that sense we all are, as Bryson says, reincarnations.

Indeed, each member of Miami's class of 2005 is related to every other member and to—facts must be faced—every graduate of Florida State. It took 2 parents to produce each of us, and 4 people to produce our parents. If we look back eight generations, to Lincoln's day, Bryson says that more than 250 people contributed to the creation of each of us. Look back to Shakespeare's day, and we are directly descended from 16,384 ancestors. Look back 64 generations, to the era of the Roman Empire, and we have a thousand trillion ancestors.

But wait. A thousand trillion people is thousands of times more than the number of human beings who have ever lived. So everyone is the product of a lot of incest—but incest at what Bryson calls "a genetically discreet remove." This extended single family—humanity—inhabits the little planet Earth, whose continents are wandering.

Bryson says Europe and North America are moving away from each other at about the speed that a fingernail grows—about two yards in a normal human lifetime. The African continent is creeping northward and someday will squeeze the Mediterranean Sea out of existence and will shove up a chain of mountains as high as the Himalayas extending from Paris to Calcutta.

The Earth is restless partly because its molten core retains heat amazingly well: It has lost only about two hundred degrees in the 4 billion years since the planet coalesced. Not that we have come close to that core: Bryson says that if the planet were an apple, our underground exploration would not yet have broken the skin.

The sun around which Earth orbits is one of perhaps 400 billion stars in the Milky Way, which is a piddling galaxy next door to nothing much. There are perhaps 140 billion galaxies in the still-unfolding universe. If all the stars in the universe were only the size of the head of a pin, they still would fill Miami's Orange Bowl to overflowing *more than 3 billion times.*

We should by now be used to strange thoughts. It has been one hundred years since June 1905, when Albert Einstein began publishing the scientific papers that taught us that gravity bends light, that space and time are warped, that matter and energy are interchangeable, that the mass of an object increases the faster it moves and that the experience of time is a function of speed.

But there is a not-at-all-strange reason that a Washington columnist would belabor Miami graduates with strange facts. It is this: The more they appreciate the complexity and improbability of everyday things—including themselves—the more they can understand the role that accidents, contingencies, and luck have played in bringing the human story to its current chapter. And the more they understand the vast and mysterious indeterminacy of things, the more suited they will be to participate in writing the next chapter.

This is so because the greatest threat to civility—and ultimately to civilization—is an excess of certitude. The world is much menaced just now by people who think that the world and their duties in it are clear and simple. They are certain that they know what, or who, created the universe and what this creator wants them to do to make our little speck in the universe perfect, even if extreme measures—even violence—are required.

America is currently awash in an unpleasant surplus of clanging, clashing certitudes. That is why there is a rhetorical bitterness absurdly disproportionate to our real differences. It has been well said that the spirit of liberty is the spirit of not being too sure that you are right. One way to immunize ourselves against misplaced certitude is to contemplate—even to savor—the unfathomable strangeness of everything, including ourselves.   [MAY 23, 2005]

An Intellectual Hijacking

Not since the medieval church baptized, as it were, Aristotle as some sort of early—very early—church father has there been an intellectual hijacking as audacious as the attempt to present America's principal founders as devout Christians. Such an attempt is now in high gear among people who argue that the founders were kindred spirits with today's evangelicals, and that they founded a "Christian nation."

This irritates Brooke Allen, an author and critic who has distilled her annoyance into *Moral Minority: Our Skeptical Founding Fathers*. It is a wonderfully high-spirited and informative polemic that, as polemics often do, occasionally goes too far. Her thesis is that the six most important Founders—Franklin, Washington, Adams, Jefferson, Madison, and Hamilton—subscribed, in different ways, to the watery and undemanding Enlightenment faith called deism. That doctrine appealed to rationalists by being explanatory but not inciting: it made the universe intelligible without arousing dangerous zeal.

Eighteenth-century deists believed there was a God but, tellingly, they frequently preferred synonyms for him—"Almighty Being" or "Divine Author" (Washington) or "a Superior Agent" (Jefferson). Having set the universe in motion like a clockmaker, Providence might reward and punish, perhaps in the hereafter, but does not intervene promiscuously, or perhaps at all, in human affairs. (Washington did see "the hand of Providence" in the result of the Revolutionary War.) Deists rejected the Incarnation, hence the divinity of Jesus. "Christian deist" is an oxymoron.

Allen's challenge is to square the six founders' often pious public words and behavior with her conviction that their real beliefs placed all six far from Christianity. Her conviction is well documented, exuberantly argued, and quite persuasive.

When Franklin was given some books written to refute deism, the deists' arguments "appeared to me much stronger than the refutations; in short, I soon became a thorough deist." Revelation "had indeed no weight with me." He believed in a creator and the immortality of the soul, but considered these "the essentials of every religion."

What Allen calls Washington's "famous gift of silence" was particularly employed regarding religion. But his behavior spoke. He would not kneel to pray, and when his pastor rebuked him for setting a bad example by leaving services before communion, Washington mended his ways in his austere manner: he stayed away from church on communion Sundays. He acknowledged Christianity's "benign influence" on society, but no ministers were present and no prayers were uttered as he died a Stoic's death.

Adams declared that "phylosophy looks with an impartial Eye on all terrestrial religions," and told a correspondent that if they had been on Mount Sinai with Moses and had been told the doctrine of the Trinity, "We might not have had courage to deny it, but We could not have believed it." It is true that the longer he lived, the shorter grew his creed, and in the end his creed was Unitarianism.

Jefferson, writing as a laconic utilitarian, urged his nephew to inquire into the truthfulness of Christianity without fear of consequences: "If it ends in a belief that there is no god, you will find incitements to virtue in the comforts and pleasantness you feel in its exercise, and the love of others which it will procure you."

Madison, always commonsensical, briskly explained—essentially, explained away—religion as an innate appetite: "The mind prefers at once the idea of a self-existing cause to that of an infinite series of cause & effect." When Congress hired a chaplain, he said "it was not with my approbation."

In 1781, the Articles of Confederation acknowledged "the Great Governor of the World," but six years later the Constitution made no mention of God. When Hamilton was asked why, he jauntily said, "We forgot." Ten years after the Constitutional Convention, the Senate unanimously ratified a treaty with Islamic Tripoli that declared the United States government "is not in any sense founded on the Christian religion."

Allen neglects one argument for her thesis that the United States is a "secular project": The Constitution mandates the establishment of a political truth by guaranteeing each state the same form of government ("republican"). It does so because the Founders thought the most important political truths are knowable. But because they thought religious truths are unknowable, they proscribed the establishment of religion.

Allen succumbs to what her six heroes rightly feared—zeal—in her prosecution of today's religious zealots. In a grating anachronism unworthy of her serious argument, she calls the founders "the very prototypes, in fact, of the East Coast intellectuals we are always being warned against by today's religious right." (Madison, an NPR listener? Maybe not.) When she says, "Richard Nixon and George W. Bush, among other recent American statesmen," have subscribed to the "philosophy" that there should be legal impediments to an atheist becoming president, she is simply daft. And when she says that Bible study sessions in the White House and Justice Department today are "a form of potential religious harassment that should be considered as unacceptable as the sexual variety," she is exhibiting the sort of hostility to the free exercise of religion that has energized religious voters, to her sorrow.

Two days after Jefferson wrote his letter endorsing a "wall of separation" between church and state, he attended, as he occasionally did, religious services in the House of Representatives. Jefferson was an observant yet unbelieving Anglican/Episcopalian throughout his public life. This was a statesmanlike accommodation of the public's strong preference, which then as now was for religion to have ample space in the public square.

Christianity, particularly its post-Reformation ferments, fostered attitudes and aptitudes associated with popular government. Protestantism's emphasis on the individual's direct, unmediated relationship with God, and the primacy of individual conscience and choice, subverted conventions of hierarchical societies in which deference was expected from the many toward the few. But beyond that, America's founding owes much more to John Locke than to Jesus.

The founders created a distinctly modern regime, one respectful of preexisting rights—natural rights, not creations of the regime. And in 1786, the year before the Constitutional Convention constructed the regime, Jefferson, in the preamble to the Virginia Statute for Religious Freedom, proclaimed that "our civil rights have no dependence on our religious opinions, any more than our opinions in physics or geometry."

Since the founding, America's religious enthusiasms have waxed and waned, confounding Jefferson's prediction, made in 1822, four years before his death, that "there is not a young man now living in the United States who will not die an Unitarian." In 1908, William Jennings Bryan, the Democrats' presidential nominee, said his Republican opponent, William Howard Taft, was unfit because, being a Unitarian, he did not believe in the Virgin Birth. The electorate yawned and chose Taft.

A century on, when the most reliable predictor of a voter's behavior is whether he or she regularly attends church services, it is highly unlikely that Republicans would nominate a Unitarian. In 1967, when Governor George Romney of Michigan evinced interest in the Republican presidential nomination, his Mormonism was of little interest and hence was no impediment. Four decades later, the same may not be true if his son Mitt, also a Mormon, seeks the Republican nomination in 2008.

In 1953, the year before "under God" was added to the Pledge of Allegiance, President Dwight D. Eisenhower declared July 4 a day of "penance and prayer." That day he fished in the morning, golfed in the afternoon, and played bridge in the evening. Allen and others who fret about a possibly theocratic future can take comfort from the fact that America's public piety is more frequently avowed than constraining.

[OCTOBER 22, 2006]

From Dayton, Tennessee, to Rhode Island's Committee on Fish and Game

John Scopes attended high school in Salem, Illinois, where his commencement speaker was the town's most famous native son, William Jennings Bryan. Their paths would cross again.

Eighty years ago, Scopes, twenty-four, a high school football coach and general-science teacher, attended a meeting in Robinson's drugstore in Dayton, Tennessee. There, to the satisfaction of community leaders who thought that what was to come would be good for business, Scopes agreed to become the defendant in a trial testing Tennessee's law against teaching "any theory that denies the story of the divine creation of man as taught in the Bible, and to teach instead that man has descended from a lower order of animals."

So began "the most widely publicized misdemeanor case in American history." That is Edward J. Larson's description of the "monkey trial" in his 1997 Pulitzer Prize–winning *Summer for the Gods: The Scopes Trial and America's Continuing Debate over Science and Religion*. With that debate again at a rolling boil, that book by Larson, professor of history and law at the University of Georgia, demonstrates that the trial pitted a modernism with unpleasant dimensions against a religious fundamentalism that believed, not without reason, that it was faithful to progressive values.

By 1925, many Christian geologists were comfortable with the fact that Earth has a long geologic history. They saw God immanent in the dynamic of appearance and disappearance of life forms. What most distressed some Christians was not the fact of evolution but the postulated mechanism—a nature-red-in-tooth-and-claw randomness that erased God's purposefulness and benevolence.

Since the publication of Charles Darwin's *Origin of Species* in 1859, religiously motivated critics of the theory of evolution by natural selection had stressed the supposed failure of paleontology to supply the "missing link" that would establish continuity in the descent of man.

Darwinism did not ignite a culture war until the 1920s, when high school education became common in the rural South, where Christian fundamentalism was strong. When school seemed to threaten children's souls, fundamentalists sought and found a champion in Bryan, a three-time Democratic presidential nominee and star of the prosecution team in Scopes's trial.

Scopes's defense, led by Clarence Darrow, stressed individual rights—academic freedom. The prosecution stressed the community's right to control the curriculum of public schools. As a young man, Bryan had been a force for progressivism understood as, Larson says, a "sunny faith in the curative power of majoritarian reforms," such as popular election of U.S. senators. So the vocabulary of progressivism served Bryan's argument that the issue was not what should be taught, but who should decide.

He, like many antievolutionists, believed that the idea of natural selection fueled merciless social Darwinism in domestic policies and militarism and imperialism among nations, justifying the survival of the fittest nations or races, and their dominion over lesser breeds. Modernists considered World War I a progressive crusade. Bryan resigned in protest as President Wilson's secretary of state.

Many scientists at the time were, Larson says, receptive to the idea that we could channel human evolution through selective breeding. Some believed that acquired human characteristics could be inherited, hence improvement of the human race could be engineered. And many evolutionary biologists embraced eugenics. By 1935, thirty-five states had laws compelling the sexual segregation and sterilization of people considered unfit—the mentally ill and retarded, habitual criminals, and epileptics.

Today's proponents of "intelligent design" theory are doing nothing novel when they say the complexity of nature is more plausibly explained by postulating a designing mind—aka God—than by natural adaptation and selection. By 1925, Larson's book notes, "Christian apologists had long regarded the intricate design of the eye as a 'cure for atheism.' "

The problem with intelligent-design theory is not that it is false but that it is not falsifiable: Not being susceptible to contradicting evidence, it is not a testable hypothesis. Hence it is not a scientific but a creedal tenet—a matter of faith, unsuited to a public school's science curriculum.

The Dayton jurors were eager to get on with their lives—"The peach crop will soon be coming in," one said—and did not even sit down before deciding that Scopes was guilty. But Bryan did not believe penalties should be attached to antievolution laws—"We are not dealing with a criminal class"—and offered to pay Scopes's $100 fine.

Bryan died five days after the trial. Scopes left to study geology—how fitting—at the University of Chicago and became a petroleum engineer. The argument about science, religion, the rights of communities' majorities, and academic freedom rolled on, but not everywhere. When an antievolution bill was introduced in the Rhode Island Legislature, it was referred to the Committee on Fish and Game.

[JULY 4, 2005]

Earth: Not Altogether Intelligently Designed

Earth, that living, seething, often inhospitable and not altogether intelligently designed thing, has again shrugged, and tens of thousands of Pakistanis are dead. That earthquake struck ten months after the undersea quake that caused the December 2004 tsunami that killed 285,000 in Asia. Americans reeling from Katrina, and warned of scores of millions of potential deaths from avian flu, have a vague feeling—never mind the disturbing rest of the news—of pervasive menace from things out of control. Too vague, according to Simon Winchester.

His timely new book, *A Crack in the Edge of the World: America and the Great California Earthquake of 1906*, teaches—reminds, really—that we should have quite precise worries about the incurably unstable ground on which scores of millions of Americans live. This almost certainly will result in a huge calamity, probably in the lifetime of most people now living.

Before the study of plate tectonics revolutionized geology just forty years ago, that science, Winchester writes, was concerned with "rocks, fossils, faults and minerals that were scattered around simply and solely *on the surface of the earth*." But the surface consists of between—depending how they are defined—six and thirty-six floating plates, which Winchester calls "rafts of solid rock." The plates' slow movements are powered by earth's molten innards, the boiling and bubbling radioactive residue of the planet's formation 4.5 billion years ago.

The plates grind against—and slide up on, or plunge below—one another. But not smoothly, which is the lethal problem. When friction freezes them for a while, stupendous energy builds up until, suddenly, plates unlock and the energy is released, sometimes in ways that seem to involve related spasms around the world.

On the last day of January 1906, that seismically dangerous year, an earthquake in Ecuador and Colombia of perhaps 8.8 magnitude on the Richter scale killed about 2,000. Sixteen days later there was a large Caribbean quake, followed five days later by one in the Caucusus, and on March 17 by one that killed 1,228 on the island of Formosa. On April 6, a ten-day eruption of the volcano Vesuvius began with rocks blown forty thousand feet into the air over Naples. Two days after Vesuvius subsided, San Francisco was knocked down, and twenty-six hundred acres of it were then devoured by three days of fires. About 3,000 San Franciscans died then, four months before a Chilean quake killed 20,000.

San Francisco's quake was smaller than the series of shocks around New Madrid, Missouri, over a few winter weeks in 1811–1812. They were strong enough to ring the bells in a Charleston, South Carolina, church that was later destroyed in that city's 1886 quake. Scores of millions of Americans now live on the unstable faults that shook mid-America in 1811–1812.

For San Francisco, the bad news is that the quake that killed sixty-three in 1989 (6.9 magnitude, compared to 8.3 in 1906) was caused not by the San Andreas fault, but by a neighboring one. So the big menace, the San Andreas, has not recently lurched, as it surely will because it is moving, sporadically, in grinding concert with the Pacific Plate. Since 1906 there have been only five major earthquakes along the 750 miles of the San Andreas, and none in Northern California. The U.S. Geological Survey estimates a 62 percent probability of a quake in that area of *at least* 6.7 magnitude before 2032. Pondering the prosperous town of Portola Valley, south of San Francisco, exactly astride two of the most active strands of the San Andreas, Winchester, like many geologists who have warned the town, is fascinated by "humankind's insistent folly in living in places where they shouldn't."

After Earth's heavings subside, they reverberate in people's minds. Winchester says that when the 1755 Lisbon earthquake killed sixty thousand, "priests roved around the ruins, selecting at random those they believed guilty of heresy and thus to blame for annoying the Divine, who in turn had ordered up the disaster. The priests had them hanged on the spot."

The 1883 eruption of Krakatoa in what is now Indonesia fueled the growth of an extremist strain of Islam, bent on purging society of impurities displeasing to God. That strain has twice recently been heard from in Bali terrorist attacks.

San Francisco's 1906 disaster prompted the explosive growth of a Pentecostal movement based in Los Angeles, a movement then embryonic but now mighty. Yet when A. P. Hotaling's whiskey warehouse survived San Francisco's postquake inferno, a wit wondered:

> *If, as some say, God spanked the town*
> *For being over frisky,*
> *Why did He burn the churches down*
> *And save Hotaling's whiskey?*

Good question. [OCTOBER 11, 2005]

Intelligent Design and Unintelligent Movies

This summer's movie stars are not the usual bipeds, but other animals—emperor penguins and grizzly bears. Their performances are pertinent to some ongoing arguments.

March of the Penguins raises this question: If an Intelligent Designer designed nature, why did it decide to make breeding so tedious for those penguins? The movie documents the seventy-mile march of thousands of Antarctic penguins from the sea to an icy breeding place barren of nutrition. These perhaps intelligently but certainly oddly designed birds march because they cannot fly. They cannot even march well, being most at home in the sea.

In temperatures of eighty below and lashed by one hundred mile per hour winds, the females take months to produce an egg while the males trek back to the sea to fatten up. Returning, the males are entrusted with keeping the eggs warm during foodless months while the females march back to the sea to fill their stomachs with nutriments they will share with the hatched chicks.

The penguins' hardiness is remarkable, as is the intricate choreography of the march, the breeding, and the nurturing. But the movie, vigorously anthropomorphizing the birds, invites us to find all this inexplicably amazing, even heroic. But the penguins are *made* for that behavior in that place. What made them? Adaptive evolution. They have been "designed" for all that rigor—meaning they have been shaped by adapting to many millennia of nature's harshness.

Speaking of harshness, Timothy Treadwell, college dropout, drug abuser, and failed actor, became a Southern California beach bum, had a heroin overdose, and then an epiphany: He must spend summers in Alaska "protecting" the grizzlies. The idea that these huge, robust carnivores need protection provided by this mentally wobbly narcissist—a developmentally arrested adolescent in his forties—would be funny, had not Alaska officials "hauled four garbage bags of people out of the bear" that devoured Treadwell and his girlfriend at the end of his fifth summer filming grizzly bears to which he gave cute names like Mr. Chocolate and Sgt. Brown.

About half of *Grizzly Man,* a documentary about Treadwell, is his film. The rest consists of interviews with, among others, a dry-eyed Alaskan who says "he got what he was asking for." Although Treadwell has been described as an "animal lover," the grandiosity of his self-praise as he preens and waxes metaphysical in front of his camera reveals that his great love was himself. His cooing of "I love you" at magnificently indifferent bears and his swooning over the warmth of bear feces ("This was just inside of her!") is as repulsive as his weeping over evidence that nature really is red in tooth and claw.

Evidence such as bear cubs killed by mature male bears so the mother will stop lactating and be sexually available. Call that the Summer of Love, Alaska-style.

Treadwell was not far from mental illness, or from a social stance— nature is sweet, civilization is nasty—not easily distinguished from mental illness. Call it Sixties Envy. So, see *Grizzly Man,* then read T. C. Boyle's 2003 novel *Drop City.*

It is about a bunch of Treadwells who, having dropped out and dropped acid, are addled but able to see that their California commune, based on "voluntary primitivism," has become overrun with inane philosophy and the communards' sewage. Also, the county sheriff is angry. So a few of them decide to found Drop City North in Alaska. As one of these pioneers explains, in Alaska there are "no rules," but there are food stamps.

There they plan "to live the vegetarian ideal," but where will the cheese come from, now that a wolverine has eaten the communal goats? When an Alaskan explains that "we eat bear and anything else we can get our hands on," a nature worshipper is horrified:

" 'But to kill another creature, another living soul, a soul progressing through all the karmic stages to nirvana'—she paused to slap a mosquito on the back of her wrist with a neat slash of her hand— 'that's something I just couldn't do.'

" 'You just did.'

" 'What? Oh, that. All right . . . I shouldn't have . . . but a bug is one thing . . . and like a bear is something else. They're almost human, aren't they?' "

The movies and novel prompt a thought: Reality's swirling complexity is sometimes lovely, sometime brutal; its laws propel the comings and goings of life forms in processes as impersonal as Antarctica is to the penguins or the bears were to Treadwell or Alaska was to Drop City North. It is so grand that nothing is gained by dragging an Intelligent Designer into the picture for praise. Or blame.

[AUGUST 28, 2005]

The Pope, the Neurosurgeon, and the Ghost in the Machine

A concatenation of three events last week—two protracted deaths and one literary birth—was, as a stimulus to reflection, remarkable. Or, some will say, providential.

In a utilitarian, if humane, place, a hospice in Florida, a woman tangled in some toils of modernity—medical technology, and the machinery of litigation and legislation—died because, after fifteen years in a vegetative state, and supposedly out of respect for her autonomy, nutrition and hydration were withdrawn from her. In any other age—even a generation or two ago—she would not have become an appendage of devices that can sustain the body, or most of it, while a part of it, the brain, has stopped performing the functions essential to personhood, as normally understood.

There was another death, in a place of purposeful splendor, the Vatican, which was built as a defiant assertion of confident authority in response to the tempest of the Reformation. The foremost contemporary steward of an ancient faith, Pope John Paul II did more than anyone in our lifetimes to make vivid the task of defining respect for life in the context of modern science.

It used to be said matter-of-factly that a person who died "gave up the ghost." But are we still confident there is, in the language of a modern philosopher, a "ghost in the machine"?

Last week a gifted novelist published a new work that is, among other things, a materialist's manifesto. Ian McEwan lives in London, where *Saturday* is set. His protagonist, Henry Perowne, has the sensibility of today's post-Christian Europe. Perowne believes we are, in a sense, machines—matter and nothing more. He thinks as those people do who say, "I do not have a body, I am a body." Perowne is a neurosurgeon.

With sharpened steel a neurosurgeon slices and splices and pares physical matter to palliate injuries to minds—to consciousness. Pharmacology also can do that. McEwan writes:

"A man who attempts to ease the miseries of failing minds by repairing brains is bound to respect the material world, its limits, and what it can sustain—consciousness, no less. It isn't an article of faith with him, he knows it for a quotidian fact, the mind is what the brain, mere matter, performs."

Perowne, the voice of scientifically sophisticated secularism, and presumably of McEwan, almost lyrically, and rightly, exhorts us to appreciate the "wonder of the real." One can, however, imagine a faint, droll smile flickering on the strong, intelligent face of John Paul II were he to have read those almost casually appended three words—"consciousness, no less." He might think to himself: The materialist must not tarry, he must hurry on, because as Emerson said, when skating on thin ice, safety lies in speed.

This pope might have read Emerson, and it is easy to imagine him, before frailty conquered his body, keeping abreast of contemporary literature, including McEwan. Before he was John Paul II he was Karol Wojtyla, a skiing poet, playwright, and philosopher. And a defining theme of his papacy was the compatibility of faith and science, the explainer of reality. The explainer, but only up to a point, so far.

Perowne reads an arresting sentence from Darwin—"There is a grandeur in this view of life"—and says, yes, indeed:

"Endless and beautiful forms of life, such as you see in a common hedgerow, including exalted beings like ourselves, arose from physical laws, from war or nature, famine and death. This is the grandeur. And a bracing kind of consolation in the brief privilege of consciousness."

But a bemused John Paul II, no stranger to materialism, dialectical and otherwise, might have responded: There you go again—that word *consciousness*. What is the grandeur in the spectacle, however interesting, of the blind, brute, violent necessity of physical laws at work? Is consciousness of an existence supposedly governed by such laws really much of a privilege?

It is, John Paul II might have responded to Perowne, one thing to say that a cosmic sneeze, aka the big bang (never mind what, or who, or Who, produced that) set all this physical-law-governed necessity in motion, and this process resulted in matter, including the cooling, unstable and sometimes lethally violent lump of it called Earth. But how much progress has science really made in explaining how some matter came to be conscious of itself?

Such arguments are not just hardy perennials in philosophy, they are part of today's political arguments. Arguments about school curricula (evolution, intelligent design). And about conundrums that modern science confronts us with concerning the end of life and the waning of consciousness. And about aborting what some people call "fetal material" as it grows toward consciousness.

Alas, death has removed from the unending and probably unendable debates about respect for consciousness and life the intellectual pope who, one imagines, appreciated the profundity, and perhaps the finality, of the philosophic jest: "Of course I believe in free will—I can't help it." [APRIL 11, 2005]

How Biology Buttresses Morality, Which Conforms to . . . Biology

Science is reshaping the argument about whether nature or nurture is decisive in determining human destinies, and about what the answer means for social policy. Consider a fascinating new report arguing the scientific evidence for the importance of "authoritative communities"—groups, religious or secular, devoted to transmitting a model of the moral life.

The report is from the thirty-three research scientists, children's doctors and mental health and youth services professionals comprising a commission jointly sponsored by the Dartmouth Medical School, the Institute for American Values, and the YMCA of the USA. The report's conclusion is in its title: human beings are *Hardwired to Connect.*

In an era of increasing prosperity, the evidence of children's failures to thrive—depression, anxiety, substance abuse, conduct disorders—is also increasing. Pharmacological and psychotherapeutic responses to such deteriorating mental and social health are necessary but insufficient. Also needed is recognition of how environmental conditions—the *social* environment—contribute to childhood suffering.

The problem is a deficit of connectedness. The deficit is the difference between what the biological makeup of human beings demands and what many children's social situations supply in the way of connections to other people, and to institutions that satisfy the natural need for moral and spiritual meaning.

The need expresses itself in religious cravings—the search for moral meaning and an openness to the possibility of a transcendent reality. The need is natural in that it arises from "our basic biology and how our brains develop." The report draws upon the science of infant attachment, and of brain development, particularly during adolescence, when the brain changes significantly.

The report argues that our understanding of children's difficulties is thwarted by the assumption that each child's problems are exclusively personal and individual, thereby ignoring social and communal factors. In fact the report argues that we are "biologically primed" for finding meaning through attachments to others.

The need for meaning is increasingly discernible in the basic structure of the brain. "The idea," says Allan N. Schore of the UCLA School of Medicine, "is that we are born to form attachments, that our brains are physically wired to develop in tandem with another's, through emotional communication, beginning before words are spoken."

Furthermore, the report says, social environments that meet—or defeat—this need "affect gene transcription and the development of brain circuitry." And "a social environment can change the relationship between a specific gene and the behavior associated with that gene." A child's "relational context," says Schore, "imprints into the developing right brain either a resilience against or a vulnerability to later forming psychiatric disorders."

"The biochemistry of connection" will seem too, well, deflating for some people's comfort. The report cites, for example, another study that says oxytocin, a hormone, enters a woman's bloodstream during sexual intercourse, childbirth, and lactation, promoting, the report says, "emotional intimacy and bonding (also sometimes known as 'love')." In men, marriage—sexual and emotional intimacy with a spouse—seems to lower testosterone levels, thereby lowering the "biological basis for violent male behavior and male sexual promiscuity."

So biology, it seems, buttresses important moral conventions. And they may have evolved in conformity to biological facts.

The scientific fact, if such it is, that religious expression is natural to personhood does not vindicate any religion's truth claims. A naturalistic hypothesis is that the emotions of religious experience have neurobiological origins: The brain evolved that way to serve individual and group survival.

In any case, the social utility of religion remains. And there may be a biological basis for religious affiliation reducing the risk of certain pathologies, and even enhancing immune systems.

The most basic authoritative community, the family, is the most crucial. Its decline weakens the other institutions of civil society. The result is a thinness of social connectedness, and what Tocqueville warned was a risk of American individualism—each person confined "entirely within the solitude of his own heart."

Hardwired to Connect suggests that there is no simple "versus" in "nature versus nurture." There is a complex interaction, which means, among many other important things, that IQ is not a simple genetic inheritance, it is a function of that inheritance and the influence on it of a context of connections.

The implication for governance is that social policies should foster the health of authoritative communities, especially given the fact that the yearning for such communities among adolescents often takes the form of gang membership. And evidently the Bush administration's belief in the wisdom of delivering social services through faith-based institutions is not just a matter of faith.

But then, the utility of faith does not establish its validity.

[SEPTEMBER 21, 2003]

The Space Program's Search for . . . Us

PASADENA, CALIFORNIA—On September 8, a spacecraft will insert into the atmosphere over Utah a glider that will spiral to Earth carrying a sealed canister containing gusts of solar wind captured over the past two years. The wind contains dust, gases, and other possible evidence of the dynamics of the solar system, dynamics that have somehow given rise to the splendor of . . . us. NASA's name for the canister project: the Genesis mission.

September 8 will be just another day at the office here on the campus of the Jet Propulsion Laboratory, where office work is not mundane but otherworldly. JPL—an appendage of, but not contiguous to, Caltech—may be the only place on the planet where you can gather around a lunch table with people who, in a sense, work on another planet.

On a recent day, some of them were behind a laboratory at a pile of sand that resembles the surface of Mars. They were trying to drive a rover, like the two currently on Mars. The JPL scientists were trying to operate one with the kind of mechanical defect—an inoperative drive wheel—that is giving a slight limp to one of the rovers on the red planet 110 million miles away.

One Mars rover was landed in a crater—what one scientist calls "an interplanetary hole-in-one." Both were expected to rove about six hundred meters, but they have covered three thousand. Their batteries are recharged daily by solar panels; they already have lasted twice as long as had been expected and may last ten times longer.

Earth, which is constantly changing, became home for life 4 billion years ago. We know neither the conditions then nor the processes by which life ignited. However, Mars may have had an early history like Earth's. One question the rovers may answer is: Were there, long ago, pools of standing water—standing for hundreds of millions of years—where life could have developed?

The rovers' arms, manipulated at JPL, put instruments in contact with rocks and read their mineral contents. By drilling into rocks, through several billion years worth of settled dust, the rovers have found sediments that were formed in bodies of water. Within the next decade, samples may be put robotically in canisters and launched off Mars to rendezvous with an orbiting spacecraft for a six-month trip to Earth.

It would be understandable if the people at JPL were jubilant, having just—after a seven-year flight—precisely inserted the Cassini spacecraft into the rings of Saturn. This multinational project will include putting instruments on Titan, Saturn's largest moon, which may have some tantalizing similarities to Earth of 4 billion years ago.

But people here know that all their marvels—JPL's deep-space control center is monitoring thirty-five space ventures—are performed against a backdrop of deepening public indifference. And cosmology's human capital is declining as young scientists choose other career paths.

The public's diminishing capacity for astonishment is astonishing. Perhaps second only to Einstein's question (Did God have a choice in the creation of the world?) is this one: How did matter, which is what we are, become conscious, then curious? Not all clues can be found on Earth.

Curiosity is why a Voyager spacecraft launched in 1977 is now 8.5 billion miles away. It is, in the scheme of things, just next door: traveling now at 1 million miles per day, it would have to continue for forty thousand more years just to be closer to another star than to our sun. Still, here in our wee solar system—our little smudge on the skies of uncountable billions of galaxies—Voyager's and JPL's other undertakings must be measured against Einstein's axiom: "All our science, measured against reality, is primitive and childlike—and yet it is the most precious thing we have."

All space programs search for . . . us. For, that is, understanding of how we came to be. Does that mean space exploration amounts to species narcissism? Yes, and that is an excellent thing. It is noble to strive to go beyond the book of Genesis and other poetry, to scientific evidence about our origins, and perhaps destiny.

The Scottish physicist James Clerk Maxwell (1831–1879), an early authority on Saturn's rings, had, as cosmologists should, a poetic bent:

> *At quite uncertain times and places,*
> *The atoms left their heavenly path,*
> *And by fortuitous embraces,*
> *Engendered all that being hath.*

The phrase "fortuitous embraces," although lovely, is not explanatory. Knowledge, tickled from the heavens, is the business of a small band of possible explainers—the people of JPL and NASA, government at its best. [AUGUST 26, 2004]

Nuclear Waste: That's Us

The Department of Transportation deals with the movement of things, which is important. The Department of Agriculture deals with food, which is vital. However, the National Aeronautics and Space Administration deals with the origin, nature, and meaning, if any, of the universe. Attention should be paid.

Space lost its hold on America's imagination after the last lunar expedition in 1972. But the really exciting research had just begun, with the 1965 discovery that the universe is permeated with background radiation which confirmed that a big bang had indeed set what are now distant galaxies flying apart.

A famous aphorism holds that the most incomprehensible thing about the universe is that it is comprehensible. It is remarkably so because of advances in particle physics and mathematics. And because of magnificent telescopes, like the Hubble, which is now eleven years old and due to cease functioning in 2010. Operating above the filter of

Earth's atmosphere, it "sees" the past by capturing for analysis light emitted from events perhaps—we cannot be sure how fast the universe is expanding—12 billion to 14 billion years ago.

Astronomy is history, and NASA's Next Generation Space Telescope, coming late in this decade, will see even nearer the big bang of 13 billion to 15 billion years ago. That was when, in a trillionth of a trillionth of a trillionth of a second, the big bang inflated from a microscopic speck to all that now can be seen by NASA's wondrous instruments.

Mankind is being put in its place, but where is that? Mankind felt demoted by Copernicus's news that this cooled cinder, Earth, is not the center of the universe. Now Martin Rees, Britain's Astronomer Royal, in his new book, *Our Cosmic Habitat,* adds insult to injury: "particle chauvinism" must go. All the atoms that make us are, it is truly said, stardust. But Rees puts it more prosaically: They are nuclear waste from the fuel that makes stars shine.

So, is life a cosmic fluke or a cosmic imperative? Because *everything* is a reverberation from the big bang, what is the difference between fluke and imperative?

Rees says our universe is "biophilic"—friendly to life—in that molecules of water and atoms of carbon, which are necessary for life, would not have resulted from a big bang with even a slightly different recipe. That recipe was cooked in the universe's first one-hundredth of a second, when its temperature was a hundred thousand million degrees centigrade. A biophilic universe is like Goldilocks' porridge, not too hot and not too cold—just right.

Here cosmology is pressed into the service of natural theology, which rests on probability—actually, on the stupendous improbability of the emergence from chaos of complexity and then consciousness. Natural theology says: A watch implies a watchmaker, and what has happened in the universe—the distillation of the post-big-bang cosmic soup into particles, then atoms, then, about a billion years ago, the first multicellular organisms that led, on Earth, to an oxygen-rich atmosphere and eventually to us—implies a Creator with a design so precise.

Perhaps. But not necessarily, unless you stipulate that no consequential accident is an accident. "Biological evolution," says Rees, "is sensitive to accidents—climatic changes, asteroid impacts, epidemics and so forth—so that, if Earth's history were to be rerun, its biosphere would end up quite different." There is a lot of stuff in the universe— the estimated number of stars is 10 followed by 22 zeros. But as to whether there are other planets with life like Earth's, Rees says the chance of two similar ecologies is less than the chance of two randomly typing monkeys producing the same Shakespearean play.

"Eternity," says Woody Allen, "is very long, especially toward the end." The end of our universe—long after our sun has died, 5 billion years from now—is certain to be disagreeable.

In his book on the universe's infancy *(The First Three Minutes)*, Steven Weinberg concludes that "there is not much of comfort" in cosmology. It indicates that Earth, "a tiny part of an overwhelmingly hostile universe," is headed for "extinction of endless cold or intolerable heat," either an unending expansion or a fiery collapse backward—a big crunch.

Yet research like NASA's is its own consolation. "The effort to understand the universe is," says Weinberg, "one of the very few things that lifts human life a little above the level of farce, and gives it some of the grace of tragedy." Not a negligible mission for NASA.

[MARCH 24, 2002]

The Loudest Sound in Human Experience

Ira Gershwin didn't know the half of it. He said the Rockies may crumble, Gibraltar may tumble. But terra firma itself is far from firm.

Even the continents are wandering, half an inch to four inches a year. Earth is a work in violent progress. The engine of its evolution is heat—boiling gas, molten rock, and other stuff—left over from the planet's formation 4.5 billion years ago. The heat frequently bursts through Earth's crust, although rarely as catastrophically as it did 120 years ago on the island of Krakatoa.

If Simon Winchester is correct in his new book—*Krakatoa: The Day the World Exploded, August 27, 1883*—the current trial in Indonesia of accused perpetrators of last year's terrorist bombing in Bali may be part of the lingering reverberation of the volcanic eruption—the loudest sound in modern human experience, heard three thousand miles away—that made an island disappear.

Billions of tons of material—six cubic miles of it—were hurled 120,000 to 160,000 feet in the air. They filtered sunlight, lowering Earth's temperature and creating spectacular sunsets that for months inspired painters and poets.

And in the East Indies outpost of the Dutch empire, where a notably relaxed and tolerant Islamic faith had long flourished, Krakatoa, by terrifying and dispossessing people, may have catalyzed the much fiercer form of Islam that fused with anticolonialism. It is alive and dealing death today.

Although the people of the East Indies will be forgiven for not appreciating this at the time, Winchester says volcanoes are part of what makes this planet hospitable to humans. They do not erupt so promiscuously as to render the planet unfit for life. And by churning Earth's mantle, they bring fertile soil and useful minerals to the surface, thereby sustaining the outer earth and the biosphere. For a while.

As Earth heads for frigid lifelessness, the leakage of heat from Earth's interior causes currents of matter to flow—movements measured in millimeters a year—above the molten core and below the crust. Just as, writes Winchester, "one sees working in a vat of vegetable soup simmering on the stovetop."

Science in the 1960s at least explained what had long pricked curiosity—the matching concavity of Africa's west coast and the convexity of South America's east coast. According to the study of plate tectonics, there are, depending on how they are defined, between six and thirty-six rigid plates on Earth's surface. In "subduction zones," where one plate slips beneath another, the descending plate pulls down untold billions of tons of material and water. This fuels white-hot seas of soup in immense chambers, from which energy seeks to break through Earth's surface.

Which is what happened in 1883 in the archipelago that now is Indonesia. Krakatoa's eruption resulted in the destruction of 165 villages and the death of 36,417 people. Most died not from the searing ash, pumice, and gas but from giant sea waves produced by Earth's spasm.

The shock wave circled Earth seven recordable times. Sea surges were detectable in the English Channel. Three months after the eruption, firemen in Poughkeepsie, New York, scrambled in search of what they thought was an immense conflagration that caused the sky to glow. Actually, the glow was light refracted by Krakatoa's debris.

The first major catastrophe to occur after the invention of the telegraph and undersea cables, Krakatoa produced an intimation of the "global village" seventy-seven years before Marshall McLuhan coined that phrase to describe the world-contracting effect of television. Krakatoa was, Winchester argues, "the event that presaged all the debates that continue to this day: about global warming, greenhouse gases, acid rain, ecological interdependence." Suddenly the world seemed to be less a collection of isolated individuals and events and more "interconnected individuals and perpetually intersecting events."

As an epigraph for his book, Winchester chose this from a W. H. Auden poem written in 1944, when the world was in agony and, unbeknownst to Auden, potentially world-shattering knowledge was being acquired at Los Alamos, New Mexico:

> *At any given instant*
> *All solids dissolve, no wheels revolve,*
> *And facts have no endurance—*
> *And who knows if it is by design or pure inadvertence*
> *That the Present destroys its inherited self-importance?*

Geology has joined biology in lowering mankind's self-esteem. Geology suggests how mankind's existence is contingent on the geological consent of the planet. Although the planet is hospitable for the moment, it is indifferent—eventually it will be lethally indifferent—to its human passengers. [MAY 22, 2003]

L = BB + pw + BC/BF

O ne hundred years ago, a minor Swiss civil servant, having traveled home in a streetcar from his job in the Bern patent office,
wondered: What would the city's clock tower look like if observed
from a streetcar racing away from the tower at the speed of light? The
clock, he decided, would appear stopped because light could not catch
up to the streetcar, but his own watch would tick normally.

"A storm broke loose in my mind," Albert Einstein later remembered. He produced five papers in 1905, and for physicists, the world
has never been the same. For laypeople, it has never *felt* the same.

In his book *Einstein's Cosmos*, Michio Kaku, professor of theoretical physics at the City University of New York, makes Einstein's genius seem akin to a poet's sensibility. Einstein, says Kaku, was able to
"see everything in terms of physical pictures"—to see "the laws of
physics as clear as simple images."

Hitherto, space and time were assumed to be absolutes. They still
can be for our everyday business, because we and the objects we deal
with do not move at the speed of light. But since Einstein's postulate of
relativity, measurements of space and time are thought to be relative to
speed.

One implication of Einstein's theories did have thunderous practical implications: Matter and energy are interchangeable, and the mass
of an object increases the faster it moves. In the most famous equation
in the history of science, energy equals mass multiplied by the speed of
light squared. A wee bit of matter can be converted into a city-leveling
amount of energy.

In the 1920s, while people were enjoying being told that space is
warped and it pushes things down (that is the real "force" of gravity),
Einstein became an international celebrity of a sort not seen before or
since. Selfridges department store in London pasted the six pages of an
Einstein paper on a plate-glass window for passersby to read. Charlie
Chaplin said to him, "The people applaud me because everyone understands me, and they applaud you because no one understands you."

The precision of modern scientific instruments makes possible the confirmation of implications of Einstein's theories—e.g., the universe had a beginning (the big bang) and its expansion is accelerating; time slows in a large gravitational field and beats slower the faster one moves; the sun bends starlight from across the sky and there are black holes so dense that they swallow light. Does all this bewilder you? The late Richard Feynman, winner of the Nobel Prize in physics, said, "I think I can safely say that nobody understands quantum mechanics."

Three years ago we learned that the Milky Way galaxy, which is next door, contains a black hole weighing as much as 2 million suns. "Thus," says Kaku, "our moon revolves around the earth, the earth revolves around the sun, and the sun revolves around a black hole." Can this story have a happy ending?

Science offers no guarantees. Astronomy evicted us from our presumed place at the center of the universe many centuries before we learned that "center" is unintelligible in an expanding universe where space and time are warped. And before nineteenth-century biology further diminished our sense of grandeur by connecting us with undignified ancestors, eighteenth-century geology indicated that seashells unearthed on mountain tops proved that Earth has a longer, more turbulent and unfinished history than most creation stories suggest. December 26, 2004, brought another geological challenge to the biblical notion of an intervening, caring God.

Einstein's theism, such as it was, was his faith that God does not play dice with the universe—that there are elegant, eventually discoverable laws, not randomness, at work. Saying "I'm not an atheist," he explained:

"We are in the position of a little child entering a huge library filled with books in many different languages. The child knows someone must have written those books. It does not know how. It does not understand the languages in which they are written. The child dimly suspects a mysterious order in the arrangement of the books but doesn't know what it is."

A century on from Einstein's "miracle year," never mind $E = mc^2$. Try this: L = BB + pw + BC/BF. Meaning: Life equals the big bang, followed by lots of paperwork, ending with either a big crunch, as the universe collapses back on itself, or a big freeze as it expands forever.

A bad ending? Compared to what? Everything, as has been said since Einstein, is relative.   [JANUARY 6, 2005]

Wonder What We Are For? Wondering

ATOP MAUNA KEA, ON HAWAII'S BIG ISLAND—On a clear day, you can see almost forever. With the help of adaptive optics, almost back to the beginning of this universe. And it is usually clear here at 13,796 feet above sea level, and above half of the atmosphere's oxygen. That is why the W. M. Keck Observatory's two telescopes, primarily operated by the University of California and the California Institute of Technology, are here, far from urban lights and above much of the atmosphere, which, although it makes the stars twinkle prettily, does so by distorting light.

Hence the need for adaptive optics. This technology became available for civilian science when the end of the Cold War led to the declassification of some devices developed for the Strategic Defense Initiative (SDI).

The Keck telescopes—the world's largest—are gathering light produced shortly (as these things are reckoned; about 800 million years) after the big bang, just under 14 billion years ago. Analysis of the light, which can be done by astronomers working anywhere, yields information about the life cycle of stars. (Grim news: our star, the sun, is doomed, so we are, too, in less than 2 billion years.) The Keck telescopes have detected more than sixty planets orbiting other stars. Ten years ago, the only planets we knew of were those orbiting our own sun.

It is axiomatic that not only is the universe stranger than we know, it is stranger than we can know. But one reason the Keck telescopes are significantly augmenting our store of knowledge is the application to astronomy of adaptive optics developed for SDI. SDI's challenge is to target, from space, ballistic missiles launched on Earth. This requires making ultraprecise measurements from space, through the distortions of Earth's atmosphere. Astronomy's challenge involves looking outward—analyzing light that is distorted by the atmosphere before it reaches telescopes on Earth.

The Keck telescopes each weigh three hundred tons, stand eight stories tall, and involve operations of more precision than those of the finest wristwatch. They can gather 13-billion-year-old light that is 500 million times fainter than the naked eye can see. They gather the light using a primary mirror ten meters (thirty-three feet) in diameter, composed of thirty-six hexagonal segments, each engineered to conform to within a millionth of an inch of single continuous surface.

But the *really* remarkable device is a mirror about the size of a man's hand. Distortions in the gathered light are removed by bouncing the light off this mirror, which has four hundred pistons operated by tiny, computer-driven motors that make adjustments in the mirror's surface 642 times *a second.*

From 1609, when Galileo built a refracting telescope (a lens assisting the naked eye), until the Hubble space-based telescope was launched in 1990, the atmosphere complicated astronomy. However, Hubble, which cost more than all other telescopes in history combined, does not make Earth-based telescopes anachronistic.

Hubble and its successors—next comes the Next Generation Space Telescope—operate in the cold vacuum that is space. But a multinational consortium has proposed an Overwhelmingly Large Telescope that would gather light on Earth with two thousand panels of mirrors in an apparatus the size of a football field. Ever-better land- and space-based telescopes will find tantalizing hints about how the expansion of the universe (actually, *this* universe; there may be many others) began— a big bang?—and whether it will continue to expand or will collapse back on itself in a big crunch.

In any case, Earth's fate is not going to be pretty, so what's the use in wondering? Because wondering is what we are for.

Mauna Kea is a dormant volcano. About forty miles southeast of here, lava from the Kilauea volcano, boiling with heat left over from Earth's formation 4.35 billion years ago, has recently been spilling across a highway and into the ocean. To stand a few hundred feet from the stream of lava plunging into the Pacific, amid the searing heat and sulfurous fumes, is to sense what the Keck Observatory, in its very different setting, explores—the violent impermanence that permeates the entire universe.

"We are curious people," says Keck Observatory director Frederic Chaffee matter-of-factly. "And the universe is an amazing place." The most amazing things in it are the curious creatures. They have evolved literally from stardust, becoming conscious beings capable of building—indeed, their glory is that they are, in a sense, incapable of not building—mountaintop telescopes, silhouetted against the edge of the atmosphere, searching for clues as to how all this started and how it will end.   [SEPTEMBER 1, 2002]

Chapter Nine

MATTERS OF LIFE AND DEATH

Golly, What Did Jon *Do?*

What did Jon Will and the more than 350,000 American citizens like him do to tick off the American College of Obstetricians and Gynecologists? It seems to want to help eliminate from America almost all of a category of citizens, a category that includes Jon.

Born in 1972, Jon has Down syndrome. That is a congenital condition resulting from a chromosomal defect that causes varying degrees of mental retardation and some physical abnormalities, such as low muscle tone, small stature, a single crease across the center of the palms, flatness of the back of the head, and an upward slant to the eyes (when Jon was born, Down syndrome people were still commonly called Mongoloids). There also is increased risk of congenital heart defects, childhood leukemia, and Alzheimer's disease. Down syndrome, although not common, is among the most common congenital anomalies—47.9 per 100,000 births (compared with 77.7 with cleft lips or palates, which also can be diagnosed in utero, and which sometimes result in abortions).

As women age, their risk of having a Down syndrome baby increases. It has become standard practice for women older than thirty-five to be offered genetic counseling and diagnostic testing. But because of the higher fertility rates of women under thirty-five, such women have 80 percent of Down syndrome babies. So new ACOG guidelines recommend that all pregnant women, regardless of age, be offered such counseling and testing.

The ACOG guidelines are formally neutral concerning what decisions parents should make on the basis of the information offered. But what is antiseptically called "screening" for Down syndrome is, much more often than not, a search-and-destroy mission: At least 85 percent of pregnancies in which Down syndrome is diagnosed are ended by abortions.

Medicine now has astonishing and multiplying abilities to treat problems of unborn children in utero, but it has no ability to do anything about Down syndrome (the result of an extra twenty-first chromosome).

So diagnosing Down syndrome can have only the purpose of enabling—and, in a clinically neutral way, of encouraging—parents to choose to reject people like Jon as unworthy of life. And as more is learned about genetic components of other abnormalities, search-and-destroy missions will multiply.

Nothing—*nothing*—in the professional qualifications of obstetricians and gynecologists gives them standing to adopt policies that predictably will have, and seem intended to have, the effect of increasing abortions in the service of an especially repulsive manifestation of today's entitlement mentality—every parent's "right" to a perfect baby. Happily, that mentality is not yet universal: 214 American families are looking for Down syndrome children to adopt.

Jon, a sweet-tempered man, was born the year before *Roe v. Wade* inaugurated this era of the casual destruction of preborn babies. And he was born just as prenatal genetic tests were becoming routine. Since then, it has become routine to abort babies like Jon, because they are like Jon. Without this combination of diagnostic advances and moral regression, there would be more people like Jon, and the world would be a sweeter place.

America has, however, become a more congenial, welcoming place for its Down syndrome citizens who have escaped "screening." On the second day of Jon's life, the hospital's geneticist asked his parents if they intended to take him home. Nonplussed, they answered that taking a baby home seemed like the thing to do.

Jon was born at the end of the era in which institutionalization of the retarded was considered morally acceptable, but in what was still an era of gross ignorance: In the first year of Jon's life, a network-television hospital drama featured a doctor telling parents of a Down syndrome newborn that their child would probably never be toilet-trained. But ignorance lingers. There are doctors who still falsely counsel parents that a Down syndrome person will never read, write, or count change. Such doctors should not try to get between Jon and his *USA Today* sports section.

In 1972, the odds were heavily against Jon's living as long as he already has lived. Just twenty-five years ago, the life expectancy of Down syndrome people was twenty-five. Today, because of better health care, better mental stimulation in schools and homes, and better community acceptance, their life expectancy is fifty-six.

Jon has a disability, but he also has some things most men would like to have—season tickets for Nationals and Orioles baseball, Redskins football, Capitals hockey, and Georgetown University basketball. He gets to and from games (and to his work three days a week for the Nationals at RFK Stadium) by himself, taking public transportation to and from his apartment.

Jon experiences life's three elemental enjoyments—loving, being loved, and ESPN. For Jon, as for most normal American males, the rest of life is details.   [JANUARY 29, 2007]

The Long Dying of Louise Will

NEWPORT BEACH, CALIFORNIA—The long dying of Louise Will ended here recently. It was time. At ninety-eight, her body was exhausted by disease and strokes. Dementia, that stealthy thief of identity, had bleached her vibrant self almost to indistinctness, like a photograph long exposed to sunlight.

It is said that God gave us memory so we could have roses in winter. Dementia is an ever-deepening advance of wintery whiteness, a protracted paring away of personality. It inflicts on victims the terror of attenuated personhood, challenging philosophic and theological attempts to make death a clean, intelligible, and bearable demarcation.

Is death the soul taking flight after the body has failed? That sequence—the physical extinguished, the spiritual not—serves our notion of human dignity. However, mental disintegration mocks that comforting schemata by taking the spirit first.

In the very elderly, the mind can come and go, a wanderer in time, and a disintegrating personality can acquire angers and jagged edges that are, perhaps, protests against a growing lightness of being. No one has come back from deep in that foreign country to report on life there. However, it must be unbearably frightening to feel one's self become light as a feather, with inner gales rising.

Dementia slowly loosens the sufferer's grip on those unique tokens of humanity, words. An early sign is a forgetfulness that results in repetitiveness, and fixation on the distant past.

For a while, one of Louise's insistently recurring memories was of spring 1918, a war year, and eastbound troop trains passing through Greenville, Pennsylvania. When the trains stopped, residents offered candy and magazines to the soldiers—but not to black units. That infuriated Louise's father, whose fury was a fine memory for Louise to have among those of a father who died at age forty-four.

To the end, even when virtually without speech, Louise could recognize her children, could enjoy music and being read from love letters written seventy-five years ago by Fred, her future husband. She could even laugh, in spite of the tormenting chasm between her remaining cognition and the prison of her vanished ability to articulate.

In 1951, in Champaign, Illinois, for her ten-year-old son, she made a mother's sacrifice: She became a White Sox fan so she could converse with the argumentative Cubs fan who each evening dried the dishes as she washed. Even after much of her stock of memories had been depleted, she dimly knew that the name Nellie Fox (a second baseman) once meant something playful.

The aging that conquered Louise was, like war, a mighty scourge, and, like war, elicited nobility from those near its vortex. The nearest was Fred Will, who died eight years ago, at the end of his ninth decade.

A few years before his death, Fred, a reticent romantic, whose reticence may have been an effect of his tinge of melancholy, shared with his children some poetry he had written for Louise, including this from 1933:

> The warm sun
> beams through the clear air
> Upon glistening leaves.

And the birds
sweep in long arcs
Over the green grass.

They seem to say,
"This might last forever!"
But it doesn't.

But it lasted more than six decades, which is forever, as foreverness is allotted to us.

A retired professor of philosophy, Fred probably knew what Montaigne, quoting Cicero, meant when he said that to study philosophy is to prepare to die. Fred was, strictly speaking, philosophic about his wife's affliction. A common connotation of "philosophic" is placid acceptance of what can be comprehended but not altered. However, Fred's philosophic response to the theft of his wife by aging was much richer than mere stoicism grounded in fatalism. It was a heroic act of will, arising from clear-sightedness about the long trajectory of Louise's life.

He understood this stern paradox: Families seared by a loved one's dementia face the challenge of forgetting. They must choose to achieve what dementia inflicts on its victims—short-term memory loss. They must restore to the foreground of remembrance the older memories of vivacity and wit.

"All that we can know about those we have loved and lost," Thornton Wilder wrote, "is that they would wish us to remember them with a more intensified realization of their reality. What is essential does not die but clarifies. The highest tribute to the dead is not grief but gratitude." Louise, released from the toils of old age and modern medicine, is restored to clarity.   [JULY 13, 2006]

ACKNOWLEDGMENTS

This collection of my writings, like the previous seven, reflects the assistance I have received from superb professionals. As an undergraduate at Georgetown University, Jed Donahue worked part-time for me in my Washington office. Now that he has become a senior editor at the Crown Publishing Group, I am, in a sense, working for him, and pleased to be. I am now in my fourth decade of writing for *Newsweek*'s back page. The magazine has never been in better hands than it is under its current editor, Jon Meachem. Alan Shearer, editorial director of the Washington Post Writers Group, makes all of my columns, and most of my paragraphs, better. Seth Meehan was an invaluable assistant in my office during most of the period covered by this volume. He has gone on to graduate school at Boston College, where he is preparing to be a professor of history. My loss is academia's gain. My current assistants—colleagues, really—are Sarah Walton and Greg Reed. They make it a pleasure to come to work in the morning and make me reluctant to leave in the evening. Mary Longnecker is now in her third decade of making my business run smoothly. Finally, Schuyler Hawkins and Daniel Phillips are the latest in a long line of very able interns I have found at Georgetown University, which has earned my gratitude for bringing such young men to Washington and to my attention.

PERMISSIONS

Grateful acknowledgment is made to the following for permission to reprint previously published material:

INDEX

Aaron, Henry, 293, 295, 314, 315, 319–21
Abraham, Spencer, 171–72
Académie Française, 117
Academy of Professional Umpiring, 324–26
Adams, Abigail, 41
Adams, Henry, 117
Adams, John, 45, 335, 336
Adams, John Quincy, 91–92
Adler, Robert, 128
Affluent Society, The (Galbraith), 33, 34–35, 111
African Americans, 119, 127, 132, 151, 158
  baseball, 286–88, 292, 293, 319–21
  basketball, 277–79
  civil rights, 24, 70–72
  cultural conservatives, 150
  Moynihan report, 31
  segregation, 104–6, 123
  welfare reform, 134–35
Ahmadinejad, Mahmoud, 123
Air America, 154
air-traffic controllers strike, 55
Alderson, Sandy, 304
Ali, Muhammad, 274
Allen, Brooke, 335–37, 339
Allen, Woody, 355
American Enterprise Institute, 61, 248–50
Anderson, Sherwood, 219
Anderson, Sparky, 330
Anglin, Margaret, 215
Antioch College, 243–45
Arafat, Yasir, 119, 192, 194, 196
Arctic National Wildlife Refuge, 171, 172
Arizona Diamondbacks, 303, 305–6
Arledge, Roone, 267
Arnold, Henry ("Hap"), 94
Arnold, Matthew, 1

Arthur Andersen, 114
Articles of Confederation, 146, 147, 337
Asplund, Lillian Gertrud, 125
AT&T, 55
Atlanta Braves, 300–301
Auden, W. H., 357
auto industry, 86–88, 108–11, 122, 203–5
aviation, 77–79, 102–4

Babbitt (Lewis), 217–18, 219
Bagwell, Jeff, 296
Barber, Red, 287
Barone, Michael, 131–33
Barra, Allen, 266–68
Barrett, Leonie, 201, 202, 203
Bartov, Omer, 200
baseball, 118, 120, 121, 123, 128, 275, 283–330
  ballparks, 329–30
  designated hitter, 240
  minor leagues, 321–23
  1908 season, 283–86
  statistics, 296–305
  steroid use, 115, 294, 295, 298, 306, 315–19, 329
  umpiring, 323–28
basketball, 120, 123, 214–15, 277–79, 306, 309, 317
Bauerlein, Mark, 241–42
Baylor, Elgin, 278
Bay of Pigs invasion, 24
Beane, Billy, 304, 307
Beat Generation, 64–65
Beatles, 123
Becker, Gary, 36
Bednarek, Janet R. Daley, 77–79
Bellesiles, Michael, 245–47
Ben & Jerry's ice cream, 173
Benton, Al, 301
Bercuson, David, 94

373